MODERN SPORTING GUNS

MODERN SPORTING
GUNS

Chief Author
JAN STEVENSON

a Salamander book
Published by Salamander Books Limited
LONDON • NEW YORK

A SALAMANDER BOOK

Published by
Salamander Books Ltd,
52 Bedford Row,
London WC1R 4LR,
United Kingdom

© Salamander Books Ltd 1988

ISBN 0 86101 234 8

Distributed in the UK by
Hodder & Stoughton Services,
P.O. Box 6,
Mill Road,
Dunton Green,
Sevenoaks,
Kent TN3 2XX

All correspondence concerning the
content of this volume should be
addressed to Salamander Books Ltd.

Credits

Project Manager:
Philip de Ste. Croix

Editor:
Richard O'Neill

Designers:
Roger Hyde
Mike Jolley

Colour photography of weapons:
Terry Dilliway © Salamander Books Ltd

Colour cutaway artwork:
The Maltings Partnership and Terry Hadler
© Salamander Books Ltd
Diagram artwork:
Chris Forsey, Terry Hadler and
The Maltings Partnership
© Salamander Books Ltd

Filmset:
H&P Graphics Ltd, England
Colour reproduction:
Scantrans PTE Ltd, Singapore

Printed in Belgium:
Henri Proost International Book Production,
Turnhout

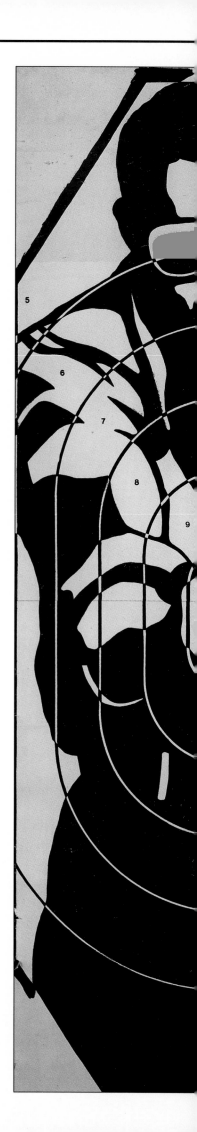

Contributing Authors

Norman Cooper, gunmaker of Bishop's Stortford, Herts, is one of Britain's foremost authorities on shotguns. A noted shooting coach, he has for many years written the shotgun column for *Guns Review* and has long been involved with the administration of international competitive clay pigeon shooting through the CPSA.

Bill Curtis, one of the leaders of the muzzleloading revival and founders of international competition in this field has, for many years, been secretary of the Muzzle Loaders' Association of Great Britain and editor of its respected publication, *Black Powder*. He has one of the finest libraries in the world of 18th and 19th century texts on firearms and shooting, the most important of which his firm, W.S. Curtis (Publishers), have reprinted.

Clay Harvey, North Carolinan, veteran of the 18th Airborne Corps, is one of America's most respected authorities on modern sporting rifles. Now freelance, he was formerly technical editor of *Rifle* and *Handloader* magazines. His book, *Popular Sporting Rifle Cartridges* (DBI Books, Inc., 1984), is indispensable.

Nigel Hinton's insatiable interest in firearms and shooting has taken him to prominence in a diversity of disciplines. Formerly a member of the British National Squad in UIT Rapid Fire Pistol, he was one of the founders of Practical Pistol shooting in Great Britain, attended the Columbia Conference that founded the IPSC and was for a number of years Director of the UKPSA. Hinton was also an early experimenter in Practical Rifle and Practical Shotgun. Today, his primary interests lie in Bench Rest, and Long Range Rifle.

Richard Munday, an historian of Christ Church, Oxford, and former captain of Oxford University's pistol team has, for the past several years, been involved in post-graduate research in defence policy. He is also assistant editor of *Handgunner* magazine.

Ken Warner is the acknowledged dean of American gunwriters—the title goes with his position as editor of *Gun Digest*. In years past, he was editor of *Gunsport*, founder, editor and publisher of *Gunfacts*, editor of *The American Rifleman* and founder of its sister publication, *The American Hunter*. Warner, who has hunted on several continents, lives in West Virginia where he can shoot out of his window.

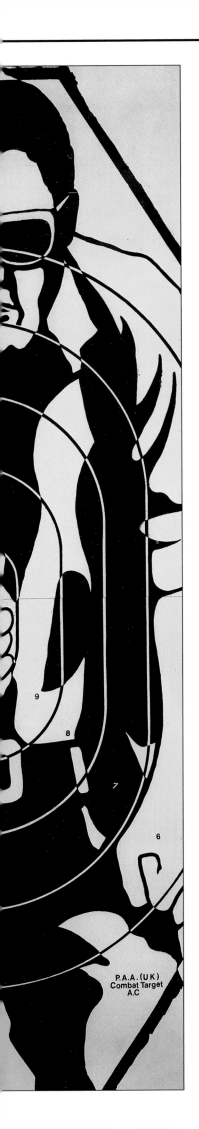

P.A.A. (U K)
Combat Target
A.C

Chief Author

Jan Stevenson is editor of *Handgunner*, one of Britain's foremost gun journals, which he founded in 1980. He has considerable experience of writing about firearms: between 1965 and 1967 he was weapons editor of the US police magazine, *Law and Order;* subsequently he became European correspondent for *Gunfacts* (1967-1969), and then handgun editor of *Guns Magazine* (1970-1975). He was co-author of *Pistols, Revolvers and Ammunition* (1972) and co-consultant to *The Book of Shooting* (1980).

Between 1973 and 1977 he studied for a D.Phil in history at Brasenose College, Oxford, and while there he won 7 half-blues for pistol shooting. His many administrative positions have included secretary of the International Practical Shooting Confederation; chairman of the UKPSA Legal Commission; member of the British Shooting Sports Council; and member of council of the National Pistol Association of Great Britain. On a more practical level, he designed the pistol training programme for the UKPSA, and was chief instructor in Practical Pistol at Delta Firearms Training Wing in Suffolk.

Apart from editing *Handgunner*, he currently runs a consultancy and forensic practice that specialises in firearms and ballistics matters.

CONTENTS

To some this may look like just another coffee table book: visually attractive, awash with colour, neatly structured and quite amazingly cheap, considering. The formula sells. Coffee table books bring a lot of pleasure and education to a lot of people, and that is a good thing. They have a reputation though, among specialists (not to say snobs), of regurgitating the commonplace and perpetuating error. A certain amount of error is inevitable in a work of this scale, despite out best efforts to weed it out. With good fortune, we shall take in corrections in a second edition.

What you will not find here is the commonplace: the potted biographies of Samuel Colt and the Reverend Alexander Forsyth of Belhelvie, the ritual recitation of the evolution of firearms by ignition systems. Our purpose, insofar as was possible with such a vast subject, has been to break new ground, or at least to take a critical look at the received wisdom. One of the problems with gun books is that they have too many

answers and not enough questions. Of course, it would be frustrating the other way round: the point of research is to push towards a conclusion, and if the author has not got one, he might have been better advised to delay publication, rather than inflicting his confusion on unsuspecting readers. But most conclusions, closely examined, are not standing on much; one cannot after all, get to a sustainable one unless the right questions have been posed in the first place. Shooting is full of received wisdom of the most dubious sort and fairly reeks of faith in the inevitability of progress.

Change is too often mistaken for improvement; there is a smugness in the present, on the part of those who cannot recall the past. Designers compulsively scale every Everest they come across, real or fancied, with results ranging from Concorde to the aerosol. It is not often recognised, even by manufacturers, how much the shooting public are creatures of fashion — not carefully contrived fashion of the *haute couture* variety, but a more diffuse sort whose trend setters are a mixed lot. Sometimes there will be a conspicuous figure — Col. Peter Hawker, Townsend Whelen, Elmer Keith,

Roy Weatherby, Jeff Cooper or Bill Ruger — whose individual influence proves substantial. Other times, the source of a trend may lie with a committee, an administration or a business; or it may be part of a larger societal or technological groundswell. To give brief examples: the NRA of Great Britain's decisions not to follow the military's adoption of a self-loading rifle in 1958 or of a small-bore service calibre in 1986, were to prove ultimately catastrophic; the NRA of America's adoption of an alibi rule led to the eventual disappearance of revolvers from the National Match Course; the UIT has tried several rules fiddles to get rid of centrefire pistol shooting altogether. On the administrative front, the FBI's espousal of the double action revolver kept the American police wedded to it for longer than would otherwise have been the case, which probably intensified the eventual backlash. And as for business, how many Colt Peacemakers, Walther PPKs and S&W Model 29s do you suppose Hollywood has sold?

Moving from the big screen to the big picture, it gets even more interesting. I have never heard a persuasive explana-

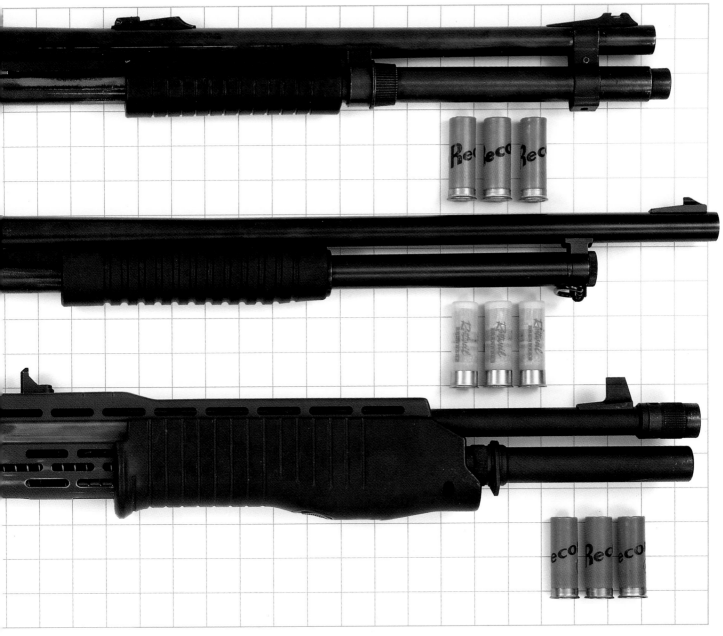

tion of why the musket replaced the bow as a military weapon. Other technological leaps forward are a lot more comprehensible, but a revisionist historian could nonetheless argue strongly to the effect that Napier was right that the Army was better off with muskets than with rifles, and that James Wolfe Ripley, the Union Chief of Ordnance, was right to prefer muzzleloaders to breechloaders.

Questions this ponderous are outside the scope of the present book; and nor are its pages strewn with iconoclasm wall to wall. The point we have been trying to make is that guns are interesting anyway, but the closer you look, the more interesting they get. What we have tried to do in the pages that follow is to give you an overview of the shooting sports and the guns involved, along with some insights as to why they are the way they are, and how they got that way. There is no pretence to completeness; even the bibliography has gaps in it. We have simply done the best we could with a big subject in the space and time available. If we have managed along the way to broaden your appreciation or give you some new perspectives on an area of knowledge that

we ourselves have always found fascinating, we shall be well enough pleased.

I had initially intended writing the entire book myself; not that I pretend to expertise across such a broad subject, but I had a lot of axes I wanted to grind, and was looking forward to the research. That was in 1986. Before the thing had progressed far, I chanced to find myself on the trajectory of an airborne automobile. Since I was standing in front of a concrete wall at the time, the splash on impact was spectacular: the wall was demolished; ditto a substantial proportion of yours truly. One of the consequences of this *contretemps* was that I was unable to complete the book on my own, and was obliged to bring in a number of specialist co-authors. I turned, naturally, to men I respect, whose books I buy and whose articles I read with pleasure, confident that they will not waste my time and may modify my point of view. And they have not done badly this time.

We have tried to make the book as nonparochial as possible. If not totally cosmopolitan, it is at least mid-Atlantic; four of the authors are British and three are American. This means the style and accent can change

markedly from chapter to chapter or spread to spread. The point of view bounces about a good bit as well. But that is all to the good.

It stands to reason that I am proud to be associated with my co-authors; I ought also to say what a splendid team Salamander had on the job. Philip de Ste. Croix was in overall charge, and nursed the project through intensive care for a very long time. Richard O'Neill was brought in as editor when I was a bit short on drive and panache, and did an excellent job. If the book looks good, it is because of Roger Hyde, who designed it, while Terry Dilliway made the colour photographs in his Bloomsbury studio. It is always interesting to watch a top professional at work.

Most of what one knows, one learns from others. We have tried to pay some of our intellectual debts in the bibliography. To all those others who have shared their knowledge and experience of firearms with us over the years, our sincerest thanks.

JAS
Brightlingsea, Essex
1988

7

HUNTING
RIFLES

Clay Harvey (Introduction) and Jan Stevenson

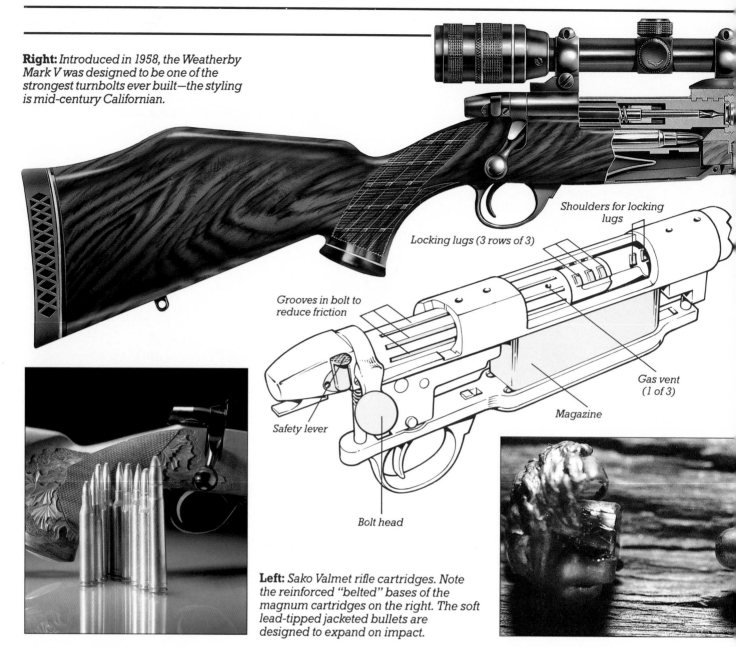

Right: *Introduced in 1958, the Weatherby Mark V was designed to be one of the strongest turnbolts ever built—the styling is mid-century Californian.*

Shoulders for locking lugs

Locking lugs (3 rows of 3)

Grooves in bolt to reduce friction

Gas vent (1 of 3)

Magazine

Safety lever

Bolt head

Left: *Sako Valmet rifle cartridges. Note the reinforced "belted" bases of the magnum cartridges on the right. The soft lead-tipped jacketed bullets are designed to expand on impact.*

Despite the reputation hunters have of being a reactionary lot, their choices in firearms — especially rifles — are trendy. Trendy, indeed. Examples? The semi-automatic flourished briefly in the early 20th century, with guns such as Winchester's Model 1905, '07, and 1910, as well as Remington's competing Models 8A and 81, finding favour among the nimrods. Then, during the time period bracketing World War II, they waned. In the 1960s, autos staged a comeback, with Ruger offering the .44 Carbine, Harrington & Richardson the Ultra Model 360, Winchester marketing their 100, Browning introducing the BAR, and Remington plugging along with the successful 742 series. Two decades later, only the BAR and the Remington survive, at least among the sporting autoloaders.

In the 1910s and 1920s, pump — or trombone — actions roamed the fields in legions. There were the Standard Arms, Remington's 14 and 141, Stevens rifles in various chamberings, Colts, and more. Today, only the Remington Model Six cum Model 7600 cum Sportsman 76 is catalogued, although Savage turned out the neat and superbly accurate Model 170 in the late 1970s.

Carbine-length boltguns, autos and levers come and go. Winchester offered a Model 70 (pre-1964) with a 20-inch (50.8cm) tube that today is quite rare, and in the late 1970s peddled a few Mannlicher-stocked snub-barrelled iterations of the post-1964 rifle. Remington periodically proffers 18.5-inch-barrelled pumps and autos; then the wind changes and they disappear for a few years. At the time of writing, in 1987, at least, they are back in the line.

Hunting-rifle cartridges exhibit the same trendiness. The .270 Winchester blossoms and fades, repeating the phenomenon every few years. The hotshot 6mm's — the .243 Winchester and .244 Remington (now known as the 6mm Remington) — virtually inundated the fine little .250-3000 and the .257 Roberts in 1955. For two decades, the .24-bores were heralded as long-range deer/antelope hunters' dream cartridges. The dust has finally settled; the new loads have been thoroughly tested in the field and often found wanting. Savage's .250-3000 and the Roberts have been picked up by several firms and are re-establishing themselves.

From time to time handgun cartridges like the .357 and .44 Magnums gain a foothold in such short, handy carbines as the Ruger auto and the Marlin lever guns. Articles appear in the sporting journals touting the antediluvian "sixgun and rifle" pairing. Some readers may believe this; others yawn, then spend their money on more practical longarms. The straight-sided cartridges wane. (Try finding a Vulcan pump-action, Winchester Model 94 .44 Mag., Marlin 336 in the same chambering, or a Remington 788 reamed to the .44 handgun round. Even today, when many dealers have Ruger Carbines, Browning B-92 lever guns in .357 Magnum, and Marlin 1894 .357's on their shelves, the death knell for these limited-use arms is sounding.)

Conversely, the .221 Fireball — originally offered in Remington's XP-100, considered a "handgun" by legal definition — has found a home in the Kimber Model 84, a neat little Mauser-type turnbolt produced in Oregon. Since the Kimber is also reamed to .222 Remington and .223, the only advantage the Fireball boasts is its quiet voice. We will see how it does.

Now it is time for an in-depth look at the present crop of hunting armament, with an eye toward current trends. The first part of this examination is concerned largely with the present trends in hunting armament in the United States of America. I shall begin with the most popular arm in this category, the turnbolt rifle.

Left: *The chrome-moly steel action of the Weatherby Mk V draws its strength from its nine forward locking lugs and a counterbored bolt which completely shrouds the head of the cartridge when it is closed.*

Right: *Wrapping it up right: this big brown bear was taken in the Yukon with a single shot from Dr. Fred Wood's 17 year old .30-06 calibre Weatherby Mk V rifle (as shown in the artwork above).*

Below: *A graphic "before and after" demonstration of the expansion of soft-nose bullets. The tremendous shocking effect of such expansion is vital for the humane dispatch of game animals.*

Bolt action

The modern sporting bolt action, king of the current scene, began its climb to fame and a devoted following with the 1898 version of Peter Paul Mauser's military rifles. (Of course the '98 was not the *first* turnbolt, nor even Mauser's initial offering. It is, however, the one that survives to this day as a superlative example of rifle design and function. It is still used to build classic, expensive hunting guns, and is the action selected by Interarms and Parker-Hale for many of their catalogued items.)

The United States' Springfield 1903 garnered quite a following, although few custom rifles are built on this action today. (Interestingly, the Parker-Hale Midland is fabricated around a modified Springfield bolt wedded to a newly-manufactured Mauser-type receiver.) For some years, the big 1917 Enfield held sway, especially for magnum-cartridge conversions, but today it is dead. Winchester's pre-1964 Model 70 is the only controlled-round feed action to rival the Mauser in lasting approbation among aficionados of the turnbolt. At the time of writing, Kimber of Oregon and a number of smaller outfits are planning to bring forth modernized permutations of the time-tested Model 70. Butch Searcy, a New

Mexican gunsmith, coverts post-1964 M70's to the older style by fitting a new bolt — complete with non-rotating Mauser side-spring extractor — coned breech, and rear-mounted ejector arm.

The foregoing characteristics are significant primarily to fans of the controlled-round feed system. Most modern hunters are quite content with the short-claw extractor (seen nearly a century ago on early Mausers), Garand-style plunger ejector, and recessed bolt face that are now fashionable. They are reliable, despite what their detractors claim. Admittedly, I have had short-claw extractors fail to yank a case free from the chamber. I have known Mauser-types fail, too. And I have had far more problems from rear-mounted ejectors than from the plunger type. From a safety standpoint, the recessed bolt face — especially when used in conjunction with a recessed barrel breech, like Remington's and Weatherby's — has it all over the Mauser, Springfield and pre-1964 M70 design, despite their vaunted gas-handling capabilities. No matter. There is room for both; each works quite well; each is safe enough for any prudent shooter or handloader.

Generally, such round-bottomed actions as the Remington 700 are considered

easier to bed properly — and *keep* bedded properly — than the slab-bottomed Model 70 or Mauser. On the other hand, the square-bellied Model 70 resists firing torque more successfully than those actions with a curved underside. The Model 70, and particularly the Mauser, uses a longer lock time (the span of milliseconds between sear release and ignition) than such modern actions as the Remington 788 and 700, and Ultra Light Arms Model 20. But then the long, heavy fall of that overweight Mauser striker provides super-reliable ignition of suspect military or aged ammunition. As you can see, everything is a trade-off. Forget esoteric comparisons; go with what works *your* way.

There are currently two significant trends, in the USA, at least. One is to very lightweight rifles. *Very* lightweight rifles. Such guns (the Mannlicher-Schoenauer, Remington Model 600 and Sako 461, to name three) have been with us for years. Some of them have achieved financial success, but on a limited basis; the rank and file did not stand in line to relinquish their cash for what they viewed as hard-kicking hunting arms of dubious accuracy, and thus limited range. But it seems that feather-heft rifles are back! And they are here to stay, I think, because of

Melvin Forbes of the Ultra Light Arms Company, as I explain below.

The new millennium for lightweight guns began with Winchester's 1981 introduction of the Model 70 Featherweight. (There had been an earlier pre-1964 Featherweight, but it was not as light as it should have been and never made sales history.) Listed in Olin's brochure at 6.75 pounds (3.06 kg), and wearing the handsomest stock ever put on a factory rifle, the new Featherweight took off. For a while, premium prices were demanded by gun shops, something virtually unheard of in those recession-ridden days. Calibres were pretty much as expected, including such perennials as the .270 Winchester, .308, and .30-06, but also catalogued was the 7 x 57 Mauser and the .257 Roberts. That surprised some people.

The Trend to Lightweights

Remington burned the midnight oil, and shortly came up with the Remington Model Seven, vaguely reminiscent of the defunct Model 600 and 660, but with a perfectly proportioned stock, skinny 18.5-inch (47cm) barrel, and cut checkering. Over the next few years, I tested all six chamberings offered and found them to be of acceptable hunting precision. The worst of them grouped five-shot strings into 1.75 inches (44mm) at 100 yards (91.44mm), and the best went not much over an inch (25mm). For jump-shooting deer in the woods, the Model Seven (preferably in 7mm-08 Remington) had, and still has, no peer, at least for the present. (Something good looms on the horizon.)

In 1984, U.S. Repeating Arms, a new company that was licensed by Olin to manufacture and sell Winchester rifles, responded to the Model Seven by adding the Model 70 Carbine to their range. It weighed in at around 6 pounds (2.72kg) in the short-action rendition, a quarter-pound (113g) less than the Model Seven. Ruger joined the fray, cataloguing the Mannlicher-stocked International at 6.25 pounds (2.835kg) and the Ultra Light Model 77 at 6 pounds (2.72kg) on the nose. The latter had a very slender handle and a 20-inch (50.8cm) rat-tail pipe; the former a slim but still man-sized profile and an equally skinny 18.5-inch (47cm) barrel.

Smith & Wesson imported their Model 1700-LS, which subsequently went to Mossberg when Smith abandoned the long-gun business (again). Browning has the A-bolt, which is not overweight — at 6.5 pounds (2.948kg) — and shoots very, very well. Weatherby markets the 6.5 pound (2.948kg) VGS and a similar synthetic-stocked version, produced by the same Japanese outfit that makes the S&W/Mossberg.

Kimber of Oregon sells the Model 84, a 6.25 pound (2.835kg) beauty. Alas, it is chambered for short, short cartridges like the .222 Remington, .223, .222 Magnum, and such wildcat numbers as the .17 Mach IV, 6 x 45, and the 6 x 47 of 1970's benchrest competition fame. I have used the last pair to take six or eight head of big game; if the little 80 and 85-grain pellets are placed *just so*, they kill neatly. Still, such limited-power cartridges are really for experts only.

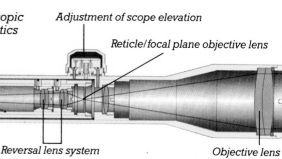

Above: *Calibrated for calibre and bullet weight, the Redfield Accu-trac enables the shooter to zoom in on the target until it fits exactly between the stadia wires, and then read off the range.*

Left: *Prime turkey taken with an Ultra-Light Arms kevlar and graphite stocked 7mm-08 sporter. The inherent strength and stability of such stocks make for robust and consistent hunting rifles.*

Below: *A Schmidt & Bender telescopic sight typical of the high quality optics used by most hunters today.*

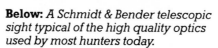

Adjustment of scope elevation

Reticle/focal plane objective lens

Eyepiece   Reversal lens system   Objective lens

The best comes last. Ultra Light Arms Company, of Granville, West Virginia, has been shipping rifles only since 1985. These rifles are destined to revolutionize the bolt-gun market. Why? There are several reasons.

First, they weigh only 4 pounds 14 ounces (2.21kg) in most short-action (.308 Winchester length) chamberings, and that's complete with scope mounts. Nothing else comes close. Further, you give up nothing ballistically, since the ULA rifles are *rifles*, not carbines, wearing Douglas Premium air-gauged barrels a full 22 inches (55.88cm) long and .56-inch (14.2mm) in muzzle diameter. (Most of the super-flyweight rigs show a .50-inch (12.7mm) diameter at the nozzle.) Better yet, these high-grade tubes are stress relieved, so they shoot to the same point of impact whether cold, hot, or lukewarm.

Second, the ULA rifles are the only affordable production rifles on the market that boast benchrest-quality machine work and action tolerances. Locking lugs are lapped until they bear evenly, 100 per cent. Only .022-inch (.0508mm) clearance is allowed between the bolt body and the interior of the receiver. That is amazing. The safety is three-position, and locks the bolt down when on "safe". The trigger is a match-grade, adjustable Timney.

Third, the ULA wears a synthetic stock, of Kevlar and graphite construction, that is stiff in the extreme, tough to the point of incredulity, well finished and fitted to the barrelled action, and so perfectly proportioned that it feels dynamic. The rifles balance perfectly. The stock is quite straight, carries a cheekpiece but no Monte Carlo, and affixed to its aft end is a thick rubber recoil pad. As a result, the guns do not transfer much recoil to their shooter's shoulder or cheekbones. And there is an optional KDF muzzle brake that tames the fierce .338 Winchester Magnum into a purring kitten.

Fourth, accuracy. Forget what I and all the other "experts" have told you about lightweight rifle accuracy. Melvin Forbes, president of Ultra Light and creator of its wares, has rescinded any physical laws heretofore governing flea-heft sporter precision. Not to belabour the point, let me just note that my ULA .22-250 averaged .54-inch (13.7mm) for five five-shot strings — benchrest, at 100 yards (91.44m) — with its pet handload, and around .8-inch (20.3mm) with Federal Blitz 40-grain hollow points. My 7mm-08 printed .875 inch (22.2mm), again for five-shot strings. The .284 Ultra Light printed three fives into .95-inch (24.1mm),

Above: *Fibre-glass stocked bolt actions such as Tim Gardiner's groundhog rifle are becoming increasingly popular not just because they are lighter but because of their better stability.*

Left: *Based on the seven shot model 70, the Marlin Papoose rimfire autoloader makes an ideal trail gun weighing just 3¾lb and with a detachable barrel that can be fitted without tools.*

and the 6.5 x 55mm with which I slew a near-Boone and Crockett black bear (18.875 inches (48cm), skull measurement; 468 pounds (212.3kg), weighed) grouped 1.25 inches (31.75mm) with my bruin ammunition, 1.2-in (30.48mm) with Norma 139-grain hollow points. My .338 Mag, a prototype, grouped right at 1.5 inches (38.1mm) with factory ammo, the 210-grain Federal Partition to be exact. That makes it the most accurate .338 I have tested, regardless of weight. (It scaled 6.25 pounds (2.835kg).)

Now we should consider a second hunting rifle trend: synthetic stock materials, and to a lesser extent, laminated wood. Despite claims to the contrary, the main advantage of a synthetic (or laminate) stock is stability, *not* light weight. (The exiguous heft is a side benefit of *some* synthetic-stocked arms, but definitely not all.) Such "plastic" materials as Kevlar, fibreglass and nylon have been used to build rifle stocks for years. Remington introduced the little Nylon 66 rimfire autoloader in the late 1950s; Steyr-Mannlicher has sold a glass-handled centrefire for quite a spell. An early example of laminated hardware is the mid-1960s-vintage Remington Model 600 Magnum.

The point is that neither synthetics nor laminates are exactly hot new items, just hot *selling* items, recently. Nearly everyone offers one or the other, or as with U.S. Repeating Arms Company, both. A laminated stock offers the traditional feel and warmth of wood and is not unpleasant to gaze upon, as some "plastic" stocks definitely are. One *caveat*: according to Alpha Arms Company's president Jim Hill, not all laminated wood is non-hygroscopic. His tests have shown that some of his competitors' woodwork will absorb moisture almost as readily as a normal wood stock. Consider this when you make your buying decision, although I have no idea how you could check it out for yourself before committing your cash. (All things considered, it is probably better simply to opt for a synthetic stock.)

Before closing on the turnbolt, it is worth noting that this action type will probably dominate the sporting-rifle market in the foreseeable future. Not because it is the best for everyone, nor the least expensive, nor the handsomest, nor yet the most reliable. But because it is demonstrably the most accurate (a nebulous attribute for the average hunter); it is entrenched; it makes up into a mouth-watering custom creation that borders on art; and it is viewed by the

public as the toughest gun going. Like it or not, those are the facts.

Semi-automatic

Aside from the amazing popularity of the military and para-military assault rifles, which shows no signs of abating, the autoloading rifle is on the downswing. It has acquired a reputation for poor accuracy, a rotten trigger, bad balance and aesthetics, and exorbitant cost. Some of which has the harsh ring of the truth. Let us look at the hunter's self-feeders, of which there are only two surviving examples, and perhaps a third sort of hermaphroditic rendition.

The sales leader is certainly the Remington series, operating under various sobriquets. Current nomenclature is Model Four, for the big spender; Model 7400, for the man with a mortgage and car payments, but with a yen for more exotic flavours than vanilla; and the Sportsman 74, for the bargain-basement shopper or the no-frills hunter. I prefer this latter piece; it does not shine, shoots as well as its up-scale brethren, and has no pretensions except as a deer killer. Unfortunately, it comes only in .30-06 at present. (Not that there is anything wrong with the ought-six, but I like a choice. Besides, a Sportsman 74 in 6mm Remington

Above: *The Winchester 94—a lever action legend. Low cost, slim action, light weight, and fast follow-up shots continue to earn the lever action big sales in North America.*

Left: *The use of military-style assault rifles, like the .308 Galil, for hunting remains controversial. But the best examples undeniably offer the accuracy to match their firepower.*

Left: *The big Browning BAR is a sporting autoloader chambered for most popular hunting cartridges. Fitted with a scope, the BAR is easily capable of printing sub two inch groups at 100 yards.*

Right: *A fine trophy taken with a scoped Marlin lever action rifle. Although unpopular outside America, the better lever guns give little away to rival action types.*

might make an excellent small-game slayer to perhaps 250 yards (230m).)

The cream of the autoloading crop is the Browning BAR. It is big but perfectly balanced, has a comb height commensurate with a telescope sight, shoots like *crazy*, and generally has an acceptable trigger pull — and often an excellent one. Its metalwork is fine, but shiny; its woodwork is equally well done, but shinier.

Incidentally, of the dozen or so 7mm Remington Magnum rifles I have fired, my BAR is the second most accurate. For example, four five-shot strings in 1.2 inches (30.48mm). Of nine handloads tried in my BAR, six printed under 1.875 inches (47.6mm) for an average. These are incredible figures.

Finally, mention should be made of the Heckler & Koch Model 770. My sample, a .308 Winchester tested ten years ago for *Guns Illustrated*, grouped under 1.5 inches (38mm) with one factory load, and well under 2 inches (51mm) with almost anything. That is the best all-round performance I suppose I have ever achieved with an auto. The trigger pull was quite good, as well. But there the accolades end.

Metal-to-wood fit was mediocre at best, horrendous in spots. The comb height was ridiculous unless used only with iron sights,

whereupon your aesthetic sensibilities were offended to the point of irritation by the gaping square holes in the receiver top, which received the detachable scope mount. The open sights were designed by a cretin, or at least someone who had never hunted, nor even read an *article* about hunting. If a scope were installed, the only correct placement for your chin (assuming you wanted to peer *through* the scope) was atop the comb. The safety location was worse. If Heckler & Koch would hire someone who knows something about hunting, about stocking, about scope use, and about *accessible* safeties, they might have something there. Until then, forget the Heckler & Koch Model 770.

Pump action

The trusty old trombone action is represented only by Remington at the present. Probably, this will long be so — maybe forever. Fortunately, it is an excellent rifle.

According to a Remington spokesman, the Model Six/7600/Sportsman 76 is as big a seller as ever, especially in its bailiwick — the northeastern United States. Certain states in that area prohibit the use of semi-automatic arms. The slide action,

being nearly as rapid in articulation as the auto, and virtually identical in looks and feel to the popular Remington series, is the obvious choice in such areas.

I have tested three or four Remingtons. The most recent, a new 7600 in .30-06, averaged 2.3 inches (58.4mm) for three five-shot strings with the 150-grain Federal soft point factory load, and 2.38 inches (60.45mm) with its runner-up, the 180-grain Hornday spire point factory number. That is pretty good, and better than any Remington autoloader I have tested.

Even more accurate was a Model Six reamed to 6mm Remington. With Remington 80-grain Power-Lokt ammo, my M6 went into 1.625 inches (41.3mm) for the aggregate. The runner-up was a handload featuring the 75-grain Speer hollow point and Hodgdon's H380 powder; with this, groups ran to 1.72 inches (43.69mm).

The pump is as reliable, in my rather limited experience, as the Remington autos. Trigger quality is comparable, as is fit and finish. Although I have no reservations about the slide action as a hunting gun, neither can I think of a reason to recommend it over any other action type. If you already own one, keep it. If you are contemplating a purchase, you will have to provide your own selling points.

Lever actions

Although the lever action has never been popular in Europe, it has long sold well in the United States. It still does, though not to the extent it once did. Marlin continues to pay its electricity bill with proceeds from Model 336 sales; U.S. Repeating Arms (formerly Winchester) catalogues several versions of the venerable Model 94; Savage trundles along with the fine Model 99; Browning lists the BLR in a broad range of chamberings, recently revived the hoary old 1886 in .45-70, and for 1987 issued a limited edition of the fabled Model 71 in .348 Winchester. Until recently, Browning offered the B-92 — a Model 92 Winchester clone — in .357 and .44 Magnums, but I understand it has been dropped. Various importers such as Allen Arms and Rossi purvey copies of ubiquitous Winchesters of yore, in such chamberings as the eccentric .44 Rimfire and the ancient .44-40 WCF. There is no dearth of lever guns.

So what are they good for, aside from playing cowboys? They are quick on the second and third shots, should you need them, but the pump and autos are quicker. They are more accurate, on average, than the self-feeder, and in some brands and calibres are more precise than the trombone action. They hold a bale of ammo in their cupboards, but so do most other action types taking similar rounds. Some examples will shift from "on safe" to "fire" with absolute quietude, but in my mind that is a moot advantage. They are reliable, but so are most other current rifles; the dead wood has been pretty well weeded out of the forest of hunting arms by this time. Bolt actions are more accurate, if slower for follow-up shots.

The fact must be faced that most levers are purchased for one (or a combination) of three reasons. Firstly, the average Model 336 Marlin or Model 94 Winchester is cheaper to buy than such turnbolts as the Remington 700 BDL or Winchester Model 70, or any of the autos or pumps. The margin may not seem great but to the shooter on a tight budget, around £30 or $50 can be a lot of money.

Secondly, the lever gun is compact for its power, thin through its midriff (especially the "traditional" carbines like the Marlin and Winchester), and easy to carry all day. (Except when scoped; then it is no handier than a similar bolt action.) For shooting no farther than 200 yards (182.88m), and in normal shooting light, the iron-sighted lever will kill plenty of venison if its user has good (or corrected) eyesight.

Finally, and maybe most importantly, lots of people simply *like* the levers, especially the classic styles. How else could Browning market so successfully the recreated .45-70 and .348 Winchester copies? They weigh too much for all-day toting; the M1886 is too long and ill-balanced for serious hunting; the cartridges are limited in range and, in the case of the .348, very hard to find. No matter; Browning are selling all they can make — to Western buffs. Of course, there is nothing wrong with that, but it has very little (actually, nothing) to do with the genre's capabilities. (This resembles the

Single shot

Such single-shot hunting arms as Ruger's delightful and handsome Number One, the new Thompson — Center TCR '83, and Browning's B-78 and current 1885, are dear to the nostalgic hunter's heart, and for good reasons. They are either unusually compact (if wearing a 22-inch (55.88cm) tube) or of moderate proportions for their barrel length (if sporting a 26- to 28-inch (66.04 to 71.21cm) pipe). Either way, delivered ballistics favour the one-shooter. Balance is generally excellent; accuracy — though not of boltgun quality — acceptable for any hunting purpose. The guns are well made, slick as a ball-bearing in operation, and denote their wielder as a gentleman. (Whether he is or not!)

Two complaints centre around single-shot arms. One, of course, is that they have no magazine, and thus offer a slow follow-up shot, which is true. There are various ways to circumvent — or at least lessen — the attendant difficulties, but none is 100 per cent satisfactory to most gunners. Single-shot fans accept the foregoing as the price they have to pay for the single's attributes.

The second criticism levelled at the one-shooters is that they are less accurate than the bolt action. This again is true, but so

what? A good single is more precise than its *user*, who needs — or can even *use* — more than that? Still, let us look for a moment at exactly how much of an advantage in accuracy the single-shot owner must yield to the average turnbolt.

Any out-of-the-box Ruger, TCR '83, or Browning (excepting possibly a.45-70) will probably group into 1.5 inches (38.1mm) for five shots at 100 yards (91.44m), on command. If you think you need better than 1.5-inch (38.1mm) groups at 100 yards (91.44m) — which means that all your shots will land within .75 inch (19.05mm) of your point of aim, assuming you do *your* part — or 3 inches (76.2mm) at 200 yards (182.88m), then you live in a rarified world of make-believe. The rest of us know better. (Of course, for long-range varminting, 1 inch (25.4mm) at 100 yards (91.44m) is necessary. Better than that is desirable but not requisite unless you hunt from one spot and shoot off sandbags. A good Browning or Ruger Number One in .22-250 or .220 Swift is fully capable of grouping right at 1 inch (25.4mm), and often under. Thus, if I miss a 300-yard (274m) groundhog, I blame myself, not my rifle.)

The single shot is not, nor ever will be, as popular with the public as the repeaters. It is a speciality gun for special hunters.

everlasting popularity of the Colt Single Action Army and the Luger pistol, neither of which was ever much good at what it was intended to do.)

Now, there are two exceptions: the BLR and the excellent Savage 99. Neither of these guns looks "Western", despite Browning's sad attempts at making the BLR do so. The BLR sells because it is *good*, not because it resembles the gun John Wayne carried in *Red River*. And the 99, despite having had its genesis when the West was *still* pretty wild, is not considered "Western" in the minds of TV and movie audiences who grew up on exposed-hammer, tubular-magazine Winchesters. Like the BLR, the Savage 99 sells every year to fans of the *gun*, not fans of the movies.

As for its capabilities in the field, any lever gun is sufficiently precise for 150-yard (137m) deer hunting, and most do well to 200 yards (182.88m). In the case of the Marlin 336, Winchester M94, Browning 1886 and M71, and the Rossi .44 Magnum, such levels of precision generally outstrip the efficacy of their cartridges. Most of these carbines will group some load or other into around 3 inches (76.2mm) at 100 yards (91.44m), though many will do better. Notable in this regard are the 7 x 30 Waters (which will print consistently under 2 inches (51mm) with iron sights), the .356 Winchester (which is also *ballistically* capable of exceeding 200 yards (182.88m)), and the .444 Marlin (which, in most examples, will group 2.25 inches (57.15mm) on a bad day).

The "modern" levers — the BLR and M99 — take longer-ranging cartridges like the 7mm-08, .308 Winchester, .243, and even the .257 Roberts in the case of the Browning. These loads will reach right out, especially the two bigger bores. Fortunately, the rifles are up to it as well. It is a rare BLR or Model 99 that cannot be coaxed under 2 inches (50.8mm), and many will print 1.5 inch (38.1mm) groups at 100 yards (91.44m). Nearly any M99 reamed to the superb .250-3000 will go around 1.375 inches (34.925mm) if introduced to even the most modest handloading skills.

Thus, the lever-action shooter has all the gun he truly needs, unless he is a very, very fine big-game shot — and maybe even then, if he chooses a BLR or Savage 99. Do not point the finger of guilt at the tried-and-true "cowboy" guns, nor scoff at them. They can do their job very well.

The European Scene

The foregoing survey of hunting armament relates primarily to the situation in the United States. In Europe, it is otherwise. Hunting there has always been a more formal and class-conscious undertaking, with a cargo of ritual designed to intimidate the uninitiated. And woe to him who disregards fashion. It is acceptable, of course, to venture afield with a downmarket rifle, providing it is the right *sort* of downmarket rifle, such as a Midland bolt action or a converted Swedish Mauser. But a levergun would be severely frowned upon; ditto a pump or semi-auto.

The latter two are virtually absent from the European scene. Lever actions are

Above: *The Browning BLR is one of the most accurate lever actions ever made. Chambered for rounds like the 7mm-08, .308 Win, .243 and .257 Roberts, it is a gun with plenty of long-range power.*

Left: *A typically European design, the Sauer over-and-under combination rifle/shotgun, allows the hunter to take whatever game presents itself during a driven shoot.*

Right: *The West German Blaser SR850 one-gun shooting system. Interchangeable barrels lock into an action that features a multi-lugged bolthead riding in a rail-mounted slide in the receiver.*

regarded as ethnic American curiosities, and while they may get a vigorous and loving workout on the range during club outings, it would take a man of standing to use one when stalking without risk of ostracism.

As far as I can recall, the Sako Finniwolf was the only sporting lever gun of European provenance. Introduced in 1964, it was discontinued after eight bleak years. Probably, it was intended for the US market, where its executive-class price tag was a robust sales disincentive. But even had the price been right, the gun was doomed by its sleek lines, Monte Carlo stock and box magazine. For apart from the 99 Savage — a classic in its own right — no non-Western-style lever gun has lasted long in the United States. The Model 88 Winchester flopped just as resoundingly as did the Finnbear, which closely resembled it.

There are two points of similarity between Europe and the USA. One is the overpowering preponderance of the bolt action and the other is the recent emergence of the single shot as a snob's gun — granted that these are lovely guns, and there are some quite congenial snobs using them. The Farquharson-inspired Ruger Number 1 action has been the vehicle for all this, and is used by Heym,

Hartmann & Weiss and even Holland & Holland as the basis for their exquisite falling blocks. And several indigenous actions, such as the Heeren, have made a recovery on the Ruger's coat tails.

A point of contrast is the eternal Continental fondness for combination guns — zweilings, drillings or vierlings, depending on the number of barrels. Any mix of calibres, gauges and barrel layout can be had. Their popularity is said to result from the prevalence of *battu* hunting, in which the shooter maintains his position, often in a blind or high seat, while the ground is beaten, and is expected to engage any game that emerges, be it furred or feathered. The same guns, with slugs in the shotgun barrels, work well on boar.

It is not, of course, that the arch-conservative European huntsman is not as much a creature of fashion as the American when it comes to choosing his hardware; it is rather that the trends sometimes differ. One in which the Continentals have led the way is the renaissance of the double rifle. The thing was more or less of a British development during the salad days of Empire, but scarcely survived the retreat from Suez. Today, the London-based firms of Purdey, Rigby and Holland & Holland,

joined lately by Hartmann & Weiss, are doing a roaring trade in the twin bores, but precious few go to Englishmen, who, economically straitened, buy theirs on the Continent, where everyone is making them as well: Dumoulin, FN-Browning and Lebeau-Courally in Belgium; Sarasqueta in Spain; Beretta and Perugini-Visini in Italy; and Heym in Germany, not to mention a host of craftsmen in Ferlach. That list probably leaves out as many as it includes: the Czechs and Finns are also making double rifles, while the Japanese produce one for Winchester, who sell it in the USA.

Granted that a heavy double rifle is the best gun for dangerous game at close quarters, precious few of today's purchasers of two-barrelled rifles will fall in that category of sportsman. Why then choose it? It is short and handy for a given barrel length, but rarely is it lighter than a comparable bolt gun. It will group both barrels only with one load and at one distance, and even then, groups will be no better than up to the job expected. Why would a man buy a Winchester 101 Double Express when, for the same outlay, he could have driven home with five or six Model 70's? The answer is snob appeal, or simple pride of ownership, depending on how you view it. Price makes the double a symbol of

conspicuous consumption. As such, its newfound popularity promises to prove durable, but the limitations and shortcomings of the machine are such that less pecunious shooters are not likely to bemoan the lack of one too pitiably.

One distinctively European trend of the past few decades has been towards the modular bolt action, which interchanges barrels and calibres, and sometimes boltheads and buttstocks as well. It seems to have started in the mid-1960s with the Gehmann-designed Mauser Model 66, later redesignated Model 660. It, and the more recent Blaser, use a multi-lugged bolthead that rides in a rail-mounted slide in the receiver. The receiver is lightly stressed, since the bolt locks into a recess machined into the breech end of the barrel itself. The result is a very short, light and handy gun. Bedding is metal-to-metal — essential if the barrel interchangeability concept is to work. The Sauer 200 uses a more conventional receiver, but has an easily (relatively speaking) dismountable butt for ease of transport.

Americans tend to dismiss these guns as prime examples of Teutonic gadgetmongery, and their North American market penetration has been precisely nil. One of the stumbling blocks has been that for the

price of a rifle and an extra barrel in another calibre, one could have bought two or three perfectly good rifles. Lately, the price has been coming more into line, so perhaps the swap-barrel concept will find a future.

The recent American enrapturement with near gravity-proof rifles has yet to arouse much enthusiasm abroad, though Parker-Hale offer a very decent representative of the genre in their 6.5 pound (2.948kg), 22-inch (55.88cm) barrelled Model 1100. The fact is that the advantage of a lightweight rifle only shows up if you have to carry it a lot. If the ghillie regards it as his job to hump your hardware, you are better off with a heavy gun. The same will be true if the furthest overland you will need to trek is the hundred yards from the road to the stand.

The near-century since Peter Paul Mauser introduced his 1898 turnbolt has been one of constant and often profound change. And the quest for improvement in sporting rifles has been as diligent as any. But, as the thoughtful Frenchman put it, *Plus ça change, plus c'est la même chose*. In neither ballistics nor the gun have we really done much more than come full circle. It is in the greater complexity and enhanced efficiency of sighting equipment that the real advance is to be seen.

Parker-Hale Rangoon oil tin

Some people will maintain, quite vehemently if the occasion requires vehemence, that falling block single-shot rifles are the most elegant firearms that have ever been made. It is a point of view to which we subscribe entirely. And the most elegant of falling blocks is the Farquarson, the lower of the two rifles illustrated, invented by, or at least named for, John Farquarson of Daldhu, a Scotsman of varied talents.

Farquarson was the most famous poacher of his age; his exploits in this respect were legendary, and subsequently filled a book. He was also a superb marksman. He won the Scottish rifle championship in 1863, but 1869 was his best year. After a series of tense tie-breaking shootoffs, he won the Elcho Shield for Scotland at Wimbledon, then journeyed to Belgium, where he won the

King's Prize at one of the most prestigious championships in Europe.

Along the way, no doubt, he thought much about rifle design, his ideas eventually coalescing in the magnificent action that still bears his name and which is widely regarded as the finest expression of the single shot. Farquarson claimed that he carved his first model out of turnips! When he patented it, he was promptly sued by Alexander Henry, the great Edinburgh gunmaker whose employ the famous poacher had recently left.

Henry was a fine craftsman and a renowned designer. His own underlever falling block was widely used by target riflemen and stalkers alike, was popular with the Volunteers, saw military service in Australia and narrowly missed adoption by British forces to replace the Snider. As it turned out, the

government adopted the Martini action, but with Henry's rifling, hence the designation Martini-Henry. Co-owners of Farquarson's patent were Sir Henry Halford and William Ellis Metford, respectively the most outstanding ballistician and engineer of their time, whose evidence to the court could not have failed to influence the jury that found in Farquarson's favour.

WILLIAM EVANS FARQUARSON ACTION

Country of origin: Great Britain
Type: Rifle
Calibre: .577-3in
Capacity: Single shot
Action: Lever operated vertically falling block
Operation: Lever under trigger guard pushes down and forward to draw breechblock downward, recocking striker and activating ejector.

Construction: All steel, colour case hardened receiver. Rifled seven grooves right hand twist, with narrow lands.
Barrel length: 26.75in (679mm)
Length overall: 43.5in (1105mm)
Weight (empty): 9.8lb (4.45kg)
Sights: Blade foresight, parade of three leaf backsights graduated 100, 200 and 300 yards
Comments: Fired 750-grain soft or solid bullets ahead of 100 grains of cordite in a 3-inch case—a classic elephant load in a 15lb double. This much lighter single shot was probably often used with comparitively softer loads.

Farquarson rifles were manufactured under licence by George Gibbs of Bristol. On expiry of the patent, the design became public property, and was manufactured by Webley and many other makers who bought their actions from Webley, who in turn got them from Auguste Francotte of

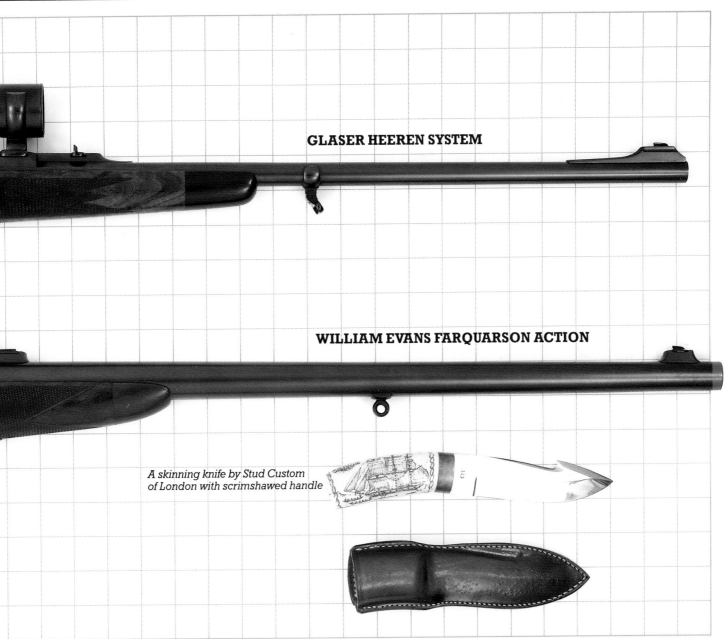

GLASER HEEREN SYSTEM

WILLIAM EVANS FARQUARSON ACTION

A skinning knife by Stud Custom of London with scrimshawed handle

Liège, Belgium. It is thought, but not proved, that all Farquarsons other than those made by Gibbs under the patent, use Francotte actions. The gun illustrated is a massive 9.8lb .577 built by William Evans of 63 Pall Mall. Using a 3-inch case and 100 grains of cordite, it fired a 750-grain bullet, either full jacketed or soft point, which was intended for use against heavy or dangerous game such as buffalo, rhinoceros or elephant. It is rifled with seven grooves on a righthand twist and carries a 3-leaf backsight with the leaves marked 100, 200 and 300 yards. The receiver is case hardened, and the fore-end has a horn tip. It was made in about 1910 for a Siamese diplomat who never called to collect it. It still has not been fired, except for proofing and regulating the sights. As might be imagined, the 300-yard sight leaf is very tall.

The Farquarson was the basis for the splendid Ruger No.1, custom versions of which are built by, among others, Hartmann & Weiss of Hamburg and London.

GLASER HEEREN SYSTEM

Country of origin: Switzerland
Type: Rifle
Calibre: 8 x 68mm
Capacity: Single shot
Action: Lever operated vertically falling block
Operation: Trigger guard serves as lever, released at front and pivots at rear to draw breechblock downward, recocking striker and activating extractor. Rear trigger pushes forward to set, though rifle may be fired by pressing forward trigger even if not set.
Construction: All steel
Barrel length: 27.5in (698mm)
Length overall: 42in (1067mm)
Weight (empty): 8.3lb (3.76kg)
Sights: Hensoldt Wetzlar Dialytan 4X scope with integral claw bases

fitted; open iron sights supplementary
Comments: Extraordinarily strong and compact design beautifully rendered

The other rifle shown is a Heeren action, which was patented in Paris, and is still built by Glaser of Zurich, and various small makers in Ferlach and Kufstein in Austria. The Heeren has an integral set trigger, and the trigger guard, hinged at the rear, forms the operating lever. The release latch is visible in the forward bow of the guard. The Heeren is a strong, efficient and extremely compact action. It lacks, on immediate acqaintance, the Farquarson's elegance, but tends to grow on one. It also lacks the Farquarson's powerful double extractor, except for the gun shown, an 8 x 68S made by

Glaser on special order from George Swenson, the designer of the Swing target rifle.

When Swenson called to pick the rifle up, he praised the workmanship. The master gunsmith who had made it was called out front, chef-like, to take the compliment. Swenson told him how delighted he was with the rifle, how he particularly liked the double extractor and wanted a .308 exactly like it. The gunsmith, a gentleman then in his '70s, promptly hurled himself to the floor and began banging the ground with his heels and fists, screaming "Nein, Nein". The proprieter, other staff, and indeed, other customers, took no notice whatever and continued their conversations without pause. Nonetheless, Swenson did not get his .308, so the old gunsmith's lack of enthusiasm for the project must have carried some weight.

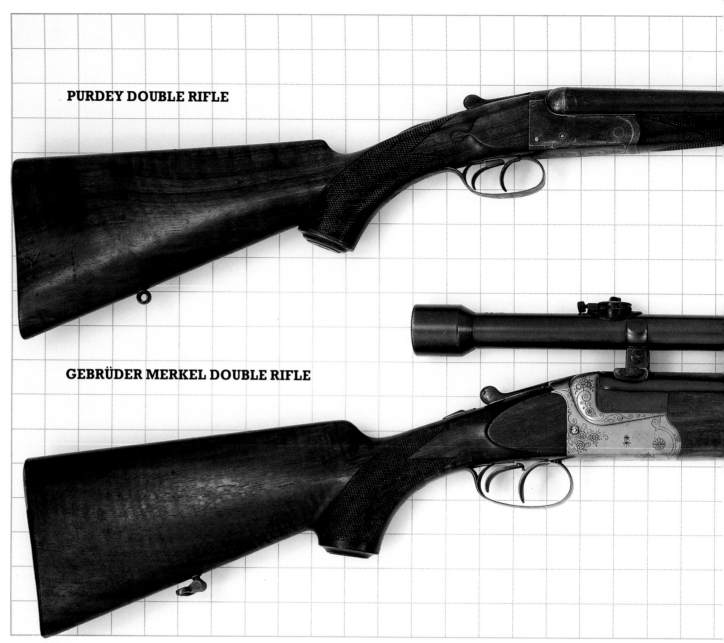

PURDEY DOUBLE RIFLE

GEBRÜDER MERKEL DOUBLE RIFLE

Double rifles have an undeniable mystique, no doubt because they are known to be the choice of professionals when faced with really dangerous game. They are not much used by anyone else because of their expense, which does no harm on the mystique front either.

Professionals use them for two reasons: absolute reliability and speed of the second shot. Both stem from the fact that the double has two of everything: two locks, two chambers, two firing pins, two mainsprings; if anything goes wrong on one side, the other is still there. The second shot only requires another trigger pressure: there is no extraction, ejection and reloading cycle with the danger of a jam or malfunction. Nor does the double suffer in a firepower comparison. A bolt action express rifle has a total capacity of four rounds: three in

the magazine and one if the chamber. Every shot requires a manual operation. After four shots, the magazine must be recharged a round at a time.

By contrast, a hunter with a heavy double goes after dangerous game with two extra rounds carried between the fingers of his left hand. After the second round is fired, his right thumb hits the toplever, the gun falls open, automatic ejectors clear the chambers, and the two spare rounds are inserted simultaneously. The barrels are slammed closed and the gun is ready to fire again. A further reload, if required, is effected, again two rounds at once, from elasticated loops on the front of the jacket. Over any number of rounds that you care to name, the double will outshoot a bolt action express rifle.

It will also prove far more reliable. Grit or debris may freeze a bolt action, but the far

greater danger is that in the heat of the moment, the shooter will short stroke the bolt, either rechambering the empty case, or jamming the top round from the magazine against the unejected empty whilst trying to chamber both. The double offers no such hazards. The double is undeniably the better weapon, and bolt actions are so widely used against dangerous game only because they are a great deal cheaper than a best double. The bolt gun is almost entirely machine made, while a double demands a great deal of highly skilled handwork on what is, in effect, two guns in one. Relatively cheaper express doubles could be made, of course, but the market is not large enough to bring them forth.

For this purpose, side-by-sides are universally preferred to over-unders, the considerations again being

reliability and speed of fire. The over-under has to hinge over a much greater arc in order to get the lower chamber even barely clear of the standing breech; it has to be closed again over that same arc. The top chamber is high enough over the hinge to put a great strain on the lower lock-up, and in effect requires an extended rib to lock into the top of the standing breech. The two-at-once reload is not as handy as with the side-by-side, and is likely to foul either on the extended rib or on the top of the standing breech.

The advantages of the double do not apply when the quarry is lighter, non-dangerous game. Greater accuracy over longer distances is likely to be required, and when precision rather than firepower is required, the double does not shine. Those who use it do so for aesthetic

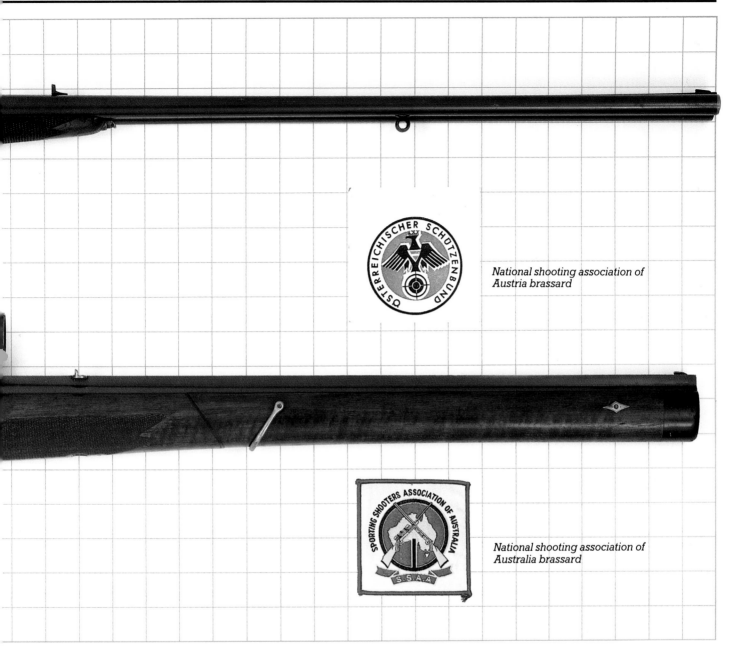

National shooting association of Austria brassard

National shooting association of Australia brassard

rather than practical reasons. Such is precisely the case with the two rifles illustrated.

PURDEY DOUBLE RIFLE

Country of origin: Great Britain
Type: Rifle
Calibre: .360x2¼in Express (.360 Miniature Express)
Capacity: Double barrel (2)
Action: Boxlock, double trigger, non-ejector, toplever opening with two underlugs and doll's head extension
Operation: Pushing toplever to right allows barrels to open on hinge, recocking internal hammers and activating extractors
Construction: All steel; case hardened receiver. Barrels rifled 7 grooves right hand twist
Barrel length: 27.125in (689mm)
Length overall: 43.25in (1098mm)
Weight (empty): 7.11lb (3.22kg)
Sights: Blade foresight and notch backsight
Comments: A very deft handling rifle built on a tiny receiver.

The upper rifle is a side-by-side hammerless boxlock by J. Purdey & Sons of South Audley Street, London. Black powder proved, it is chambered for the rimmed .360 x 2¼in Express, sometimes called the "Miniature Express" which threw a 190-grain bullet, often paper patched, at about 1,700 feet per second. Dating from the 1890s, this rifle was probably used for culling fallow deer in the park of some great house. Its tiny receiver makes it muzzle-heavy but very deft in handling.

GEBRÜDER MERKEL DOUBLE RIFLE

Country of origin: Germany
Type: Rifle
Calibre: 7 x 57R
Capacity: Double barrel (2)
Action: Boxlock over/under, double triggers

Operation: Moving toplever to right allows barrels to open on hinge, recocking internal hammers and activating ejectors
Construction: All steel
Barrel length: 25.5in (648mm)
Length overall: 42.25in (1073mm)
Weight (empty): 9.3lb (4.22kg)
Sights: Zeiss Jena 4X scope with single pillar adjustments, 3-post reticle and integral claw mounts fitted, open iron sights supplementary
Comments: A superb rifle. The full-length fore-end is unusual.

The over-under, glass sighted Merkel, made in Germany before the last war, is rather a different proposition. The problem with doubles, as far as accuracy goes, lies in regulating the two barrels to shoot to the same point of impact. There is also the consideration that the barrels will converge (if at all) only at the precise range for which they were regulated, and only

with the precise load with which they were regulated.

The Merkel is chambered for the 7 x 57R *Normaliziert*, a round especially loaded by Dynamit Nobel and guaranteed for ballistic uniformity. With loads of comparable uniformity, this rifle will pattern shots from alternate barrels into 1.5in (38mm) at one hundred metres, and will hold excellent groups even further. It was probably used for chamois stalking, where accuracy is all. It did not disappoint.

The rifle illustrated is fitted with a telescopic sight made by the well known German firm of Carl Zeiss. This four power scope features a 3-post reticle, and it is fitted to the rifle by means of the integral claw mounts shown. The full-length wooden fore-end is another note-worthy feature, giving the Merkel a highly distinctive appearance.

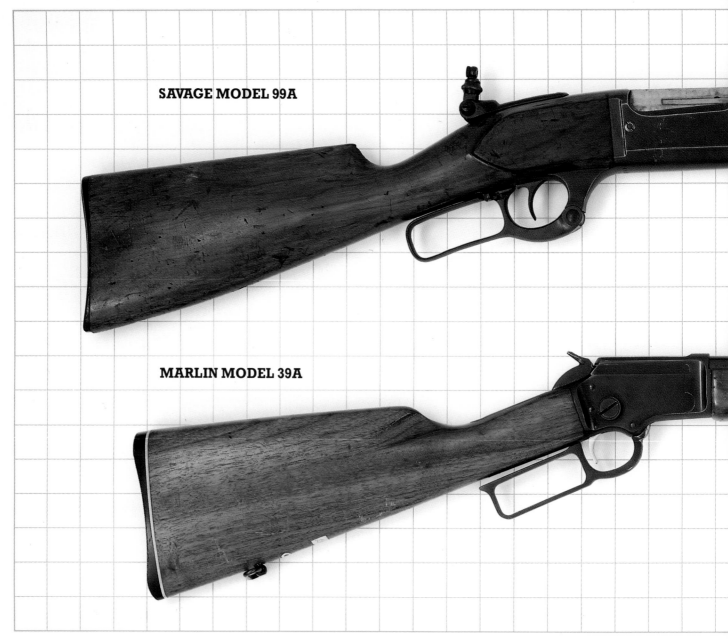

SAVAGE MODEL 99A

MARLIN MODEL 39A

Bolt action sporting rifles came onto the market towards the end of the last century, but did not find the immediate acceptance in the United States that they did in Europe, where they seemed the natural successor to the single-shot and double rifles then in use (except where dangerous game might be encountered when the double retained preference).

Americans did not follow this swing to the bolt gun, because by the time it arrived, they had been using lever actions for half a century and liked them very much. Six and a half million Model 1894 Winchesters and four million Marlin Model 336s (1893) later, they are still happily using lever guns. Granted that after ninety years, the bolt action has made some headway.

Lever actions became immediately popular in the

United States because of a perceived need for firepower. In Europe, the rifle was either a military weapon—simplicity and ruggedness were the criteria here—or a sporting implement. In either case, the single shot served admirably, although boar hunters preferred a double. In America, the rifle was a working tool, carried constantly, used to protect stock and to feed the family and the dogs. It was also the means of personal defence in half a continent when the nearest law might be several days away and problems, such as Indians, rustlers or bandits, might come in bunches. No wonder that the lever action, with the fifteen or so fast follow-up shots in a tubular under-barrel magazine seemed such a necessity to daily existence. It was also short and flat and carried in a saddle scabbard.

In the Eastern USA, where rifles were more strictly sporting in application than in the West, most hunting was in dense cover for game which quickly bounded out of view. Here too, the lever guns' agility and fast second or third shot were much appreciated.

The lever action, by the turn of the century was also in the vanguard of ballistic progress. The .30-30 Winchester, introduced in the Model 94, was the first smokeless powder cartridge loaded in the US. It was also ideal for most North American game. When the bolt actions followed along, they were widely regarded as slow, cumbersome and overpowered.

SAVAGE MODEL 99A

Country of origin: United States
Type: Rifle
Calibre: .30-30 Winchester

Capacity: 5 rounds
Action: Lever
Operation: Tipping bolt, rotary magazine. Closing lever lifts rear of bolt to lock against the face of the receiver. Magazine inspection port on side, indicator pin on top of receiver. Safety pushes forward to engage, locks lever shut.
Construction: All steel. Brass follower, lever case hardened and bolt engine turned.
Barrel length: 20in (508mm)
Length overall: 39.5in (1003mm)
Weight (empty): 6.34lb (2.875kg)
Sights: Replacement coloured plexiglass foresight with Parker-Hale tang mounted aperture backsight. Original barrel-mounted open backsight missing.
Comments: Current production (Model 99C) uses a detachable box magazine—a pity.

One could name a dozen lever rifles that Americans hold in affection. The Savage 99 and Marlin Model 39A are two of

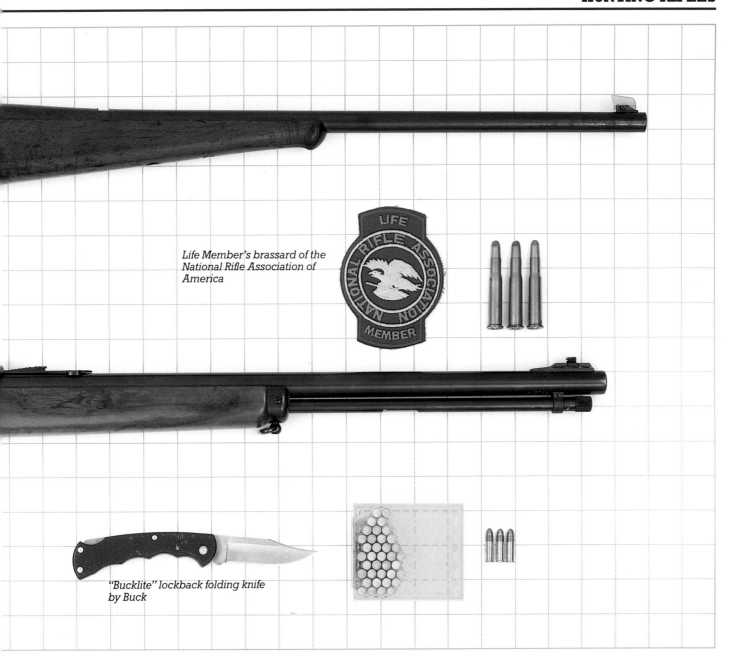

Life Member's brassard of the National Rifle Association of America

"Bucklite" lockback folding knife by Buck

the editor's favourites. The Savage was introduced in 1895 and improved in 1899 (hence the name) and is still, 1½ million guns later, going strong. Designed by Arthur Savage, it broke sharply with the prevailing aesthetic of "Western" styling, hence took a while to gain acceptance. But the astuteness of its design was such that it won a devoted and increasing following.

For the first fifteen years or so, the '99 was chambered for the usual run of low-pressure lever action cartridges: .30-30, .25-35, .32-40. The break came in 1915, with the introduction of the .250-3000 cartridge, which put the '99 in a class of its own. Charles Newton designed the .250 on a cut-down .30-40 Krag case as a useful deer cartridge. Harvey Donaldson, another leading ballistic experimenter of the day, suggested basing it on the .30-06 instead, while

Arthur Savage, always with a keen eye to publicity, cut the bullet weight from 100 to 87 grains, which enabled him to launch the first commercially loaded American cartridge with a muzzle velocity in excess of 3,000 feet per second—hence the name.

Later in 1921, the case was blown back out to .30 calibre, trimmed slightly, and introduced as the .300 Savage, a proto-.308 that came within 100 feet per second of matching .30-06 ballistics. The .250-3000 and .300 Savage were both excellent cartridges but have, in recent years, been elbowed aside by the more widely distributed but ballistically similar .243 and .308 Winchester. So that is what the Savage 99 now chambers. The fact that it can do so (while the Winchester 94 cannot) is due to its extremely solid tilting-bolt lock-up, and its

receiver-housed rotary magazine (tubular magazines are unsafe with sharply pointed bullets).

MARLIN MODEL 39A

Country of origin: United States
Type: Rifle
Calibre: .22 Short, Long or Long Rifle
Capacity: 19 rounds in Long Rifle, 26 in Short
Action: Lever
Operation: Nose of lever locks bolt. Pulling down and forward on lever drives bolt rearward, overriding and cocking hammer, extracting and ejecting spent case, and raising cartridge lever elevating a round from the magazine for chambering as the lever is closed.
Construction: All steel; most parts machined from forgings.
Barrel length: 20.5in (521mm)
Length overall: 36.5in (927mm)
Weight (empty): 6lb (2.72kg)
Sights: Bead foresight, open notch backsight with notched elevation

ladder, drift adjustable for windage.
Comments: Large screw on right of receiver allows disassembly into two parts for easier transport.

The .22 Marlin Model 39A, introduced in 1891, is another well-loved classic, and has been in continuous manufacture longer than any other American sporting firearm. More than a million of them have been produced, and it is still going stong.

The 39A was innovative, way back there. It was perhaps the first .22 repeater to work interchangeably with Shorts, Longs and Long Rifles, and introduced the front-loading tubular magazine, with an interior tube that draws forward during loading, housing the follower and spring—a system since widely copied. It is a thoroughly excellent rifle, selling on its quality and style.

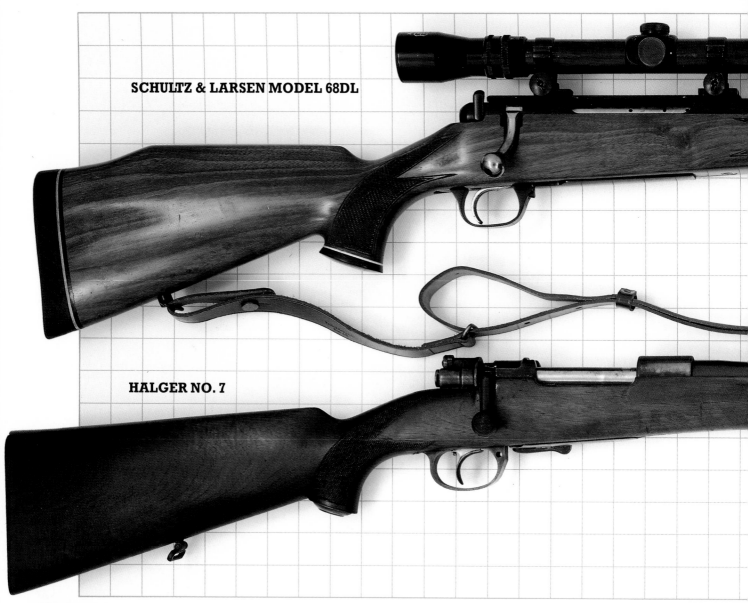

SCHULTZ & LARSEN MODEL 68DL

HALGER NO. 7

SCHULTZ & LARSEN MODEL 68DL

Country of origin: Denmark
Type: Rifle
Calibre: .264 Winchester Magnum
Capacity: 3-round internal box magazine
Action: Turning bolt action, rear locking, 4 lugs
Operation: Manual bolt, feeds from internal box magazine; 54° bolt lift; cocks on opening
Construction: Steel. Cylindrical receiver turned from bar stock with soldered recoil lug. Bolt machined from bar with cast handle welded on. Bolt and receiver ground to extremely close fit. Plunger ejection.
Barrel length: 26in (660mm)
Length overall: 46in (1168mm)
Weight (empty): 9.7lb (4.39kg)
Sights: 4-10X Pecar variable scope fitted; no provision for iron sights
Comments: Exceptional strength and quality; unusual design, heavy and difficult to load, few made.

HALGER NO. 7

Country of origin: Germany
Type: Rifle
Calibre: .244 HV Magnum
Capacity: 5-round internal box magazine
Action: Turning bolt action, Mauser type front locking, 2 lugs
Operation: Manual bolt, feeds from internal box magazine, cocks two-thirds on opening and final third on closing. Bolt rotates 90°.
Construction: All steel forgings
Barrel length: 26.25in (667mm)
Length overall: 47.75in (1213mm)
Weight (empty): 7.8lb (3.55kg)
Sights: Notch backsight and blade foresight; no provisions for scope mounting
Comments: Heavy, single-stage trigger. Built on Mauser 1898 action. Fancy ballistics in a rather plain rifle.

The rifles illustrated, unprepossessing at first glance, are actually of extraordinary interest. The pre-war .244 Halger Magnum (bottom) was the ballistic progenitor of the epoch-making post-war Weatherbys, whose exuberant styling is given a mercifully pale relection in the technically sophisticated but commercially ill-starred Danish Schultz & Larsen (top) of the late 1960s.

The decades following 1886, and the invention of smokeless powder by the French chemist, Paul Vielle, were ones of intense experimentation as firearm designers took advantage of the lack of fouling to design automatic mechanisms while ballisticians devoted themselves to rolling back the velocity barriers. Calibres fell from 11mm to 6mm, and the 2,000, then the 3,000 feet-per-seond barriers were soon breached. Four thousand feet was the next hurdle, but it was never quite reached, though some came close. Harold Gerlich claimed, in the early 1930s to have achieved 3,770fps with his 87-grain .244 HV Magnum, and 3,900 with a 100-grain .280 Magnum. Whether he actually did or not is a matter of controversy. Since Halger only made about 150 rifles, and no loaded cartridges survive, as far as we are aware, the matter is not easily resolved.

The lingering doubt is due to Philip Sharpe, who reported in 1949 that he had been unable to reach even 3,000fps with his loads in Halger's 7mm which, he said, was nothing other than a .280 Ross with a compressed powder charge. "This baby is a phoney, pure and simple," he concluded. Gerlich was assuredly a showman and Sharpe, just as assuredly, was the foremost authority of his day. His books, notably *The Rifle in America* and *Complete Guide to Handloading*, are authoritative and comprehensive; they can be read with much profit, even today. Sharpe was also, according to many who knew him, a vindictive man. But the reason for his vindictiveness towards Gerlich, who died in 1934, is barely explicable on grounds other than ballistic envy. Sharpe's own 7 x 61mm never lived up to the claims he made for it, and he claimed less than Gerlich.

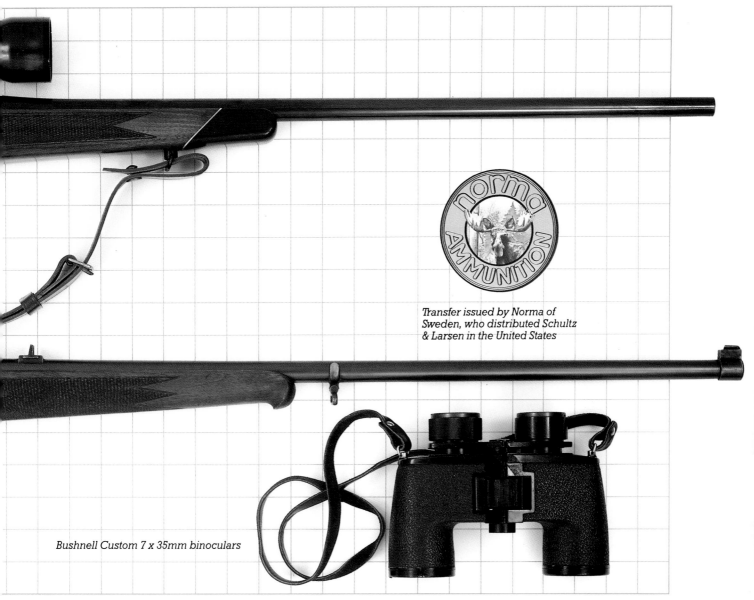

Transfer issued by Norma of Sweden, who distributed Schultz & Larsen in the United States

Bushnell Custom 7 x 35mm binoculars

Gerlich traded as Halger. Some say it was a contraction of the first three letters of his surname with the diminutive of his Christian name. More likely it arose from a brief partnership with his brother-in-law, whose surname was Halbe. Gerlich was American born and it was a matter for his everlasting consternation that he was denied enlistment in the German army in 1914 on that account, even though he was an artillery reservist. His father, in fact, a diplomat, had been the German Consul in St. Louis at the time of Harold's birth; the family returned to Germany about four years later. Harold Gerlich put his knowledge of English to use throughout his career. For some years before the Great War, he ran an import business in London where one of his better known customers was Walter Winans, whose double barrelled .22 High Power Running Deer rifles he supplied. And for some eighteen months after 1930,

only a few years before his death, Gerlich was employed at the Royal Laboratory, Woolwich, presumably in a research capacity, and probably already gripped by the passion for ever higher velocities that some riflemen find irresistably beguiling.

The current feeling is that Gerlich may have got close to the velocities he claimed. His bullets were aerodynamically sophisticated and his powders were custom made for him, a few pounds at a time, by RWS (he had connections there). The rifle shown is a crude vehicle for the cartridge, with a rough trigger, non-adjustable iron sights, and no provision for scope mounting. It was designed to sell for $90. Part of Halger's downfall was that his rifles were priced at more than $1,000 by their American importers.

The rifle at top is the Danish Schultz & Larsen Model 68DL, one of the finest but least successful sporting rifles ever

made. Originally designed by Uffe Larsen, son of the firm's founder, in the years following World War II, it was introduced in 1954 in match target and hunting versions, as the Model 54. Two subsequent variations were meant mostly to make it more appealing to the American market, and involved notably a change from cock-on-closing to cock-on-opening operation, a faster lock time and stocking in a mercifully subdued version of the garish California style of the time. The choice of chamberings was also increased to fourteen.

The Schultz & Larsen was one of the most accurate, safest and smoothest operating rifles ever made. The metallurgy was excellent and the workmanship exquisite. The key to the design were the four equidistantly spaced locking lugs mounted just ahead of the bolt handle. This permitted an extremely stiff, enveloping receiver which guided the ground-and-lapped bolt

throughout the operating stroke, eliminating the flop, slop and binding characteristic of bolt actions. The absence of forward locking recesses meant that the bolt could be ground to a hermetic and wholly supported fit in the receiver ring. This, combined with excellent gas venting and a back deflector shield, made the Schultz & Larsen exceptionally strong and safe. The short (54°) bolt lift combined with excellent camming, made it ideal for use with telescopic sights.

Why then did it not succeed? Only about 3,000 of all models were made, and only about 200 of the perfected Model 68DL were delivered to North America. The gun was expensive, to be sure, but not overpriced: it was finally discontinued when Schultz & Larsen discovered that they were losing $50 a gun. It suffered from a wholly groundless prejudice against rear locking actions.

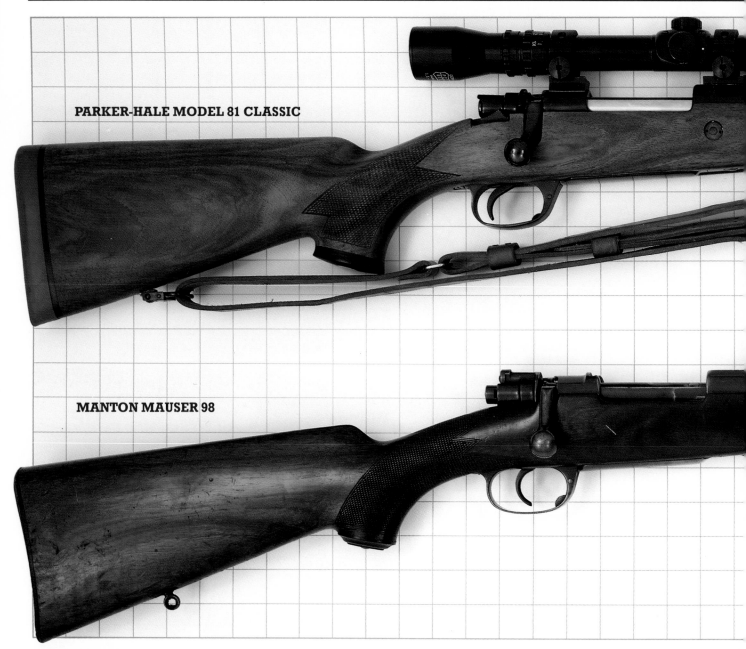

PARKER-HALE MODEL 81 CLASSIC

MANTON MAUSER 98

Aside from the fact that most of them nowadays are telescopically sighted, serious hunting rifles have not changed very much in close on a century, as this fine pair so clearly demonstrates, for neither mechanically, ballistically nor stylistically do they significantly differ. Both are built on Mauser 1898 actions, are stocked in what has now come to be called the classic manner, and chamber the .30-06 cartridge introduced in 1906. Yet the telescopically-sighted gun was introduced by Parker-Hale only some three years ago, while the lower one was built by Manton & Co. of Calcutta and Delhi in the salad days of the British Raj.

The aesthetics of classic stockmaking derive from pure functionality. Rifles, like motor cars, went through a garish phase in the 1950s, when the fins and chrome of the auto-mobile were paralleled by white-line spacers, roll-over cheek pieces, skip-line-chequering, back-raked fore-end tips and plough-share pistol grips of the rifle. Mercifully, it eventually dawned on the makers that all this gruesome frosting contributed nothing to function, and we are now happily returned to the style of stocking popularized several generations back by such famous sporting shots as Theodore Roosevelt and Stuart Edward White.

Sporting rifles have been built on every type of action devised by human ingenuity, but the turnbolt mechanism has maintained its overwhelming popularity because of its unique balancing of the factors of accuracy, strength, reliability, lightness and repeat shot capability. Other actions—lever, pump, single shot or self-loading—stress one or two of these factors, but only the bolt action blends them together so perfectly.

In recent years there have been bolt actions that have introduced supposed improvements, but most of these innovations prove, on examination, to have been tried and rejected by Peter Paul Mauser prior to 1898.

A bolt action can be heavy, or it can be miraculously light. When it is heavy, the weight is there for strength or rigidity; it is not just a function of a lot of machinery that is needed to work the gun.

PARKER-HALE MODEL 81 CLASSIC

Country of origin: Great Britain
Type: Rifle
Calibre: .30-06
Capacity: 4-round magazine
Action: Mauser Model 98 type bolt action

Operation: Cocks primarily on opening; side-mounted rocking safety; hinged floorplate
Construction: All steel
Barrel length: 24in (610mm)
Length overall: 44.5in (1130mm)
Weight (empty): 7.75lb (3.52kg) stripped; 9.25lb (4.2kg) as shown here
Sights: As supplied: gold bead foresight and Williams semi-buckhorn U-notch backsight; backsight adjustable for windage and elevation
Comments: This rifle is aptly named "Classic".

The Model 81 Classic (top) is built by Parker-Hale in Birmingham, using their hammer-forged barrels, and is based on new commercial receivers made by the La Coruna arsenal in Spain, one of two extant sources of new Mauser 98 type actions (the other being in Yugoslavia).

Parker-Hale are Britain's

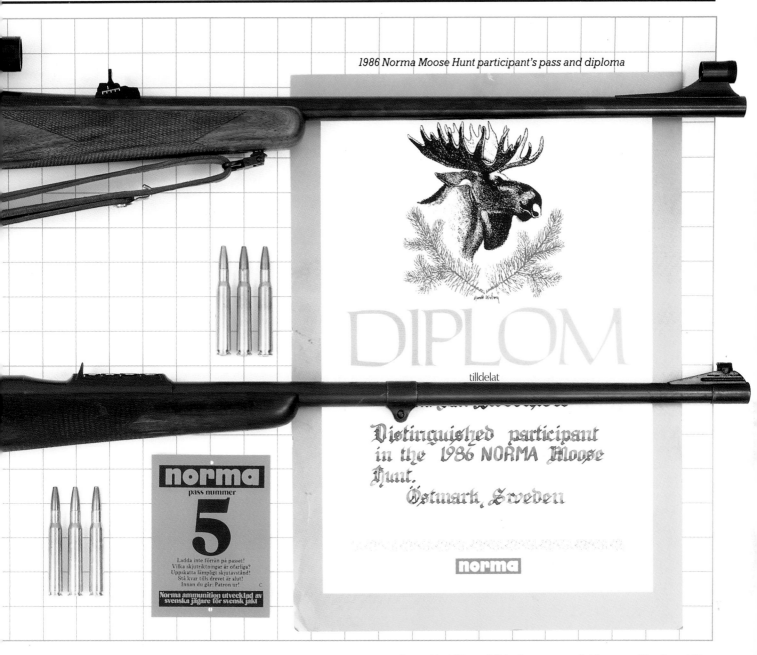

1986 Norma Moose Hunt participant's pass and diploma

DIPLOM

tilldelat

Distinguished participant in the 1986 NORMA Moose Hunt.
Östmark, Sweden

norma
pass nummer
5
Ladda inte förrän på passet!
Vilka skjutriktningar är ofarliga?
Uppskatta lämpligt skjutavstånd!
Stå kvar tills drevet är slut!
Innan du går: Patron ur!
Norma ammunition utvecklad av
svenska jägare för svensk jakt

norma

foremost rifle makers, and it is a great compliment to their basic workmanship that the famed London firm of Rigby are now marketing the Model 81 under their own cachet. Rigby, of course, put in a little extra work to make the rifle a Rigby, but it is much to their credit that they leave Parker-Hale's name on it, merely adding their own.

The Model 81 is a fine rifle, satisfying to own and to use. The only notable modification on the example shown is the side-mounted safety, which is necessary if a 'scope is to be used. The telescope shown on the rifle is a Pecar 1 x 4 variable, which has proved to be ideal.

MANTON MAUSER 98

Country of origin: India
Type: Rifle
Calibre: .30-06
Capacity: 4-round magazine

Action: Mauser Model 98 bolt action
Operation: Front-locking turnbolt action, two lugs, cocks on opening; clip guides on receiver bridge
Construction: All steel
Barrel length: 23.75in (603mm)
Length overall: 44.75in (1137mm)
Weight (empty): 7.66lb (3.47kg)
Sights: Gold bead foresight and five-leaf parade of backsights in 100-yard graduation; foresight drifts for windage correction
Comments: This rifle was made or supplied by Manton of Calcutta from Mauser commercial parts. The Mauser crest appears on the receiver ring, while the floorplate is marked "Made in Germany". It bears crowned B, U and G proofmarks.

The Manton Mauser 98 (bottom) retains the original "flag" safety and has the Mauser crest on the receiver ring. The backsight has five folding v-notch leaves, each with a gold inlaid centreline,

graduated in 100-yard (91m) increments. The foresight is a gold bead, drift adjustable for windage. In comparison with the Parker-Hale rifle (top), the much lower comb on the stock positions the eye to engage the sights, while the Parker-Hale's higher comb lifts the eye to the axis of the 'scope.

Joseph Manton, who was at first apprenticed to his older brother, John (formerly the foreman to the famous maker T. Twigg, but working under his own name from 1780), founded his own firm in 1792 and thereafter became the most celebrated gunmaker of his generation. A designer of genius, and a kindly man, he defined the form of the classic English shotgun, which remains essentially unchanged to this day. In his time, a Manton gun cost a minimum of 70 guineas (£73.50; $110.00)—a stupendous sum in those days

—and this was willingly paid by the best wingshots of the day.

Sadly, Manton's gunmaking genius was not matched by his business acumen; during his life he served two stints in a debtor's prison, and he died poor. His first bankruptcy occurred in 1826, the year after he had sent his son, Frederick, to Calcutta to found the Indian branch of the business. This fared better than the British, for Manton's became gun-makers by appointment to successive Viceroys.

The eulogy that appears on Joseph Manton's tombstone was written by the famous sportsman Colonel Peter Hawker (who claimed, in his book *Instructions to Young Sportsmen*, that he himself had made significant contributions to certain of Manton's designs). All the records of the firm were subsequently sent out to Calcutta and were lost.

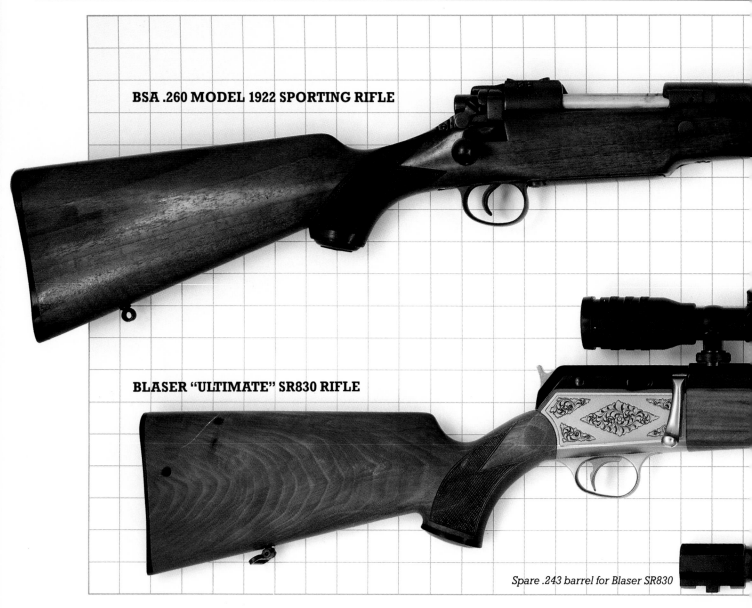

BSA .260 MODEL 1922 SPORTING RIFLE

BLASER "ULTIMATE" SR830 RIFLE

Spare .243 barrel for Blaser SR830

If Holland & Holland's or Parker-Hale's approach to the sporting rifle is rigorously classic, applauded by all men of good taste, circumstances or ambition may lead one to follow other routes, as the two guns shown here, one old and one new, serve to demonstrate.

BSA .260 MODEL 1922 SPORTING RIFLE

Country of origin: Great Britain
Type: Rifle
Calibre: .26 BSA Rimless Nitro Express
Capacity: 5-round magazine
Action: Mauser-type turnbolt action, cocks on closing
Operation: Twin-lugged, front-locking, rotating-bolt design, adapted from World War I Pattern 14 action; two-stage trigger
Construction: All steel
Barrel length: 26.5in (673mm)
Length overall: 48in (1219mm)
Weight (empty): 8.25lb (3.74kg)
Sights: Post foresight; two aperture backsights, one for 200yds (183m) and one for 400yds (366m), fold into the receiver bridge

Comments: Ballistically sophisticated, this anticipated the .264 Winchester Magnum and the 6.5mm Remington Magnum (all three use the .375 H&H case) by nearly half a century.

The BSA Model 1922 sporting rifle (top) reminds one powerfully of Remington's Model 30: both were leftover Pattern 14's or M1917's, as the case may have been. The 1898 Mauser made Britain's Lee, adopted a decade earlier, look somewhat inferior, so Ordnance decided to have designed a new rifle, super-strong, rigid and robust, for a new, rimless .280 cartridge. This was the Pattern 13, which was quickly redesignated the Pattern 14 and chambered for the old .303 round when hostilities began in 1914. Production was contracted to the United States, who in turn rechambered the rifle for the .30-06 round under the designation M1917. At the war's end, Remington were

making 4,000 of these rifles every day, and doubtless had a huge parts inventory. It was not surprising, therefore, that they should use this action as the basis for their post-war line of bolt-action sporting rifles.

Why BSA should have done likewise is less easy to decide, because, so far as we are aware, the Pattern 14/M1917 was never manufactured in Great Britain. BSA may have bought over-run parts from the USA, or they may have converted surplus Pattern 14's. In any event, their Model 1922 sporter was not notably more successful than Remington's Model 30 and Model 720. None of these guns is often encountered. American shooters did not like the dog-leg bolt handle, nor the fact that it cocked on closing.

Although those were matters of taste or preference, and rectifiable in either case, the real problem with the pattern 14/M1917 as a sporting rifle was that it was huge. The receiver

alone weighed 58oz (1644g)—10oz (283g) more than the Winchester Model 70—and measured 8.875in (225mm) long with a bolt throw of 4.74in (120mm). The magazine was 3.4in (86mm) long, and could be made still longer. Receiver ring diameter was 1.385in (35mm), compared to the Springfield's 1.305in (33mm).

The action was massively strong, but only made sense when chambered for large cartridges: it converts into an excellent .458 and, with the magazine lengthened, is ideal for the .375 or .300 H&H Magnums. Remington should not have been surprised that no one wanted it in .257 Roberts.

The Model 1922 shown here is more interesting. The barrel is stamped, "For BSA .260 HV Cartridge", presumably referring to the .26 Rimless Nitro Express round designed by BSA especially for this rifle. The .26 was a .375 H&H necked down to 6.5mm and cut back to 2,391 l.o.a., driving a 110-grain

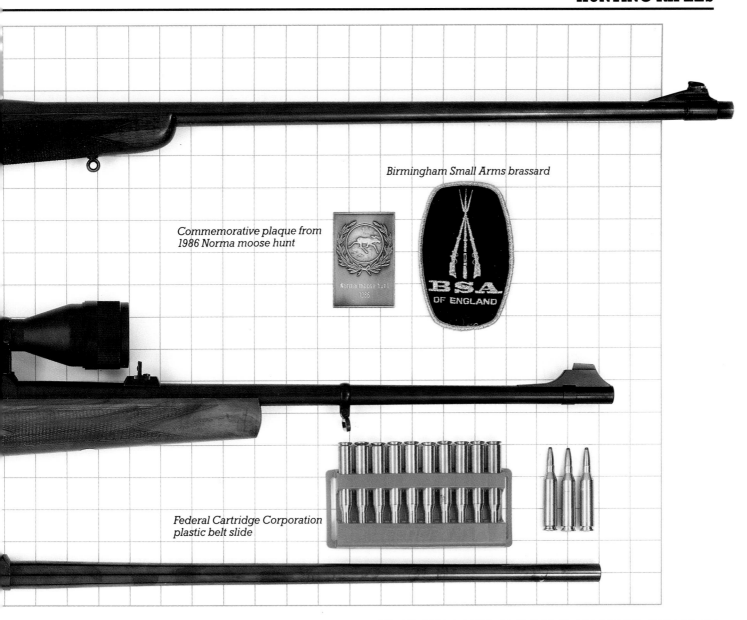

Commemorative plaque from 1986 Norma moose hunt

Birmingham Small Arms brassard

Federal Cartridge Corporation plastic belt slide

(7.13g) bullet at 3,100 f.p.s. (945 m.p.s.). That amount of ballistics was, by modern reckoning, largely wasted in a rifle not fitted with telescopic sights—but British shooters were slow to appreciate the 'scope.

BLASER "ULTIMATE" SR830 RIFLE

Country of origin: West Germany
Type: Rifle
Calibre: .270 Winchester, with a spare .243 Winchester barrel shown; ten chamberings are currently offered
Capacity: 2 rounds in magazine; 1 in chamber
Action: Turnbolt action, forward locking with three equidistant lugs locking into barrel extension
Operation: Conventional, except for safety system. Round button on right detensions mainspring rearward; push forward on "hammer spur" to retension it. Rocking bar on right sidelocks bolt handle down. Vertical plunger under base of bolt depresses to release slide assembly

Construction: Aluminium receiver, slide and trigger guard; other parts are steel
Barrel length: 22in (559mm)
Length overall: 40.25in (1022mm)
Weight (empty): 7.7lb (3.49kg) as shown; spare barrel weighs 2.7lb (1.22kg); Magnum barrels heavier
Sights: Square post foresight and U-notch backsight supplied; 'scope mounting points integral with barrel
Comments: An example of superb precision workmanship.

The Blaser "Ultimate" (bottom) is an opposite case in every respect. Designed by Horst Blaser of Isny, Bavaria, and introduced in 1984, the Ultimate incorporates some novel and sensible design features in the longstanding search for a take-down rifle that works. We have had take-down rifles for a very long time, but their accuracy was usually poor.

Mauser re-entered the field some 25 years ago with a Gehmann design they called the Model 66. It had no receiver

in the traditional sense, but rather a set of rails that carried a bolt head mounted on a pistol-like slide. The bolt head locked into the barrel extension and all the stress of discharge was taken there. The barrel indexed on a brass plate in the fore-end channel, which worked poorly because fore-end timber is dimensionally unstable. Recoil transfer to the stock was a problem that took several re-designs to solve.

Blaser has built shrewdly on Mauser's experience. He uses a two-piece stock, a bolt-bearing slide mounted on an aluminium receiver with the

Above: *Blaser SR830 with action open and cartridge in feed position.*

barrel mounted on a forward extension of the receiver. It seems to work: the gun comes apart in a moment; barrels interchange with a hex screw and are said to return to zero and to shoot sub-minute-of-angle groups. If you change barrels, you may as well change calibres: ten are currently offered, from .22-250 to .375 H&H Magnum. Two bolt heads suit two calibre families: these are the .30-06 and .375 H&H.

Fine sporting rifles have an aesthetic which their admirers feel is unmatched by any other firearm. Contemplating this magnificent group of Holland & Holland rifles, it is difficult not to be swept into agreement with this viewpoint and easy to identify with those who espouse it wholeheartedly.

Of course, it takes deep pockets to accommodate such tastes. However, the rich, like the poor, are always with us, and in recent years the collection of custom-built, classic sporting rifles has become a pastime of the fortunate, particularly in the United States, whose custom rifle makers are today almost without compare.

The problem, if you wish to see it as such, is that these guns are *never* carried afield. Holland & Holland could no doubt equal the best American craftsmanship if they wished to do so. They have chosen instead to build the finest rifles that one could dare to contemplate actually *using*.

The three guns shown here, all built on Mauser 98 actions, form a typical African battery. They are chambered (top to bottom) for .375 Holland & Holland Magnum, .458 Winchester Magnum and .264 Winchester Magnum respectively—an eminently suitable and highly appropriate selection.

In the early years of this century, Holland & Holland designed the most thoroughly useful range of sporting rifle cartridges ever created—and the reader may consider that there is some question as to whether we have made much progress since then.

HOLLAND & HOLLAND .375in MAGAZINE RIFLE

Country of origin: Great Britain
Type: Rifle
Calibre: .375 H&H Magnum
Capacity: 4-round magazine
Action: Mauser 98 turnbolt action; two forward lugs locking in receiver ring
Operation: Primary extraction and most of cocking on upstroke of bolt handle; single stage trigger; rocking safety on right of receiver
Construction: All steel
Barrel length: 24.5in (622mm)
Length overall: 45.75in (1162mm)
Weight (empty): 10.03lb (4.55kg) with 'scope; 8.97lb (4.07kg) without 'scope
Sights: Gold post and folding "big bead" foresights provided, along with two-leaf backsights marked 50/200yds and 350 yds respectively. The example shown here carries a Zeiss Diatal-C 4 x 32 telescopic sight, which may be a little strong for the calibre, in the author's view
Comments: A superlative rifle. Like its companions in the set of Holland & Holland rifles shown here it is a credit to British gunmaking

The best known of the Holland & Holland series of cartridges was the .375in—as used in the rifle shown (top)—introduced in 1912. Jack O'Connor eulogized it; Clay Harvey called it "the King": the finest all-round cartridge for heavy game ever created. Some regard it as borderline for elephant, rhino or Cape buffalo, although it has taken many. For big bear, tiger or lion, it is ideal.

In 1925, the firm announced the .300 H&H Magnum, which soon toppled all 1,000-yard target records in the United States and is still regarded as the finest "heavy .30" available. The .300 was simply the .375 Holland & Holland cartridge necked down.

HOLLAND & HOLLAND .458in MAGAZINE RIFLE

Country of origin: Great Britain
Type: Rifle
Calibre: .458 Winchester Magnum
Capacity: 3-round magazine

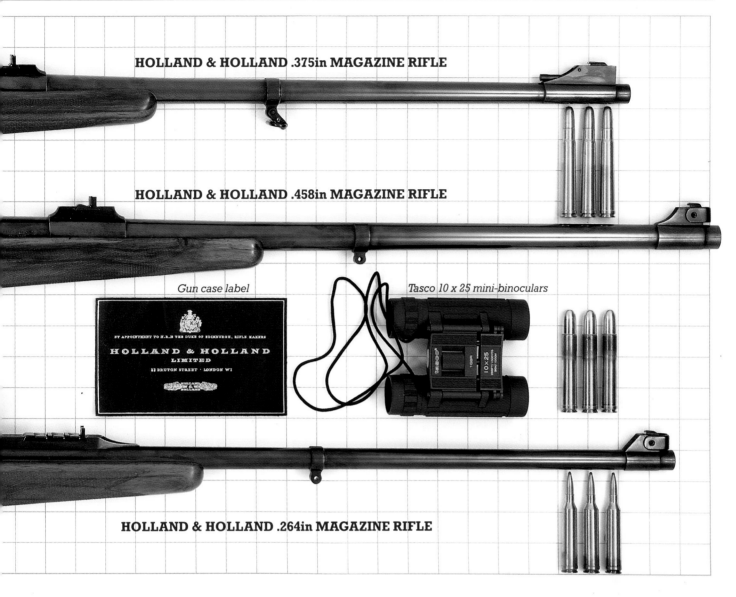

HOLLAND & HOLLAND .375in MAGAZINE RIFLE

HOLLAND & HOLLAND .458in MAGAZINE RIFLE

Gun case label

BY APPOINTMENT TO H.R.H THE DUKE OF EDINBURGH, RIFLE MAKERS

HOLLAND & HOLLAND
LIMITED

13 BRUTON STREET · LONDON W1

Tasco 10 x 25 mini-binoculars

HOLLAND & HOLLAND .264in MAGAZINE RIFLE

Action: Mauser 98 turnbolt action; two forward lugs locking in receiver ring
Operation: Primary extraction and most of cocking on upstroke of bolt handle; single stage trigger; rocking safety on right of receiver
Construction: All steel
Barrel length: 24.75in (629mm)
Length overall: 46.25in (1175mm)
Weight (empty): 10.06lb (4.56kg)
Sights: Gold bead foresight with folding guard; two-leaf backsight marked, respectively, 50-200yds and 350yds.
Comments: Marked: "1985 Sesquicentennial Rifle".

When Winchester decided, in around 1955, to seek for themselves a slice of the African market, the cartridge case the firm looked to was the venerable belted rimless from Bruton Street. Winchester engineers blew the .375 H&H out straight-walled, trimmed it back to 2.5in (63.5mm) l.o.a., and thus arrived at the .458in—as used in the rifle shown (centre)—which has become the world standard in this category.

Part of the reason for the .458's popularity lay in its dimensional compatibility with standard-length bolt-action receivers; another part concerned the excellent performance of its 510-grain (33g) bullets—one a reliable soft-nose and the other a tough, steel-jacketed solid that quickly established a fine reputation. This combination of affordability and performance soon overwhelmed all competition.

HOLLAND & HOLLAND .264in MAGAZINE RIFLE

Country of origin: Great Britain
Type: Rifle
Calibre: .264 Winchester Magnum
Capacity: 4-round magazine
Action: Mauser 98 turnbolt action; two forward lugs locking in receiver ring
Operation: Primary extraction and most of cocking on upstroke of bolt handle; single stage trigger; rocking safety on right of receiver

Construction: All steel
Barrel length: 24.5in (622mm)
Length overall: 46.25in (1175mm)
Weight (empty): 9.625lb (4.37kg) with 'scope; 8.125lb (3.69kg) without 'scope
Sights: Gold bead foresight with folding guard, along with parade of four V-notch leaf backsights on quarter-rib, provided. The example shown carries a Zeiss Diavari-ZA 1.5-6 x 42mm 'scope: an excellent choice for the cartridge
Comments: A superb rifle in the English style. Any American rifle of the same type would have a longer, fuller, fore-end with the forward sling swivel mounted in the woodwork.

The .264in Winchester round—as used in the rifle (bottom)—is also ultimately of Holland & Holland parentage—it is nothing more than the .458 necked to 6.5mm. The capacious case is doubtless somewhat over bore capacity, but the ballistics are nevertheless impressive: the standard load throws a 100-grain (6.5g) bullet at 3,700 f.p.s. (1128 m.p.s.), or a 140-grain

(9.1g) bullet at 3,200 f.p.s. (975 m.p.s.). Excellent sectional density helps the projectile hold its velocity and deliver a very flat trajectory. With the heavier bullet, it should be suitable for most plains' game. The .375 and .284 rifles shown here both carry Zeiss 'scopes, although the latter also has a parade of four V-notch backsights mounted on a quarter-rib and graduated to 450yds (411m). The Monte Carlo comb on the .458 is intended to lessen the risk of the comb's impacting the cheekbone during recoil.

Holland & Holland's Bruton Street, London, showroom is a Mecca for lovers of fine firearms the world over. The firm was founded in 1835 by Harris J. Holland and took its present name in 1877.

Holland & Holland are as well known for their shotguns as for their rifles. On present form, Holland & Holland will be the flag bearer of best British gunmaking well into the 21st century.

TARGET
RIFLES

Nigel Hinton (Introduction) and Jan Stevenson

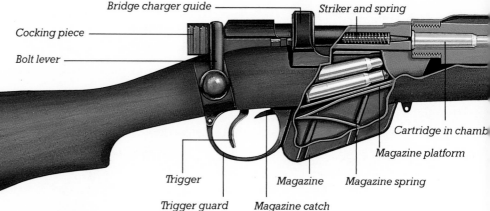

Bridge charger guide

Cocking piece

Bolt lever

Striker and spring

Cartridge in chamb

Magazine platform

Trigger

Trigger guard

Magazine

Magazine catch

Magazine spring

Butt

Butt disc

Lower sling swivel

Below: A painted pot-lid of an 1868 rifle meeting at Wimbledon—a range opened with a shot fired by Queen Victoria.

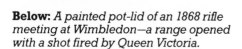

Traditionally, many countries use the sport of target-rifle shooting as a basis for training an additional line of defence for the country: a defence which can be called upon in a time of crisis. In the United Kingdom, this tradition can be traced back to the early 14th century when, as Roger Ascham described in *Toxophilus* in 1545, every English village was required to provide for archery competition among its able-bodied males. So highly was the use of the bow regarded that King Henry VIII retained Ascham as a tutor for his daughter Elizabeth, later Queen Elizabeth I, to school her in the skills of archery.

With the adoption of the musket, much of the tradition of local defence training appears to have been lost. Because of the musket's relative innaccuracy, volume fire was virtually mandatory and individual accuracy had become a thing of the past. To counter the threat posed by cavalry, the infantry had evolved the tactic of fighting in squares. But in the American War of Independence, the British found that they suffered heavily at the hands of Colonial sharpshooters; so much so that they had to resort to an old stand-by upon which so much of the British Empire was founded — mercenaries. These were raised in the German states to fight in the colonies as the

60th Royal American Regiment, later to become the King's Royal Rifle Corps, a regiment that has remained famous for its marksmanship up to the present day. The reason that the RAR was held in such high regard was that its men, armed with German flintlock rifles, were capable of hitting an enemy with the 400-grain (26g), .50-to-.70 calibre lead ball out to 200 yards (183m), or about 125 yards (114m) farther than the range at which a musket was effective. A 12in (305mm) group at 100 yards (91m) was just about within the rifle's capability, compared to the smoothbore musket's group of 40in (1016m) or more at the same range.

Early Rifling

The musket, with its ballistically poor spherical projectile, precluded accurate shooting. The first major advance was the invention of rifling. No one knows who invented rifling, but documents dating from the end of the 15th century have survived from such disparate centres as Leipzig, Vienna and Nuremburg, in which mention is made of grooves being cut into gun barrels. Like many major advances, the concept was not exploited immediately, because of manufacturing complexity and

also because of the authorities' innate conservatism. It was mercenaries, like the Germans mentioned above, who first gave rifles their well-deserved reputation, when mercenary soldiers with rifled weapons were employed as sharpshooters to pick off enemy officers. But despite the spin imparted by the rifling, the ball still tended to yaw in flight; this was overcome by elongating the projectile into the bullet shape recognizable today. It is interesting to note that both the United States and the United Kingdom still refer to their standard service cartridges as "ball" ammunition, as opposed to specialist loadings such as tracer or armour piercing.

Until the middle of the 19th century, weapons were still being loaded from the muzzle, but the introduction of the bulleted cartridge permitted far more rapid rates of fire. This posed two other problems: fouling from the black powder propellant, and the lead fouling deposited by the bullet on its travel up the barrel at a velocity in excess of some 1400fps (427mps). A Swede, Alfred Nobel, founder of the Peace Prize, invented a smokeless propellant to solve the powder-fouling problem, and a Swiss Army major, Jochim Schmidt, came up with the idea of covering the bullet with a coating of copper, thus reducing diameter and

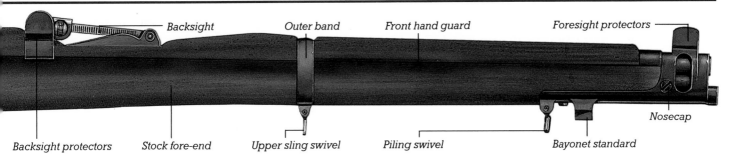

Backsight — Outer band — Front hand guard — Foresight protectors

Backsight protectors — Stock fore-end — Upper sling swivel — Piling swivel — Bayonet standard — Nosecap

Right: *Robin Piser adopts the supine position for a long shot at Bisley. Despite the strain on back and neck, many shooters find this the most secure of all firing positions.*

Left: *This satirical cartoon of 1875 finds no trouble in hitting its mark, commenting succinctly on the visual absurdity of some of the new techniques developed by civilian riflemen.*

1. Rifle is loaded, with the striker cocked and the bolt closed.

2. Pressure on the trigger sends the striker forward to ignite the primer.

3. The bolt is unlocked and drawn back, withdrawing the spent cartridge case.

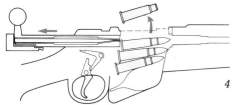

4. The empty cartridge is ejected and the striker is re-cocked.

5. Closing the bolt strips a live round from the magazine and chambers it.

increasing velocity. The accurate volume-fire cartridge had arrived.

By the 1870s, it was obvious that the potential for a higher rate of fire and longer-range shooting was far greater with rifles using the bulleted cartridge, although the military strategists, ever slow to exploit technological advances, still thought in terms of forming squares. To further the development of marksmanship, the volunteer regiments in the United Kingdom, (roughly the equivalent of the present-day Territorial Army) took a prominent part in the formation of the National Rifle Association in 1860, although it may be noted that they made it a fairly exclusive establishment: farm labourers, for instance, were not representative of its membership.

The new Association received the blessing of the War Office, and could almost be perceived as a Quango: the whole thing was run on military lines, and during national meetings the ranges took on the appearance of an army camp. It is understandable that most competitions reflected military influence: the rifle was the tool of the soldier's trade, and all the important posts in the NRA were filled by naval and military (and, much later, RAF) personnel. At that time, the citizen army was a widely-held concept throughout the world, if for no other reason than that it was an extremely cheap method of retaining an army at minimal cost. Nations were also extremely tribal in their outlook, and patriotism was held in high esteem. The NRA would have had few civilian members, since all but a few of its 19th century membership would have served in the forces at some time. So when competition conditions decreed past or present membership of the armed forces, that encompassed all those likely to be entering.

The NRA ranges were first established at Wimbledon Common , in the suburbs of London, and the first target was shot at by Queen Victoria, using one of the famed muzzle-loading Whitworth rifles in a cradle rest. It was well set up, for she scored a bull. Although shooting at NRA level had little to do with the man in the street, an awareness of the importance of marksmanship began to take root. Lord Roberts, speaking at Bisley (where the NRA had moved in 1883), noted the growing need for riflemen to be trained in the ability to engage targets of opportunity – that is, in snapshooting – at distances up to 150 yards (137m). It is interesting to note that many of the courses of fire then taking place under the NRA banner were what today would be

considered Practical Shooting. Commonly, distances at which competitions were shot were 200, 600 and 900 yards (183, 549 and 823m), with volley-fire at 400 yards (366m). A 200-yard (183m) target was 40in (102cm) wide and had an 8in (20cm) bull. At 500 yards (457m) the bull was 22in (56cm) in diameter, while at 1,000 yards (914m) it had widened to 36in (91cm), only 12in (30cm) wider than the present size.

In 1885, the Mullens Trophy was donated to encourage field shooting. A section of six men, including not more than one officer, in Full Marching Service Order and carrying Martini-Henry or Snider rifles at the trail, started at 500 yards (457m) and advanced at the double to between 400 and 300 yards (366 and 274m) where, in any position, they fired as many rounds as possible in one minute. Then they moved forward to 200 yards (183m) to fire three rounds volley-fire from the kneeling position. Finally, they moved forward to 100 yards (91m) to fire from the standing position. Another competition, the Running Man, was a sporting (sic) rifle shoot, although the mind boggles at what the target represented to the 19th-century sportsman. The trophy for this competition was presented by Walter Winans, the famed revolver shooter; he was also a

strong advocate of rapid-fire shooting with the rifle.

By 1895, competition commands were being sounded on the bugle, with calls to retreat in addition to the advance. Cyclists were considered important enough to warrant their own competition, with members of the cyclist section of a battalion riding about 0.75 mile (1.2km) over rough grass, before shooting. Nor was the horseman forgotten: a team of six mounted scouts had to gallop 1 mile (1.6km), dismount, and fire from 800 and 500 yards (732 and 457m) at Sectional Targets (targets representing a group of men). A superior force was then considered to have appeared on the horizon, upon which our heroes had to retreat in good order. Points were awarded for scouting, fieldcraft and manner of approach, as well as concealment and efficiency in securing the horses.

By 1914, the Running Man had been reduced to the status of Moving Target and its speed reduced to a walking pace. In an effort to encourage rapid-fire shooting, Winchester were offering a .351 self-loading rifle as a prize for the marksman achieving the highest score at 200 yards (183m), shooting as many rounds as he wished in a two-minute period.

On the battlefield, during the latter part of the 19th century, the sniper had assumed greater importance, the American Civil War having shown the value of the lone marksman and the psychological effect of one-shot kills. More recently, the British had been at the receiving end of precision shooting by the Boers in South Africa, who had been armed with the then new, magazine-fed, 8mm Mauser rifles. In an effort to encourage snap-shooting, the Duke of Westminster Cup was offered for shooting through loopholes at 450 yards (411m). This competition was restricted to "Efficient Volunteers". Competitors were supplied with cover in the form of sandbags and ammunition boxes, and range officers were responsible for deducting points if a shooter should expose more of his body than necessary while firing. The McQueen Cup, also a sniper event, was introduced in 1931. This was competed for by teams of two, one man acting as a spotter and the other firing, with the two changing places after 10 rounds. The distance was at first only 200 yards (183m); this was later extended to 600 yards (549m).

In the late 1920s, the Queen Mary Cup was donated for a competition that has remained a favourite until the present day. This shoot is now the foundation of the

Left: *A squad of servicemen reload their L1A1 SLRs during competiton at Bisley. Requiring physical fitness as well as marksmanship, such events provided the basis for civilian Practical Rifle shooting.*

Right: *Heckler & Koch's delayed roller lock bolt system showing bolt locked (top) and unlocked (bottom). The camming action of the rollers, just after firing, balance recoil and promote greater accuracy.*

Below: *The Great Butt at Bisley showing the mantlets, or movable screens of the markers. Targets were raised and lowered by hand, holes patched and scores signalled using a special form of semaphore. A recent photograph (below right) shows that remarkably little has changed over the years.*

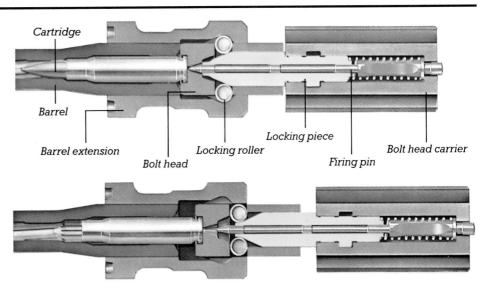

Service Rifle Championship. It started out at 600 yards (549m) — the distance has since been reduced to 500 yards (457m) — with ten rounds of precision fire on the army silhouette target. There are then a series of 45-second exposures, during which the shooter runs successively to 500, 400, 300 200 and 100 yards (457, 366, 274, 183 and 91m), firing two rounds at each distance from prone, kneeling, sitting and standing positions. The third stage was originally a rapid-fire set of 10 rounds in 40 seconds; in deference to self-loaders, this time has since been reduced to 30 seconds. The competition is nominally open to civilian competitors, but service entrants get preference and this leaves little opportunity for civilian entrants.

Practical Shooting

In an effort to redress this situation the United Kingdom Practical Shooting Association has developed this style of shooting, and all courses of fire now consist of stages which, commensurate with range safety, are of a practical nature. Shooting starts at 1,000 yards (914m), with snap shooting, where a high degree of precision is required, since the IPSC silhouette targets are only 18in (46cm) wide. Another

course follows in the wheeltracks of the competitors' forefathers, as the shooters cycle round the rougher tracks of Bisley Camp on mountain terrain bicycles, with rifles slung across their backs. So precision-orientated has the long-range event become that it is encouraging the development of specialized weapons, usually chambered for one of the high-intensity Magnum cartridges, such as the wildcat .30/378 Weatherby Magnum or the more traditional .300 Winchester Magnum. The competitors in this event are called upon to shoot to horizontal half-minute-of-angle accuracy, since the centre five is only some 6in (15cm) wide. To achieve this degree of precision, the shooter needs to draw heavily upon bench-rest techniques when assembling his ammunition. Rifles are fitted with high-power telescopic sights, usually in the 16X-to-24X range, although even 36X is not unknown.

From the turn of the century, competition at Bisley had been split into two categories, military and civilian type shooting. The two categories were classified as SR (Service Rifle) and TR (Target Rifle), a distinction which still exists. The competitors were using essentially the same weapon, although in TR small modifications were

permitted. A major reason for the distinction was that competitions required a high standard of physical fitness, for such shoots as the Queen Mary, and it was not possible for older, civilian competitors to last out the 500-yard (457m) run.

Despite exhortations from such notables as King's Prize Winner Arthur Fulton, who wrote in the *NRA Journal* in 1913 calling for more realism in the competitions, most competitors appear to have concentrated on slow-fire shooting. Writing in the same publication, Major W. Donald Smith, captain of the Indian team, complained that NRA competitions were too easy and, further, that the Stickledown Range was admirably suited to surprise-fire targets. One of his suggestions was that falling plates might be considered. Much of the prejudice against shooting rapidly would appear to derive from fear that damage might be caused to the barrel from deposits of nickel left by the bullets. Arthur Fulton suggested that this might be eliminated if shooters were to use a proper bullet lubricant.

Towards the end of the 19th century, efforts were made to reduce the cost to the Treasury of training soldiers. It was realised that the use of "sub-calibre" training rifles would lead to economies in terms of time, transport, maintenance, range space and

Above: *A Peter Taylor 6 x 47 mm Bench Rest rifle with 416R stainless steel barrel. The 10x scope is underpowered —20 to 36x scopes currently dominate.*

Below: *Adjustability is the key quality of bizarre looking rifles like this Walther KK Match with its thumbhole stock, palm rest and counter weights.*

Right: *Shooting prone, the spine should be straight, the right leg angled at 45° and the left elbow to the side of the barrel. A kneeling or sitting position demands a secure base. Care must be taken to avoid bone to bone contact. When standing, body should be 90° to the target, feet shoulder-width apart and left hand at rifle's point of balance.*

ammunition costs. The first attempts at miniaturization involved the use of the old Rook Rifle cartridges, the .300 Rook and the .297 Rook, obsolete blackpower loadings. The brass was necked down to .23 calibre, and the reserve Martini-Henry falling-block rifles were sleeved with a reduced calibre adaptor known as the Morris Tube. The Rook Rifle cartridges were soon replaced by the now universal .22 Long Rifle. Almost all shooting with these "sub-calibre" weapons was at a black circular aiming mark; the British Army did, however, use the .22 training rifle to practise snap-shooting at the black semi-circular aiming mark, which was supposed to represent the helmet of an enemy appearing over a trench.

This period saw the founding of the Society of Miniature Rifle Clubs (SMRC), which later became the National Small-Bore Rifle Association (NSRA). The SMRC was very different from the NRA: its membership was largely drawn from what was then considered to be the "working class" —for some reason, railway workers seemed to be predominant among members. The SMRC fired only .22 rifles and pistols, a practice that the NSRA continues. Patriotism was a very real force at the time of the formation of the SMRC, before World War I and immediately after the debâcles of the Boer War. The fervour of the era can be gauged by reading contemporary authors such as C. W. Thurlow Craig, who writes of going to the gun shop in his local market-town as a 14-year-old boy and buying a box of .22 Lesmoke cartridges, to stave off the invading Hun.

American Competitions

Because of its geographic location, the United States, even more so than the United Kingdom, has tended to be isolated from the rest of the shooting world. Thus, competition has developed there along somewhat different lines. The National Rifle Association of America was founded in 1871 because of a perceived inadequacy of marksmanship among the National Guard, particularly the volunteer regiments from the State of New York; marksmanship in the regular Army simply did not exist. The success of the NRA in turning around this state of affairs may be judged by the fact that the importance of developing and maintaining the skills of rifle marksmanship was enshrined in an Act of Congress.

Very early on, there was considerable rivalry between the United States and the member countries of the United Kingdom. Competition in those days was usually at long range, typically 1,000 yards (914m). The most beautiful custom rifles were built specifically for the matches: names such as Farquarson, Gibbs, Henry and Whitworth were made famous by these shoots. A series of cartoons brought the competitions to wide public attention. The great rivalry that has always existed between the United States and Great Britain in shooting was never more apparent than in the latter part of the 19th century, when a series of competitions took place between the two nations. The rivalry was far more intense than that of today's Americas Cup.

The forthcoming competition soon took on the overtones of a duel between tradition and modernity, between muzzleloading and breechloading. Experience in the American Civil War had suggested that breechloading weapons, the most famous being Sharps and Remington, could be as accurate as muzzleloaders. A boost for long range shooting was given to the Americans by a challenge from the Irish team, which had been victorious against all comers at the Wimbledon matches. The match was held at Creedmoor Ranges on Long Island and, to the chagrin of the Irish, was won by the Americans. The blaze of publicity that surrounded the run-up to the shoot ensured that long range shooting was put on the

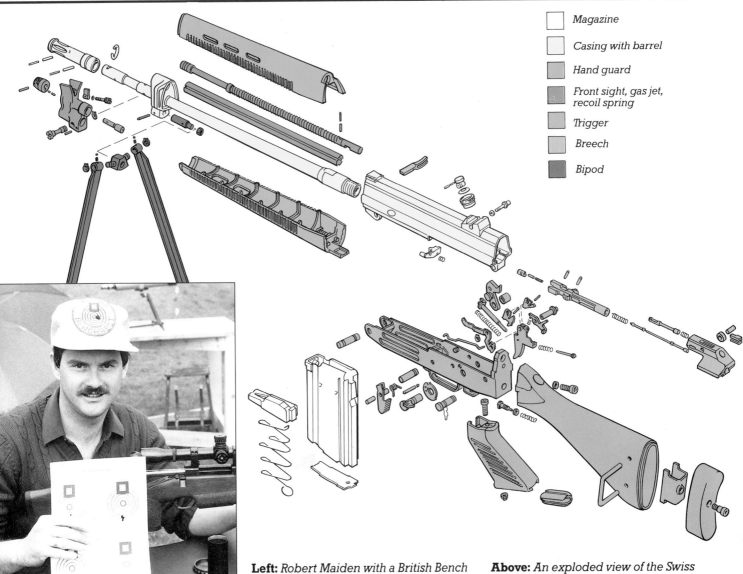

	Magazine
	Casing with barrel
	Hand guard
	Front sight, gas jet, recoil spring
	Trigger
	Breech
	Bipod

Left: *Robert Maiden with a British Bench Rest championship winning .36" five shot group shot with a .22-250 Tikka.*

Above: *An exploded view of the Swiss SIG 542. Semi-automatic weapons are widely used in Practical Rifle competitions.*

map in the United States. The event spurred much development of specialist weapons, both in the USA and in Britain, resulting in superbly crafted rifles that, even in their obsolete blackpowder loadings, achieved results that would not shame a modern target rifle.

The great conservationist and statesman Theodore Roosevelt further strengthened the fledgling American NRA by establishing the National Board for the Promotion of Rifle Practice as part of the War Department Appropriations Bill in 1903. Progress was swift, and in September of that year the first National Match was held at New Jersey. Initially, the matches were run as separate civilian and military events. Not unitl 1916 did the two categories compete alongside each other: an officer was given special responsibility for civilian marksmanship, with authority to dispense military rifles and ammunition. This state of affairs existed until the late 1960s, when the wave of anti-gun feeling that swept the United States led to the suspension of the programme. Such was the strength of the NRA, however, that it managed to survive this crisis. Today, the events are even more strongly supported, with active participation by the various branches of the armed forces.

Compared to British competitions, the American courses of fire have always contained an element of practicality. The service rifle competition begins with the shooters in the standing position at 200 yards (183m) firing 10 rounds in 10 minutes, followed by 10 shots from the sitting position in 50 seconds. Competitors then fall back to 300 yards (274m) for 10 shots prone in 60 seconds; finally, they fire 20 shots prone at 600 yards (549 m) in 20 minutes. The time limits include reloading time, and the time necessary to get into position from a standing ready position to the rear of the firing point. In this competition considerable dexterity was needed to master the bolt throw with the cock-on-opening Springfields of the US Army.

Automatic Weapons

Now that most nations have adopted automatic weapons as their primary infantry arm, shooters in many countries have found themselves disbarred from owning a current issue service pattern rifle. Switzerland is one of the few nations to treat its population as responsible citizens and allow them to keep full-automatic weapons at home. Among the countries which permit their citizens to participate in target shooting, ownership of rifles has been, in many cases, limited to bolt-action weapons, while elsewhere semi-automatics may be allowed. Courses of fire necessarily reflect the weapons in use: generally, slow fire requiring only single loading is paramount.

The United Kingdom probably leads the world in practical rifle shooting as far as formal competition is concerned. Courses of fire, though written afresh, bear a remarkable resemblance to what was taking place at Bisley before the turn of the century. In the southern hemisphere, South Australia, with its reasonably enlightened firearms laws, seems to be top contender. Naturally, in the United States, with its strong tradition of firearms ownership, the sport has an active following, but its organization is fragmented, split by survivalist factions all waiting for doomsday so that they may take to the woods! It will probably call for all the organizational talents of the American NRA to promote some sort of cohesion.

The International Practical Shooting Confederation specifically allows a free choice of weapon to be used; the only restrictions apply to the power of the cartridge. A rifle is either of "major" or "minor" calibre, but regulations are still a little hazy regarding the dividing line. A calibre of 5.56 x 45 is minor, while 7.62 x 51 is classified as major; it is yet to be decided what happens when a

competitor arrives with something obscure, like the 7.35mm Terni.

The new NATO 5.56 x 45 SS109 loaded with the heavier 63—grain (4g) bullet looks to have some potential in Practical Shooting. On its first outing at the 1985 UK Practical Rifle Championships, it swept the board and won the title for its user. Even out to 600 yards (548m), reports indicate a high degree of accuracy with good wind-bucking ability. Taking into account also the light weight of the rifle a shooter should gain considerable advantage over someone carrying a 14lb (6.35kg) Heckler & Koch 91C (with all accessories).

Almost without exception, the semi-automatic rifle has been adopted for Practical Rifle shooting. Unfortunately, many of the courses of fire encourage large-capacity magazines, causing some shooters to try to substitute firepower for accuracy. In recognition of the IPSC principle of not restricting weapons by types, thought needs to be given to the encouragement of accurate shooting. Courses of fire need to be exhilarating, but they also need to be designed in such a manner that the shooter is required to think before shooting. For example, a shooter might be shown a series of symbols and then be confronted by targets bearing a variety of designs, with instructions to

shoot only at the designated targets.

Because of accuracy requirements, the sniper events are developing into a specialist category. The military, because of logistical considerations, have almost universally adopted their standard service cartridge as a sniper round. In the case of the NATO countries, this has been the 7.62 x 51. The Eastern Bloc have a problem; they use a cartridge in the Kalashnikov assault rifle that is not suited to the sniper role. The 7.62 x 39 has a low muzzle velocity, a light bullet and a consequent poor trajectory for long-range work. Consequently, they have had to fall back on their obsolescent rimmed round, the 7.62 x 54R. As might be expected, most civilian shooters are using the NATO round for sniper competition in the same weapon that they use in other stages of a competition; among the most common are the M14 or its derivatives, the G3 family and the FAL series. The M14 offers considerable potential for accurizing, and the US Army has made its field manuals on this subject available. In its accurized form, the M14 was adopted as the US M21 sniper rifle and, when fed a diet of 7.62 x 51 match ammunition, it is capable of superb accuracy. Over long range—1,000 yards (914m) or more—the draw-back is the relatively low power of the cartridge. Although it is superior to the

Russian assault rifle round, there is a marked curve in the NATO bullet's trajectory, and it is also highly susceptible to crosswinds: a drift of 20 feet (6m) at 1,000 yards (914m) is not unusual.

The demanding IPSC courses of a sniper stage usually commence at a minimum of 600 metres (656 yards), with the target often being no larger than the 150mm x 150mm (6in x 6in) head box. With the increasing effect of wind, the course becomes progressively more difficult as it goes back to 1,000 yards (914m). As well as the problems of wind and bullet trajectory, there are other factors, such as mirage, with which to contend. At the 1,000 yard (914m) stage, the target is given progressively decreasing exposures and the shooter is required to fire one round at each of two targets during the exposure. There is little opportunity to let the wind ease. One would expect that with the advantages to be gained from the self-loader, it would be the popular choice. In terms of weapons on the firing line, this is the case, but the higher positions are now being infiltrated by custom-built bolt-action rifles. These are often chambered for high-intensity .30 calibre Magnum cartridges, with velocities around the 3,000fps mark.

It is sad to see that many of the younger generation entering the sport do not wish

Above: *Ian MacIntyre with a scoped .223 calibre AR15 and Colin Toose with an iron-sighted 7.62 Parker-Hale T4 highlight the variety of equipment used by competitors in Practical Rifle.*

Above right: *Using a 7.62 calibre Steyr, a shooter tackles a 300 metre standing shot. Despite the difficulty of this discipline a Swiss shooter has recorded an unmatched 393 ex 400.*

Right: *UIT 300 metre Free Rifle shooting requires 40 shots to be taken standing in 2 hours. Free rifles can be up to 8 mm in calibre but otherwise are virtually free from design restrictions.*

Left: *Practical Rifle shooting with military-style weapons such as the Armalite AR180 and 7.62 mm L1A1 SLR is one of the most exciting and demanding of the rifle disciplines.*

Below: *Telescopic sights are permitted for running boar and stag shooting. This competition was organized by the Deutsche Jagdschutz Verband. A typical target decorates the firing point partition.*

to serve their apprenticeship by graduating from slow-fire deliberate shooting to rapid-fire. To quote again from Arthur Fulton: "Any-one who aspires to become a really good shot should not be content with deliberate shooting. Rapid fire is most interesting in itself and no shooting man's education is complete if he is not good at rapid." How-ever, Fulton noted that he had never come across a person who was proficient at rapid who had not first learnt to shoot slow fire. Young shooters today feel the need for considerably more activity than is to be found in traditional target shooting, and this has led to a resurgence in interest in the sort of competition shot in the 19th century. Many newcomers enter the sport with-out preconceived notions of target shooting and thus they will readily adapt to some of the more exciting events.

Practical Rifle competition offers these aspects aplenty and is, in many respects, a return to the sources of competitive rifle shooting. It is also the type of competition that is practised, under the auspices of the International Practical Shooting Confedera-tion, both in the USA and the UK, thus forming a bond of common experience between the shooting communities in the two countries.

Competitive shooting in both countries,

as we have seen, had its origins in a desire on the part of volunteer reservists to raise the level of marksmanship both in the militia and in the regular forces, where standards generally were even more to be deplored. The object was to inculcate into and dis-seminate among the population a skill which the nation would have need of in time of war. Regular competition would be a spur to excellence, a generator of enthusiasm and an edifice of permanence.

The nature of the competitions them-selves, though, differed. In Britain, the mili-tary and civilian components bifurcated, with the civilians finally doing nothing but slow fire, prone, medium and long range work, with single shot bolt guns, while the military shot from holes and ran up and down the range with semi-autos.

In the United States, service and non-service shooters both used a middle-of-the-road course of fire that combined speed with accuracy at known distances. It is tremendously demanding, and may be described as a semi-practical undertaking.

But there is a spirit of innovation in all branches of shooting these days. Besides Practical Rifle, there has developed a tremendous enthusiasm for Metallic Sil-houette shooting, a discipline that was imported from Mexico and is fired from the

standing position only, with sporting type rifles. This splendid undertaking has yet to reach Britain; on the other hand, the USA has nothing to equate to British Sporting Rifle competitions, which comprise running deer and sitting hare events with realistic field equipment.

Running almost at counter-cadence to the ossified as well as the dynamic factions of domestic rifle shooting in both the USA and the UK, are the UIT events (for Union International de Tir, the world governing body), which constitute the programme of the Olympic Games and traditional world and regional championships. There is only one fullbore rifle match extant in UIT com-petition, and it is a three-position shoot at 300 metres (328 yards). Running boar used to be a fullbore event, but now is .22 and air weapon only. Biathlon used to be a full-bore event, but now is .22 only. Fullbore is no longer shot at the Olympics. The UIT would like to eliminate fullbore altogether and, having done so, would no doubt phase out cartridge weapons in favour of air weapons.

The Anglo-Saxon countries are fortunate to have such rich traditions of domestic riflery, firmly based in a concept of civic duty, and to have built innovation onto these solid foundations.

WINCHESTER SINGLE-SHOT MUSKET

VICKERS MINIATURE RIFLE

A Boer rifleman, it was often said at the time, seldom used more than two shots to kill an English soldier, whereas it took a ton of British lead to kill a single Boer. The Second Boer War of 1899-1902 was a rude shock to British self-esteem. The British Army had invaded a sparsely-populated nation of farmers, with no military establishment of its own, and was being soundly thrashed! The question very much in the public consciousness was whether a European army that had invaded Britain would meet with a similar reception.

The consensus was that it would not. If British regular soldiers, by and large, could not shoot and had no mastery of fieldcraft, what might one expect of an army of national defence that had been hastily recruited from the factory floor? General Baden-Powell, hero of

Mafeking and later the founder of the Boy Scout movement, returned from South Africa determined to promote fieldcraft; Field Marshal Lord Roberts, commander in South Africa in 1900, returned determined to teach marksmanship, and he encouraged Major-General Charles Edward Luard to found the Society of Working Men's Rifle Clubs (SWMRC).

By that time, rifle clubs were springing up across the length and breadth of the United Kingdom, and the British Rifle League, founded by Vere d'Oyly Noble, editor of *The Regiment*, a popular paper devoted to military affairs, had enrolled 10,000 members. However, most of these were probably drawn from the middle classes, and General Luard's concern, shared by Lord Roberts, was to make

riflemen from the kind of workingmen who would form the rank and file of a hastily-raised mass army.

After the Prime Minister had given the movement strong support in a speech delivered at the Albert Hall, London, on 9 May 1900, General Luard had little difficulty in assembling powerful sponsors. Lord Dudley, the Duke of Norfolk and the Duke of Westminster all made substantial contributions: the Duke of Norfolk agreed to be Chairman of the new association, while Lord Roberts, now Commander-in-Chief, agreed to accept the presidency on his retirement from the army.

The inaugural meeting was held at the Mansion House at the invitation of the Lord Mayor of London, and was attended by, among others, the Archbishop of York and the

Lord Mayor of Liverpool. According to *The Times*, "...the scheme would be a co-operative one, that is, the gentlemen of the country would contribute to the funds, whilst the working men could be expected to join the clubs and make themselves efficient in the matter of rifle shooting."

Both General Luard and Lord Roberts felt strongly that the skills of marksmanship could be developed to a high order with the aid of "miniature rifles"; that is to say, with .22in rimfire, which could be used all year round on easily-constructed indoor ranges. The inaugural motion at the Mansion House meeting was: "That the foundation of The Society of Working Men's Rifle Clubs, for facilitating rifle shooting, more especially in the evening, with small-bore rifles and inexpensive ammunition, as an

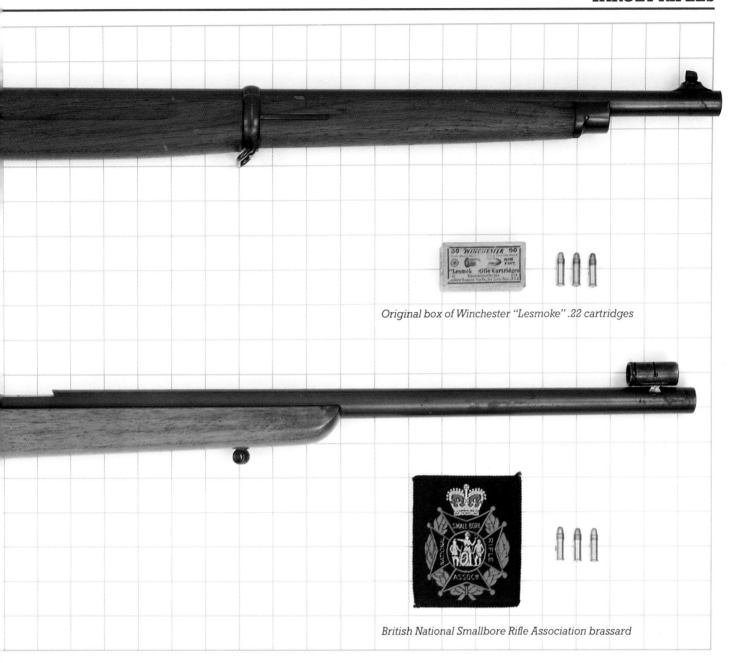

Original box of Winchester "Lesmoke" .22 cartridges

British National Smallbore Rifle Association brassard

ordinary branch of recreation by working men's and working boy's clubs and institutes, be now proceeded with."

VICKERS MINIATURE RIFLE

Country of origin: Great Britain
Type: Rifle
Calibre: .22 LR
Capacity: 1
Action: Martini-type tipping block, underlever operated
Operation: Pushing the underlever down and forward tips the front end of the breechblock down, ejects the case and cocks the striker
Construction: All iron or steel; one-piece stock
Barrel length: 26.25in (667mm)
Length overall: 43in (1092mm)
Weight (empty): 7.57lb (3.43kg)
Sights: Not original; see text below
Comments: This was one of the first rifles to be designed for the patriotic smallbore rifle movement in Great Britain.

The Vickers Miniature Rifle (bottom) was typical of the guns —"miniature rifles" in .22 calibre, suitable for use on indoor ranges—which the patriotic movement outlined above brought forth in its efforts to improve marksmanship in Great Britain. Built on a Martini action, but with a one-piece stock, it is inscribed "Vickers Miniature Rifle" and was marketed by Vickers Ltd., Broadway, Westminster. As the heavy barrel witnesses, it was already evolving into a specialized target gun. At some time in its career, the open backsight originally fitted to the example shown here has been replaced by a BSA micrometer rear sight with a six-aperture disc. The original foresight has been filed down and a tunnel foresight with interchangeable elements has been welded to the base.

WINCHESTER SINGLE-SHOT MUSKET (2nd MODEL HIGH WALL MUSKET)

Country of origin: USA
Type: Rifle
Calibre: .22 LR
Capacity: 1
Action: Falling block, underlever operated
Operation: The underlever pushes down and forward to drop the breechblock and extract the fired case; the exposed hammer cocks on closing
Construction: All steel or iron
Barrel length: 28in (711mm)
Length overall: 43.75in (1111mm)
Weight (empty): 8.36lb (3.79kg)
Sights: Post foresight; tang-mounted Lyman aperture backsight
Comments: This is one of a host of "miniature rifles" that were on the market at the time. A later "Low Wall" version was purchased by the US government for training purposes during World War I.

The National Rifle Association of America, publicly supported by President Taft, had been making vigorous efforts to have .22in riflery included in the schools' curriculum. The Winchester .22in Musket (top) was one of many similar guns developed for the purpose. The term "musket" in this context referred to the military-style woodwork, and not to any lack of rifling.

The gun shown here is a 2nd Model High Wall, built on an action designed by John Moses Browning and introduced by Winchester in 1885. It was a lever-operated, dropping-block, single-shot, and was the first of many Browning designs to be made by the New Haven firm. Over 28 years production, some 109,327 of these elegant rifles were built in a variety of configurations and fifty-nine calibres.

Smallbore rifle shooting has progressed a long way since the Winchester High Wall and the Vickers Miniature Rifle—or sunk a long way, depending on one's point of view. General Luard would have hated it, for today's smallbore target rifle is a study in irrelevance, a barely man-portable remote control paper punch, onerously expensive and calculated to appeal to as few as possible, notably to prosperous masochists. Worse, the skills involved in its expert use are only tangentially related to marksmanship with a "real" rifle.

The pressure of competition and the search for improvements in equipment have entailed an evolution that is well illustrated by the rifles shown here: a turn-of-century Vickers Jubilee (lower), already a sophisticated target rifle, and tne Schultz & Larsen UIT "Free Rifle" (upper) of the 1960s which reached a stage of specialisation and sophistication that has only marginally been exceeded.

VICKERS ARMSTRONG JUBILEE MODEL

Country of origin: Great Britain
Type: Rifle
Calibre: .22 LR
Capacity: 1 round
Action: Lever operated tipping block single shot rifle
Operation: Swinging lever down and forward causes front of breechblock to rotate downward, exposing chamber and activating extractor
Construction: All steel. Barrel and receiver one piece. Quick demountable action.
Barrel length: 29in (737mm)
Length overall: 44.5in (1130mm)
Weight (empty): 9.57lb (4.34kg)
Sights: Micrometer adjustable aperture backsight. Tunnel foresight with 9 interchangeable elements stored under capscrew at fore-end tip.

Comments: The leading target rifle of its day. Vickers' Miniature Rifle and Empire models were of similar design. Patents 419459 and 13034 refer.

SCHULTZ & LARSEN UIT FREE RIFLE

Country of origin: Denmark
Type: Rifle
Calibre: .22 LR
Capacity: 1 round
Action: Turning bolt
Operation: Lifting bolt handle unlocks breech and cocks striker. Single shot, manual operation.
Construction: All steel; aluminium buttplate assembly and forward handguard.
Barrel length: 28.25in (718mm)
Length overall: (as shown) 45in (1143mm)
Weight (empty): (as shown) 13.9lb (6.29kg)
Sights: Micrometer adjustable aperture backsight; tunnel foresight with interchangeable elements
Comments: Introduced in the late 1940s and manufactured, with improvements, into the 1970s. State of the art when introduced; exquisite workmanship. Butt prong and forward handrest not shown.

The difference between these two rifles is only partially one of evolution over time; they also represent, to some extent, different philosophies and traditions of marksmanship. In Anglo-Saxon countries, the function of competitive rifle shooting has been to develop skills that would be of service to the nation in time of war. The Schützen tradition of the Germanic countries was much more a purely sporting one, and by the mid-nineteenth century, the equipment was highly specialised, with hook buttplates, extended forward handrests and hairtriggers the mode. In fine weather, the big guns were shot outdoors; throughout the winter,

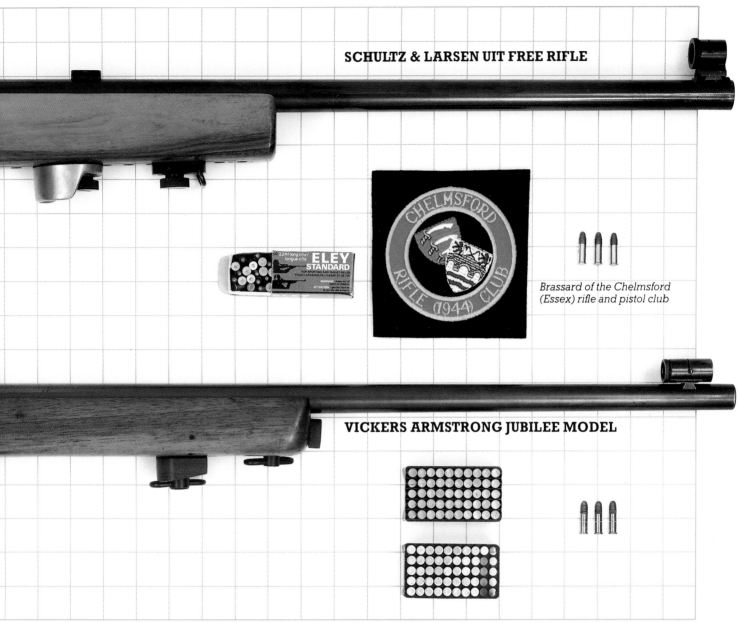

SCHULTZ & LARSEN UIT FREE RIFLE

Brassard of the Chelmsford (Essex) rifle and pistol club

VICKERS ARMSTRONG JUBILEE MODEL

smallbores with light charges were shot indoors. In both cases, German beer flowed in abundance. The cold-weather performance was a Teutonic parallel to British pub darts, with about as much self conscious military relevance.

Another distinction was that the German shot standing while the Englishman shot lying down. When international competition was developed, during the long period of peace between 1872 and 1914, an effort was made to bridge these disparate traditions. The newly formed UIT (*Union International de Tir*, International Shooting Union) in Paris adopted a competition they called the English Match, which consisted of 60 rounds, all fired from prone. The other major component of the new international programme was the 3-positional match of 120 rounds, 40 each from standing, kneeling and prone.

Meanwhile, the United States developed its own indigenous programme of 4-positional shooting: standing, prone, sitting and kneeling. The rules forbade gadgetry, applied a tight upper weight limit and required a 3-pound trigger pressure. The result was a good rifle that required solid mastery of basic marksmanship skills. The same held true for Britain, except that all shooting was on the deck. A good prone rifle, however, is a good all-round rifle, while a specialist standing rifle cannot be fired from any other position unless comb height is adjusted and the forward handrest is removed. For many years, the UIT has approved any safe improvement in equipment (except telescopic sights) that would enhance accuracy. That is why the guns have grown so grotesque.

The Vickers Jubilee was reckoned the best British smallbore target rifle of its time which, judging from the name, must have been bang on the turn of the century, when "miniature rifle" was in lift-off stage. Surprisingly little is known of the gun. Vickers is a heavy armaments firm, whose dalliance in small arms is sporadic. They made a lot of Maxim-type machine guns, a few Luger pistols on contract, and experimental Pedersen self-loading rifles. The Jubilee, is a lever operated, tipping block, single shot of vaguely Martini pattern with two eccentricities: the stock is one piece, which made it easier to bed, the receiver and barrel are one piece as well. A wing screw on the right side frees the action to drop out for cleaning or adjustment.

A brass capscrew on the fore-end top houses nine interchangeable foresight elements. Ring foresights of various diameter were used at different ranges and in differing light conditions, while a post foresight was used in "Mad Minute" exercises, which involved logging as many hits as possible within sixty seconds.

The Schultz and Larsen Free Rifle (above) is as far from the Jubilee philosophically as it is mechanically. It is for a fundamentally different kind of shooting, and was one of the finest rifles, in terms of quality of workmanship, of that type ever built, and was the last rifle made by a firm that had been dedicated to Match Rifle production since its foundation at the beginning of this century. The Schultz & Larsen never achieved the popularity its quality deserved, largely because it was designed to give optimum perfomance with Finnish Lapua ammunition while all the winners were using Eley Tenex. The S & L set trigger was also a bit crude.

Spanner and Allen key set

The UIT Free Rifle—the one they shoot at the Olympics—is a marvellously sophisticated tool, more so than a Bench Rest rifle really, for a great deal of mechanical ingenuity has gone into compensating for lack of a solid rest. One may either stand in awe of its refinement or disdain it for not being a gun, in the proper sense, at all. In fact, one can do both.

In order to understand the terms of debate you must look at the upper gun pictured, and imagine it under full sail. For the photograph shows it stripped —drydocked as it were. Set up for shooting, it would have a long armpit prong extending from the butt plate, a black elastic tape, about two inches wide, stretched the length of the barrel from foresight to receiver ring (to break heatwaves), an antenna-like

prod extending forward from the fore-end tip, with adjustable weights on it, a spade-handle palm rest mounted (for standing position) and a leather sling to attach the rifle firmly to the shooter.

A Free Rifle is so called, because it is relatively free of restriction. It must not have optical sights, the pistol grip may not contact the sling, all-up weight limit is 17.6lb (8kg), butthooks are limited to 6in (153m) in length and the forward palm rest must not extend more than 7.9in (200mm) below the centreline of the barrel. And that is about it. There is specifically no trigger weight requirement in case you wondered. The Free Rifle may be a prime example of evolution to the rules, but it is also heir to a distinguished German target shooting tradition that concentrated on precision shooting from the

standing position.

But no matter how it had got that way, the Free Rifle was undeniably grotesque, so much so that the UIT determined to phase it out. The new Standard Rifle rules banned buttplate extensions, external adjustable weights, thumbhole stocks, adjustable palmrests and cheekpieces and forward hand rests. The weight limit was lowered to 11lb (5kg). Samples were shown at the Cairo World Championships in 1962, and the first competitions took place the following year. According to schedule, the Free Rifle would be phased out by 1966. However, it did not happen. Parallel competitions —Free Rifle and Standard Rifle categories at the same match—were held until 1974, when the project fizzled out. The situation at present is that ladies shoot Standard Rifle

while men and juniors shoot the Free Rifle.

The reasons for the failure of the Standard Rifle programme, despite the backing of UIT head Ernst Zimmerman, and the fact that the proposed rules were very similar to national rules in Germany, Britain and the United States, is a question of some moment. Certainly there was an outcry from a number of top competitors, who had paid a lot of money for their Free Rifles and claimed to object vehemently to this proposed expropriation. Object they did, but the real reason is more likely that the Free Rifle requires a subtle technique which they had mastered, and few others would. Their positions at the top of the target shooting world were protected both by a price barrier and a skill barrier. Stripped of the clap-trap, their rifles would have qualified. But

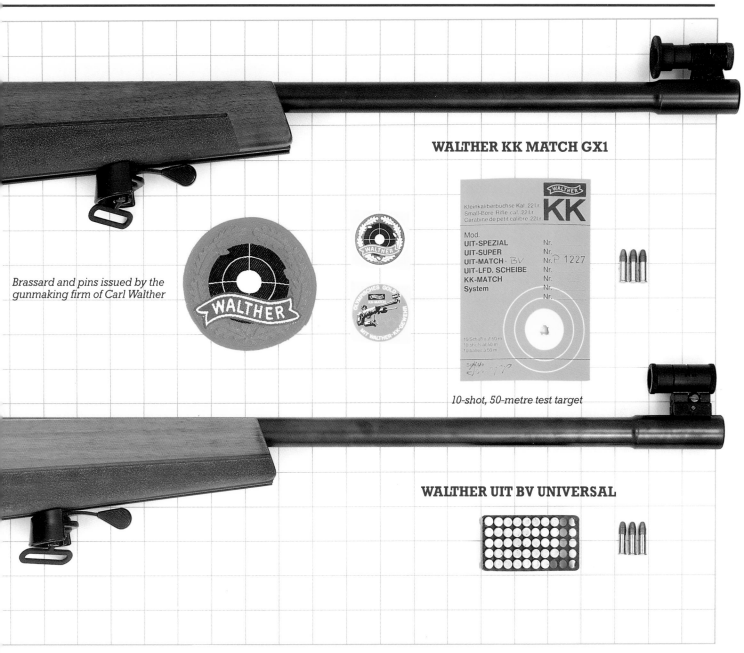

WALTHER KK MATCH GX1

Brassard and pins issued by the gunmaking firm of Carl Walther

10-shot, 50-metre test target

WALTHER UIT BV UNIVERSAL

Free Rifle techniques, which involve a delicate balancing act, with as little physical contact with the gun as possible, would no longer work. The Standard Rifle would have to be shot like a rifle, and against a lot of other riflemen.

Whatever the rules, the rifles that win and have won for decades are made by Anschutz in Germany. Non-German guns do not rate much in UIT smallbore events, but lately Anschutz has been hard pressed by Walther and Feinwerkbau.

WALTHER KK MATCH GX1

Country of origin: West Germany
Type: Rifle
Calibre: .22 LR
Capacity: 1 round
Action: Turning bolt, striker fired single shot
Operation: Lifting bolt handle

unlocks action and cocks striker. Fresh round must be placed on loading tray by hand.
Construction: All steel. One piece walnut stock.
Barrel length: 25.75in (654mm)
Length overall: 43.25in (1098mm)
Weight (empty): (as shown) 12.4lb (5.64kg)
Sights: Micrometer adjustable aperture backsight and tunnel foresight with interchangeable elements and a spirit level.
Comments: Top quality UIT Free Rifle. Mauser-type wing safety. 11in (279mm) accessory rail in fore-end. Stock adjusts via ten hex bolts; hinged buttplate on dovetail mounting.

WALTHER UIT BV UNIVERSAL

Country of origin: West Germany
Type: Rifle
Calibre: .22 LR
Capacity: 1 round

Action: Falling block action, sidelever operated
Operation: Pulling lever to side forces breechblock downward and operates extractor. Fresh cartridge must be hand fed into the chamber.
Construction: Aluminium receiver; most other parts steel.
Barrel length: 27.5in (698mm)
Length overall: 43.25in (1098mm)
Weight (empty): (as shown) 10.45lb (4.75kg)
Sights: Micrometer adjustable aperture backsight; tunnel foresight with interchangeable elements.
Comments: UIT Standard Rifle. Electronic trigger capable of any desirable adjustment. 11.5in (292mm) accessory rail in fore-end.

The rifles shown are both by Walther of Ulm/Donau. The one at the top is their KKM (for Kleinkaliber Match) Model GX1 Free Rifle. Quality is exquisite and the gun, when

introduced, was notable for its range of adjustments and for the fact that the barrel was set more deeply in the stock than the norm, thus reducing recoil disturbance of the sight picture. The cheekpiece, buttplate and handrest adjust vertically, horizontally and rotationally, and the first skill a Free Rifleman masters is that of changing the adjustments each time he changes position.

The lower rifle is Walther's BV-E built to Standard Rifle configuration. The cheekpiece and buttplate are capable of considerable adjustment, but once set, must be locked in place for duration of the match. The BV-E (the "BV" stands for Blockverschluss) is a radical design—a sidelever operated falling block with a hard anodized aluminium receiver. The "E" refers to the electric trigger system, which has not proved to everyone's liking.

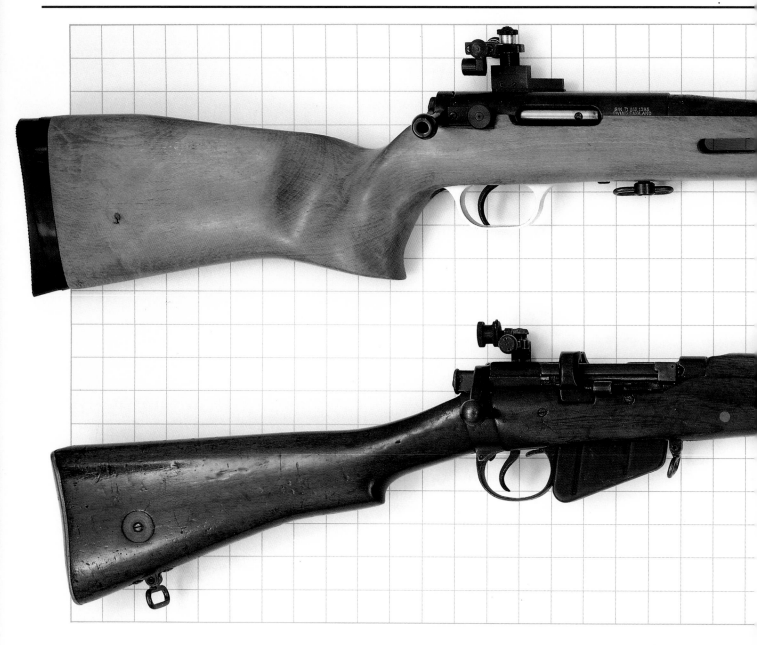

ENFIELD SMLE MK III

Country of origin: Great Britain
Type: Rifle
Calibre: .303
Capacity: 10 rounds
Action: Turning bolt. Cocks on closing; rear locking.
Operation: Lifting bolt handle unlocks breech. Striker recocked at end of forward stroke, chambering fresh cartridge and relocking breech.
Construction: All steel; brass buttplate and stock disc
Barrel length: 25.25in (641mm)
Length overall: 44.25in (1124mm)
Weight (empty): 9.4lb (4.26kg)
Sights: Parker-Hale 5A adjustable aperture backsight replaces tangent adjustable open sight on barrel. Post foresight behind protective wings.
Comments: The Lee bolt action, adopted in 1888, is still the mainstay of UK target shooting.

When, in 1888, Britain adopted the box-fed, bolt action Lee-Metford to replace the

Martini-Henry, it was a move to the front of the small arms queue, neatly overtaking France, who had only adopted the tubular magazine Lebel two years earlier. A decade later Germany's 1898 Mauser, massively strong, with a clip-fed internal box magazine, made everything else seem archaic. The Lee's chronic bedding problems, wood mounted trigger, rear-locking bolt and asymmetrical receiver all looked dated; Britain began work on a new, Mauser-type, stiff-actioned rifle to replace the Lee.

Meantime, the World War intervened, and the Lee turned out to be a superb combat rifle. It also turned out to be a quite remarkable target rifle with the bizarre proclivity to shoot better and better, the further away the target was. The rifle shown is the World War I standard SMLE Mk III with a Parker-Hale aperture backsight fitted for

Bisley target shooting.

While not threatening the hegemony of the Lee, stiff actioned rifles from the Ross to the Wichita have been in constant use at Bisley; regulated Pattern 14s have been particularly popular across the years as economy short range guns. Indeed, all of them shot extremely well back to the 600-yard (549m) limit of Century Range. It was "over the hill", on Stickledown, with its firing lines to 1,200 yards (1,097m), that stiff-actioned rifles proved vulnerable. Or at least that was the case until very recent years, when George Swenson introduced the Swing, the stiffest target rifle ever.

SWING SIN 71 M5

Country of origin: Great Britain
Type: Rifle
Calibre: 7.62mm NATO (.308 Winchester)

Capacity: 1 round
Action: Turning bolt
Operation: Lifting bolt handle unlocks breech and cocks striker. Four-lug front locking bolt.
Construction: All steel with titanium components in striker assembly. Beech stock.
Barrel length: 27.75in (705mm)
Length overall: 46in (1168mm)
Weight (empty): 11.2lb (5.07kg)
Sights: Swing micrometer adjustable aperture backsight; tunnel foresight with interchangeable elements.
Comments: The leading British target rifle, and the apotheosis of the stiff action approach. Introduced 1970. Set up here for NRA Target Rifle rules.

There is some question as to how much of the Swing's success (most of Britain's top riflemen now use it) is due to the extraordinary symmetry and rigidity of the action, and how much to a general improvement in the ammunition issued. Two

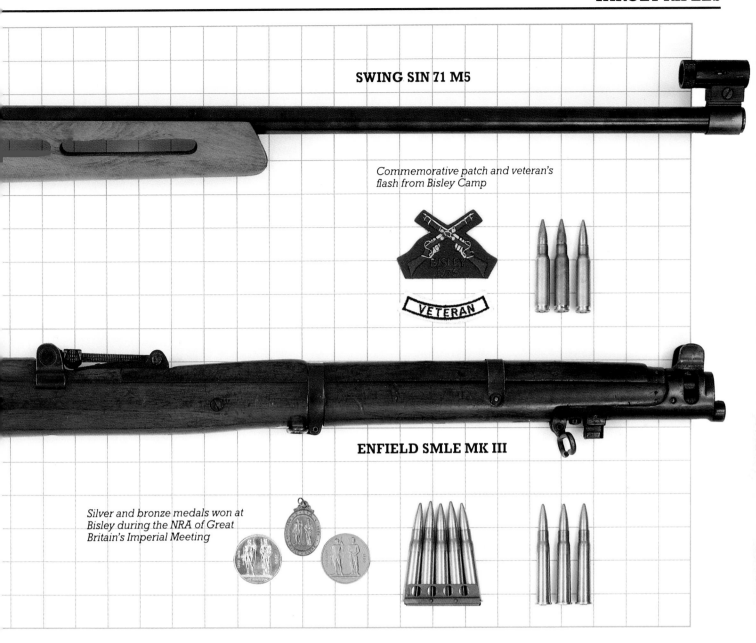

SWING SIN 71 M5

Commemorative patch and veteran's flash from Bisley Camp

ENFIELD SMLE MK III

Silver and bronze medals won at Bisley during the NRA of Great Britain's Imperial Meeting

crucial factors are that, all things being equal, any front-locking rifle will outshoot a Lee if selected or handloaded ammunition can be used—hence their success at 1,200 under Match Rifle rules. Under Target Rifle rules, however (the Queen's Prize, and most of the rest of British fullbore riflery), only issued military ammunition may be used.

Military ammunition, like any other, may be more or less consistent. Inconsistency manifests itself most significantly in velocity variations from round to round. At closer ranges, the effect on grouping may be slight. But at 1,000 yards (914m), when midrange trajectory will carry the bullet some feet above the line of sight, the fall of shot will be very considerably affected. Whether by accident or by design—far more likely the former—the substantial flex of

the Lee action on firing tended to iron out these shot-to-shot variations. A shot at lower velocity would depart with the muzzle whipped slightly up, while a higher velocity one would exit with the muzzle on the downwhip. This rather miraculous effect had long been recognised. What few besides George Swenson understood was that the Mauser 98, and all the similar front-locking, twin-lugged designs that followed it, decompensated. The Mauser, in fact, locks up with the lugs at 6 o'clock and 12 o'clock and in consequence produces vertically elliptical groups. At extreme ranges, the effect is dire.

What Swenson wanted was a rifle that would beat anything made at any range, and match the Lee with off-the-wall ammunition at one thousand. He visualised an ultra-stiff action delivering dense, round

groups, with a very fast lock time to minimise shooter-related departure error.

The result was the Swing, a *tour-de-force* of accuracy engineering, a massively rigid round-bottomed action, with the smallest possible loading/ejection port, and with two massive recoil lugs; one at the back, underneath the bolt handle, and the other just to the rear of the locking engagements. Vertical bedding bolts engage each lug. The rifle is Devcon bedded up to the bore line, and the positioning of the recoil lugs is intended to minimise torquing of the receiver within the bedding. The bolt head carries four massive, equally spaced locking lugs, with a plunger-ejector. The extractor is set into the right lug and by using titanium components and a massive mainspring, Swenson has got the lock time down to 1.24 milliseconds

while retaining 100 per cent reliability on military primers.

The Swing trigger unit, which Swenson says is an adaptation of a Montari design of the 1930s, is adjustable down to 1 pound, and is a much sought-after item in its own right, as are the Swing's micrometer sights. The rifle is normally fitted with 28in or 30in Schultz & Larsen barrels.

With its gargantuan mainspring and short lift, the Swing is not a pleasant gun to operate. The camming angles are steep, and the bolt requires a bit of manhandling on the cocking stroke. What its users like is the way it shoots. This year's winner of the Queen's Prize switched to a Lee at 1,000yds because it was a particularly nice day. Had a cloud strayed over the horizon, he would have stayed with the Swing he had used at the other distances. Lees and rain don't get on.

LEE-ENFIELD NUMBER 4 MARK 1 (T)

Country of origin: Great Britain
Type: Rifle
Calibre: .303in
Capacity: 10 rounds
Action: Bolt action repeater
Operation: Rear-locking bolt;
cocks on closing
Construction: All steel; most parts
machined from forgings
Barrel length: 25.2in (640mm)
Length overall: 44.5in (1130mm)
Weight (empty): 11.5lb (5.22kg)
all up
Sights: Number 32 Mark II
telescope; 3X magnification
Comments: The standard British
sniping unit throughout World War
II and the Korean War; excellently
rated. Most Number 4 Mark 1 (T)
rifles were set up by Holland &
Holland from Number 4 Mark 1
rifles produced by BSA-Shirley.

Old soldiers, it is said, never
die—and the two rifles shown

here have not even faded away.
The bolt-action Lee—of which
the Lee-Enfield Number 4
Mark 1 (T) version is shown
(top)—was adopted in 1888 and
is still, in its L42A1 sniper
version, in first-line service with
British forces, pending its
eventual replacement by the
Accuracy International Model
PM.

The L1A1 SLR (Self Loading
Rifle) (see below) was adopted
in 1958 and awaits eventual
replacement by the 5.56mm
bullpup L85A1. Good guns die
hard—and these are good
guns.

James Paris Lee was a Scots-
born American citizen whose
bolt-action rifle was for several
years produced, with no great
success, by the Remington
Arms Company of Ilion, New
York, before its submission for
the British trials to choose a
successor for the hopelessly

obsolete Martini-Henry tipping-
block single-shot.

The Lee-Metford (Metford
designed the rifling) was
Britain's first small-bore,
magazine-fed service rifle. The
Mark 1 .303, which used a
compressed charge of black
powder, was replaced in 1890
by an improved Mark II version
and in 1891 by a cordite Mark I
load. The Chitral campaign of
1895, however, proved that the
new combination, for all its
enhanced firepower, was
woefully lacking in terminal
effectiveness. Various
expanding bullets—generally
termed "Dum-Dums", after the
development programme
undertaken by the Indian
arsenal of that name—were
tried, but were eventually
abandoned in the face of
international disapproval. The
spire-point, backward-
weighted Mark VII load of 1910

proved to deliver the desired
performance on all
parameters.

During a service life that now
approaches a century, the rifle
itself underwent a number of
permutations. The Lee-Metford
and Lee-Enfield (the rifling was
changed) were "long rifles",
with carbine versions for
cavalry and artillery. The 1903
US Springfield was an
intermediate length for all
services, and the Boer Wars
indicated that the idea had a lot
of merit. The SMLE (Short
Magazine Lee-Enfield) of 1903
was the standard infantry
weapon of World War I. Some
7,000,000 were manufactured,
and they are easily
recognizable by the massive
muzzle cap that incorporated
the bayonet mount; the post-war
Number 4 rifle used lighter

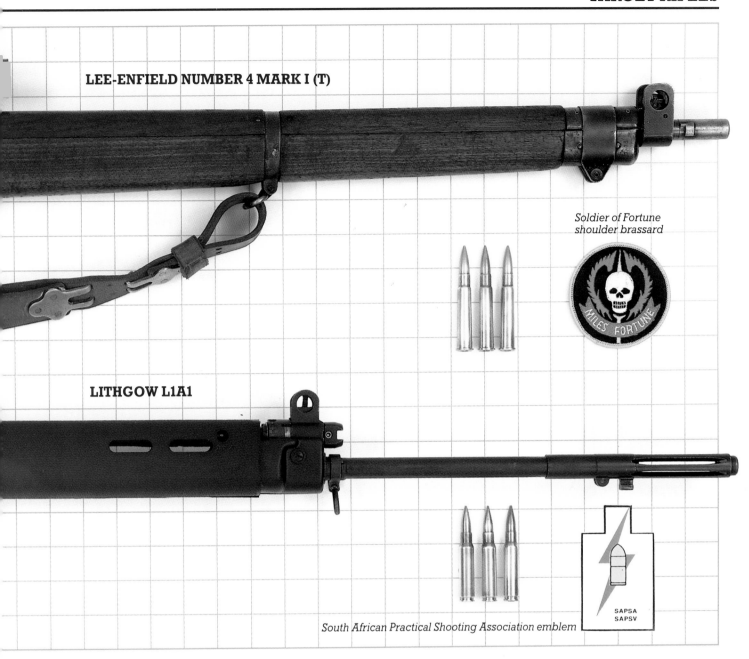

LEE-ENFIELD NUMBER 4 MARK I (T)

Soldier of Fortune shoulder brassard

LITHGOW L1A1

South African Practical Shooting Association emblem

SAPSA
SAPSV

furniture and had an aperture rear sight.

There was much to criticise in the Lee. The receiver was light, asymmetrical and springy, and so was the rear-locking bolt; torsional flexing on firing was immense. Compared to the 1898 Mauser, the Lee looked rather silly, and it would soon have been replaced by the massively robust, Mauser-derived Pattern 13 had not World War I intervened.

War, however, was the Lee's element and, to the surprise of practically everyone concerned it proved to be probably the best rifle of the conflict. Despite its myriad parts and strange vibrations, it was tough, reliable, fast and accurate. In fact, it was unbeatable at long range, for it vibrated in such a fashion as to compensate for the normal dispersion of the shots. Only in

very recent years have stiff-actioned guns been able to match the Lee at a range of 1,200yds (1097m).

LITHGOW L1A1

Country of origin: Australia
Type: Rifle
Calibre: 7.62mm NATO
Capacity: 20 rounds
Action: Semi-automatic; locked breech; gas operated
Operation: Short stroke piston impulses bolt carrier to unlock tipping bolt
Construction: Steel, machined from forgings, with pressed steel topcover. Furniture of ICI Maranyl nylon
Barrel length: 24.35in (618mm)
Length overall: 45in (1143mm)
Weight (empty): 9.8lb (4.45kg)
Sights: Post foresight; aperture rear sight
Comments: The most widely distributed full-power military rifle of the post-World War II period; now obsolete.

The gun that replaced the Lee was the Belgian *Fusil Automatique Légère* (FAL), designed by Dieudonne Saive, John Browning's gifted pupil, at Fabrique Nationale (FN) in Liège, Belgium. Britain, at that time, had developed the bullpup EM2 for a .280 calibre intermediate round, and briefly adopted it under the Atlee government. Churchill, for the sake of NATO unity, rescinded the adoption and accepted the full-power 7.62mm cartridge upon which the USA insisted. The FN FAL seemed to be the best rifle of that chambering—a conclusion which the 80 or so nations that subsequently adopted it must have shared. Its ubiquity over the past quarter-century of cold war has earned the FN FAL the sobriquet of "The Free World's Right Arm".

The FAL is gas-operated with a tipping bolt and a short-stroke

piston that acts on the bolt carrier. Lock-up is against a shelf in the lower receiver. The gas regulator has six adjustments, so that rifle and ammunition can be matched quite exactly. The recoil spring is in the butt, and the cocking handle is on the left of the receiver.

The axis of the bore is as low as could be achieved without turning to a straight stock with raised sights. This was an option that FN considered but rejected on the grounds that it would not allow the rifleman to make adequate use of cover, a point that subsequent guns like the M16 have illustrated.

The gun shown here is the Australian service version, with plastic furniture, the Lithgow L1A1 (bottom), so called from its place of manufacture. It is very similar to the British L1A1 produced at Enfield.

United Kingdom Practical Shooting
Association—Scotland brassard

U.K.P.S.A. SCOTLAND

STERLING AR180

SCHWEIZERISCHE INDUSTRIE-GESELLSCHAFT (SIG) SG510

Country of origin: Switzerland
Type: Self-loading rifle
Calibre: 7.62mm NATO (.308in)
Capacity: 20-round magazine standard
Action: Recoil operated roller-locked breech
Operation: Casehead thrust against the bolthead is diverted laterally into vertical rollers which lock into the receiver walls and which reconvert the energy into thrust against the bolt body; fires from closed bolt
Construction: All steel; pressed metal receiver. The Swiss service model has a rubber buttstock
Barrel length: 19.8in (503mm)
Length overall: 40in (1016mm)
Weight (empty): 9.375lb (4.25kg)
Sights: Post foresight laterally adjustable for windage zero; aperture backsight adjustable on click ramp for elevation
Comments: A superlative piece of

equipment. The version shown here does not have the grenade-launching facility, but note the bipod folded along the top of the barrel. The Stgw.57 was chambered for 7.5mm Swiss.

"Switzerland," Metternich is said to have observed, "does not have an army: it is an army." Indeed, the militia system has kept the Helvetian Confederation free from conflict for close on two centuries, during which no aggressor since Napoleon has dared to cross the Swiss borders. The Confederation's greatest test was undoubtedly during World War II, when the country's geographical location forced the Axis advance to take an inelegant loop through Austria. This was a tense and trying time, when Switzerland was the only country of mainland Europe whose preparation was sufficient to keep Hitler at bay.

Switzerland's introduction of the radical Stgw.57, of which a target rifle version is shown here (top), in 1956 seemed to underline the country's determination to survive a possible World War III as successfully as it had negotiated World War II. The introduction of the Stgw.57 coincided with a massive tunnelling programme designed to convert the country into a sub-alpine rabbit warren fit to withstand whatever nuclear holocaust the super-powers might unleash overhead.

If that should happen, the Swiss, burrowing back topside after the Geiger counters had quietened down, would dominate whatever they found, for the Stgw.57 was a terrain-compatible rifle, a generation ahead of anything else. It shocked at first sight. It was damnably heavy, weighing 12.25lb (5.56kg)

empty, and had an integral bipod and a semi/full-automatic selector lever. It had a rubber buttstock to withstand grenade launching, and was straight-line stocked to control burst fire and permit instantaneous follow-up shots on semi-automatic.

The Stgw.57 reflected the strength of the defence; it embodied the Pétainist post-World War I doctrine: "*Le feu tue.*" Guderian, the German panzer leader of World War II, may have blown holes in this philosophy—but he did not do so by driving tanks up Alps. The Stgw.57 very substantially enhanced the deterrent value of the Swiss militia. The rifle was eventually superseded not because it had become operationally obsolescent, but because it had become too expensive to manufacture.

About 600,000 Stgw.57's have been manufactured and

SCHWEIZERISCHE INDUSTRIEGESELLSCHAFT (SIG) SG510

International Practical Shooting Confederation emblem

I.P. S.C.

Schützenverein Rheinpfalz (West Germany) Practical Shooting Club brassard

issued to Swiss militiamen. They are kept in the militiaman's home and remain the property of the individual when his service obligation is concluded (as we have noted, Switzerland is a country that treats its people as responsible citizens!). Perhaps a further 100,000 were manufactured for export. The gun, using a roller-locked breech, was the Rolls-Royce of service rifles.

The gun illustrated here is the AMT (standing for "American Match Target") model, with walnut furniture and bereft of the grenade-launching facility. The white tab on the receiver shows that the full-automatic capacity has been blocked out.

STERLING AR180

Country of origin: Great Britain
Type: Self-loading rifle
Calibre: 5.56mm (.223in)
Capacity: 20-round magazine standard
Action: Gas operated; short-stroke piston; rotary-locking bolt
Operation: Operating rod impulses bolt carrier, which cams rotating bolthead out of lockup in the barrel extension
Construction: All steel, with plastic furniture; extensive use of sheet steel pressings for the upper and lower receiver bodies and for a number of internal and external parts
Barrel length: 18.25in (464mm)
Length overall: 36.4in (925mm) extended; 29in (737mm) with stock folded
Weight (empty): 7lb (3.18kg)
Sights: Post foresight adjusts for zeroing; two-leaf aperture backsight click adjustable for windage
Comments: An excellent mechanical design, adapted for

Great Britain's L85A1 rifle. The gun shown has been fitted with an extended magazine.

The Armalite AR18, of which a British-manufactured version is shown (bottom), designed by Arthur Miller after Eugene Stoner and the AR15 had both gone to Colt, is an opposite case to the Swiss rifle. Its pressed steel receiver, we are told, was meant to be easily manufacturable by Third World countries that might lack the tooling to cope with the forged aluminium receiver of the AR15. However, the AR18, or AR180 as it was later known, is an extremely good mechanism. It was manufactured variously by Armalite, Inc., of California, USA, Sterling Armament of Dagenham, Great Britain, and Howa Machinery Co. of Japan.

Despite its engineering

excellence, the AR18 never found the official acceptance that perhaps it deserved. The basic mechanism, however, was refined, simplified, and adopted as the new British service L85A1 in a bullpup configuration.

The AR18/L85A1 uses a seven-lugged rotating bolt locking into the breech end of the barrel. A short-stroke piston impacts the bolt carrier, impulsing it rearward. Twin recoil springs, running on guides through the upper part of the carrier on either side, give a well-supported, straight-line return from recoil, permitting a rigid, folding buttstock to be fitted on non-bullpupped versions. The admirable simplicity of this system has no doubt contributed to the rather spectacular success of the L85A1 in recent NATO inter-service competitions.

COLT AR15

COLT AR15

Country of origin: USA
Type: Self-loading rifle
Calibre: 5.56 x 45mm (.223)
Capacity: 20-round box magazine standard
Action: Self loading
Operation: Gas operated, direct deliver system. Gas tube above barrel jets gas against face of bolt carrier, which cams multi-lugged bolthead rotationally out of lockup in the barrel extension
Construction: Forged aluminium receiver; polymer furniture; most other parts steel
Barrel length: 20in (508mm)
Length overall: 39in (991mm)
Weight (empty): 7.241lb (3.28kg)
Sights: Post foresight; adjustable aperture rearsight in carrying handle
Comments: AR15 is the commercial designation for the US service M16 and M16A1 rifles, save that the AR15 is semi-automatic only, the M16 is selective fire and the M16A1 offers either semi-automatic fire or 3-round bursts, but not full automatic fire.

The modern era in military small arms was perhaps unwittingly ushered in when US Secretary of Defense Robert McNamara abruptly halted M14 production at the end of 1963 and let a contract to Colt for 85,000 AR15's for the Army and 19,000 for the Air Force. The M14 was .30 calibre, while the AR15 fired a light, high velocity projectile of .223 (5.56mm) calibre: a "woodchuck round", it was rightly said. The ensuing period was one of uncertainty, but on 6 December 1966, General William Westmoreland formally requested 100,000 M16's (as the AR15 was by then known, after its USAF designation) for his troops in Vietnam. A further 100,000 were ordered in the following year. Early in 1967, the little black rifle was adopted by the US Army as the M16A1; the US Government purchased

manufacturing rights from Colt and let contracts for a further 500,000 units.

The M16A1 had a chequered career in Vietnam, where between 50,000 and 200,000 rounds were required to produce an enemy casualty—astonishing figures, especially in view of the notorious frequency at which the gun refused to shoot at all. Jams and malfunctions were legion. The microscopic hit ratio was due to an almost complete lack of fire discipline; the malfunctions were caused by an equally comprehensive absence of field maintenance. The Army appeared to believe that the M16 did not require cleaning or regular inspection, and most soldiers did not even possess a cleaning kit. In fact, the M16 required more constant maintenance than any previous infantry weapon of

the smokeless powder era. This was due to endemically weak magazines and a gas system that delivered heavy fouling to the breech mechanism with every pull of the trigger.

Rather than a piston and operating rod system (which vented the gases to the atmosphere at high pressure) as used on the M1 and M14, the M16 employed a gas delivery pipe that spewed the half-cooled gases directly into the breech, where they impulsed the bolt carrier and then coagulated. This arrangement had worked well on the Swedish AG42 Eklund-Ljungmann, the Egyptian Hakim and the French MAS 49 and 49/56 rifles; it also worked well on the M16, until the IMR powder for which the rifles had been designed was dropped in favour of a colloidal ball

STEYR AUG

British Forces reduced "Figure 11" silhouette

powder that left treacle-like residue.

Today, however, recently readopted as the M16A2, the black rifle is the most tried, proved and improved battle rifle of the Western world—an excellent piece of equipment.

STEYR AUG

Country of origin: Austria
Type: Selective-fire rifle
Calibre: 5.56 x 45mm
Capacity: 30-round box magazine standard
Action: Self loading
Operation: Gas operated, offset short-stroke piston impulses bolt carrier to rotate multi-lugged bolthead out of lockup in receiver ring
Construction: Hammer forged barrel; machined steel block mounts barrel and provides locking engagements for bolthead; die cast aluminium receiver with steel inserts; stock, magazine, receiver housing and many parts are of high strength polymers

Barrel length: 21.625in (549mm); 25.75in (654mm)
Length overall: 31.5in (800mm) with shorter barrel
Weight (empty): 9.37lb (4.25kg)
Sights: 1.5x Swarovski scope built into carrying handle; rudimentary open sights moulded into top
Comments: Quick-change barrels permit formats from sub-machine gun to section support weapon. Insulated forward grip is attached to barrel, protecting hand from burns during change-over. Two-stage trigger pull: initial stage for semi-auto, all the way through for full auto.

The M16's most formidable competitor in world markets is probably the Steyr AUG. The abbreviation stands for *Armee Universalgewehr*, or universal army rifle: in its various guises it replaces the rifle, sub-machine gun and section support weapon. A futuristic-looking contrivance, making extensive use of advanced plastics

technology, the AUG is in the currently fashionable "bullpup" format, with the pistol grip forward of the magazine and the breech mechanism alongside the user's face. The advantage is a short overall length, which makes the gun easy to rack in armoured vehicles or to handle in tight quarters. The disadvantage is that it cannot be fired around cover from the opposite shoulder.

The AUG has a solid, indestructible feel and is said to be extremely reliable; accuracy runs about 1.5-2 MOA from a benchrest and with a target scope. In service trim, it has a 1.5x Swarovski scope in the carrying handle. Barrels interchange quickly and lock into a machined steel ring, contained within the cast aluminium breech housing; the bolthead locks into the same steel ring.

The gun uses a rotating bolt that recoils along two substantial guide rods, the right one housing the operating rod. Both rods impinge on recoil springs contained within the buttstock.

The use of polymers extends to the firing unit, most components of which are plastic though there has recently been some substitution of metal parts, probably in order to increase hammer impact. An excellent weapon, its primary vice seems to be a gruesome 10-pound (4.5kg) trigger pull that makes the attainment of its inherent accuracy a somewhat arduous process.

The AUG has been in service in Austria since 1977 and has since been adopted by the armed forces of Oman, Saudi Arabia and Australia. Its adoption in Scandinavia is said to be pending.

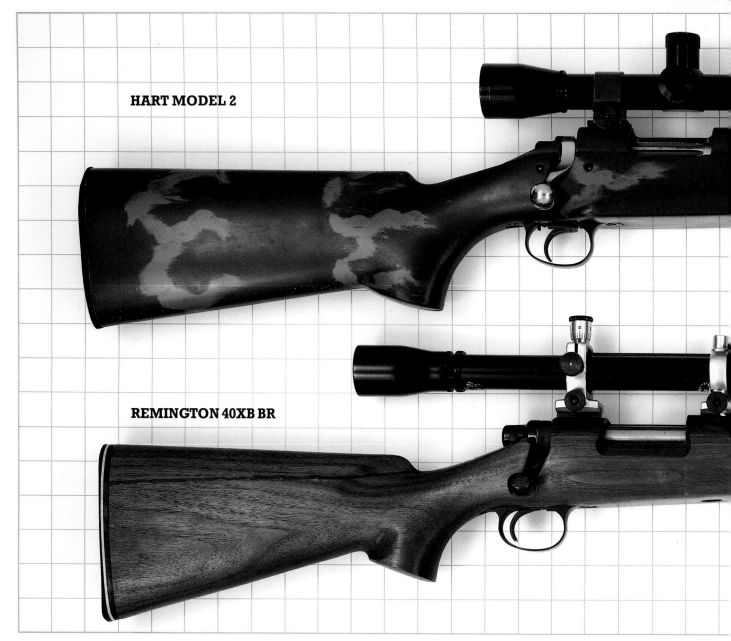

HART MODEL 2

REMINGTON 40XB BR

The shooting sports are tests of skill. The group on the target is a measure of neuro-muscular co-ordination achievable only by years of dedicated practice, constant self-examination, diligent fault correction and painstaking refinement of technique. All the shooting sports except one, we might say. For Bench Rest is devoted precisely to the elimination of anything to do with skill. The goal is pure accuracy: accuracy demands consistency and skill implies nothing if not a whole zone of variables that mask just the sort of equipment variables that Bench Resters are dedicated to isolating and correcting. Bench Rest is the ultimate equipment sport, a pure contest in engineering. A properly crafted cartridge, Bench Resters reckon, should group into less than .03 minute of angle—maybe even .02. The

problem lies in crafting a rifle that will add nothing to that.

The inevitable result was the "rail gun", a sort of miniature fieldpiece fired by remote control, that does not much look like a rifle at all. This all was getting a bit remote for a lot of people who regarded themselves essentially as riflemen, and most of the competitive activity today is in the categories known as light and heavy varmint and sporting. Light means a maximum all-up weight of 10.5lb (4.76kg), (heavy allows 13.5lb, 6.12kg). Varmint allows .22 centrefires, while sporting requires a minimum bullet diameter of .243in (6mm). Both the rifles illustrated fall in the "light varmint" category.

Skill still comes into it insofar as perfecting one's bench technique goes, and in judging, or at least coping with, wind. But a bullet launched

from a rail gun is no more proof against wind drift, and it is a tribute to the shooters that groups in light varmint do not lag significantly behind those to be found in the heavier categories.

REMINGTON 40XB BR

Country of origin: United States
Type: Rifle
Calibre: .222 Remington
Capacity: 1 round
Action: Turning bolt
Operation: Lifting bolt handle unlocks breech and cocks striker
Construction: All steel; stainless barrel
Barrel length: 20in (508mm)
Length overall: 38in (965mm)
Weight (empty): 10.47lb (4.76kg)
Sights: 20-power Remington-Unertl telescope with adjustments in back mount
Comments: The first great "light varmint" Bench Rest competition rifle. Uses special Remington 2oz trigger.

The guns pictured illustrate successive generations of light varmint equipment. The lower rifle is the Remington Model 40XB BR in .222 Remington calibre that dominated the sport for a decade. Introduced in 1969 and offering immediate out-of-the-box accuracy of .04 minute of angle, it was very much the creation of Mike Walker, the Ilion firm's remarkable chief of research and development. Walker designed the Models 721 and 722 bolt actions which Remington launched with crossed fingers into the unpredictable post war market; he redesigned them as the Model 700, and later, in match target trim, as the Model 40X.

He also designed the .222 cartridge, using an entirely new case with a .378in head diameter and 1.7in length. Introduced in 1950 and situated ballistically at midpoint

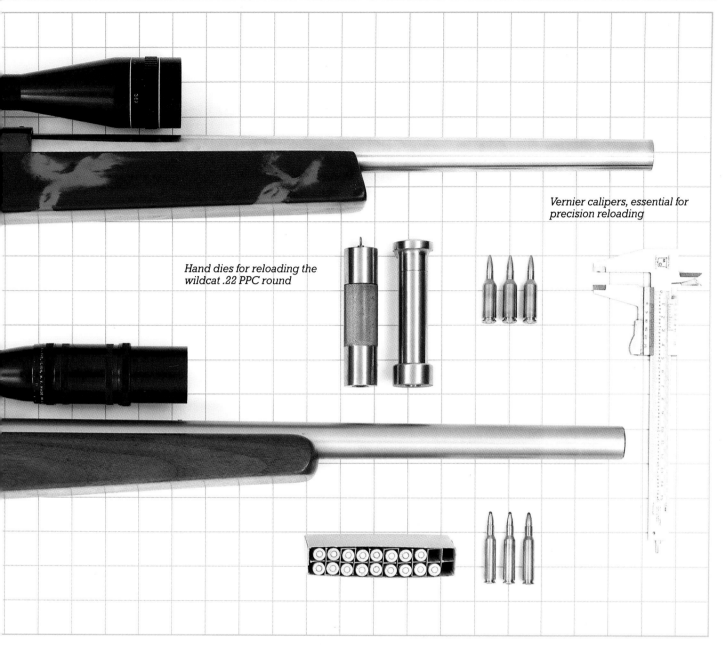

Hand dies for reloading the wildcat .22 PPC round

Vernier calipers, essential for precision reloading

between the gentle .22 Hornet and the barrel-eating .220 Swift, the .222 established an immediate reputation for outstanding accuracy and promptly became the overwhelming Bench Rest favourite. Today, the .222 Remington is regarded as perhaps the most accurate factory cartridge ever produced, and has won more Bench Rest titles than any other. A slightly lengthened version, with the shoulder moved forward, was adopted as the US, and subsequently NATO, standard service rifle cartridge, the 5.56 x 45mm.

The 40XB BR as shown typifies the light varminter of the 1970's with its short, massive free-floating stainless steel barrel, glass bedded action and walnut stock with a broad, flat fore-end to lie steadier on the sandbags. Factory cartridge cases have to have

the necks lathe-turned for a precise fit in the tightly dimensioned chamber throat. The telescope is a 20-power Remington-Unertl with external adjustments in the rear mount as shown.

HART MODEL 2

Country of origin: United States
Type: Rifle
Calibre: .22 PPC
Capacity: 1 round
Action: Turning bolt
Operation: Lifting bolt handle unlocks breech and cocks striker. Each round must be placed in the breech by hand, there being no magazine.
Construction: All steel; stainless barrel. Glass fibre stock.
Barrel length: 20in (508mm)
Length overall: 39.25in (997mm)
Weight (empty): 10.38lb (4.71kg)
Sights: 36-power Leupold telescope in Weaver mounts
Comments: Top rated Bench Rest rifle in its class

The top rifle is the 40XB BR's 1980's successor and differs essentially in calibre, sights, stocking, bedding and receiver. Based on the 40XB BR and built by Robert W. Hart of Pennsylvania, it uses a fluted bolt (to save weight) and a massive action. Note the thickness of the receiver walls, and the length of the receiver ring, which is nearly twice that on the Remington.

The barrel unscrews by hand, but all of the engagements of barrel, bolt and receiver are machined to be absolutely true. The fashion nowadays is to glue the extended tang into the stock, leaving the barrel and receiver both free to vibrate. The former practice was to free float the barrel, while using vertical screws to seat the receiver firmly into a glass bed. The problem was that even using a torque wrench, the tension

exerted by the screws could never be exactly uniform. For similar reasons, the trend today is towards fibreglass stocks—wood is too vulnerable to changes in humidity, while laminates are too heavy.

The Hart is chambered for the .22 PPC, designed by toolmaker Ferris Pindell and vascular surgeon, Dr Lou Palmisano, hence the acronym. The "C" stands for cartridge. The .22 PPC derives from a necked-down 7.62 x 39mm Soviet case and was based on computer calculations concerning the most efficient combustion chamber configurations for given projectiles. Chronograph tests show phenomenally low velocity variations. The 6mm PPC, based on the same case, is often used at 300 yards or, if the wind rises, at 100 or 200 yards as well, these being the three standard ranges.

Rear sandbag which is moved to make fine adjustments when aiming the rifle.

Bench Rest shooting, as a national sport in the US, is conducted at 100, 200 and 300 yards' range, though the famous 1,000-yard shoots at Williamsport, Pennsylvania are much envied. Long range shooting of any sort is something of an eccentric interest, however, and it was not until the sport crossed the Atlantic that Long Range Bench Resting found the congregation it deserved.

In the UK shooting vernacular, 600 yards is still "short range", and somewhat socially inferior as well. When Bench Resting arrived in 1972, the 100, 200 and 300-yard stages, which are what the sport is all about in the US, attracted appropriate interest, but soon became a bit of a sideshow to the main event—the 1,000 yard stage, where groups ran the better part of a foot—which was felt to be something you could get more of a grip on.

Bench Rest at this distance exerted a strong attraction on Bisley's "over the hill" contingent, the "Match Rifle" competitors who shoot out to 1,200 yards, but never closer than 1,000, and who had long since allowed optical sights, handloads and non-standard calibres into their competitions —all out of bounds to the British marksman under "Target Rifle" rules. "Match" riflemen constituted a corps of a long range ballistic experimenters and equipment fiddlers whom the new sport could not fail to attract. And it is this pre-existing community that has stood the sport somewhat on its head in the UK. Over the course of time, no doubt, the comparative rarity of 1,000-yard ranges will inhibit expansion of this discipline to the relative benefit of the short-range side of the sport.

There are differences between the two: long range is more about skill and ballistics while short range emphasises mechanical precision. A bullet for short range must be absolutely concentric; for long range, ballistic co-efficient (sectional density and aerodynamic form) is more important. Wind and mirage are problems at close range; at 1,000 yards they are *the* problem. For 300 yards and in, the choice of cartridge is pretty cut-and-dried; for the longer ranges, there are keen adherents to every calibre from 6.5-300 to .30-378. Studied closely, however, there is not all that much disagreement between proponents of these various calibres. Everyone is looking for very heavy bullets in whichever calibre (in order to maximize ballistic co-efficient) in a cartridge that will give high velocities with optimum ballistic efficiency for uniform velocities and minimum muzzle disturbance. One's freedom of choice in this respect is somewhat restricted to those

calibres for which top quality heavyweight match bullets are available, and that, in turn, leads one most commonly to .30 and 7mm.

REMINGTON 40XB RANGEMASTER TARGET

Country of origin: United States
Type: Rifle
Calibre: .30-338 Magnum
Capacity: 1 round
Action: Turning bolt
Operation: Lifting bolt handle unlocks breech and cocks striker. Forward locking with dual opposed lugs, plunger ejector, C-clip rotating extractor inset in bolt face. Each round must be fed into the breech by hand. Uses Remington 2-ounce set trigger.
Construction: All steel. Stainless barrel.
Barrel length: 27.25in (692mm)
Length overall: 47in (1194mm)
Weight (empty): 13lb (5.6kg)
Sights: Weaver T16 Micro-Trac telescope with pedestal mounting onto a single piece bridge mount.

REMINGTON 40XB RANGEMASTER TARGET

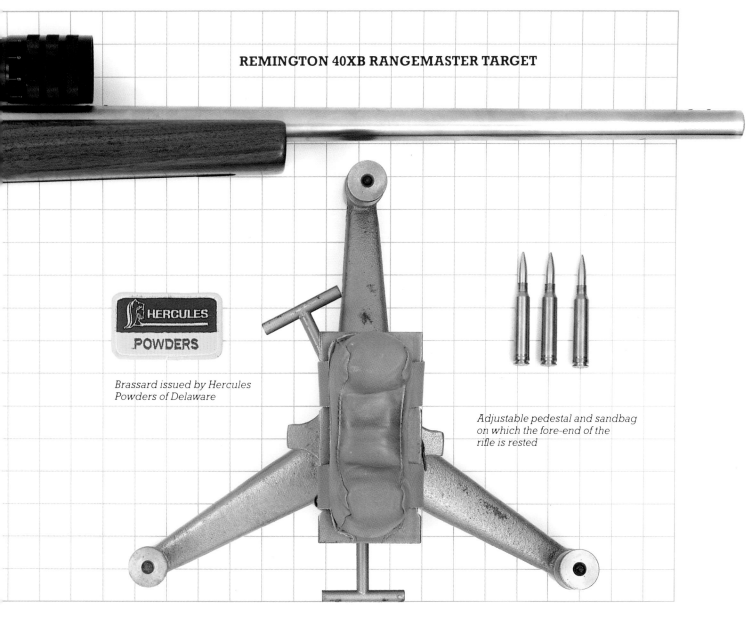

HERCULES
POWDERS

Brassard issued by Hercules Powders of Delaware

Adjustable pedestal and sandbag on which the fore-end of the rifle is rested

Comments: 1,000 yard Bench Rest Rifle in a wildcat calibre consisting of .338 Winchester Magnum necked to a .30 calibre.

The Model 40XB is built in Remington's famed Custom Shop on Model 700 receivers snatched from the production line as early as possible, i.e. before the magazine opening is cut. They are then lathe turned to very tight standards of concentricity, and fitted with special barrels, with barrel and receiver being trued square and adjusted for minimum headspace. The bolt lugs are lapped for full bearing contact, and most of these guns carry Remington's 2oz trigger. They come with three 5-round test targets, with guaranteed accuracy of a minute of angle or less. In .222 or .223, Remington guarantee .45in (11mm) groups, and in 7.62mm, .75in (19mm) groups at 100 yards. The rifle illustrated is a

Remington Model 40X in .30-338—a .38 Winchester Magnum necked to a .30 calibre, or alternatively a .458 Winchester Magnum necked to .30 cal., since the .338 itself is a necked-down .458. The advantages are several. The cartridge is short for its power, which permits a relatively beefier, stiffer receiver than a .300 H&H or .300 Winchester Magnum, with much less vibration on discharge, and more sheer mass in the barrel and action. And while, theoretically, a 6.5mm ought to be advantageous—greater sectional density for a given weight—the fact is that, as of last look, no smaller calibre bullet came close to the .556 ballistic co-efficient of the 200-grain, 30-calibre spitzer. This splendid co-efficient, combined with the availability of premium quality bullets and efficiently designed cases, makes .30 calibre the first choice, with the 168-grain,

7mm a close second.

The disadvantage, of course, is recoil. An extended bench session with one of these guns can become punishing. Most long-range Bench Resters have taken to placing a sandbag or lead-shot bag between the buttplate and the shoulder as a form of physical protection against the recoil forces.

Bench Rest rifles are all, of course, single shot, since a magazine recess in the underside of the receiver would make a turning fork of it. Several things are sacred to the sport, but none more so than a stiff receiver.

As at closer ranges, the rifle is fired with the fore-end resting across a saddle-shaped leather sandbag on a heavy, cast iron pedestal. The pedestal offers coarse and fine adjustments—as many as nine in all—so that the rifle may be laid to the shooter's preference. The toe of the stock is supported by another

sandbag, of "bunny ears" shape. This rear sandbag is used to aim the rifle. It is slid forward or back to adjust elevation and from side to side for windage. Some shooters make the final adjustment by slightly pinching the sandbag, but others fear that such treatment will affect the recoil characteristics of this rifle from shot to shot, and hence accuracy.

With short range guns, many competitors touch only the trigger, allowing the rifle to recoil entirely unhindered. With a gun like the .30-338, such a technique is not practical. There must be firm, consistent, shoulder, cheek and hand contact. Trigger pressure is normally two ounces. Technique is important. But the real challenge lies in making the cartridges and judging the wind. Long Range Bench Rest is just British Match Rifle with a few variables ironed out.

SPRINGFIELD ARMORY M1A RIFLE

WINCHESTER M14 US SERVICE RIFLE

Country of origin: USA
Type: Rifle
Calibre: 7.62mm NATO
Capacity: 20-round magazine
Action: Selective fire (most rifles were issued with the selector blocked to semi-automatic)
Operation: Gas operated; long-stroke piston with self-metering feature, operating two-lugged, front-locking, rotating bolt. This is similar to the M1 Garand, with a different piston head and without the en-bloc clip feed system
Construction: All steel; aluminium buttplate; timber stock with glass fibre upper handguard. Some were made with synthetic buttstocks
Barrel length: 22in (559mm)
Length overall: 44.14in (1121mm)
Weight (empty): 8.7lb (3.95kg); (loaded) 10lb (4.5kg)
Sights: Square post foresight; aperture backsight, click

adjustable for windage and elevation
Comments: Excellent accuracy; good reliability; very effective.

The service rifle, as much as the flag, is the emblem of a nation, and it is rarely changed without an aftermath of vociferous public discord. The short-lived M14 rifle (bottom) was no exception: it was viewed by some as the last gesture of doomed ballistic diehards and by others as the best service rifle the United States ever had. There is merit in both views. What is less pardonable than a robust opinion on either side of the technical argument is the fact that the 7.62mm cartridge was rammed down the throats of America's NATO allies, while the tests were slanted to disadvantage competing rifles, notably the Belgian FAL.

The M14 is essentially a box-magazined M1 Garand with a modified, self-metering gas system. A more compact propellant (ball powder) allowed the cartridge case to be shortened by 0.5in (12.7mm) while conserving full power, thus permitting a shorter receiver and a somewhat lighter gun.

The M14 has all the Garand's reliability in a better-balanced, more agile package. It handles and snap-shoots like a shotgun. A friend of the author, a fine marksman and a former company commander in Vietnam, regarded it as a much better jungle gun than the M16 and always put M14's in point position on patrols. The shotgun-like handling was one reason for this; the brush-chopping quality of the cartridge was another.

In short, the M14 was a rifleman's rifle. It was a superb

match target performer, splendidly accurate, especially when tuned, and without the M1's propensity to go spontaneously and inexplicably out of tune.

The US Army, however, despite having originally gone all out to adopt the rifle, seemed to be doctrinally incapable of capitalizing on its advantages. Instinctive shooting and random-hit probability were all the rage, and the M14 was expected to fulfil multiple roles when it was only good at one. All M14's were built with selective fire capability (the light infill visible near the back of the receiver on the example shown here marks the former position of the selector—but the M14 was ineffective on full-automatic, since this caused it to climb uncontrollably and thus made it about as lethal as a sack full of thunderflashes. Even if the

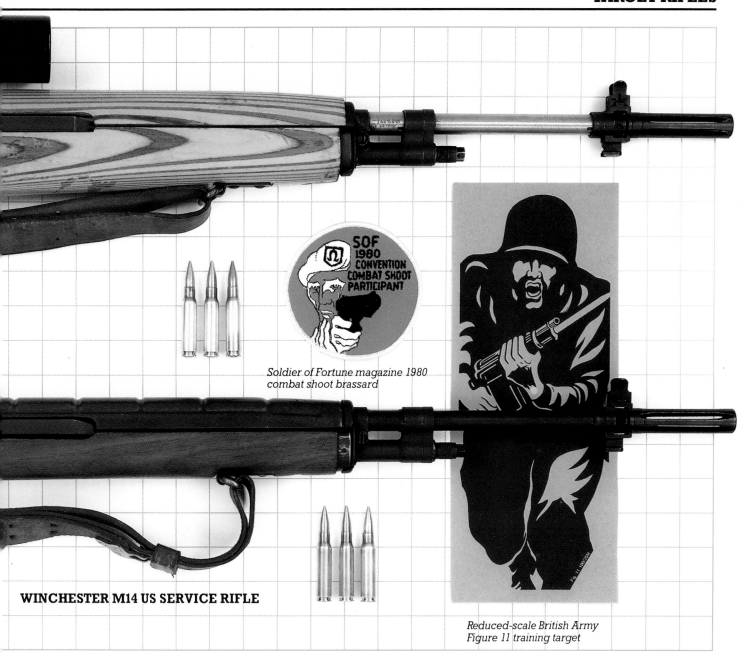

Soldier of Fortune magazine 1980
combat shoot brassard

WINCHESTER M14 US SERVICE RIFLE

Reduced-scale British Army
Figure 11 training target

muzzle could have been held down, the barrel would have overheated and very quickly burned out. Perforce, the M60 light machine gun was drawn into the section support role, while politics and history caught up with the M14's other roles.

The M14 had been the culmination of the US Army's post-World War II "Light Rifle" programme—and, by definition, could scarcely have failed to disappoint. Meanwhile, a development programme designated SPIW was expected to yield the weapon of the future in fairly short order. In January 1963, Secretary of Defense Robert McNamara abruptly cancelled M14 production after only 1,380,346 of the rifles had been made. In the following year he announced his decision to close Springfield Armory as well. Neither of these

decisions, taken as the Vietnam War was in the process of being intensified, has ever been satisfactorily explained.

In any event, the SPIW programme was a failure and the US Army, left rudderless and rifle-less, followed the US Air Force down the smallbore, M16 path. The US Marine Corps held on to their M14's for a while longer, but today the US Navy is the only service still using the M14. Since they use more rifles than either the US Marines or the US Air Force, the US Navy's reluctance to be blown off course by what is perhaps best described as a ballistic fad is particularly noteworthy. And, of course, the United States Navy's continuing use of the M14 provides a large part of the answer to those who may be tempted to wonder just what happened to close on 1.4 million rifles.

SPRINGFIELD ARMORY, INC., M1A RIFLE

Country of origin: USA
Type: Rifle
Calibre: 7.62mm NATO
Capacity: 20-round magazine
Action: Self-loading rifle (semi-automatic)
Operation: Gas operated; long-stroke piston with self-metering feature, operating two-lugged, front-locking, rotating bolt. A copy of the US Army M14 rifle
Construction: All steel; laminated stock
Barrel length: 22in (559mm)
Length overall: 44in (1118mm)
Weight (empty): 13.5lb (6.12kg)
Sights: Service aperture and post provided; gun shown here mounts a Schmidt and Bender telescopic sight
Comments: This is strictly a match machine, barely man-portable but extremely accurate and consistent. The rifle shown has been modified by its owner.

After its closure, described above, the name "Springfield Armory" was sold to a light engineering firm in Illinois. They lost little time in putting the M14 back into production, this time for the civilian market. As we have already mentioned, this second-generation Garand rifle was a superb target performer, and its aborted production run meant that too few were released to satisfy a growing civilian market.

Today, the M1A (top), as the rifle is called in commercial production, is pre-eminent in Practical Rifle competiton, where it is challenged only by the G3. The gun illustrated belongs to Peter Sarony, known as the father of Practical Rifle, who uses it to great effect, having carried out the modifications himself. It has a replacement barrel, telescopic sight and massive laminated stock.

HECKLER & KOCH MODEL HK-94

A sub-machine gun (SMG) is a selective fire carbine chambered for a pistol cartridge. The first of the type to appear was the Bergmann SMG of 1918: the German answer to the American riot gun as a trench sweeper. After World War I the SMG achieved wide popularity in European armies, tending to replace the pistol, which few servicemen could use effectively. Whether anyone could use the SMG effectively seems not to have been the subject of much enquiry; however, the fact that the SMG made much more noise than the pistol was indisputable, and this tended to be good for morale all round.

The shotgun, being incapable of point fire at intermediate ranges unless time is available to substitute slug for shot, has usually been a supplement to the handgun rather than a replacement for it.

The primary advantage of the SMG over the shotgun is that it can provide point fire or area fire capability (single shots or full automatic) at the flip of a thumb-lever. A second advantage, given a skilled operator, is that the SMG can give variable area coverage, depending on the situation: it can cut a broad swathe or it can maintain a succession of short bursts into quite a small area. The shotgun, on the other hand, for a given choke, is entirely a prisoner of distance as far as shot dispersal goes.

The disadvantages of the SMG are its gross over-penetration in urban circumstances, relatively poor stopping power, and, as compared to the shotgun, the considerably greater training needed to acquire reasonable proficiency with the SMG. But both guns are, in practice, expected to fill the same role,

so the argument as to which is to be preferred is often a heated one—as might be expected, given their considerable dissimilarity.

Simplicity is a virtue that most SMGs carry to an extreme that results in poor single-shot accuracy unless great care is taken to follow through. This is because of the lurch, jolt and lag involved in firing from an open bolt. Slam-fire, or "advanced primer ignition" as it is more politely known, may make for economy—but it does not make for precision.

STERLING MARK VI

Country of origin: Great Britain
Type: Carbine
Calibre: 9mm Parabellum
Capacity: 34 rounds (10-round magazine optional)
Action: Semi-automatic; unlocked breech
Operation: Blowback operated; fires from closed bolt

Construction: All steel; seamless tubular receiver
Barrel length: 16.125in (410mm)
Length overall: 35.125in (892mm) with stock extended; 26.75in (679mm) with stock folded
Weight (empty): 8.5lb (3.86kg)
Sights: Post foresight; double-leaf aperture backsight
Comments: A semi-automatic version of the selective-fire Mark IV SMG, with action extensively redesigned to fire from a closed bolt. A very heavy recoil spring backs the 1.5lb (0.68kg) bolt.

The Sterling SMG (top) was developed by George Patchett during the closing days of World War II, and it is still standard with the British, Canadian and many Commonwealth armies, albeit it is now distinctly showing its age. It was used by both sides during the Falklands War and, because of its extreme reliability in adverse

STERLING MARK VI

atal Practical Shooting
ssociation emblem

N.P.S.A.

circumstances, it is also popular in the Middle East. Indeed, reliability and workmanship are the Sterling's strong points; it is, in a manner of speaking, a Sten Gun as built by Rolls-Royce. Design-wise, it is old fashioned, with a long receiver and all of the bolt behind the barrel. In most of the more recent designs, the breechblock envelops the back end of the barrel to economize on length.

As well as quality and robustness, three factors contribute to the Sterling's reliability. First, slam-fire guns are virtually misfire-proof. Second, the helical ribs machined on the bolt scrape the receiver walls clean of sand, fouling or debris of any kind. Third, the side-mounted magazine with its reinforced feed lips and roller-bearing follower is extremely positive and dependable; vertical

magazines, on the other hand, have to fight gravity, friction and fouling—not always successfully. A 30- or 40-round stack of cartridges is quite heavy, and the magazine spring has only a fraction of a second to lift the stack so that the top cartridge is in feed position when the bolt returns.

The Sterling Mark VI shown here has been re-engineered to fire from closed bolt only, putting it in the same league as the HK-94 (below) for single-shot accuracy. Both guns are semi-automatic only, and both have c.16in (406mm) barrels to meet the requirements of the US sporting market. The extra barrel length makes the Parabellum's muzzle ballistics even more impressive. Both carbines will give excellent results when they are fitted with a low-powered scope or Aimpoint sight.

HECKLER & KOCH MODEL HK-94

Country of origin: West Germany
Type: Carbine
Calibre: 9mm Parabellum
Capacity: 15 rounds
Action: Semi-automatic; recoil operated
Operation: Roller locked; delayed blowback
Construction: Steel; extensive use of heavy-gauge precision blankings
Barrel length: 16.5in (419mm)
Length overall: 33.5in (851mm) with stock extended; 27in (686mm) with stock retracted
Weight (empty): 7.6lb (3.45kg)
Sights: Post foresight; aperture backsight mounted on elevating drum
Comments: A semi-automatic version of the selective-fire MP5 sub-machine gun, using a roller-retarded action; a scale-down of the German G3 rifle.

The Heckler & Koch MP5, of which the semi-automatic

Model HK-94 is shown (bottom), represents such a significantly radical departure in SMG design that it might better be regarded as a selective-fire carbine, like the American M-2. It uses a roller-locked bolt similar to that used on the G3 rifle and fires from closed-bolt position. Thus, the lock time is incomparably faster than that of a conventional SMG, with the expected improvement in point fire accuracy; and the recoiling masses are much lighter, which should both aid control and make possible a much lighter weapon. On the negative side are greater expense in manufacture and greater complexity, the latter making the possibility of malfunction more likely. Nevertheless, the MP5, like the Sterling, is a splendid tool: with the British weapon, it is among the three or four best SMGs current.

HUNTING
PISTOLS
&
REVOLVERS

Ken Warner (Introduction) and Jan Stevenson

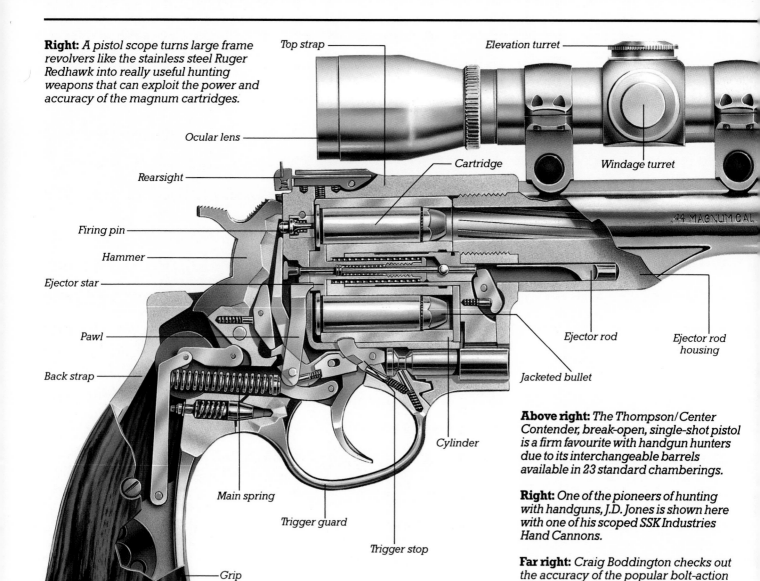

Right: *A pistol scope turns large frame revolvers like the stainless steel Ruger Redhawk into really useful hunting weapons that can exploit the power and accuracy of the magnum cartridges.*

Top strap

Elevation turret

Ocular lens

Windage turret

Cartridge

Rearsight

.44 MAGNUM CAL

Firing pin

Hammer

Ejector star

Pawl

Ejector rod

Ejector rod housing

Back strap

Jacketed bullet

Cylinder

Main spring

Trigger guard

Trigger stop

Grip

Above right: *The Thompson/Center Contender, break-open, single-shot pistol is a firm favourite with handgun hunters due to its interchangeable barrels available in 23 standard chamberings.*

Right: *One of the pioneers of hunting with handguns, J.D. Jones is shown here with one of his scoped SSK Industries Hand Cannons.*

Far right: *Craig Boddington checks out the accuracy of the popular bolt-action Remington XP-100. Its super strong action easily handles the 200 grain hollow points.*

Twenty-five years ago, acting on the advice of Maynard Buehler, I buckled a 4-power scope onto a Smith & Wesson K-22 revolver chambered in the then-not-too-old .22 Winchester Rimfire Magnum and sallied forth to handgun hunt. The rig worked well at Florida woods' ranges on gray squirrels, there charmingly called "cat" squirrels, and on crows. I wrote an article about it—and that was more or less the end of the business for me.

It was not so for other handgunners, who are now in their myriads travelling all over the world and taking, in fair chase, everything up to elephant. These people, among whom I know some of the masters, like J.D. Jones, constantly amaze me. Of course, anyone who shoots very well amazes me, and hunting handgunners have to do that. Remember, too, that they must also spend tens of thousands of pounds (or dollars) going hither and yon in search of bigger and better beasts to slay, and you must agree that they are a remarkable set of people.

Their hardware, too, is remarkable. It is rarely possible, when it comes to firearms, to say anything without fear of contradiction, but in this one tiny area it is possible to state, categorically, that there have never been handguns like these handguns.

For instance, I own a Thompson/Center Contender—quite an old one, but a very nice gun. For it, I have three barrels: a Hot Shot .44 Magnum barrel, which handles .410 bore-class shot cartridges; a .35 Remington barrel, wearing its original iron sights; and one of J.D. Jones's .45-70 barrels, scoped in a Jones T'SOB mount. In practice, the Hot Shot barrel is the spare for whichever of the others I have with me.

The basic purpose of the .35 Remington barrel is to be a very portable spare hunting arm. On several occasions, one or another hunting companion has been glad there was a spare gun in camp, particularly one with the undeniable potential of the .35 Remington Thompson/Center. And I am always glad to have it with me, for when the rifle has done its work and the hunt is over, but the time allotted is not, pottering around in the hills and bushes is a lot easier when you do not have to carry a rifle.

Role of the XP-100

What I think of as the big bore, the .45-70, is itself a principal hunting arm. And well it might be: the .45-70 is a very impressive cartridge, no matter what firearm it is shot from. The .35 Remington barrel was chronographed as part of a test prgramme

and produced velocities only 150 feet per second less than those from a 20-inch (508mm) Marlin carbine which was shot at the same time with the same lot of ammunition.

Thompson/Center is now indeed at the forefront when it comes to hunting handguns, but it was not so at the very beginning of the handgun hunting fever. Three other guns led the way. They were the Smith & Wesson and Ruger .44 Magnum revolvers, and the Remington XP-100 bolt action single shot pistol. A small clique of enthusiasts used Ruger's Hawkeye pistol, but eventually the collectors outbid the hunters for that unique piece of Rugeriana.

It is likely that the XP-100's role in the story of hunting handguns will forever be understated. This much, however, is true: it was the XP-100 that showed us all how a handgun could shoot. I remember shooting away all the ammunition at hand from the benchrest at 100 yards (91.44m) the first day that I ever had my hands on an XP-100. Punching out 1-inch (25mm) five-shot groups often enough to keep one interested was a real thrill in those days, with any hunting-class firearm, but doing the same thing with a genuine, Federally-defined handgun, one that was

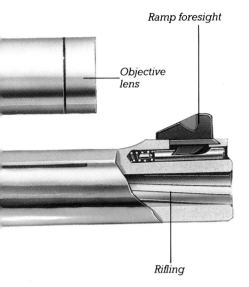

Ramp foresight

Objective lens

Rifling

bulky but really would fit into a holster and ride on a belt, was really something new—and something that caught the imagination of a great many people.

Remington still make the XP-100, so sales must have been moderately good. I do not think it has ever been the great success that the later Thompson-Center Contender proved to be, but if they were not selling some of them, Remington would not still be making XP-100's.

Against odds, therefore, the handgun hunting fever began. It was, in this writer's view, more a matter of extension of hardware not previously available than it was the case of enterprising manufacturers finding an undiscovered market. Until those guns were in hand, nothing really got going. The fever did not rise until a significant number of shooters realized that, while even these handguns were not in a class with normally suitable rifles in terms of power, they did offer enough to get the job done at sensible handgun ranges.

Then it started. And as the indefatigable American experimenters tinkered more and more foot pounds out of less and less, such attractions as my small battery of Thompson-Center barrels became commonplace. Indeed, among the most

dedicated handgun hunters, my equipment might be regarded as being suitable for an old fuddy-duddy—but not what the really macho shooter would carry to do battle in the fields of sport.

Before further discussion of hardware and ballistics, the contribution to the sport of one splendid and legendary man ought to be credited. His name was Elmer Keith; his accomplishments with handguns were great; and as much as any other single man, he brought the idea of the successful handgun hunt to the public in the United States.

Elmer Keith's Deer Kill

Many stories have been told of Elmer Keith's 600-yard (550m) mule deer kill. It is legendary now—but it happened; and it happened just as Elmer Keith first said it did. He had a wounded mule deer in clear sight at a considerable distance and kept holding up more and more front sight until he brought it down on the fourth round or so.

Had Elmer had the least idea that there was anything unusual about making such a shot with a handgun, he would never even have mentioned it. He told me so himself. Keith was more than a little annoyed at the fuss over that shot, mostly because he did

not understand why anyone should doubt his word in the matter. When it became clear to him that they *were* going to doubt his word, he got a surveyor, went out to the place he shot from, and had the surveyor measure how far away the deer's remains were. It came out to 600 yards (550m). So Elmer knew he was right, but his last word on the subject was: "Ken, if I knew that there was going to be all that fuss, I would have just killed the buck and forgot about it."

Turning to another aspect of handgun hunting hardware, there is another fellow who deserves a lot of credit that he never received. His name is Maynard Buehler, and it was he who first made it relatively simple to join a telescopic sight and a handgun. What is routine now was by no means so in the early 1960s. Buehler's mounts, particularly those for the Smith & Wesson, were absolutely essential to the development of handgun scopes, telescopic sights designed to be held out at arms-length. In the early days of the sport, I shot the Smith & Wesson K-22 with an ordinary rifle scope on it—something that one could get away with because the recoil effect was manageable.

There were once two, and now there are three, main hardware styles in the handgun hunting fields. First, and nearest to my own preference, there are the shooters who get up close with more-or-less standard handguns like Smith & Wesson Model 29's, Ruger Super Blackhawks and the like. They shoot these firearms uncluttered with optical equipment. The next group are those who shoot standard revolvers, autoloaders and standard single shots, scope-equipped. This is the biggest group of handgun hunters, in my opinion, and it is very likely that more of them shoot single shots than shoot repeaters. Finally, there is a very enthusiastic group of handgun hunters who do their shooting with made-to-measure firearms. most of them one or another form of single shot in the Thompson/ Center and Remington XP-100 category, but a few with such de luxe hand-tailored items as Larry Kelly's Stalker series, or the remarkably well-made handguns of Dick Casull, in the augmented .45 Colt calibre called .454 Casull. These hunters are the wild ones, the elephant shooters, and every one of them is totally dedicated to the pursuit of his sport.

Cartridge Development

Among the latter group, the wildcat cartridge—notably the Herrett series and J.D. Jones's Hot Shots—is supreme. To get what these shooters obtain from such types of ammunition as a .444 Marlin case necked down to .375, handgun hunters have to be very canny handloading technicians. So the way in which ammunition has developed is another important aspect of the story of hunting handgunning. Beginning with the elite group of elders known as the .44 Associates, led in spirit in the 1930s and 1940s by Elmer Keith, and ranging through the commercial exploits of Lee Jurras, who taught the handgun world that, when it came to handgun cartridges, more was more, to the ineffable J.D. Jones himself, ammunition has made as many demands on firearms and shooters as shooters and firearms have in their turn made room for new kinds of ammunition.

And among the major influences on handgun hunters is a game. Under one word—silhouette—we practise a number of disciplines in the United States. One of these has its own association and is especially popular among the most dedicated handgunners, the ones who prefer to pull the trigger on a really powerful piece. In the silhouette game, you have to knock down big steel targets—and you cannot do that with a gun that lacks punch.

Handgun silhouettes are engaged out to 200 meters (218.7yds), so you can be sure that there is some healthy ballistical stuff happening on any handgun silhouette firing line. There may even be some unhealthy ballistical stuff going on, because the average silhouette shooter would sell his soul to get two or three more targets down during a 40-target series.

Thus, in its quarter-century of history, handgun hunting has seen several notable personalities, some remarkable firearms (even more remarkably tinkered with in

some cases), and some all-out ammunition put together because of new opportunities on the competitive firing line and in the woods. That is handgun hunting in the United States.

It is not the story of handgun hunting across the world, of course, although American shooters do go everywhere that they are allowed to try out their big and bellowing toys. That means Africa, mostly. Many years ago, John Pondoro Taylor carried a Webley .455 wherever he went, or so he wrote. On at least one instance, sleeping out with his Arab companions, he potted a passing lion with no more trouble ensuing than from a rabbit similarly shot. But Pondoro was not a handgun hunter—and he might very well have been fascinated by what such folk now carry to the Zambesi, if they can get there.

Preparing for a Safari

Around twenty years ago, I was permitted to accompany one of the early experts of the high-velocity big-booming handgun while he prepared for a forthcoming African safari. That safari was probably among the very first properly planned handgun hunting expeditions to Africa. The expert was Lee Jurras, of

Above: *Hal Swiggett feeling the hefty punch of the Freedom Arms .454 Casull. This massive single action revolver is chambered for one of the world's most powerful handgun cartridges.*

Left: *Kord Hupe and his dog track a wounded boar through heavy brush. It is a situation where the fast-handling handgun excels and Kord has a .357 Smith & Wesson Model 28 at the ready.*

Right: *The rugged simplicity of the revolver is perfectly demonstrated by this round-butt .44 Special Smith & Wesson Model 624, shown with grip and sideplates removed.*

Super-Vel fame, and although Jurras was in earnest about his preparations, in retrospect, those preparations were laughably primitive.

The occasion was considerably enhanced by the fact that Jurras owned an ammunition factory. We took approximately 200lb (90kg) of .44 Magnum Super-Vel ammunition, and one gun, out to a nearby quarry. Expertly positioning his pickup truck about 100 yards (91.44m) from a rock wall, Jurras then showed how it was done. We simply stood in the truck, behind the cab, laid out as much ammunition as we felt like shooting, and opened fire on an assortment of cans, plastic bottles, chunks of rock and marks on a rock wall. Jurras' chosen load was his 180-grain (11.7g) .44 Magnum round; his chosen gun was a Ruger Super Blackhawk; and we both shot it hot that afternoon.

Backed by the entire output of a reasonably substantial ammunition factory, one can become quite a good shot—and Lee Jurras had done so. Astonishingly enough, I too discovered that, if I chose to do it, I could hit reasonable targets at a range of 100 yards (91.44m). Certainly the gun could hit them and so could the ammunition, and a string of shots with the Super-Vel 180-grain (11.7g) load was not

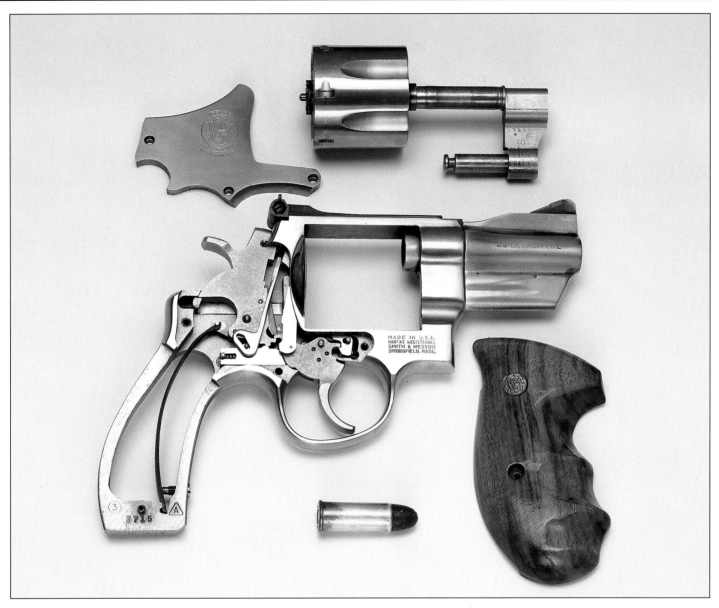

nearly so punishing as .44 Magnum loads with heavier bullets were. So it all made sense then, as it does now.

Lee Jurras did indeed go to Africa and knocked over zebras and other beasts. His exploits were then emulated both in the United States and abroad, and while I would hesitate to assign to Jurras the responsibility for everything that has happened since, there is little doubt that his remarkable and adventurous handgun loads and his willingness to try them in Africa marked a watershed of sorts.

Of course, an even more clearly-marked watershed arrived somewhat earlier in the form of the Ruger Super Blackhawk. If there is a basic gun in the whole phenomenon, it is this immensely sturdy outdoorsman's handgun. Jurras, as I have said, used it in Africa; many others have relied on the sturdy single action since the first time they had the urge to go seriously in search of game with a holstered sidearm. So far as I know, the occasions when a Super Blackhawk has failed in the hands of a reasonable man (but remember, we are not dealing solely with reasonable men here!) are rare indeed. I have no wish to denigrate the Smith & Wesson Model 29 in .44 Magnum, but the Smith was for rich folks and the Ruger was for Everyman.

There are a number of semi-technical reasons for that. The first, of course, is price. At the time, anyone who wanted to own a Smith had virtually to pay a premium, while the Rugers were normally priced. It is assumed that the Ruger's classic plough handle grip and balance is easier on the hand, and wide experience indicates that this very well may be so. There is a belief—not founded, so far as I know, on any formal testing—that the Ruger would, in the immortal words of the wristwatch commercial, "Take a licking and come up ticking" more regularly than the more complex Smith. And, in the hunting field, the Ruger's fire control system was as fast as need be—double-action simply is not needed.

Using Standard Handguns

Now, of course, the "with-it" safari-maker would not take something as simple and reliable as a Ruger—or perhaps even as a Smith—out to Africa, even as a backup. One has to go with something genuinely special in the way of a "pocket rifle". That is not true of every shooter, of course, for in support of his own services the redoubtable Larry Kelly always carries much-modified double action and single action revolvers. Still, with

all the power options available in modified Remington bolt actions, in speciality guns of one sort or another, and in rebarrel-led Thompson-Center Contenders, the simpler sidearm is now somewhat old hat.

Handgun hunting, regardless of with what or at what, remains a game of "Get as close as you can—and then get ten yards closer", although for some that means closing from 200 yards down to 190 yards! On that basis, it has all come full cicle. And it has become, in some circles, unremarkable. A handgun of suitable accuracy and suitable power is regarded as an entirely adequate hunting tool within its newly-discovered limitations of range and likely opportunity. When one seriously wishes to get within about 50 yards (45m) of game animals, one changes one's approaches and, often enough to keep it interesting, one succeeds.

That is how we have come to where we are. Large numbers of hunters have discovered that they can succeed with the handgun. The consequence is that although they may use specialized handguns when they can, they have brought the use of standard handguns to the point where succeeding with them is simply a matter adopting the correct tactics and making use of all the power available.

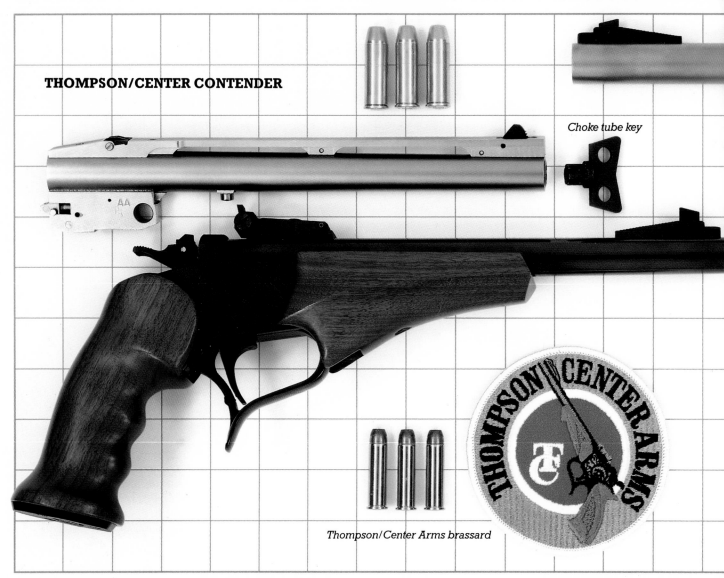

THOMPSON/CENTER CONTENDER

Choke tube key

Thompson/Center Arms brassard

THOMPSON/CENTER CONTENDER (Left)

Country of origin: USA
Type: Single-shot pistol
Calibre: 357 Magnum
Capacity: 1
Action: Single action, break open
Operation: Forward pressure on trigger guard spur releases barrel to hinge down from frame for loading and unloading
Construction: All steel. Investment cast receiver; many action components also investment cast.
Barrel length: 9.9375in (252mm); nominal 10in (254mm)
Length overall: 14.25in (362mm)
Weight (empty): 48oz (1361g)
Sights: Square post foresight; square notch backsight click adjustable for windage and elevation
Comments: Shown above the pistol is a replacement barrel, with folding backsight, in .45 Colt/.410 shotshell chambering, with a removable screw-in choke for shot loads which must be removed when firing ball ammunition. Note that plated barrels will fit only onto plated receivers; likewise, blue-finished barrels will interchange only on blued receivers.

THOMPSON/CENTER CONTENDER (Right)

Country of origin: USA
Type: Single-shot pistol
Calibre: .30-.30 Winchester
Capacity: 1
Action: Single action, break open
Operation: Forward pressure on trigger guard spur releases barrel to hinge down from frame for loading and unloading
Construction: All steel. Investment cast receiver; many action components also investment cast.
Barrel length: 13.9375in (354mm); nominal 14in (356mm)
Length overall: 18.125in (460mm)
Weight (empty): 61oz (1729g)
Sights: Square post foresight; square notch backsight adjustable for windage and elevation
Comments: This pistol is intended for Metallic Silhouette shooting, and would normally be equipped with telescopic sights.

When Ken Thompson and Warren Center introduced the Contender in 1967, the prospects of recovering their investment could scarcely have given rise to transports of optimism. Every previous American single-shot pistol, of whatever format, had failed, usually calamitously. The one exception was the Remington XP-100—and that was scarcely setting sales records. However, the Contender managed to find a niche as a sort of ballistics experimenter's test bed, and soldiered on until it became a cult object. Today, sales have long since passed the quarter-million mark and are progressing steadily towards half a million. There is a specialist Thompson/Center Collectors' Association that diligently catalogues the varieties (of which there are many). At least two other firms offer aftermarket spare barrels: one catalogues 70 calibres, the other 34.

Thompson/Center estimate that most people who buy a gun add about five extra barrels—and they estimate also that in the last two decades they have produced about 236 miles (380km) of pipe for this purpose. If you add SSK and Bullberry production to the total, you could lay Contender barrels end to end across the widest part of Great Britain and still have a few crates of them left over!

Thompson/Center themselves currently offer 23 chamberings: .22 LR and .22 WMR in rimfire; .32 H&R Magnum, 9mm Parabellum, .357 Magnum, .357 Maximum, .41 Magnum, .44 Magnum and .45 Colt in standard handgun rounds; .22 Hornet, .222 Remington, 5.56mm, 7-30 Waters, .30 Carbine, .32-20 WCF, .30-30 and .35 Remington in standard rifle calibres; 6mm TC/U, 6.5mm TC/U, 7mm TC/U, .30 Herrett and .357 Herrett in wildcats; and .410 in shotshell. The TC/U cartridges (for Thompson/Center-Ugaldi) are based on .223 brass, while the Herrett cartridges are made up on .30-30 cases. The aftermarket firms, which both have excellent reputations for quality, offer some amazing confections, of which the show-stopper is probably the .411 JDJ—a .444 Marlin case necked to .41 calibre. Another

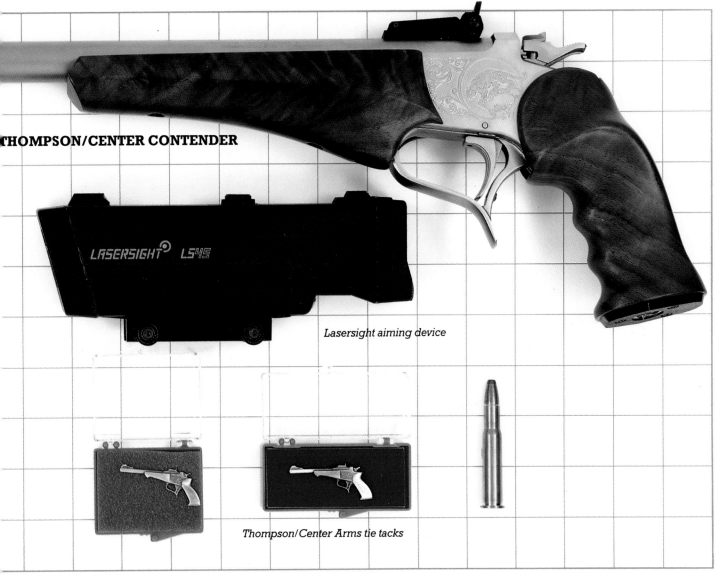

Lasersight aiming device

Thompson/Center Arms tie tacks

THOMPSON/CENTER CONTENDER

J.D. Jones wildcat opens a .225 Winchester case to .264 calibre and drives a 120-grain (7.8g) bullet at 2,185fps for sub-minute-of-angle accuracy —certainly heady stuff for a handgun.

For a while, Lee Jurras, the founder and former proprietor of the Super Vel Cartridge Corporation, was offering an enormous heavy barrelled custom version of the Contender that he called—with singular aptness—the Howdah Pistol. This particular version used massive barrels with beam welded underlugs mounted on specially heat-treated frames. These awesome pistols were chambered for a range of wildcat cartridges based on the old .577/500 Nitro Express case shortened and necked variously to .375, .416, .460, .475 or .500, or straight-walled in .577, each intended to drive solid bullets for deep penetration of heavy and potentially dangerous game in the field.

Very few of the Jurras guns were built, but they were exotic enough to generate a lot of comment, and J. D. Jones' Marlin-based wildcats followed soon after to reap the benefit of the considerable interest that Jurras' creations had aroused.

Cheap calibre changeover and unprecedented ballistics are, after all, what the Contender is about. The former comes from careful design and up-to-date manufacturing processes, while the latter derives from the great strength and the total casehead support that the gun affords. Handgun power is usually strictly limited by the strength of the brass cartridge case, which is unsupported over a semi-automatic pistol's feed ramp. Even a revolver requires a degree of play at the back end so that the cylinder may rotate. A detonating load, of course, will still blow up your gun. But you will not lose a Contender, as you would an autopistol, because a thin web of brass has yielded under marginally excessive pressure.

The Contender was the gun that made handgun hunting a recognized specialist avocation. The Smith & Wesson Model 29 .44 Magnum got the sport off the ground, but it was the scope-sighted Contender in high-intensity wildcat chamberings that really fired the enthusiasm of the purists.

At this providential juncture, someone decided that metallic silhouette shooting, recently imported from Mexico, was altogether too good to leave to riflemen. Handgun Metallic Silhouette is one of the great success stories of modern sport, and the Contender was just what it needed—an affordable gun that scope-mounted easily, shot like a dream, and sledge-hammered iron animals. The Contender also opened the gate to as much ballistic experimentation as one could ever decently wish to do.

It is precisely as a test bed for all manner of things that the Contender has, perhaps, served shooting best. If the average customer accumulates five spare barrels for his Contender, then the really keen customers must have scores of them—and they do, each in a different calibre. No one who is at all interested in load development could imagine life without a Contender. The practice is to try out anything on the gun. The laser sight shown beneath the Contender on the right in the photograph actually turned out to be much more useful on speed shooting pistols—but to bolt it initially onto a Contender seemed the natural thing to do under the circumstances.

As the photograph shows, the Contender is currently offered in two barrel lengths—10in (254mm) and 14in (356mm)—and in two finishes, blued or Armalloy. The latter, a hard-wearing plated finish, seen in the gun on the right in the photograph and the spare barrel (left), involves a build-up on critical dimensions. Thus, white barrels do not fit onto blue frames, and vice versa.

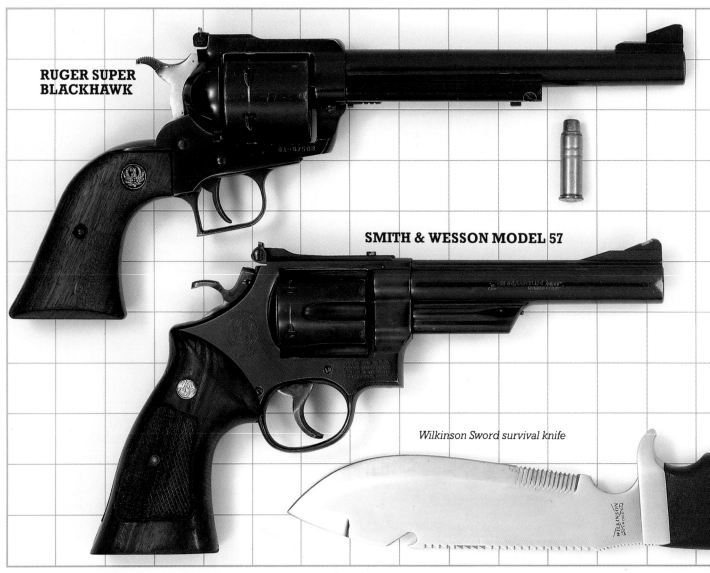

RUGER SUPER BLACKHAWK

SMITH & WESSON MODEL 57

Wilkinson Sword survival knife

Most guns are tools, but some are more like tools than others—and none more so than the heavy-calibre handgun of the man whose life or livelihood keeps him outdoors, and whose enemies are likely to have more than two legs. Such creatures as bulls and bears are very big, and often unpredictable. They will rarely attack a man—but not rarely enough to make the risk negligible. The guns shown here are among the classic outdoorsmen's sidearms.

RUGER SUPER BLACKHAWK

Country of origin: USA
Type: Revolver
Calibre: .44 Magnum
Capacity: 6
Action: Single action with transfer bar ignition
Operation: Gate loading; rod ejection
Construction: All steel; extensive use of investment castings
Barrel length: 7.5in (190mm)
Length overall: 13.4in (340mm)
Weight (empty): 48oz (1361g)
Sights: Square ramp foresight;

square notch backsight click adjustable for windage and elevation
Comments: Simple, reliable and immensely strong.

The Ruger .44 Magnum Super Blackhawk (top left) is the linear descendant of the Colt Peacemaker, and a worthy successor to it. It is a single action gun, with a mechanism engineered for durability. Several weak parts and fragile flat springs of the original Colt have been replaced, while nylon plug-locks keep the gun's superabundance of screws from working out, as they used to on the Peacemaker. The traditional plough-handle grip slips on recoil, which takes the sting out of the recoil and also positions the thumb to cock the hammer for the next shot. It also enables the gun to be made light for its power. However, we would prefer the standard Blackhawk, which is 8oz (227g) lighter still, in this calibre.

The Blackhawk was introduced in 1955, with the

Super Blackhawk following in 1959. Both guns received the New Model interlocked mechanism in 1973. For some time after the Super Blackhawk's introduction, the standard model was not chambered for .44, but that is no longer the case.

RUGER REDHAWK

Country of origin: USA
Type: Revolver
Calibre: .44 Magnum
Capacity: 6
Action: Selective double action
Operation: Hand ejection; crane-mounted cylinder swings out of frame to left
Construction: All stainless steel; extensive use of investment castings
Barrel length: 7.5in (190mm)
Length overall: 13in (330mm)
Weight (empty): 52.5oz (1488g)
Sights: Square ramp foresight with interchangeable coloured inserts; square notch backsight click adjustable for windage and elevation
Comments: An excellent hunting revolver, but too heavy to carry otherwise.

The Ruger Redhawk (top right) was introduced in 1979, for the benefit of those who preferred a double action mechanism—which one might, if being gored by a bull. The gun shown is made of stainless steel, which makes excellent sense outdoors and in the wilderness.

The Redhawk is a massively robust and reliable gun: it sins only by its very considerable weight. Recently introduced heavy-barrelled versions with moulded-in scope mounting points—which soon evolved into the Super Redhawk, with an extended frame reinforcing the breech end of the barrel—confirmed the feeling that the Redhawk was really more of a compact carbine than a beltgun.

ISRAEL MILITARY INDUSTRIES DESERT EAGLE

Country of origin: Israel
Type: Semi-automatic pistol
Calibre: .357 Magnum
Capacity: 9-round magazine
Action: Single action

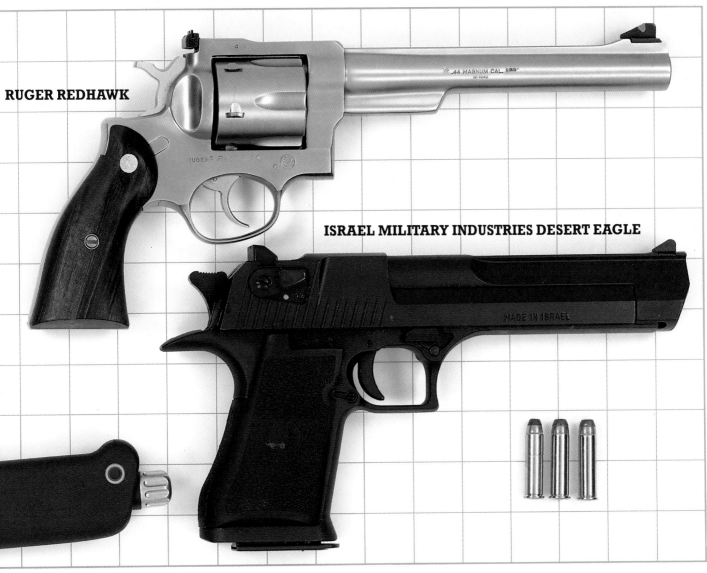

RUGER REDHAWK

ISRAEL MILITARY INDUSTRIES DESERT EAGLE

Operation: Locked breech; gas-operated, with three-lug rotating bolt
Construction: All steel; alloy frame version available
Barrel length: 6in (152mm)
Length overall: 10.25in (260mm)
Weight (empty): 60oz (1701g); aluminium-framed version weighs 52oz (1474g)
Sights: Square post foresight; square notch backsight. Adjustable unit interchanges.
Comments: Also available in .44 Magnum with a 7-round magazine.

The American-designed and Israeli-manufactured Desert Eagle pistol (bottom right) is both huge and heavy—and no amount of advertising showing it being whipped from beneath a sports-jacket by an alert bodyguard is going to persuade anyone that it is a viable proposition as a beltgun, let alone as a concealment gun. Its 10-round capacity and .357 Magnum chambering were also fairly underwhelming: the Desert Eagle has become much more interesting now that it is available in .44 Magnum.

The gun is unusual in being gas- rather than recoil-operated. This ought to obviate the need for a heavy slide, and permit a light and compact design, but it does not seem to have worked out that way, although a recently-introduced aluminium-framed version has brought down the weight somewhat. The static barrel should also make a contribution to accuracy.

SMITH & WESSON MODEL 57

Country of origin: USA
Type: Revolver
Calibre: .41 Magnum
Capacity: 6
Action: Selective double action
Operation: Simultaneous hand ejection; cylinder swings leftward on crane out of frame when thumblatch is pushed forward
Construction: All steel
Barrel length: 6in (152mm)
Length overall: 11.375in (289mm)
Weight (empty): 48oz (1361g)
Sights: Square ramp foresight with red inset; square notch backsight click adjustable for windage and elevation

Comments: Except for calibre, the Model 57 is identical to the Smith & Wesson .44 Magnum Model 29. It is an excellent all-round heavy-calibre revolver.

The best all-round outdoorsman's sidearm is probably the Smith & Wesson N-frame (bottom left), available either in .44 Magnum as the Model 29 or, as shown here, in .41 Magnum as the Model 57. The Model 29 weights 47oz (1332g) with a 6in (152mm) barrel, or 44oz (1247g) with a 4in (102mm) barrel (add 1oz (28g) for the .41 Magnum Model 57 in each case, because of the smaller borings).

There is probably no functional difference between the two calibres. The .41's better ranging power does not count at working distances, where the .44's slightly harder blow would. However, the advantage is strictly marginal.

The Smith & Wesson has an excellently-designed mechanism and is usually finely crafted. It is not as robust as the Ruger, but nor is it as bulky and burdensome. It will take a lot of shooting to show up the difference. If one practises with mid-range loads, reserving full-power rounds for occasional sighting-in and actual defensive use, the Smith & Wesson gun's comparative fragility will not prove a problem.

The Smith & Wesson Model 29, introduced in 1956, was the first of the .44 Magnums, just as the Smith & Wesson Model 57 of 1964 inaugurated the .41 Magnum. The N-frame itself dates from 1907, when the New Century hand-ejector appeared in the new .44 Special chambering. One may say that, after 80 years, it is a well-proven design. In its stainless steel rendition it offers, along with the Ruger Blackhawk, the most sensible power-to-weight ratio the outdoorsman can find. Either gun would be well matched with the Wilkinson Sword survival knife, also shown here, which is an excellent design.

RUGER NEW MODEL BISLEY BLACKHAWK

Natal Practical Shooting Association emblem

COLT NEW FRONTIER

Joint Services Pistol Club (Scotland) brassard

ELEY CLUB

WARNING keep out of reach of children

The single action versus double action question had been a topic of heated debate in British military circles since the Crimean War and the Indian Mutiny, both of which had highlighted the contrasting advantages of the single action Colt and the double action Adams (the latter fired with a long, sweeping pressure on the trigger, whereas the former required only a light pressure, but had to be thumb cocked first). Robert Adams must, therefore, have been particularly pleased when he bought Frederick Beaumont's 1855 patent which incorporated both modes of fire in the same mechanism. In the following year, the British Army adopted the Adams-Beaumont as its service revolver.

The logic of selective double action was so clear that Adams, and the British, must have been somewhat mystified when the US Army adopted a single action Colt in 1860, and altogether baffled when another single action Colt was adopted to replace it in 1873.

The simple answer is that, by then, Americans had acquired a fondness for single action Colts that has never left them; as late as the Korean War, young officers were still going off to battle with privately purchased single actions.

COLT 1873 SINGLE ACTION ARMY

Country of origin: USA
Type: Revolver
Calibre: .357 Magnum
Capacity: 6
Action: Single action only
Operation: Solid frame, gate loading, rod ejection. With hammer at half cock, swing loading gate on right of frame out to load or unload each chamber individually. Sprung ejector rod in housing on right underside of barrel. Carry all Colt single actions with five chambers only loaded, and hammer down on empty sixth chamber
Construction: All steel, with colour case hardened frame
Barrel length: 5.5in (140mm)
Length overall: 11in (280mm)
Weight (empty): 38oz (1980g)
Sights: Milled notch in topstrap and blade foresight

Comments: Introduced 1873. Production suspended in 1942 and resumed in 1955. Series manufacture ceased in 1982, but the gun is still available from Colt as a special order item. The 1873 was offered in around 36 calibres and in barrel lengths from 3in (76mm) to 12in (305mm), in finishes to order.

The archetypal American single action is the 1873 Colt (lower right), known as the Single Action Army, Peacemaker, or, in .44-40, the Frontier Model. The SAA had the almost magical characteristic of feeling just right in anyone's hand: a triumph of ergonomics more than a century before the term became fashionable. Quality was beyond reproach and the balance was exquisite. The gun also had a superficial ruggedness that inspired confidence. In truth, it had a surfeit of screws and several fragile internal parts, but these were minor faults that scarcely impaired its popularity. The Colt was an integral and indeed indispensable part of the romance of the American

West. It remained in production until 1941. By then, some 357,859 had been manufactured in around 36 calibres. Production was resumed—by sheer pressure of public demand—in 1955, and the Model P is still available from Colt as a special order item.

COLT NEW FRONTIER .22

Country of origin: USA
Type: Revolver
Calibre: .22 LR
Capacity: 6
Action: Single action only
Operation: Solid frame, gate loading, rod ejection. Uses frame mounted floating firing pin. Otherwise, operation is as for the 1873 Single Action Army
Construction: All steel, with light alloy grip straps and trigger guard
Barrel length: 4.375in (111mm)
Length overall: 9.875in (251mm)
Weight (empty): 29.5oz (836g)
Sights: Click adjustable square notch backsight and ramp foresight
Comments: Available with 6in (152mm) or 7.5in (190.5mm) barrels and in .22 Magnum rimfire or with

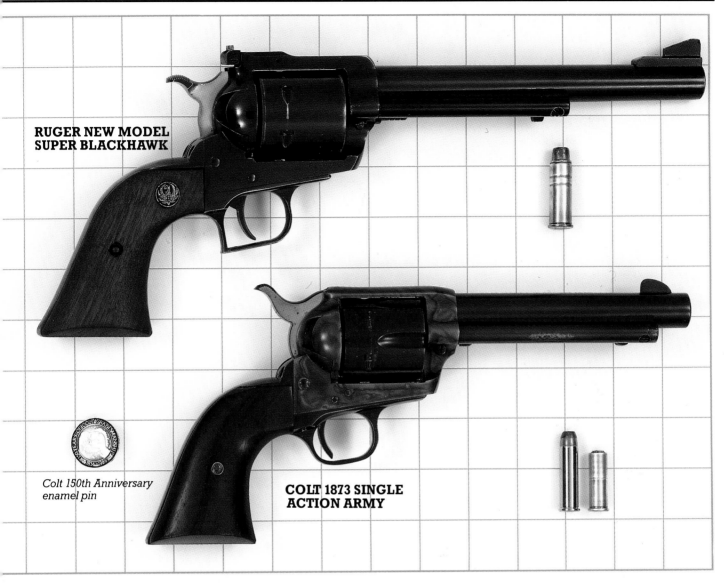

RUGER NEW MODEL SUPER BLACKHAWK

Colt 150th Anniversary enamel pin

COLT 1873 SINGLE ACTION ARMY

dual cylinders. A ⅞-scale copy of the flat top Single Action Army with Colt's incomparable colour case hardening on the frame.

In 1973 Colt introduced a beautiful ⅞-scale version of the century-old single action in .22 rimfire (lower left). Called the New Frontier, after John Kennedy's campaign slogan, it had a redesigned mechanism, but was otherwise pure legend. Sadly, the New Frontier could never match price with Ruger's vastly popular .22 Single Six, and hence never enjoyed the popularity that its quality and charm deserved. It was dropped in 1975, but reintroduced in 1981.

RUGER NEW MODEL SUPER BLACKHAWK

Country of origin: USA
Type: Revolver
Calibre: .44 Magnum
Capacity: 6
Action: Single action only
Operation: Solid frame, gate loading, rod ejection. Uses Ruger New Model interlock mechanism

and transfer bar ignition whereby the loading gate freezes the hammer and releases the cylinder to rotate for loading and unloading. 1873 pattern sprung ejector rod in housing on lower right side of barrel
Construction: All steel. Investment cast frame and heavy use of investment cast action components
Barrel length: 7.5in (190.5mm)
Length overall: 13.375in (340mm)
Weight (empty): 48oz (1361g)
Sights: Click adjustable Patridge backsight and .125in (3.2mm) ramp foresight
Comments: Super Blackhawk introduced in 1959; New Model introduced in 1973.

Sturm, Ruger & Co. have made most of the running with single actions in recent years. Their .22 Single Six, introduced in 1953, was followed by the .357 Blackhawk in 1955. A .44 Magnum chambering appeared in 1956 but was deleted in 1959 with the introduction of the heavier .44 Magnum Super Blackhawk (upper right). About 1973, all Ruger single actions were

replaced by equivalent models using a new mechanism featuring transfer bar ignition, so that all six chambers could safely be carried loaded. Single action revolvers had traditionally (and very wisely) been carried with five chambers loaded and the hammer down on the empty sixth chamber. The changeover was probably forced by a worsening public liability situation, and was unpopular in conservative quarters since the mechanical aesthetics were not at all the same.

RUGER NEW MODEL BISLEY BLACKHAWK

Country of origin: USA
Type: Revolver
Calibre: .357 Magnum
Capacity: 6
Action: Single action only
Operation: Solid frame, gate loading, rod ejection. Loading gate on right of frame swings out, locking hammer and depressing the cylinder stop, freeing the cylinder to rotate for loading or unloading. 1873 pattern ejector

rod in housing on lower right side of barrel
Construction: Chrome molybdenum investment cast steel frame; extensive use of investment cast action components
Barrel length: 7.5in (190.5mm)
Length overall: 13in (330mm)
Weight (empty): 44oz (1247g)
Sights: Click adjustable Patridge rearsight with ramp foresight
Comments: Patterned after the turn-of-century Colt Bisley Model, designed for Edwardian period competitive target shooting. Introduced 1985. Also available with non-fluted, roll engraved cylinder.

Ruger's recently introduced Bisley Model (upper left), is visually a near-copy of Colt's highly successful *Belle Epoque* target piece. The more upright handle and the dropped hammer spur enable it to be recocked by the right thumb without shifting the grip, a considerable advantage for timed strings of shots. Otherwise, it is all Ruger, and utterly reliable. Made in two frame sizes, it is available in .22 LR, .32 H&R Magnum, .375, .41 and .44 Magnums, and .45 Colt.

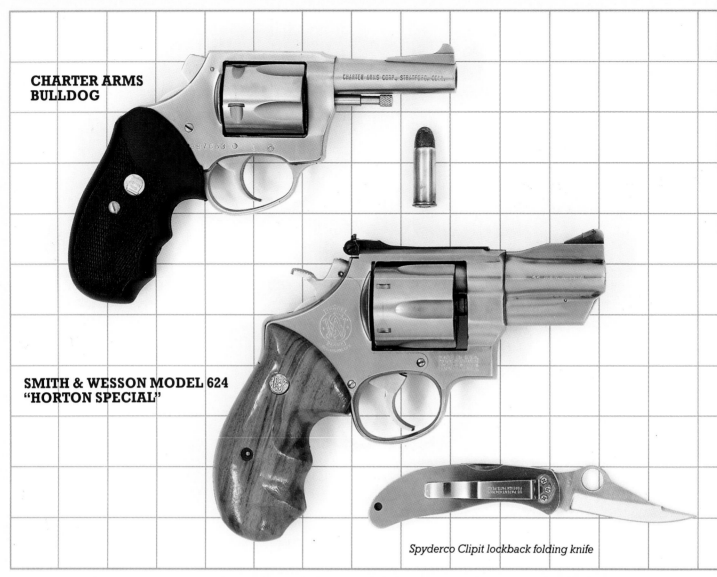

CHARTER ARMS BULLDOG

SMITH & WESSON MODEL 624 "HORTON SPECIAL"

Spyderco Clipit lockback folding knife

The .44 has always been an accurate, versatile and useful calibre which, on merit, probably deserves more popularity than it has enjoyed. The .44 Special, introduced in 1907, succeeded the .44 American and Russian rounds and was intended primarily as a target cartridge, with secondary service and sporting roles. But the military adoption of the .45 automatic in 1911, and the NRA's subsequent development of a National Match Course dominated by the service pistol, effectively cut much of the .44 Special's intended ground out from under it. It found devotees, but they were few in number.

The .44's most noteworthy champion was Elmer Keith, Idaho cowboy, big-game guide, ballistic experimenter and gun writer, whose handloads in the .44 Smith & Wesson Outdoorsman pushed back the frontiers of the possible and led directly to the introduction of the .44 Magnum in 1956.

The Magnum was, at that time, the world's most powerful production handgun, and the publicity and mystique surrounding it focused interest and attention on the .44 Special as well. The physical difference between the two rounds was a small one of length, so that the less powerful .44 Special will chamber and fire in .44 Magnums, but not vice versa. Many Magnum owners shoot .44 Specials for practice, or download the Magnum case to Special velocities (about 750fps), reserving the full loads for occasions that actually require them. This approach is easier on the gun and easier on the shooter as well, for in guns of this size, the .44 Magnum can be uncomfortable to shoot.

CHARTER ARMS BULLDOG

Country of origin: USA
Type: Double action revolver
Calibre: .44 Special
Capacity: 5
Action: Selective double action; outside hammer
Operation: Solid frame, hand ejection. Crane mounted cylinder

swings out to left for loading and unloading. Thumblatch on left of frame
Construction: All stainless steel
Barrel length: 3in (76mm)
Length overall: 7.6in (193mm)
Weight (empty): 24oz (680g)
Sights: Square concave ramp foresight. Square notch backsight milled in top of receiver
Comments: A prime defensive revolver and very powerful for its weight; the rubber grips are really necessary. It points beautifully. Note the massive, spurless hammer, for positive ignition and to avoid snagging on clothing.

Practice aside, the .44 Special's primary role these days is defensive, and the gun most often selected is the Charter Arms Bulldog (top left), shown here in a stainless steel rendition with neoprene grips. Introduced in 1973, the .44 Bulldog has proven a phenomenally successful gun: more than half a million have been made, and production has averaged about 37,000 a year, compared to a historical average of about 700 .44

Specials per year for Smith & Wesson. The Charter Bulldog has given the .44 Special a new lease of life. Attempts to upgrade the .38 Special with high-velocity, hollow-point loads proved less than wholly successful; on the other hand, the .44 Special gives solid, dependable performance in a similar package.

The Charter Arms Bulldog is less than half the weight of the Horton Special (see below), and recoils accordingly. When it was first introduced, factory cartridge crimps would not stand the jolt, and the gun would often stall after the fourth shot, with the fifth bullet pulled forward out of the chamber. The tendency of late is to lighter bullets at rather higher velocities, which suits the gun better.

SMITH & WESSON MODEL 624 "HORTON SPECIAL"

Country of origin: USA
Type: Double action revolver
Calibre: .44 Special
Capacity: 6

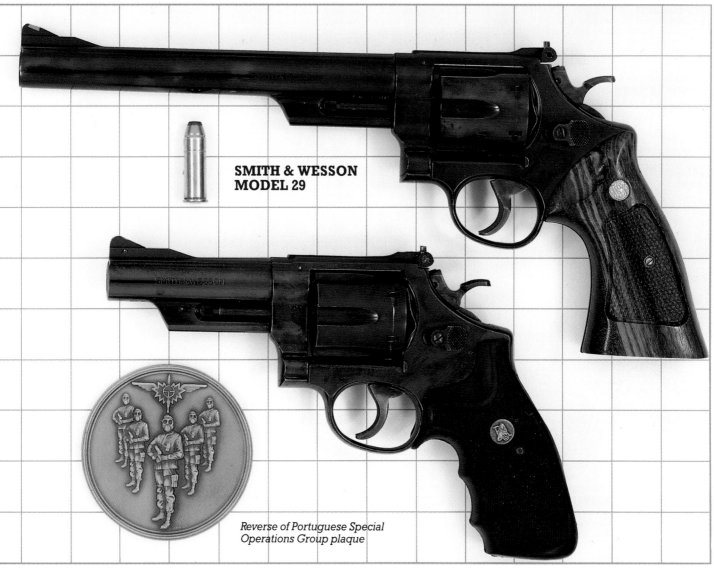

SMITH & WESSON
MODEL 29

*Reverse of Portuguese Special
Operations Group plaque*

Action: Selective double action; outside hammer
Operation: Solid frame, hand ejection. Crane mounted cylinder swings out to left for loading and unloading. Thumblatch on left of frame pushes forward
Construction: Stainless steel
Barrel length: 3in (76mm)
Length overall: 7.75in (197mm)
Weight (empty): 40oz (1134g)
Sights: Square ramp foresight. Square notch backsight click adjustable for windage and elevation
Comments: One of a run of 5,000 revolvers specially produced for Lew Horton Distributors of Massachusetts.

In the .44 Special market, things have been picking up a little lately for Smith & Wesson. The Model 24 was reintroduced in 1983, after an absence of nearly 25 years, and an initial run of 7,500 sold out within months. The stainless steel Model 624 followed in 1985, in a run of 10,000 units, along with a further 10,000 Model 24's and 624's ordered by Lew Horton Distributors of Massachusetts.

The "Horton Special" (bottom left), as it became known, was built to a distinctive and proprietary pattern, with a 3in (76mm) barrel and smooth-finished, birdshead grips with deep finger grooves. So far as is known, this was the first time that N-frames had been produced with round butts. The Horton is easy shooting and, albeit bulky, is quite tolerable to carry about with you in a medium threat environment.

SMITH & WESSON MODEL 29

Country of origin: USA
Type: Double action revolver
Calibre: .44 Magnum
Capacity: 6
Action: Selective double action; outside hammer
Operation: Solid frame, hand ejection. Crane mounted cylinder swings leftward out of frame for loading and unloading. Thumblatch on left of frame pushes forward
Construction: All steel; frame and most components machined from drop forgings

(top right)
Barrel length: 8.25in (210mm); nominal 8.375in (213mm)
Length overall: 14in (356mm)
Weight (empty): 54oz (1531g)
Sights: Square ramp foresight. Square notch backsight click adjustable for windage and elevation
Comments: Useful for deer or boar hunting, but otherwise too much gun or not enough.

(bottom right)
Barrel length: 4in (102mm)
Length overall: 9.5in (241mm)
Weight (empty): 48oz (1361g)
Sights: Square ramp foresight. Square notch backsight click adjustable for windage and elevation
Comments: An excellent gun when needed; heavy for a beltgun, but of manageable proportions.

The original .44 Magnum was the Smith & Wesson Model 29 (top right; bottom right), which is shown here in two barrel lengths and with wooden (top) and rubber (bottom) stocks. This is the gun immortalized by Clint Eastwood in the "Dirty Harry" films, and the revolver which made handgun hunting a recognized sport.

The Model 29 is a big gun by most people's standards—but it is dwarfed by more recent .44's, such as the Dan Wesson or the Ruger Super Redhawk, which are intended specifically for hunting and metallic silhouette shooting. In their favour is ruggedness: they will withstand an unlimited diet of top-end loads and their weight makes them reasonably comfortable to shoot. But one really might as well carry a rifle.

The Model 29 is man-portable; the shorter of the two is, indeed, an excellent holster gun, concealable under a jacket. It is not often chosen for police or security use, in part because the recoil is such as to require a measurable recovery period between shots. Some élite formations, however, notably the French Gendarmerie's Intervention Group (G.I.G.N.), have expressed keen interest in the Model 29. They like the idea of wrapping the whole job up with one shot.

TARGET
PISTOLS
&
REVOLVERS

Jan Stevenson

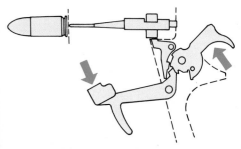

Above: *Decocking levers clear the sear from the full cock notch while themselves engaging the hammer (Astra A-80).*

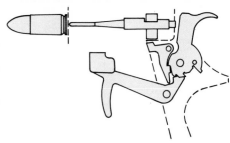

Above: *The hammer rides the lever to "at rest" position with its broad safety notch resting on the sear. Firing pin is blocked.*

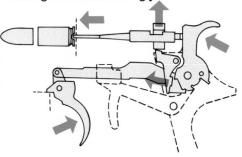

Above: *Top of sear lifts firing pin block out of engagement as sear notch releases the hammer from full cock.*

Above: *A daring young man in his flying machine, as a British Long Range Pistol shooter's portable seat and rest are known. This is the 100 yard stage on Bisley's Century range with the silhouette-shaped Wessex targets up.*

Pistol shooting, like economics or theology, is more complicated than it really ought to be, too prone to faction, too subject to schism, too populated by cliques of sporting zealots on the one hand, keen to make rules for others or, on the other hand, oblivious to or disdainful of alternative confessions. But it too has its wets, its middle-of-the-roaders, its post-monetarists and ecumenists anxious to draw the broad church together, to polish the mosaic and to emphasize the common bonds of fellowship and mutual interest. Theirs is a task, for so many chapels are involved.

To give an example, the most broadly based of handgun contests is the British National Pistol Association's annual meeting at Bisley each Whitsun holiday in May, which includes some thirty-six separate, different squadded matches, from flintlock to Practical. Parenthetically, the NPA itself is the most purposefully ecumenical of organisations, a federation of governing bodies (like the Muzzle Loaders' Association of Great Britain and the UK Practical Shooting Association) or of powerful interest groups (like the British Pistol Club, Marylebone Rifle & Pistol Club, the Welsh Pistol Association and the British Women's Pistol Association). Founded in 1980, the NPA,

was the formalization of an ad hoc group formed in 1977 to hold a great multi-disciplinary competition (Pistol '78) and who subsequently took upon themselves the goal not only of drawing together the various complexions of handgunning under a common umbrella, but of offering the hand of fraternity to riflemen and shotgunners as well, in the long-odds hope that one day there would be a single national association representing British shooters. Long odds, indeed.

To walk round Bisley over the Whit weekend is to sense the kaleidoscopic variety of the handgun sports. From one range to the next, one crosses zones of space, time and mentality, from the austere, cloistered, Zen-like world of the Free Pistol competitor to the urban combat scenarios of Practical, to the technical and ballistic fastidiousness of Long Range, via the Georgian-to-Edwardian eccentricities of Muzzle Loading and Classic, the latter fired with the original guns on resurrected glory days courses of fire. Our forebears, we discover, were very keen on ambidextrous (most courses involve a weak-handed stage) and used targets with a white centre scoring seven points. And along the route, we should have encountered two Police Pistol events, several for Service Pistol

(current and past British Army qualification courses) as well as man vs. man contests on falling targets.

But the NPA meeting perforce leaves out far more than it encompasses. While it has, in recent years, included almost as an afterthought (event no. 62 in the catalogue) the most widely practised domestic discipline (NSRA Club Pistol), it still does not include the most elegant and imaginative of them (British Duelling). Nor does it include the most widely practised overseas discipline (American National Match Course), nor the most vigorous of current handgun sports (Metallic Silhouette), nor some of the most interesting foreign courses such as the Mexican Defence Course, the *Deutscher Jagdschutz-Verband's Jäger* pistol course or the *Tir d'Assaut* from France. Also conspicuously absent are such significant current disciplines as the Bianchi Cup course, its "official" derivative, NRA Action Pistol, or indeed its Welsh variant, PP III. The Steel Challenge, Second Chance Skittles or the S&W Masters' Course could have further enriched the programme.

Competitive pistol shooting is indeed a *mille fleurs* tapestry of incomparable variety; no one in fact knows how many events, disciplines, courses — call them

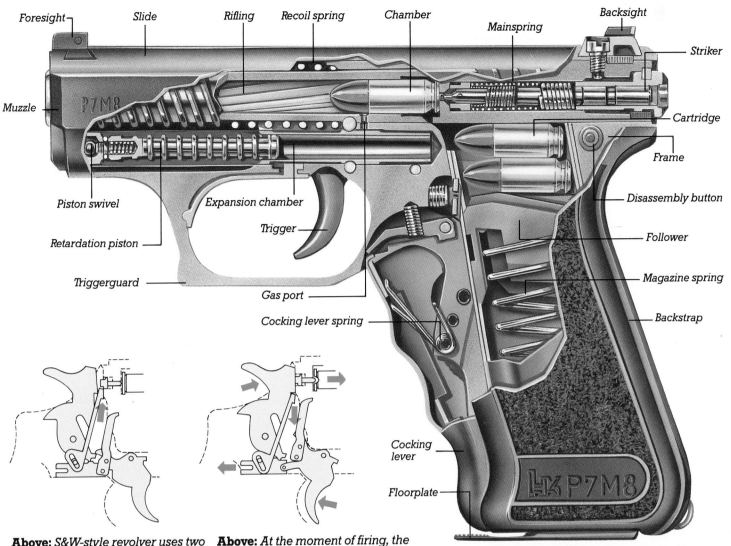

Foresight · Slide · Rifling · Recoil spring · Chamber · Mainspring · Backsight · Striker · Muzzle · Piston swivel · Expansion chamber · Trigger · Retardation piston · Triggerguard · Gas port · Cocking lever spring · Cartridge · Frame · Disassembly button · Follower · Magazine spring · Backstrap · Cocking lever · Floorplate

Above: *S&W-style revolver uses two safety blocks: the foot of the hammer rests on the rebound slide while a steel bar blocks the striking face.*

Above: *At the moment of firing, the rebound slide is fully rearward, while the block has been lowered out of the hammer's path.*

Above: *The HK P7 is a squeeze-cocking, striker fired, gas retarded, delayed blowback self-loading pistol.*

what you may — are shot on a formal, competitive basis round the globe. There are about a dozen that are truly worldwide, with world championships, international governing bodies and so forth, or, like Skittles, Long Range or the FBI course, are widely practised under varying conditions of formality.

A Multitude of Disciplines

If we add to the international disciplines those practised on a national basis in the developed countries, then the total must be at least a hundred, and perhaps several hundred. And if we go beyond the widely practised competitive and recreational courses to include police and military qualification courses (which are constantly being devised to rectify perceived shortcomings in previous or standard courses) and ad hoc competitive courses (concocted at club level because someone had an idea that seemed fun or worthwhile) then the count probably rises into the thousands.

One remarkable aspect is that all these things are of comparatively recent coinage. Flintlock and Percussion Pistol, billowing black powder smoke, may look convincingly antique, but the competition

dates only from the 1960s. Practical started in the late 1950s, Police Pistol only achieved a widespread competitive following in the early 1960s, the first British Long Range contest was in 1971, while Handgun Metallic Silhouette was launched in the US in 1975 with a match in Tucson, Arizona. In Central Lake, Michigan, that same year, Rich Davis held the first Second Chance skittles shoot. The oldest competitive handgun programme is Classic, whose courses of fire, disinterred in 1979 after half a century of disuse, date from the late 1890s. From the point of view of historical perspective, it is baffling and somewhat unsatisfactory.

It would be satisfying if we could follow the evolution of target pistol shooting from the outset, to see how the various strands have evolved. However, beyond a fairly recent point, we cannot. This is in contrast to shotgunning, which has been copiously reported since the development of the flintlock made wingshooting feasible, and riflery or musketry, which can be traced archivally back to the late Middle Ages, when international matches (or, more properly, inter-municipal ones, since the nation-state was then embryonic, and much of the evidence relates to the Germano-Swiss area were the occasion of vast

festivity, and maidens, livestock and the like were awarded as prizes. Was anyone shooting pistols?

Of course they were. They just were not writing about it. We do not run into much in the way of documentary evidence until the latter part of the nineteenth century. What we have prior to that is an assortment of beautiful but frustratingly mute artefacts. There are a lot of extant target pistols from the late flint and percussion eras. They are not duellers, nor horse pistols nor officers pistols, nor greatcoat pocket pistols, nor even travelling pistols. They can only be target pistols, but we know practically nothing of the circumstances under which they were shot, save for the occasional presentation piece which identifies the recipient as the regimental pistol champion, or what have you.

We know that personages as diverse as Prince Rupert, Wild Bill Hickock, Lord Byron and Andrew Jackson were all excellent pistol shots. They practised assiduously and to serious purpose. Contests and competitions, which no doubt took place as well, at least at local level, were regarded as a comparatively trivial pastime and went unreported.

An anonymous "New Yorker", writing in 1875, remarks on the "singular fact that

Left: *Wild Bill Hickock was an excellent pistol shot whose practice sessions have been described. The costume was not his normal garb, but the 1851 Colt Navies worn butt forward were.*

Above: *Walter Winans made Englishmen take their pistol shooting seriously. This is the revolver line on Century Range, Bisley at the 1910 Imperial Meeting during a precision fire event.*

notwithstanding the enormous number of pistols in the hands of the public (he estimated that they outnumbered shotguns ten-to-one) no book giving simple and plain directions for their selection and use has even been published." That there were numerous books on shotgunning but none on pistol shooting was probably due to the fact that the pistol, as a recreational implement, was not worth serious exposition while, as a fighting tool, the subject seemed "…too brutal and horrible to admit of quiet discussion". What was missing was the middle road of organised sporting competition.

But this would not be long in coming, for at the time "New Yorker" wrote, public interest in competitive shooting was developing a momentum that would soon carry the sport to a level of popularity that it had not experienced since the 16th century.

There were numerous strands contributing to this crescendo of interest. Wingshooting had become the favoured sport of the gentry and monied society in Britain. In an age of heavy gambling, live pigeon shooting from traps became a natural object of wager, and artificial targets — clay pigeons — soon put shotgun sports within reach of the middle classes.

A series of international long range rifle matches between Ireland, Britain and the United States attracted enormous attention in the popular press in all three countries. Invasion fears in 1859 had led to the formation of Rifle Volunteer corps throughout Britain, and the National Rifle Association was launched in 1860 in order to give the movement permanence. During the following decade, similar movements emerged in France, Belgium, the United States and in a number of other countries.

By the last quarter of the century, shooting had become a patriotic, popular and highly publicised pastime. Exhibition shooting fitted naturally into this context, both fuelling popular interest and catering to an already widespread public curiosity. There were perhaps a dozen American professional shooters touring Europe during this period, the best known of whom was Buffalo Bill Cody, whose Wild West Show was a great sensation. Most of the professionals moved easily between stage, circus and competitive arenas where, particularly in live pigeon shooting, there was a lot of prize money and wager money to be had. W. F. "Doc" Carver and Captain A. H. Bogardus were both leading figures on the pigeon circuit.

These men (and women) were splendid

shots, recognised and admired as such. The young Kaiser Wilhelm let Annie Oakley shoot the ash off a cigarette he held in his lips, much to the gratification of the audience. The king of Portugal, himself a keen shooting man, so admired Ira Paine's performance that he knighted him. One of Paine's students, Dr Eduard Thomas of Vienna, was made a Privy Councillor of the Austro-Hungarian Empire largely on the strength of his shooting.

The Great Showmen

It is often forgotten how much the shooting sports today owe to these flamboyant 19th century showmen. Captain Bogardus, for example, invented the ball trap and was one of the first promoters of clay pigeon shooting. Chevalier Ira Paine, as he was known, might well be regarded as the father of target pistol competition.

Paine never hesitated either to put his reputation on the line or to pass on all his vast knowledge of marksmanship to those who wished to learn. A master of trick and fancy shooting of all sorts, he was nonetheless always ready to face up to the line and shoot slowfire groups against anyone. In September of 1885, Eduard Thomas arranged a meeting, billed as a

European pistol championship, between Paine and the Austrian gun designer, Josef Schulhof. It was a .22 slowfire match at 15, 20 and 30 metres for a prize of 2,000 gulden, which Paine, using a Stevens Lord Model single shot, won by 100 x 120, five points ahead of Schulhof. Dr Thomas went on to become a leading figure in Austrian, and indeed, pan-Germanic, target shooting. He founded a pistol club in Vienna in the wake of visits by Paine and Doc Carver, and the well established *Wiener Schützenverein* formed a pistol section shortly thereafter.

The following year — indeed, it stretched on for two years — Paine got himself involved in a series of matches with the Bennett brothers for the title of Champion of the United States. The shooting took place at the Walnut Hill range, just outside Boston, and at the Springfield Revolver Club, both in Massachusetts. This amazingly protracted contest drew a great deal of publicity, and not a little controversy, and concluded finally when Paine withdrew in favour of W. W. Bennett.

Aside from Dr Thomas, Paine's greatest student was Walter Winans, a Russian-born American who spent most of his life in England and became a vice-president of the National Rifle Association. Winans inaugurated competitive pistol shooting in Britain, set tremendously high standards of scoring, and wrote a number of books on the subject which ensured him a durable influence. When Paine died (whilst performing at the *Folies Bergères* in Paris and probably from something he drank) Winans inherited his guns and used them often. His own revolvers were gold, silver or copperplated to identify them as regulated for a specific load and distance.

Winans was a man of wealth, leisure, talent, energy and determination; his accomplishment was considerable. It was his influence that got pistol competitions included at the NRA's annual meeting at Wimbledon in 1885, after a quarter century of unalleviated riflery; and by 1908, he had been British champion for twelve years.

The first regular handgun competition of any consequence in the United States was the *Army & Navy Journal* Revolver Match introduced at the US National Rifle Association's championship meeting at Creedmoor, Long Island, in 1882 and fired on the "tramp" target which represented a disappearing deadbeat. It must not have found much of a following, since it was dropped from the programme after only a few years. The revolver match was reintroduced in 1895, by which time the annual meeting had moved to Sea Girt, New Jersey. This time, it was a great success, and by 1900, handgun matches accounted for a quarter of the total programme.

The last decade and a half of the 19th century, then, saw pistol shooting established as a competitive sport, following some twenty years after the popularisation of rifle shooting. The national titles and competitions were established during this period, and so were the great clubs. Members of the Massachusetts Rifle Association, whose famed Walnut Hill range was near Boston, were probably the first to be heavily involved in handgunning; it was they who

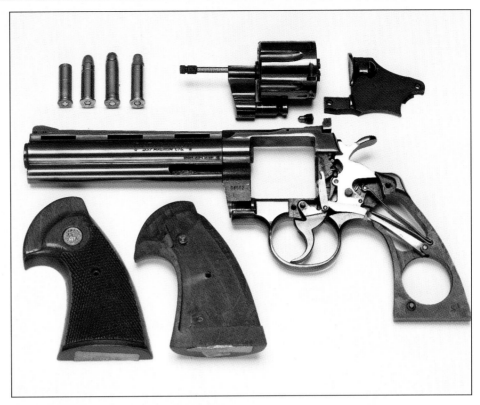

Above: *Colt's top-of-the-line Python is a fine combination of class and utility. It serves in rôles as varied as competition target work, police and military service, and hunting. The cylinder and crane dismount as an assembly. Removal of the sideplate exposes the action, which uses a V-type mainspring, the upper leg of which powers the hammer while the lower one acts on the trigger and hammer rebound lever.*

Left: *Nose-heavy Python fired from braced kneeling still bucks in recoil.*

devised the American practice (still followed) of conducting pistol competition at 25 and 50 yards, using the 200-yard rifle target as a mark. The Springfield Revolver Club, founded in 1886, is the oldest known exclusively handgun-shooting club (as opposed to mixed rifle and pistol clubs) in the US. From 1886 to 1921 they contributed more members to American interational and Olympic pistol teams than any other club.

European Developments

In 1890, a pistol match was included for the first time in the German Union shooting championships in Berlin, in the wake of which a number of clubs and associations sprang up. In 1900, the *Deutsche Pistolenschützenbund* was formed to administer the new sport nationwide. The most prestigious and vigorous of the German clubs was Major Ackermann's *Bärenswinger* pistol club in Berlin, which worked hard to diversify the national pistol programme which, by 1909, included nine events, from 50-metre precision to the more entertaining "disappearing poacher," who was fired at, at will, during 30-second exposures at 35 metres. Another 35-metre shoot, this time on a ring target, involved fire-at-will on 20-second exposures.

In England, the two most noteworthy clubs were the pistol sections of the North London Rifle Club (shooting at Ilford) and the South London Rifle Club (shooting at Runnymede), whose pistol rules date from 1898 and 1900 respectively. Both clubs are now resident at Bisley, the South London's turn-of-century courses of fire and current day patronage forming the armature and foundation of the Classic disciplines. Another London club that has proved tremendously influential in recent years, Marylebone, was founded in 1900. There were also revolver sections in many of the rifle clubs round the country that were associated with Volunteer units. Few of these would have predated 1859, and it is doubtful if they were much involved with pistol shooting prior to its introduction, at the instigation principally of Walter Winans, at Wimbledon in 1885.

Target shooting in France developed out of national humiliation at their defeat in the Franco-Prussian War of 1870-71 and the loss of the provinces of Alsace and Lorraine. By 1900, the *Union des Sociétés de Tir* had 677 affiliated clubs with a combined membership of 120,000. Most of these were riflemen, but there were more than 600 entries to the pistol matches at Satory that year. Though billed as an Olympics, the great bulk of the

Above: *Long Range exemplifies the late 20th Century explosion of interest in pistol shooting. The first competition* was in 1971, and the first national championship in 1975. It now caters for seven categories of pistol, and embraces interests from the functional approach of Service Pistol to the techno-gamesman hobby flavour of Free Pistol.

entry was local — there were 1,600 competitors in the rifle events!

The growth of shooting clubs was a consequence of the development of the sport as an adjunct to national defence; the ranges used were, for the most part, built and maintained by the military, or benefitted from official or private patronage of some sort. After the turn of the century, many industrial firms and municipalities provided premises for works-based or local clubs.

Where, one might wonder, did one shoot before this sort of philanthropy became available? In rural areas, one shot where one pleased; natural backstops abounded. Even in towns, revolver practice in the back garden was commonplace and, providing one took care to stay on good terms with one's neighbours, unlikely to generate complaints. In any case, the country was near to hand.

In cities, there were commercial ranges, or "galleries," for the purpose. In 1890, there were at least ten commercial ranges — indoor and outdoor — in New York City, offering facilities for practice from 50 feet to 200 yards. The best known were Conlin's and Zettler's. There were probably as many in London. Captain Hugh Pollard recommended King's Gallery, off Panton Street,

Haymarket, next to the Prince of Wales' Theatre.

Pollard himself, along with Winans, Paine and every other pistoleer of note, rarely missed an opportunity to visit the most famous gallery of them all, Gastinne-Renette's in Paris, founded in 1835 and still going strong. Gastinne-Renette's was an elegant establishment, lavishly decorated. It marked the transition from the *salles de combat* of the 18th and 19th century duelling schools to commercialized sport, and also fostered international competition not only by serving as a *rendez-vous* for the leading shots of the day, but by issuing a challenge to Conlin's Gallery in New York. It was, of course, promptly taken up, and there ensued, in June of 1900, the world's first telegraphically relayed international shooting match, which the Americans won by a narrow, but not precarious, margin.

The French challenge had an electrifying effect in the US. There was a nationwide selection trawl to form the best possible team, and the US Revolver Association was formed to administer it. The USRA, for many years thereafter, was in charge of selection of the American Olympic pistol team.

The first Olympics had been held in Athens only four years previously. John B. Paine of Boston (no relation to Ira Paine)

decided to go along for the pistol shooting, stopping in Paris en route where he met his brother, Sumner Paine, at Gastinne-Renette's. They spent a few days there working up loads and getting their kit together. Not being quite sure what the course of fire was, they entrained for Athens with six pistols and 3,500 rounds of ammunition. In fact, they only fired 96 rounds altogether, and took first and second places in the Military Revolver match. Sumner Paine additionally took the gold medal in the Any Revolver competition.

The high point of Olympic pistol shooting was the 4th Games, in 1906, again in Athens in which there were six pistol events: Army Revolver at 20 metres; M1873 Service Revolver at 20 metres; Any Revolver at 25 metres; Any Revolver at 50 metres; Duelling "au visé" at 20 metres and Duelling "au commandement," again at 20 metres.

The Olympic pistol programme today has been trivialized beyond redemption. The 50-metre Any Revolver event of 1906 is now UIT Free Pistol, using a sophisticated .22 single shot with a wrap-around grip that one puts on like a glove, and an electrical or multi-lever mechanical set trigger that can be adjusted to fractions of an ounce. As in Free Rifle, the shooter tries to have as little

Above: *An inspector checks a Hämmerli 208, the most successful .22LR target pistol ever. Note recoil spring (under barrel) and internal hammer (white).*

Right: *Precision pistol shooting may not have changed much since 1910 but the shape of the shooters has! This is the "offhand stance"—a hard way to shoot.*

Above: *A flying machine and scope sight make it easier. Terry O'Dwyer of Wales has just shot a 200-yard possible.*

physical contact with the gun as possible; the techniques, for the most part, are non-transferrable.

UIT Events

The UIT Rapid Fire event first appeared in the Olympics in 1924, and was based on a French "defensive fire" revolver course, in which the shooter faced a bank of six silhouettes at 25 metres. There were no scoring rings — it was a hit or miss situation. Each competitor began by firing 18 rounds (one shot per target on each of three 10-second exposures). Those with *no misses* went on to try one pass (6 shots) at 8 seconds, then at 6 seconds and finally at 4 seconds. If there was anyone left, there would be a 3-second stage and very occasionally it would take a 2-second stage to settle matters. It was a splendid course.

Today, the silhouettes are gone and we have scoring rings on a black rectangle. The course is fired with virtually recoilless .22 shorts with wrap-around stocks and no restrictions on trigger weight. It is a game, with little relevance outside itself. The skills developed are useless ones, which is doubtless why the IOC likes it.

There are two other UIT handgun events that do not figure in the Olympics:

Centrefire and Standard Pistol. Centrefire is a splendid course, consisting of 30 rounds precision at 25 metres on the ring target, followed by 30 rounds duelling "au commandement", one shot per 3-second exposure of the silhouette. The interval between exposures is 7 seconds. The same course of fire, but using .22 pistols, is called Sport Pistol, and is shot by ladies and juniors.

The Centrefire course has been around from the outset; Standard Pistol, on the other hand is a recent creation, adopted by the UIT in 1969 at the urging of the Americans, whose domestic course it resembles. Shot at 25 metres on the precision target, it consists of 60 shots in 5-round sets at 150 seconds, 20 seconds and 10 seconds, each set beginning with the gun arm depressed to 45 degrees. A 2.2lb (1kg) minimum trigger weight and a ban on wrap-around stocks do a lot to make this event a test of marksmanship.

The initial fluster of innovation during the 1880s and '90s was followed by a half-century or so of stability and consolidation as far as the handgun sports were concerned. Most of the European countries adopted the UIT programme for national competition with the Anglo-Saxons characteristically going their own way. Britain and

the United States each developed a programme of domestic competition and paid scant attention to what anyone else did anywhere.

American competition was all built around the NRA's National Match Course — or 2700 Course, as it was known, since that was the maximum score when the full 270-round exercise was shot. While the 2700 Course was mind-numbingly repetitive, it involved a thoroughgoing wring-out of marksmanship skills in testing circumstances. It took a full day to shoot, at the end of which you had done a real day's work.

The whole thing was built of 5-shot sets of slow, timed and rapid fire. Slow was two sets of five in 10 minutes; timed and rapid were five in 20 seconds and 10 seconds respectively. One was allowed to come on aim before the signal to fire was given. Slowfire was shot at 50 yards, with timed and rapid at 25.

Three guns were used, and the full course consisted of 90 rounds each with .22, Centrefire and .45. The centrefire was, for many years, undertaken with a .38 revolver, but from about 1960 to 1980, most competitors used the .45 auto for that stage as well, while since 1980 the trend has been to use a European .32 target auto for centrefire.

The National Match Course was variously jigged to suit circumstance. There was a Short Course with a reduced slowfire target for those whose range stopped at 25 yards. And winters were mostly spent shooting the Gallery Course at 50 feet with .22 pistols. But the format was always the same: slow, timed and rapid, shot the hard way.

New Competitions Emerge

In Britain, things were duller still. The only shooting most people got fell under the aegis of the NSRA, and consisted of .22 slowfire, using indigenous single shot pistols for the most part, fired variously at 15, 20 and 50 yards. Meanwhile, the NRA's Imperial Meeting at Bisley each July, behind the façade of riflery, remained a pistoleer's treasure chest, with leftover Victorian entertainments such as the Advancing Men (shot on three charging silhouettes with fixed bayonets), rundowns, tile shoots, service pistol, police pistol and so forth.

A minor mystery is why so little of this splendid fare got transported back to the clubs. One reason, no doubt, was that most clubs shot on borrowed ranges and were restricted to .22 only. Be that as it may, the revolt against the domestic programme, when it came, took the form of a campaign

for UIT events, which seemed exotic by comparison. The British Pistol Club was founded in 1957 specifically as a vehicle for UIT competitions.

The BPC prospered and prospers still, but restless spirits moved on. In 1975, Practical Pistol was introduced in Britain, and immediately found an enthusiastic following. Many clubs, however, though unsatisfied with the status quo, were intimidated by the complexity of Practical. They tended to seize upon Police Pistol or Service Pistol as a convenient halfway house.

Such ebullience provided the ideal environment for fresh thought, and the next few years saw the creation of Long Range, British Duelling, Splinter Silhouettes, Combat Snub, Falling Men and so forth, along with the renaissance of Classic and the increasing popularity of Black Powder. Britain, against all expectation, had become a world centre of innovation and leadership in handgunning sports.

Meanwhile, the United States was experiencing similar changes. The launch period was likewise the late 1950s, with dissatisfactions concentrating on the hegemony of the 2700 Course. The FBI had, for some years, been panhandling their own qualification course to police

departments up, down and across the continent, and this was inevitably seized upon by bored shooters everywhere, who found it much more entertaining than the nose-to-the-stone NMC.

Practical Pistol was launched as an intellectual reaction against both the NMC and the FBI course, on grounds that if one's goal was to achieve the highest possible level of expertise with the handgun, one's path was blocked by the established courses of fire, each of which, by stipulating stance and position, and by imposing cadences through time allowances, effectively outlawed the sort of open-minded quest that would, one might hope, have led to the discovery of more efficient techniques. Moving from a sporting to a service perspective, if it is true that under pressure, one reacts as one is trained to, then clearly the NMC and the FBI's PPC inculcated suicidal reactions.

Practical rejected the entire "course of fire" approach, basing competitions on conflict scenarios, written afresh for each occasion. One had to evaluate the situation one was placed in, and then contrive one's salvation as best one could. Shooting was "freestyle", in the happy expectation that a lack of constraint in these matters would lead to breakthroughs in technique. So it

Above: *A modern indoor range with wrap-around soundproofing and TV monitored targets. Gastinne-Rennette's, a century earlier, was a lot plusher and also had impact recording targets.*

Left: *As Richard Davis was the first to realize, shooting at bowling pins is a lot more fun than rolling large balls at them. The picture shows walk-up skittles bashing at Bisley.*

Above: *Practical Pistol is freestyle, but requires the shooter to adapt to circumstance. Targets here must be engaged through either aperture and round either side of the barricade.*

Below: *World Champion Jimmy von Sorgenfrei reloading. Practical tests gunhandling under pressure.*

did, and a whole range of new concepts: the isometric stance, the flash sight picture, the compressed surprise break and so forth, gradually defined themselves.

Practical was founded by Jeff Cooper, a retired Marine colonel, in the late 1950s, and was refined over the next decade and a half through constant, hard fought competition in a federation of California clubs called the Southwest Pistol League. Over the years, the new sport was adopted in many countries, and 1976 saw the foundation of the International Practical Shooting Confederation.

The face of sport was changing, and the NRA of America wished to change with it. If people wanted to shoot Practical, the NRA wanted to offer it and, parenthetically, run it. In 1982 they issued a provisional *Practical Shooting Rules* that drew vehement protest from practitioners of the sport who saw in the NRA's zeal for euphemism and keeness to fudge the issues, a profound and fundamental misunderstanding of what the sport stood for. The NRA responded by renaming their confection, Action Pistol.

Action Pistol was nothing more than Bianchi repackaged, and the Bianchi Cup match, in turn, was Practical sanitized for mass marketing. That, indeed, was what the NRA wanted.

These are all worthy undertakings that deserve to prosper but may, we fear, be doomed by an inbuilt propensity to trivialize, and the consequent arrival of funny guns. The problem with funny guns is, first, that they make the undertaking look silly and second, that they are dauntingly expensive. Part of the tremendous success of Handgun Metallic Silhouette has lain in its determination to preserve the bulk of the sport for people with sensible, affordable, out-of-the-box equipment.

John Bianchi's thinking in the late 1970s, that led him to inaugurate and administer the annual cup match bearing his name, was to the effect that the shooting sports could either adapt to an age of mass marketing and mass media, and use those techniques and facilities to reach a host of potential participants, or else be eradicated by those same tools of communication and influence wielded by those who bear us ill.

His initiative has recently been seconded by Smith & Wesson, with the Masters' Cup, a multidisciplinary contest that draws in elements of Practical, Long Range and pure, precision bullseye work. It is a challenging course.

Target pistol shooting today is a sport of incomparable richness and variety. Long may it remain so.

SMITH & WESSON MODEL 14-4 K-38 MASTERPIECE

SMITH & WESSON MODEL 41

For nearly half a century, from the 1930s to the 1970s, the average American pistol shooter's battery consisted of three guns: a .22 self-loader, a .38 revolver and a .45 auto. Wintertime shooting was over the .22 gallery course at 50ft (15.24m), comprising 5-round sets of slow fire, timed fire (20 seconds) and rapid fire (10 seconds). In warmer weather, everyone moved outdoors to compete on the National Match Course at 25 and 50 yards (22.86 and 45.72 metres).

The National Match Course was an awesome 270-shot affair that took a full day to complete and involved 90 shots with each gun. Slowfire (30 rounds per calibre) was shot at 50yds (45.72m), while timed and rapid were at the same target but at the nearer distance.

SMITH & WESSON MODEL 41

Country of origin: USA
Type: Self-loading pistol
Calibre: .22 LR
Capacity: 10

Action: Single action; internal hammer
Operation: Self-loading; unlocked breech (blowback)
Construction: Steel
Barrel length: 5.5in (140mm)
Length overall: 9in (229mm)
Weight (empty): 44.5oz (1262g)
Sights: Undercut square post foresight; square notch backsight click adjustable for windage and elevation
Comments: Introduced around 1957 for US National Match Course competiton; also suitable for UIT Standard Pistol, Standard Handgun and Ladies' Match. Upright grip angle duplicates that on the .45 service pistol and is regarded as disadvantageous for UIT events.

The Smith & Wesson Model 41 (bottom left) set the fashion for rimfire target pistols with a grip angle duplicating that of the .45. High Standard soon followed suit with upright handles on their very popular and successful Supermatic Trophy and Citation Models.

With its backsight mounted on a rib that extended rearward from the barrel, the Smith & Wesson Model 41 also set

another fashion. Henceforth, slide-mounted rear sights tended to be viewed with dark suspicion. High Standard soon began mounting theirs on a frame-mounted stirrup that encircled the rear of the slide, much the same as the system that was used by Hämmerli on their Model 208.

SMITH & WESSON MODEL 14-4 K-38 MASTERPIECE

Country of origin: USA
Type: Revolver
Calibre: .38 Special
Capacity: 6
Action: Selective double action; hand ejection
Operation: Crane mounted cylinder swings leftward out of frame for loading and unloading.
Construction: Steel
Barrel length: 6in (152mm)
Length overall: 11.125in (283mm)
Weight (empty): 37oz (1049g)
Sights: Square post foresight; square notch rearsight click adjustable for windage and elevation
Comments: Probably the world's most popular and successful target handgun.

Centrefire, until the 1960s, was undertaken with a .38 revolver, and by far the most popular was the Smith & Wesson K-38 Masterpiece (top left). Most competitors shot single action, and necessarily became very clever at thumbcocking on the rapid fire sets. A few, however, shot double action on the timed and rapid fire series, and proved that, provided the shooter mastered the technique, the gun would produce the desired results.

COLT GOVERNMENT MODEL

Country of origin: USA
Type: Self-loading pistol; locked breech; recoil operated
Calibre: .45 ACP
Capacity: 7+1
Action: Single action; outside hammer
Operation: Link-mounted barrel locks two ribs into corresponding mortises in roof of slide; breech of barrel swings down after a short distance of locked travel
Construction: Steel
Barrel length: 5in (127mm)
Length overall: 8.5in (216mm)
Weight (empty): 39oz (1106g)

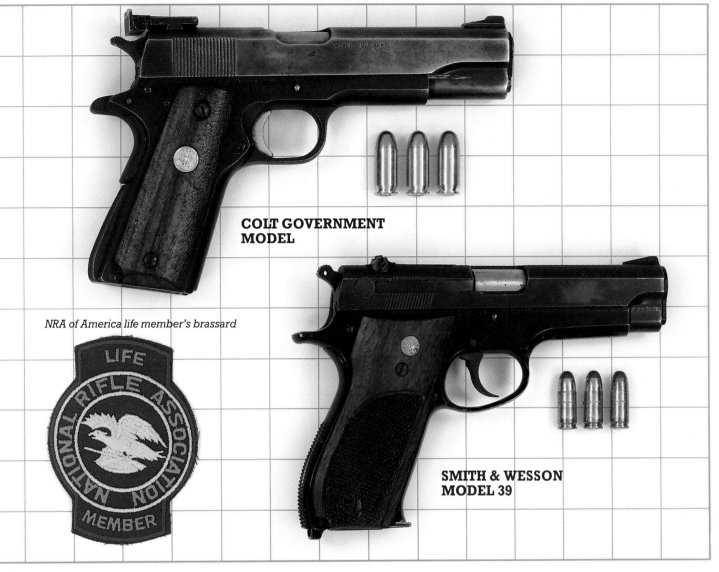

COLT GOVERNMENT MODEL

NRA of America life member's brassard

SMITH & WESSON MODEL 39

Sights: Square post foresight; square notch backsight click adjustable for windage and elevation

Comments: Gun shown is made up with a 1911A1 slide on a commercial Mark IV frame, with non-Colt target sights.

The .45 section of the NMC was perforce undertaken with the Colt Government Model (top right) suitably modified, or, later, the Gold Cup version, which had most of the desired features ex-factory. The permissible and desirable changes from service specification included a lighter, creep-free, backlash-free trigger release, larger and more visible adjustable sights, and internal accuracy tuning.

The gun may not have looked beautiful, but if the work was properly done, it shot fabulously. So well, in fact, that by the 1960s most competitors had stopped using .38's for the centrefire stage and now shot the NMC with two guns: 90 rounds with the .22 and 180 with the .45.

In recent years the tables have turned: European .32 UIT autoloaders are increasingly used in the centrefire match; one might just as well fire 180 rounds of .22 and 90 rounds of .45 for all the challenge the .32 poses.

The .38 revolver, however, had no sooner been deleted from the National Match battery than police style shooting—the PPC course—swept to nationwide popularity, in part, no doubt, because every shooter had a K-38 he was no longer exercising. The PPC broke the monopoly which the NMC had long exercised over competitive pistol shooting, and in its wake came a host of new disciplines: Practical Pistol, Bowling Pin Shooting, Metallic Silhouettes and so on. Then there was the Bianchi Cup over a semi-Practical course that evolved into NRA Action Shooting.

The old National Match Course three-gun battery was no longer either adequate or ideal, but it coped remarkably well. The .45,

particularly, proved to be an extraordinarily versatile gun, hard to beat on either skittles or steel plates.

SMITH & WESSON MODEL 39

Country of origin: USA
Type: Self-loading pistol; locked breech; recoil operated
Calibre: 9mm Parabellum
Capacity: 8+1
Action: Double action for first shot; subsequent shots are single action
Operation: Breech of barrel locks into roof of slide and is cammed downward to unlock after a short distance of locked travel.
Construction: Aluminium alloy receiver; other parts steel
Barrel length: 4in (102mm)
Length overall: 7.44in (189mm)
Weight (empty): 26.5oz (751g)
Sights: Square ramp foresight; square notch rearsight click adjustable for windage only
Comments: Introduced in 1954 for possible military adoption. The original Model 39 has been superseded by a variety of models on the same basic design, some with larger capacity (double column) magazines, and some of all stainless steel construction.

As a result of the developments described above, there was a great deal of experimentation going on, and most shooters were adding pieces to their battery. The 9mm proved useless on bowling pins, but aroused a lot of interest nonetheless, as NATO standardized on it. The Smith & Wesson Model 39 (bottom right) was the first successful American gun in this (at the time, rather exotic) European chambering. Introduced in 1954, the Model 39 enjoyed an immediate popularity, and its longer-term prospects were much enhanced when it was adopted by the Illinois State Police.

Subsequent models have introduced improved sights, extractors and slide bushings, as well as large capacity magazines (Model 59) and stainless steel construction (Models 639 and 659).

The Smith & Wesson was the only serious American contender for the US service pistol contract, and the decision against it in favour of the Beretta has remained controversial.

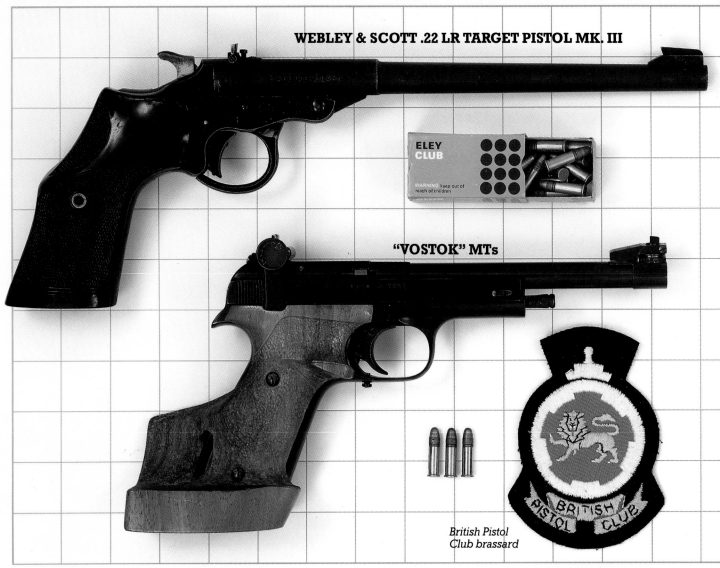

WEBLEY & SCOTT .22 LR TARGET PISTOL MK. III

"VOSTOK" MTs

British Pistol Club brassard

If you had gone through the kit of any British pistol shooter of the mid-20th century, these are the guns you would most likely have found. The Webley Single Shot shown at upper left is the patriarch of the quartet, dating from an era when, as Lord Cottesloe put it, gentlemen really did not shoot pistol. Whoever did (and they were not many) used the workhorse Webley tip-open or, if they aspired to the officer class, the elegant Webley Mk. IV revolver (lower right), which offered the same feel as the .455 or .380 service revolver. The one shown here belonged to the Oxford University Pistol Club.

WEBLEY & SCOTT MK. IV .22 LONG RIFLE

Country of origin: Great Britain
Type: Revolver
Calibre: .22 LR
Capacity: 6
Action: Selective double action
Operation: Stirrup latch releases barrel and cylinder assembly to pivot downward at the muzzle, rotating on the hinge at the front of

the frame. Ejection is automatic.
Construction: All steel; black plastic grip panels
Barrel length: 5.9375in (151mm)
Length overall: 11.125in (283mm)
Weight (empty): 34oz (964g)
Sights: Square format; backsight adjustable for windage and elevation by opposing screws
Comments: Very few made. A lovely revolver that deserved better sights. Stirrup springs chronically broke.

The Mk. IV Webley .38 was introduced in 1929 with the police market foremost in view, since the firm had recently lost the military contract to Enfield. The .22 version (as shown at lower right) followed in 1931, and although it remained in the line until the firm ceased handgun production in 1968, the numbers made were never large. Its price was a disincentive, as was the fact that no recognised competition really required it. The Single Shot was cheaper and better suited to domestic courses of fire.

Or, rather, *the* domestic

course of fire, which was known as NSRA Club Pistol and consisted of 10 shots slowfire, or multiples thereof, at 20 yards (18.29m). For the British Championships at Bisley, the range was increased to 50 yards (45.72m) and the ammunition requirement inflated to marathon proportions. But it was all slowfire at the ring target and, over the course of decades, many people found this awfully boring. There was also the fact that Britain was quite alone in enduring this self-inflicted tedium.

The British Pistol Club was formed in 1957 to popularize Continental-style "UIT" shooting, which would give British marksmen better chances abroad, while allowing them to shoot a more varied and entertaining competitive programme at home. The UIT courses called for rapid fire sets, so that the tendency, already underway, to replace the single shots with self-loaders accelerated.

This was a pity, inasmuch as

the single shot was an elegant and distinctively British type of pistol with a visible line of descent from the duellers of an earlier age; unlike the Continental Free Pistol, which had long since been refined to absurdity. It would have taken a re-design of the course of fire by the NSRA, to make it more engaging, and some interest on Webley's part in preserving the market, to save the single shot. Neither the organization nor the firm was intellectually up to it.

WEBLEY & SCOTT .22 LR TARGET PISTOL MK. III

Country of origin: Great Britain
Type: Single shot pistol
Calibre: .22 LR
Capacity: 1
Action: Single action
Operation: Pressing forward on trigger guard releases barrel to tip downward at the muzzle, pivoting on the hinge at the front of the frame. The hammer must be cocked for each shot
Construction: All steel; two-piece moulded plastic grips

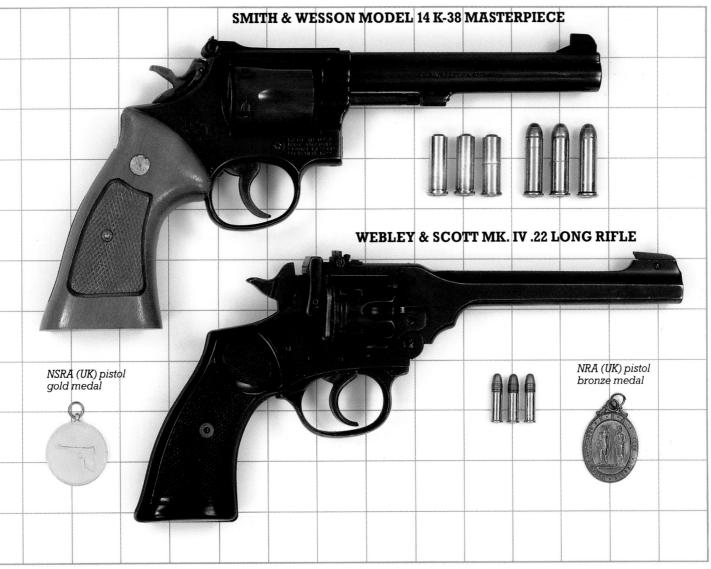

SMITH & WESSON MODEL 14 K-38 MASTERPIECE

WEBLEY & SCOTT MK. IV .22 LONG RIFLE

NSRA (UK) pistol gold medal

NRA (UK) pistol bronze medal

Barrel length: 9.9375in (252mm)
Length overall: 14in (356mm)
Weight (empty): 38.5oz (1091g)
Sights: Square format; backsight windage and elevation adjustable by opposing screws
Comments: A robust and well loved classic, sadly missed. A few were made in centrefire.

The Webley Single Shot (upper left) was introduced in 1909 and discontinued in 1965; there were grip variations in 1938 and 1952, but the front end and action never changed at all. The gun was famed for the simplicity of its mechanism, which consisted of the hammer, trigger and mainspring guide. What killed the Single Shot was Webley's comprehensive apathy. The gun never had trigger adjustments; it never had decent sights; it was never offered in a choice of barrel lengths or weights. Because it was light and rather whippy, most shooters taped spare wheelweights under the barrel in an attempt to tame these characteristics..

"VOSTOK" MTs

Country of origin: Soviet Union
Type: Self-loading pistol
Calibre: .22 LR
Capacity: 6
Action: Single action
Operation: Unlocked breech, blowback operated, external hammer
Construction: All steel
Barrel length: 7.375in (187mm)
Length overall: 10.875in (276mm)
Weight (empty): 37oz (1049g)
Sights: Square foresight click adjustable for elevation; U-notch backsight click adjustable for windage
Comments: Very well made. Came with additional barrel and muzzle weights. This pistol is marked with an "arrow in shield" crest, which is believed to indicate that its place of manufacture was the Soviet state arsenal of Tula.

While top level competition shooters turned to American or European selfloaders, club level shooters more often chose the Soviet MTs pistol (lower left), which commended itself by its price no less than by its quality and workmanship. Its defects were its rather light

overall weight (though muzzle weights helped) and a general air of mechanical complication due, perhaps, to its having been designed by a blind man, Mikhail Margolin. Universally known in Britain as the Vostok, the MTs was a good gun and gave good service.

SMITH & WESSON MODEL 14 K-38 MASTERPIECE

Country of origin: USA
Type: Revolver
Calibre: .38 Special
Capacity: 6
Action: Selective double action
Operation: Thumblatch on left of frame releases cylinder to swing leftward out of frame on its yoke. Hand ejection
Construction: All steel
Barrel length: 6in (152mm)
Length overall: 11.1in (282mm)
Weight (empty): 38.5oz (1091g)
Sights: Square format; backsight click adjustable for windage and elevation
Comments: The world's most successful target revolver, superlatively versatile and excellent value for money.

Part of the UIT package was centrefire—and once shooters had had a taste of the bigger bang, they liked it. UIT Centrefire produced a knock-on effect in heightening interest and participation in Police and Service Pistol events, the more so since the best gun for the lot was the ubiquitous Smith & Wesson K-38 (upper right), combining excellent design with a very reasonable price.

Although the wheel of fashion has recently turned as the century nears its end, and Webleys and Vostoks have been replaced by more sophisticated equipment for the new courses of fire favoured by a much more vigorous handgunning community, a good .38 revolver still covers a lot of bases. It will do handsomely for Service Pistol B in Britain, for all the Police Pistol courses, for Practical Revolver, Skittles (2nd Chance Match), Bianchi-style (NRA Action Pistol) competitions, Long Range and UIT Centrefire.

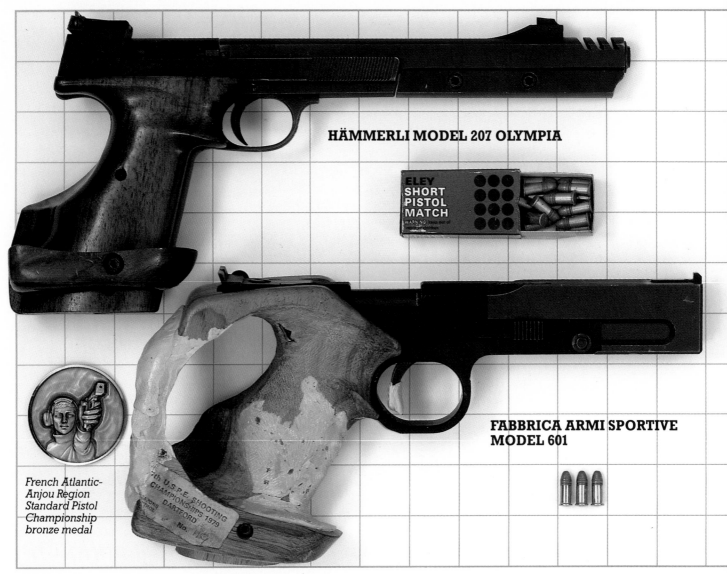

HÄMMERLI MODEL 207 OLYMPIA

ELEY SHORT PISTOL MATCH

FABBRICA ARMI SPORTIVE MODEL 601

French Atlantic-Anjou Region Standard Pistol Championship bronze medal

The pistol events administered by the *Union International du Tir* (UIT) involve speed and precision components, to use the UIT's terminology. Free Pistol is precision only; Rapid Fire is speed only; Standard Pistol, Ladies' Match, Standard Handgun and Centrefire involve both. It goes without saying that the speed events still require precision of a high order, and that the challenge concerns accurate shooting within fairly tight time limits. In the case of Rapid Fire, this means lifting the pistol from a 45° depressed position and firing one shot at each of five silhouettes 25m (27.34yds) distant, all within four seconds.

HÄMMERLI MODEL 207 OLYMPIA

Country of origin: Switzerland
Type: Pistol
Calibre: .22 Short
Capacity: 8
Action: Semi-automatic; unlocked breech; blowback operated
Operation: Gas pressure in bore and chamber uses the cartridge case as a piston to drive the slide rearward
Construction: All steel; machined from solid
Barrel length: 7.06in (179mm)
Length overall: 12.9in (328mm)
Weight (empty): 38.8oz (1100g)
Sights: Square post foresight; square notch backsight click adjustable for windage and elevation
Comments: Derived from the pre-World War II Walther Olympia model.

For many years, the gun to use was one of Hämmerli's 200-series. The Model 207 Olympia (top left), introduced in 1964, replaced the Model 205 of 1960, which in turn succeeded various models, all quite similar, going back to the Model 200 of 1952, itself a direct descendant of the Walther Olympia (some parts interchanged) which had been designed to help ensure a Teutonic triumph at the Berlin Olympics of 1936.

The design objective of all Rapid Fire pistols is to minimize muzzle lift on discharge so that the sight picture is as undisturbed as possible. They are chambered for .22 Short cartridges, and gentle ones at that. The Hämmerli 207 carries a rather heavy barrel weight as well as a muzzle brake that is meant to deflect high-pressure gases upward, thus pushing the muzzle down against recoil forces. In addition, a series of ports are drilled downwards through the top of the barrel into the bore, thus venting peak pressure gases upwards throughout the bullet's travel down the bore.

FABBRICA ARMI SPORTIVE MODEL 601

Country of origin: Italy
Type: Pistol
Calibre: .22 Short
Capacity: 5
Action: Semi-automatic; blowback operated
Operation: Gas pressure in bore uses cartridge case as a piston to drive the slide rearward
Construction: Aluminium receiver; much use of advanced manufacturing techniques
Barrel length: 6in (152mm)
Length overall: 11.3in (287mm)
Weight (empty): 40oz (1134g)
Sights: Square post foresight; square notch backsight click adjustable for windage and elevation
Comments: Highly sophisticated: one of the first of the current generation of low bore axis competition pistols. Magazine inserts from top of gun, through ejection port.

Modern Rapid Fire pistols such as the Italian Fabbrica Armi Sportive (FAS) Model 601 (bottom left), which was introduced in the early 1970s as the IGI Domino, dispense with the muzzle brake is superfluous but incorporate larger ports running the length of the barrel, with the venting adjustable by plug screws.

Other notable design changes in the Model 601 involve more hand support, a more steeply raked grip and, most importantly, a much lower bore line, which significantly reduces muzzle torque on recoil.

The Model 601 was designed, like the Walther GSP,

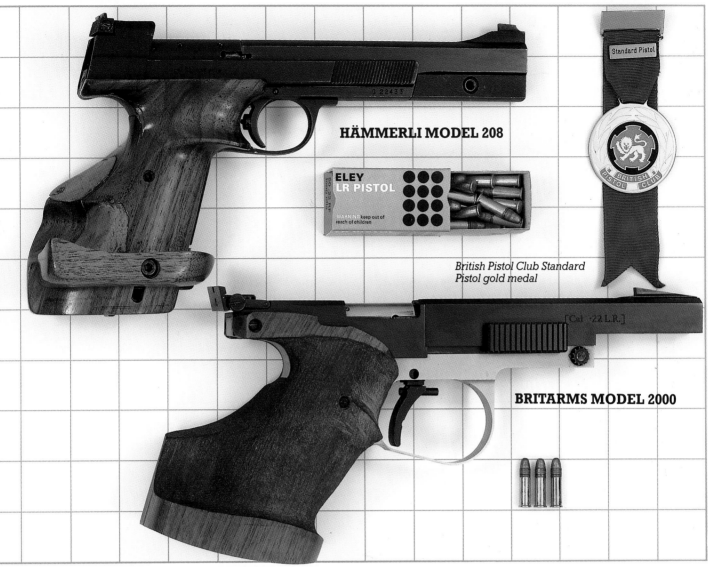

HÄMMERLI MODEL 208

ELEY LR PISTOL

British Pistol Club Standard Pistol gold medal

Standard Pistol

BRITISH PISTOL CLUB

[Cal .22 L.R.]

BRITARMS MODEL 2000

to combine optimum performance with essentially cheap manufacture, thereby ensuring an attractive margin of profit. Early examples were plagued by parts breakages: it took several years fully to debug the design of what has become a top-level competition gun.

HÄMMERLI MODEL 208

Country of origin: Switzerland
Type: Pistol
Calibre: .22 LR
Capacity: 8
Action: Semi-automatic; unlocked breech; blowback operated
Operation: Gas pressure in bore and chamber uses the cartridge case as a piston to drive the slide rearward.
Construction: All steel, machined from solid
Barrel length: 6in (152mm)
Length overall: 10in (254mm)
Weight (empty): 34.7oz (984g) without muzzle weight
Sights: Square post foresight; square notch backsight click adjustable for windage and elevation
Comments: For the past two decades—the gun that wins.

Recoil, or loss of sight alignment, is also a problem in Standard Pistol, which involves sets of five shots in ten seconds at the international precision target at 25m (27.34yds). This is a small mark and requires very tight grouping for a good score. The .22 Long Rifle cartridge is mandatory.

The Hämmerli Model 208 (top right), introduced in 1958, still holds the world record and is still the gun to beat, but competitors nowadays have to clamp rather massive barrel weights onto it to hold the muzzle down during the shot.

The Model 208's remarkable hegemony is constantly challenged by more recent designs like the FAS Model 602 (the LR version of the Model 601 illustrated) or the Britarms Model 2000 (see below). Hämmerli themselves have recently unveiled the Model 280, the gun they intend to replace the Model 208. Constructed largely of carbon fibre, the Model 280 is a bold venture and, necessarily, a big gun. When Hämmerli come

forth with a winner, it goes on winning for a long time, but it must be said that their record of new model launches is not altogether lemon-free.

BRITARMS MODEL 2000

Country of origin: Great Britain
Type: Pistol
Calibre: .22 LR
Capacity: 5
Action: Semi-automatic; unlocked breech; blowback action
Operation: Gas pressure in bore uses cartridge case as a piston to push slide rearward
Construction: All steel, machined from solid
Barrel length: 5.9in (150mm)
Length overall: 11in (279mm)
Weight (empty): 42oz (1191g)
Sights: Square post foresight; square notch backsight click adjustable for windage and elevation
Comments: In many respects, an upmarket FAS.

The Britarms Model 2000 (bottom right) was designed by Chris Valentine in the early 1970s as a state-of-the-art

Standard Pistol. Much influenced by the IGI (whose internal magazine it copies), the Britarms may be broadly described as a carriage-trade FAS. It is a sophisticated design, rendered in the finest steels, and is highly regarded. The firm has been plagued by changes of ownership and low volume production, as a result of which, despite having been on the market for more than a decade, the gun is still not altogether de-bugged.

However, now that it is under the ownership of former British champion and professional engineer Alan Westlake, the Britarms looks better every day. As far as the performance aspects of design are concerned, the Britarms Model 2000 is still unsurpassed.

Westlake's immediate ambition is to malfunction-proof the Model 2000. That done, he is confident that his recently-patented recoil-damped experimental gun, if approved by the UIT, will give Hämmerli a hard run for their money into the 21st century.

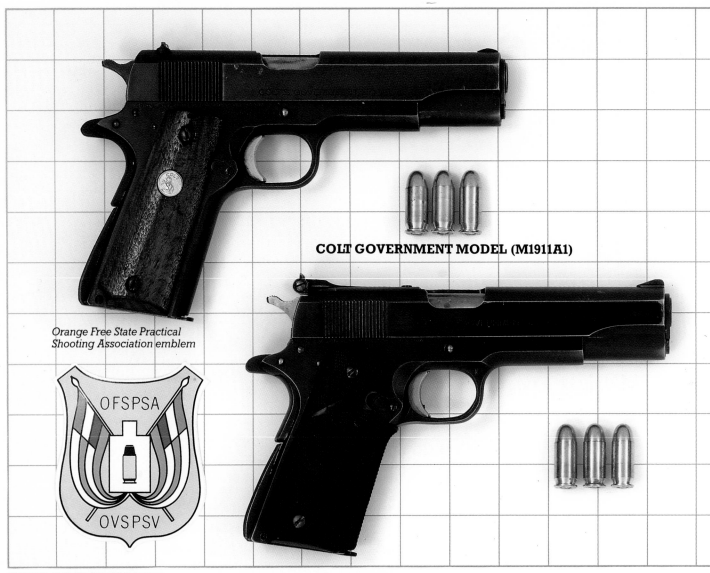

COLT GOVERNMENT MODEL (M1911A1)

Orange Free State Practical Shooting Association emblem

COLT GOVERNMENT MODEL (M1911A1)

Country of origin: USA
Type: Self-loading pistol
Calibre: .45 ACP
Capacity: 7 + 1
Action: Single action
Operation: Locked breech, recoil operated, link-unlocking pivoting barrel, drops down at breech to unlock ribs on top of the barrel from mortises in the roof of the slide
Construction: All steel
Barrel length: 5in (127mm)
Length overall: 8.75in (222mm)
Weight (empty): 39oz (1106g)
Sights: Square format. Backsight drift adjustable for windage
Comments: A splendid weapon which supports an industry of accessories' manufacturers and custom modifiers. Available from Colt in four calibres (.22 LR, 9mm Para, .38 Super, .45 ACP) in four formats (compact, semi-compact, standard and match target) and steel or aluminium frames.

Colt's .45 Government Model of 1911 is unquestionably the most successful automatic pistol ever introduced. Its advantages are compactness, ease of handling, reliability,

robustness, accuracy, ease of reloading and dependable stopping power without excessive recoil. Other pistols may claim many of these virtues, but none put them together as well as the 1911. It was the US service pistol for three-quarters of a century, and many would contend that its retirement was premature. It was also adopted by the Mexican, Argentinian and Norwegian armed forces and was the RAF sidearm.

More than three million Government .45's have been manufactured by Colt, Springfield Armory and licenced wartime contractors. This figure does not include Mexican, Argentinian and Norwegian production; it does not include the versions in 9mm, .38 Super, .38 Spl. and .22 LR produced by Colt; it does not include recent copies by up to a dozen firms, including Detonics, Randall, AMT and Arminex; nor does it take in the vast quantities of 1911 derivatives manufactured by Star and Llama in Spain.

The Government Model is so popular because it is good at so many things. One-third of the gruelling 270-round US National Match Course must be shot with the 1911; the other two-thirds are split between .22 LR and any centrefire. Such was the scoring ability of the .45, however, that most competitors during the 1960s and 1970s had given up on .38's for centrefire and used the Government .45 for that stage as well.

The 1911 pistol dominates the sport of Practical Pistol shooting, now practised in nearly 20 countries. Unlike conventional target shooting, which breaks marksmanship into components, Practical creates realistic scenarios and seeks the best combination of tactics, technique and equipment for dealing with them. It was the Government Model's overwhelming success in this competitive environment that led to the growing conviction that it had no peer as a combat or defensive sidearm. Its adoption

by the Los Angeles Police SWAT unit presaged its acceptance by many other elite formations.

Skittles (bowling pin) shooting is another recent discipline which the .45 dominates, as it does the NRA's Action Pistol event, based on the Bianchi Cup course of fire. There is even a British Long Range match for .45's, fired at 100 and 200 yards (91.44 and 182.88m), the results of which definitively dispel the old myth that the 1911 was useful only at rock-throwing ranges.

The Government Model is a recoil operated, single action, self-loading pistol carrying its ammunition in a box magazine in the grip. The magazine is released by a pushbutton on the left of the frame behind the trigger. Thus the thumb of the gun hand can activate the release while the other hand reaches for a spare magazine. With practice, the reload can be acomplished in about one second.

Regulations permitting, the piece is carried "cocked and

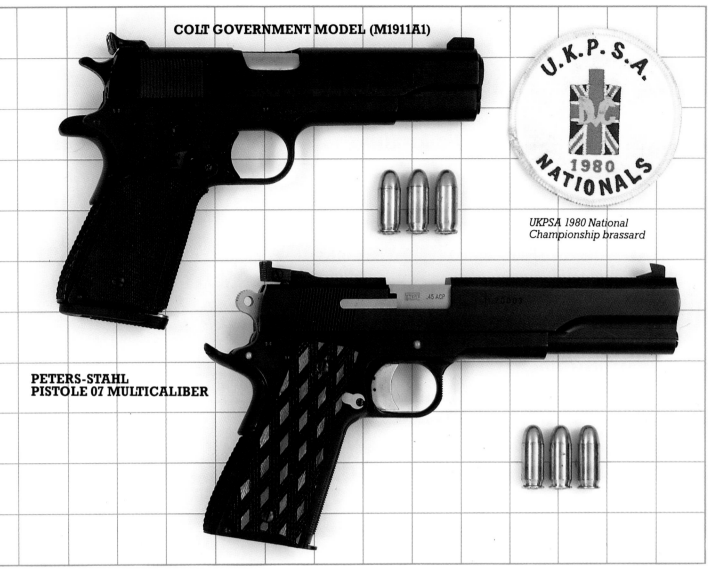

COLT GOVERNMENT MODEL (M1911A1)

PETERS-STAHL PISTOLE 07 MULTICALIBER

UKPSA 1980 National Championship brassard

locked"; that is, with the chamber loaded, the hammer cocked and the manual safety engaged. The safety lever lies under the thumb on the left of the frame, and wipes off naturally as the gun comes on target. No pistol is faster on the first shot than a cocked and locked .45. Military regulations often require the gun to be carried with the chamber empty. In these circumstances, the slide is racked by the left hand as the right hand punches the gun towards the target. Trained US sentries can get a semi-aimed shot off in this way, from the military flap holster, within about two seconds.

The guns illustrated show the .45 in various degrees of modification. At top left is a Colt Mk. IV, absolutely ex-factory, albeit well used. It differs from previous models in having a collet bushing that maintains spring tension on the muzzle—to doubtful benefit. The owner is not particularly sold on it, and cites as other defects: sights too small and hard to see, trigger around a

half-pound too heavy, and lack of the magazine bumpers that would make seating a fresh magazine on a speed reload a much surer proposition.

The black-handled guns show conservative modifications for Practical Pistol, defensive or police duty use. The Pachmayer rubber stocks, now in vogue, give what some criticize as too secure a grip, so slip-proof are the handles, since an off-centre hold on the draw is hard to correct on aim. The gun at lower left retains the steel backstrap surface to make shifting the hold easier. Smith & Wesson K-frame sights have been fitted, offering a larger, clearer sight picture, as well as the convenience of click-adjustment, while remaining reasonably unobtrusive. The gun at upper right has a rubber coat on the mainspring housing (the lower half of the backstrap) and carries a rubber magazine bumper, both to cushion the ejected magazine's impact on the ground and to help ensure that the fresh magazine is

pushed fully into engagement. The replacement sights are a high-visibility fixed set from Millett's.

PETERS-STAHL PISTOLE 07 MULTICALIBER

Country of origin: West Germany
Type: Self-loading pistol
Calibre: .45 ACP
Capacity: 7 + 1
Action: Single action
Operation: Recoil operated, cam unlocking, tilting barrel, locks shelf ahead of the chamber against the forward edge of the ejection port
Construction: All steel. Early production built on Caspian Arms 1911 receivers. Hammer-forged barrels with polygonal form rifling.
Barrel length: 6in (152mm)
Length overall: 9.5in (241mm)
Weight (empty): 43oz (1219g)
Sights: Square format. Interchangeable post foresight; backsight click adjustable for windage and elevation.
Comments: Converts to 9mm Parabellum, .38 Super or .38 Spl. Wadcutter by changing barrel and magazine; same breechblock and recoil spring used throughout. .38

unit is blowback operated, others locked breech. Base of recoil spring guide rod carries locking cams on upper surface. Introduced in 1986.

The gun at lower right is a longslide match pistol by Peters-Stahl of West Germany. It uses a Caspian Arms 1911 receiver, but the upper structure is a new design manufactured by Peters, which replaces the Colt's link unlocking system with cams. As one would expect, the sights are click adjustable to fine increments, with the undercut front post giving a dead black Patridge picture. The trigger has been finely tuned, and the long slide shifts the centre of balance forward, helping the gun hold more solidly on target and dampening the recoil of light loads. A replacement .38 Spl. barrel (unlocked breech) adapts the gun for UIT centrefire, while in .45 it suits for skittles, Long Range or National Match work.

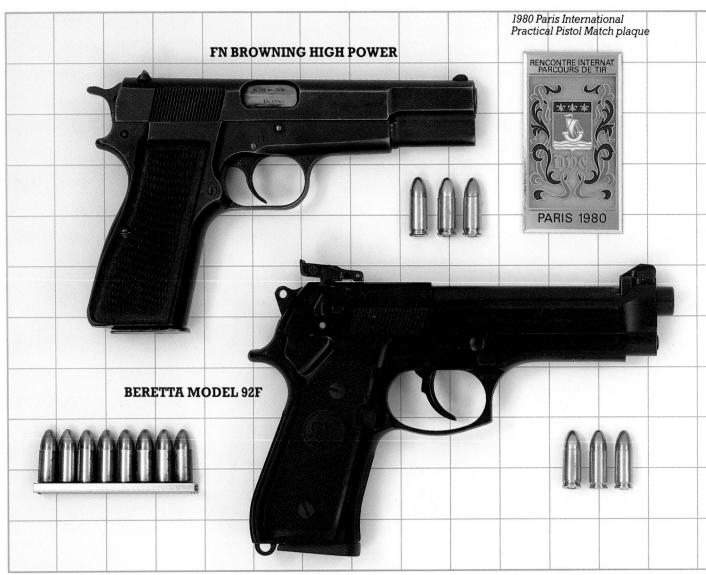

FN BROWNING HIGH POWER

RENCONTRE INTERNAT.
PARCOURS DE TIR

PARIS 1980

BERETTA MODEL 92F

The 9mm Parabellum has, in recent years, become almost the world standard military pistol and submachine gun cartridge, outside the Communist bloc. Its use as a sporting or defensive round has grown alongside, or slightly in the wake of, its official popularity.

The Parabellum (the name derives from the German manufacturer's telegraph code) dates from the turn of the century, and was originally a bottleneck 7.65mm (.30 cal.) round chambered in the freshly introduced Parabellum pistol, designed by Georg Luger as a modification of the previous, ungainly, Borchardt.

However, colonial experience with the slightly more powerful 7.63mm Model 1896 Mauser pistol had persuaded the German military that the new breed of high velocity .30's lacked stopping power. In order to accommodate this misgiving, Georg Luger and his engineers blew the 7.65mm case out to straight-wall (slightly tapered,

actually) configuration, and 9mm is what it turned out to be. That must have been what the service chiefs had in mind, for it was in this chambering that the German forces adopted the Parabellum pistol in 1904 (Navy) and 1908 (Army). They have since changed guns, but not changed cartridges.

Although many harbour well-founded doubts about the 9mm's terminal effectiveness, there is definitely something about the cartridge that seduces the military mind, at general staff level in any event. The 9mm Parabellum's virtues, in fact, are largely logistical. A high intensity, very compact round, it packs and transports efficiently and is sparing of critical materials. It is also an excellent sub-machine gun cartridge, while its modest dimensions permit the use of high capacity, double-column magazines in pistols.

It is precisely the firepower factor that has led many American police departments, as well as sporting shooters worldwide, to favour the 9mm.

Modern 9mm pistols offer from 14 to 19 rounds compared to 8 rounds (7+1) for the .45.

FN BROWNING HIGH POWER

Country of origin: Belgium
Type: Self-loading pistol
Calibre: 9mm Parabellum
Capacity: 13+1
Action: Single action
Operation: Recoil operated, locked breech, cam unlocking. Ribs on top of barrel at breech end lock into roof of slide
Construction: All steel
Barrel length: 4.625in (117mm)
Length overall: 7.75in (197mm)
Weight (empty): 32oz (907g)
Sights: Notch backsight drift adjustable for windage; blade foresight
Comments: The first of the high-capacity 9mms, and the most widespread military service pistol of the postwar era, still in service worldwide.

The first of the modern generation of 9mm battle pistols was the FN Browning High Power (upper left),

introduced in 1935 and immediately adopted by the Belgian Army. When German forces overran Liège in 1940, most of Fabrique Nationale's management and engineers fled to Britain, whence they were sent to Canada to place the P35 in production at the John Inglis plant in Toronto. Inglis production—about 200,000 pistols—went to arm Nationalist Chinese, Greek, Australian, Canadian and British forces. In the meantime, FN continued production under German control. The 1935, redesignated the P640(B), became substitute standard and most of the production, estimated at a further 200,000 units, seems to have gone to Waffen SS formations on the Eastern Front. Today, the High Power, though showing its age, remains in production and is still the issue sidearm of UK, Commonwealth and many NATO and non-aligned armed forces. Suitably modified, it is a top-ranking competitive pistol for IPSC matches.

BERNARDELLI P018/9

I.P. S.C.
DVC

International Practical Shooting Confederation emblem

HECKLER & KOCH P7M13

BERETTA MODEL 92F

Country of origin: Italy
Type: Self-loading pistol
Calibre: 9mm Parabellum
Capacity: 15+1
Action: Double action first shot, single action thereafter
Operation: Recoil operated, locked breech. Straight recoiling barrel using P38-type locking block under barrel that is cammed downward to release slide
Construction: Aluminium alloy frame; other parts steel
Barrel length: 4.92in (125mm)
Length overall: 8.54in (217mm)
Weight (empty): 33.5oz (950g)
Sights: Millett click adjustable backsight with accurizer foresight assembly; not original equipment
Comments: Adopted, controversially, as the US service pistol. Excellent reputation for reliability. Introduced in 1977. Design derives from the single action Beretta Model 1951.

The Beretta Model 92F (lower left) is the recently adopted US service pistol, and reflects modern preferences in its features: double action trigger, ambidextrous controls, and massive capacity (15+1). The gun shown has click-adjustable sights, but the lightweight frame and lack of single-action first-shot option handicap it competitively. It has established for itself an excellent reputation for reliability and durability.

BERNARDELLI P018/9

Country of origin: Italy
Type: Self-loading pistol
Calibre: 9mm Parabellum
Capacity: 16+1 (Factory recommends 15 in magazine)
Action: Selective double action
Operation: Recoil operated, locked breech, cam unlocking. Ribs on top of barrel at breech end seat in roof of slide
Construction: All steel. Major components machined from forgings. Nose of slide keyed and brazed in place
Barrel length: 4.8in (122mm)
Length overall: 8.4in (213mm)
Weight (empty): 35.7oz (1012g)
Sights: Post foresight; square notch backsight laterally dovetailed, adjusts for windage with Allen key

Comments: No hammer trip. Thumb safety for optional cocked-and-locked carry. Introduced 1984. An excellent pistol, strongly resembling the Swiss P210 in some respects, but selective double action. Also available in .30 Luger calibre, and in a compact model in either calibre.

The recently introduced Bernardelli P018 (upper right) increases the firepower by one round, while countering the objections to the Beretta with a steel frame, a speed safety, and a cocked-and-locked override so that the first shot may be taken either single action or double action.

HECKLER & KOCH P7M13

Country of origin: West Germany
Type: Self-loading pistol
Calibre: 9mm Parabellum
Capacity: 13+1
Action: Single action, squeeze cocking
Operation: Unlocked breech, gas retarded delayed blowback. Gas is bled through a port immediately ahead of the chamber through the lower barrel wall into an expansion chamber beneath the barrel, where it acts against a piston attached to the nose of the slide. Squeezing a lever in the frontstrap cocks the striker for the first shot. Recocking is automatic as long as the lever is held depressed: releasing it decocks the piece
Construction: All steel
Barrel length: 4in (102mm)
Length overall: 6.9in (175mm)
Weight (empty): 35oz (992g)
Sights: Square format with 3-dot low light system. Both sights mounted in lateral dovetails
Comments: Extremely accurate. Used by state police forces in West Germany and USA.

The Heckler & Koch P7M13 (lower right) is a gas retarded, squeeze cocking pistol of radical design and great technical merit. It and its single-column variant, the P7M8, have a fine reputation for accuracy and reliability, and are in service with many West German police units, as well as a number of American departments, including the New Jersey State Police.

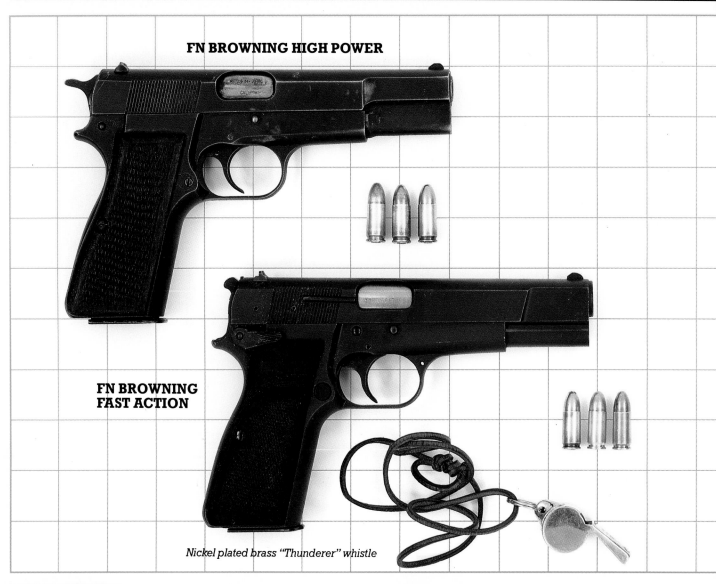

FN BROWNING HIGH POWER

FN BROWNING FAST ACTION

Nickel plated brass "Thunderer" whistle

FN BROWNING HIGH POWER

Country of origin: Belgium
Type: Self-loading pistol
Calibre: 9mm Parabellum
Capacity: 13 + 1
Action: Single action; outside hammer
Operation: Recoil operated, locked breech, cam unlocking, Browning system. Lugs on top of barrel lock into mortises in roof of slide; breech end of barrel cams down to unlock
Construction: All steel
Barrel length: 4.8in (122mm)
Length overall: 7.6in (193mm)
Weight (empty): 31oz (879g)
Sights: Blade foresight; U-notch backsight drift adjustable for windage
Comments: The world's most successful and widely distributed military service pistol.

Introduced in 1935, the Browning High Power (top left) was used about equally by both sides in World War II, and is unquestionably one of the world's most successful military sidearms. It has served scores of armies and is still the official

service pistol in Britain, the Commonwealth and many other countries. Its most recent major campaign was the Falklands War where, once again, it served both sides with its customary reliability.

Despite this impressive longevity and ubiquity, the wheel of fashion has turned—and the fact is that the High Power is an old design and that governments are not going to keep on ordering it forever. They will all, in due course, change to a more modern design, which means, initially, one that is not single action on the first shot and one that has some means other than the trigger for getting the hammer down when a shot is not desired.

SIG-SAUER P220

Country of origin: Switzerland/West Germany
Type: Self-loading pistol
Calibre: 9mm; also available in .45 ACP
Capacity: 9 + 1
Action: Selective double action; no cocked-and-loaded carry

Operation: Recoil operated, locked breech, cam unlocking. Shelf on outside of barrel ahead of chamber locks against forward edge of ejection port; breech end of barrel cams downward to unlock.
Construction: Light alloy frame with steel inserts. Slide is a heavy-gauge blanking with machined nosepiece welded on and breechblock keyed and pinned in place
Barrel length: 4.3in (109mm)
Length overall: 8.1in (206mm)
Weight (empty): 29.5oz (836g)
Sights: Square post foresight; square notch backsight drift adjustable for windage
Comments: The service pistol of the Swiss Army, with P225 and P226 variants in use by many West German and American police forces. Extremely accurate, reliable and easy handling, although inclined to break trigger return springs.

The new breed of service auto-pistol, of which there are a score or more on the market, is exemplified by the Swiss Army's SIG-Sauer P220 (bottom right), which was an extremely close runner-up to the Beretta

for US service adoption. A compact version was adopted by the Dutch national police and a number of West German police forces, while the .45 and large capacity 9mm versions are popular with US police.

The P220 is built on a tough aluminium frame and uses a heavy-gauged, stamped slide with the nosepiece welded on. The breechblock is a separate machined part that is keyed into the slide and retained by a rollpin. The first shot is double action, with subsequent shots single action. The pistol shown here has the magazine release on the heel of the butt; later production models use a pushbutton on the side of the frame.

There are three controls on the left of the frame. Just under the thumb is the slide latch; immediately forward, and working on a much longer arc, is the decocking lever. The disassembly lever is amidships, ahead of the trigger. There is no need to touch the trigger except to fire a shot.

FEG P9R

*Obverse of Portuguese
Special Operations Group plaque*

SIG-SAUER P220

The P220 series, which includes the compact P225 and the large-capacity P226, conforms to a requirement made by the West German Police in 1975, for a self-loading pistol with the reactive qualities of a revolver. That is to say, that it could be carried with absolute safety from accidental discharge, and drawn and fired without having to disengage a manual safety by means of crossbolts, levers, or what have you. Of course, the Walther PP, which they wished to replace, already met this requirement.

FN BROWNING FAST ACTION

Country of origin: Belgium
Type: Self-loading pistol
Calibre: 9mm Parabellum
Capacity: 13 + 1
Action: Single action with self-cocking safety hammer
Operation: Recoil operated, locked breech, cam unlocking, Browning system. Lugs on top of barrel lock into mortises in roof of slide
Construction: All steel
Barrel length: 4.75in (121mm)
Length overall: 7.5in (191mm)
Weight (empty): 34.5oz (978g)
Sights: Square ramp foresight; square notch backsight drift adjustable for windage
Comments: A brilliant design, but unlikely to be produced.

Fabrique Nationale of Belgium have not to date come up with a replacement for the 50-year-old High Power. They ran a zero-series of a gun called the BDA (Browning Double Action), which cannot have impressed them because it is still not in production, although Japanese blank-firing replicas of it have been available for at least two years.

Another attempt towards a successor was the so-called Fast Action pistol (bottom left), of which only around a dozen prototypes were built. The Fast Action was meant to afford the safety in carry of a double action arm, while preserving the speed and accuracy on the first and second shots of a cocked-and-locked single action.

In brief, the hammer is mounted round a large hub which carries the sear engagement. The hammer is pushed forward over a latch for carry; the first pressure on the trigger releases it to spring back round the hub before the sear is released to fire. Trigger pressure, therefore, is light and easy for each shot, rather than being rough and heavy for the first shot with a drastic change of system for the next one, which is the case with most double action pistols. However, the indications are that the Fast Action was too novel to succeed.

FEG P9R

Country of origin: Hungary
Type: Self-loading pistol
Calibre: 9mm Parabellum
Capacity: 14 + 1
Action: Selective double action; outside hammer
Operation: Recoil operated, locked breech, cam unlocking, modified Browning system. Lugs on top of barrel lock into mortises in roof of slide; breech end of barrel cams down to unlock
Construction: All steel
Barrel length: 4.75in (121mm)
Length overall: 7.75in (197mm)
Weight (empty): 37oz (1049g)
Sights: Square post foresight; square notch backsight drift adjustable for windage only
Comments: Well designed and constructed; a sound update of the basic Browning pistol.

If FN have appeared hesitant about the path forward, such is scarcely the case with FEG, the Hungarian state works, who introduced a blatant High Power copy for commercial export in 1982 and followed it shortly thereafter with a double action version called the P9R (top right).

The double action version required extensive redesign. The Hungarian engineers deleted the High Power's transverse cam bar, camming the barrel into lockup with the back of the recoil spring guide rod, which is secured in place by the slide latch crosspin. The P9R is a good pistol which will appeal to frustrated Browning enthusiasts.

DETONICS COMBAT MASTER MARK I

WALTHER TPH

King Leather inside waistband holster

Small auto-pistols of "vest pocket" format, in .25 or .32 calibre, have been popular in Europe for personal defence for around ninety years. More recently—in fact, very recently—chopped down 9mm or .45 self-loaders have tended to displace the snub .38 revolver in the same role in the United States. The difference in emphasis, however, has not entirely altered. The Europeans, while becoming more power conscious, have not fundamentally abandoned the view that any gunshot wound is horribly dissuasive: therefore, convenience is the main criterion for them. Americans, on the other hand, regard crushing power as vital, and therefore try to incorporate this into an easily portable package.

In Great Britain, all the guns shown here find a place in Combat Snub and Long Range Pocket Pistol competitions, where techniques of marksmanship with these particularly challenging arms get a thorough testing.

WALTHER TPH

Country of origin: West Germany
Type: Self-loading pistol
Calibre: .25 ACP; .22 LR also available
Capacity: 6 + 1
Action: Selective double action; outside hammer
Operation: Fixed barrel, blowback operated. No provision for cocked and locked carry. Hammer trip safety on left of slide
Construction: Light alloy frame; other parts steel
Barrel length: 2.75in (70mm)
Length overall: 5.5in (140mm)
Weight (empty): 11oz (312g)
Sights: Square post foresight with white dot inset. Square notch backsight drift adjustable for windage; white rectangle under notch for low light use
Comments: Introduced c.1969; excellent handling characteristics.

The .25 Walther TPH (bottom left) is representative of a new breed of gun in the European tradition. The designation stands for *Taschenpistole mit Hahn* (pocket pistol with hammer). It is double action on the first shot, with a hammer trip

safety. Its excellent sights, adequate trigger reach and easy release distinguish it from previous pistols of the type. The TPH is also available in .22 LR, and in either calibre it is capable of remarkable accuracy up to 100 yards (91.44m).

SMITH & WESSON MODEL 469

Country of origin: USA
Type: Self-loading pistol
Calibre: 9mm Parabellum
Capacity: 12 + 1
Action: Selective double action; no facility for cocked and locked carry
Operation: Recoil operated locked breech, cam unlocking. Rib on top of barrel ahead of chamber locks into mortise in roof of slide. Rear of barrel cams downward to unlock. Browning system. Hammer trip safety on left of slide
Construction: Light alloy receiver; other parts steel
Barrel length: 3.6in (91mm)
Length overall: 6.9in (175mm)
Weight (empty): 26.5oz (751g)
Sights: Square ramp foresight. Square notch backsight click adjustable for windage only
Comments: Note the bobbed

hammer. An excellent gun of its type, giving maximum firepower for the size.

The TPH dates from the mid-1960s. During the same period, Bob Angell, in New York, was experimenting with bobbed and shortened Model 39 Smith & Wessons, while in Chicago, Major George C. Nonte was trying to reduce the 1911 .45 pistol to the minimum possible weight and dimensions.

Angell's pioneering work was picked up by Paris Theodore of Seventrees, and marketed as the Asp. The firm has since changed ownership, but the Asp is still available as a semi-customised and very finely finished gun.

The market having been well tested and proved, Smith & Wesson included a chopped 9mm in their profuse range. Called the Model 469 "Mini-Gun" (bottom right), it is based on the 14-shot Model 459, whose magazine it will accept, although the 469's

SIG-SAUER P225

SMITH & WESSON MODEL 469

*Smith & Wesson handcuffs with Seventrees
concealment belt pouch*

standard magazine is a shorter one of 12-round capacity with a Walther-type finger hook on the front. The barrel is 0.5in (12.7mm) shorter, while bobbing the tang and using a spurless hammer helped achieve a reduction in overall length of 0.8125in (20.6mm). This was about all that could be done while still retaining a conventional recoil spring. Note that the .45 Detonics (top left) used two recoil springs, one working within the other, while the SIG P225 (top right) uses a braided wire spring.

DETONICS COMBAT MASTER MARK I

Country of origin: USA
Type: Self-loading pistol
Calibre: .45 ACP
Capacity: 6 + 1
Action: Single action; outside hammer
Operation: Recoil operated. Colt/Browning type link-unlocking barrel locks ribs on top of barrel ahead of chamber into corresponding mortises in roof of slide
Construction: All steel
Barrel length: 3.44in (87mm)

Length overall: 7in (178mm)
Weight (empty): 30oz (850g)
Sights: Square post foresight. Square notch backsight drift adjustable for windage
Comments: The first of the ultra-compact production autos, it has an excellent reputation.

The Detonics Combat Master Mark I (top left), which draws on Major Nonte's experiments, was introduced in 1977 and is the classic of its type. Eight years later, it was to a considerable extent (bushing and spring system) copied by Colt's Officers' ACP. The Detonics arm, however, is still 5oz (142g) lighter than the Colt, and 0.5in (12.7mm) shorter. For those who are concerned about weight—and that probably includes most people who want a gun of this size— Colt offer the Officers' ACP with a light alloy frame.

SIG-SAUER P225

Country of origin:
Switzerland/West Germany
Type: Self-loading pistol

Calibre: 9mm Parabellum
Capacity: 8 + 1
Action: Selective double action; no provision for cocked and locked carry
Operation: Recoil operated, locked breech, cam unlocking. External shelf ahead of chamber locks against forward edge of ejection port, breech end cams down to unlock. Browning system. Hammer trip lever on left of frame
Construction: Light alloy receiver; other parts steel. Stamped slide with nosepiece welded in and machined breech-block keyed and pinned in place
Barrel length: 3.88in (99mm)
Length overall: 7.1in (180mm)
Weight (empty): 29oz (822g)
Sights: Square post foresight. Square notch backsight drift adjustable for windage. Foresights interchange for elevation correction.
Comments: Breaks trigger return springs.

The SIG-Sauer P225 (top right) had a light alloy frame from the start. It is a foreshortened and redesigned version of the Swiss service P220: a factory modification designed to

conform to the dimensional maximum specified for a new West German police sidearm. Against competition from Mauser, Walther and Heckler & Koch, the P225 immediately passed a 10,000-round endurance test—the only gun to do so.

The P225 (or P6, as it is known to the German police) has largely set the fashion for what a modern pistol should be. It can be used instantly, without having to disengage catches; on the other hand, the finger need only press the trigger to shoot. The controls on the left of the receiver are the slide holdopen (farthest back), then the decocking lever that lets the hammer down safely. Beneath that is the pushbutton magazine release, while amidships lies the takedown lever. The single-stack eight-round magazine may be thought to be short on firepower by contemporary standards, but it permits the shooter to be offered a very comfortable and compact grip, which is a most desirable characteristic.

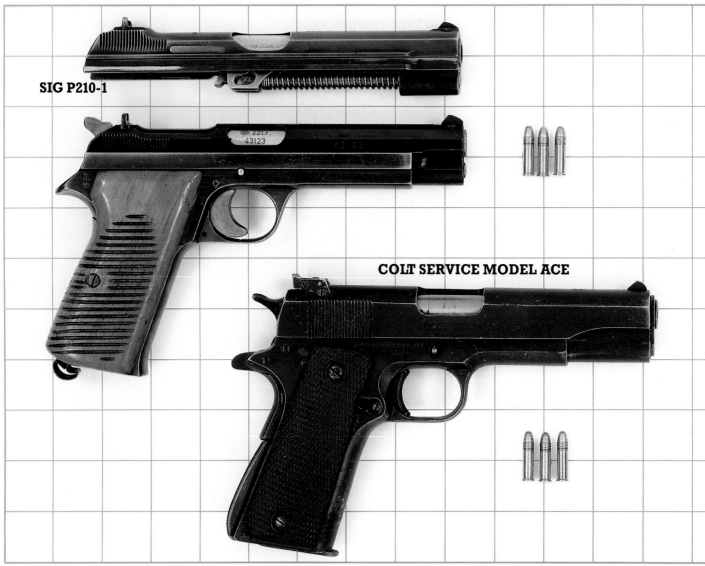

SIG P210-1

COLT SERVICE MODEL ACE

"I actually prefer pistol," a veteran rifleman once said, "but the consequences of going out of training are so painfully conspicuous. With the rifle your group may open up by 50 per cent; with the pistol it is more like 300 per cent." The rifle is held in both hands and is braced by the shoulder and cheek; sometimes it is strapped to the body by a sling as well. The pistol, in contrast, is just stuck out in the air, where the slightest imperfection of pull or surge in trigger pressure will throw it off aim. It also appears, to the shooter, to wander across the target constantly and never to settle down steadily.

To the beginner, this sense of instability is demoralising, and it is only one of many reasons why the pistol is so much more difficult a weapon than the rifle with which to develop a useful degree of skill. And that skill, once developed, must constantly be maintained by assiduous and regular practice, lest it deteriorate markedly.

In other words, it takes a lot of shooting to produce a competent handgunner and a lot more to keep him competent. The cost of ammunition can be intimidating. One cost-mitigating approach is to do most of one's practice with sub-calibre weapons which resemble, or duplicate, the fullbore gun in all respects save calibre. Alternatively, one can convert a fullbore weapon to subcalibre by exchanging parts or using units such as the Morris tube inserts with which British forces trained until recently.

SIG P210-1

Country of origin: Switzerland
Type: Self-loading pistol
Calibre: .22 LR
Capacity:
Action: Single action
Operation: Unlocked breech, blowback operated
Construction: All steel; en-block firing unit lifts out of frame when slide is removed. Slide runs in full-length railing within the frame

Barrel length: 4.75in (121mm)
Length overall: 8.625in (219mm)
Weight (empty): 30.5oz (865g)
Sights: Square foresight, U-notch rear sight, both drift-adjustable for windage correction
Comments: Superlative quality; an impeccable gun.

The best of the conversion units is that for the Schweizerische Industrie Gesellschaft (SIG) P210 (upper left) which involves swapping self-contained slide assemblies. Removing the disassembly pin allows one unit to be slid forward off the frame and the other to be slid on in its place. Magazines, of course, also exchange. The .22 unit is shown on the gun, with the 9mm assembly above it. The .22 rimfire is blowback operated, uses a lighter recoil spring, and has the slide machined to be as light as possible. Note the "saddle" ahead of the back-sight, where enough steel has been removed to shed another ounce or so from the weight of the slide.

COLT SERVICE MODEL ACE

Country of origin: USA
Type: Self-loading pistol
Calibre: .22 LR
Capacity:
Action: Single action
Operation: Unlocked breech, assisted blowback operation using Williams' patent floating chamber
Construction: All steel
Barrel length: 5in (127mm)
Length overall: 8.75in (222mm)
Weight (empty): 44oz (1247g)
Sights: Square format; backsight adjusts for windage and elevation
Comments: An excellent trainer; gun illustrated is ex-US service.

Colt was working on a similar unit for the 1911 .45 as early as 1910. There were problems, and the .22 Ace, as it was called, was not introduced until 1931; about 11,000 were made. The Service Model Ace (lower left) was offered in 1937, either as a complete gun or as a conversion unit. The former is the better idea. The Service Model Ace uses "Carbine" Williams' patented floating chamber, which effectively

COLT TROOPER

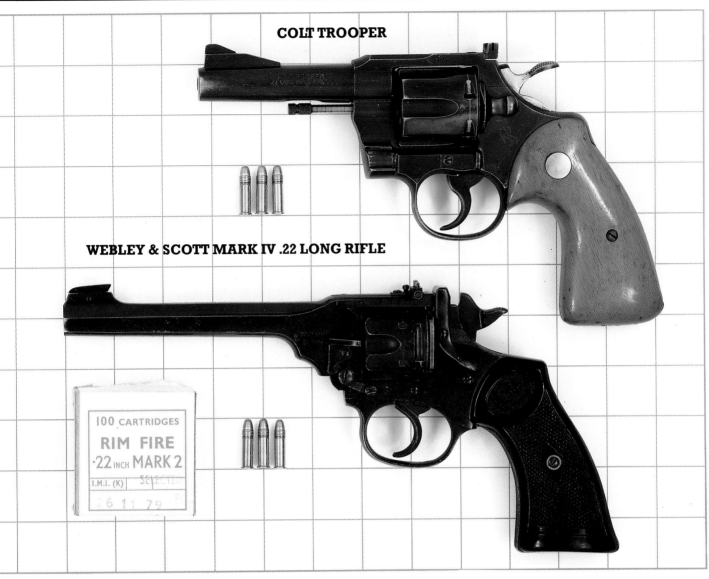

WEBLEY & SCOTT MARK IV .22 LONG RIFLE

100 CARTRIDGES
RIM FIRE
·22 INCH MARK 2
I.M.I. (K) SELECTED
26 11 79

magnifies the breech thrust of the .22 cartridge to the point that it will cycle the full-weight slide with full-strength springs. The only disadvantage is that the changeover is somewhat fiddly, since the ejector tries to fall out while the slide is being run on. It is much more convenient to mount it permanently on a frame and have a complete .22 understudy. The Ace is the only .22 in the Colt line at present.

COLT TROOPER

Country of origin: USA
Type: Revolver
Calibre: .22 LR
Capacity: 6
Action: Selective double action
Operation: Thumblatch on left of frame releases cylinder to swing out on its yoke; hand ejection
Construction: All steel
Barrel length: 4in (102mm)
Length overall: 9.25in (235mm)
Weight (empty): 40.5oz (1148g)
Sights: Square format; backsight click adjustable for windage and elevation
Comments: Perhaps the author's favourite gun.

Conversion units for revolvers—barrel-lining tubes and cylinders with subcalibre chambers that turn corners to get the rim underneath the firing pin—come and go. It is much better to buy a proper .22 revolver on the same frame as the centrefire. The .22 Colt Trooper (upper right) is a superb specimen of the type and served the author for years as understudy to a Python .357. Thousands of rounds were fired through it whilst practising hip-shooting against a clay bank, and thousands more were fired whilst practising each position of the PPC. Fire with movement, ambidextrous shooting and shooting at moving targets were all extensively practised with rimfire before fullbore practice began. The advantage of a conversion unit is that the balance, heft, trigger action, sights and grips of the primary weapon are preserved. Of these factors, grip configuration, grip angle and trigger action are the most important, particularly if one is practising

a semi-instinctive or reactive style of shooting. With an understudy, one wants to duplicate these elements as closely as possible. Sometimes, as in the case of the Smith & Wesson K22 and Combat Magnum, they can be duplicated exactly; at other times, as with a Beretta Model 71 understudying a Model 951, there will be significant differences—in this case, weight. But even if the identity is only approximate the use of a sub-calibre training gun has always proved to be of enormous benefit.

WEBLEY & SCOTT MARK IV .22 LONG RIFLE

Country of origin: Great Britain
Type: Revolver
Calibre: .22 LR
Capacity: 6
Action: Selective double action
Operation: Stirrup latch releases barrel and cylinder assembly to pivot downward at the muzzle, rotating on the hinge at the front of the frame. Ejection is automatic
Construction: All steel; black plastic grip panels

Barrel length: 5.9375in (151mm)
Length overall: 11.125in (283mm)
Weight (empty): 34oz (964g)
Sights: Square format; backsight adjustable for windage and elevation by opposing screws
Comments: A fine revolver which deserved much wider popularity. As is normal for Webleys, the stirrup latch spring frequently broke.

The problem with .22 understudies is that most people do not realise how valuable they can be. Demand is insufficient and they go out of production. The .22 version of the Trooper has not even reached the reference books, and the rimfire Mk. IV Webley (lower right) is at least equally rare.

Revolvers of this type currently available include the Colt Diamondback and the Smith & Wesson K22. Colt still offers the Williams' Patent .22 conversion unit for the Government Model, but it really needs a dedicated frame underneath for convenience, and that is not hard to obtain.

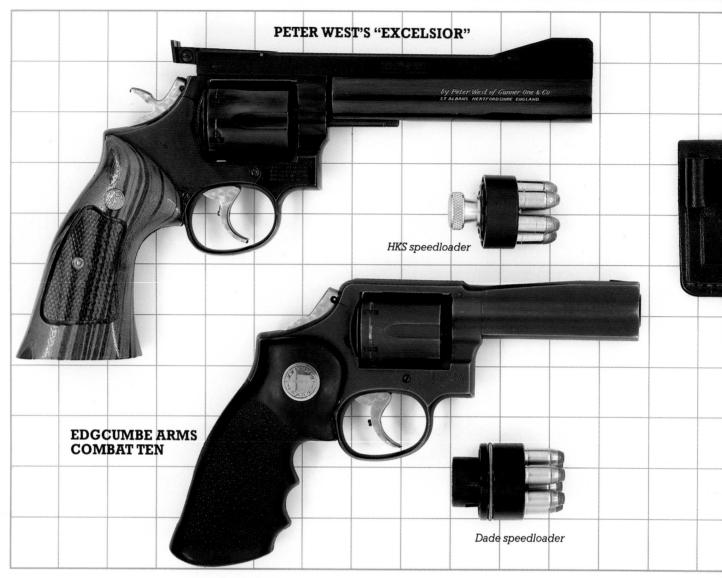

PETER WEST'S "EXCELSIOR"

HKS speedloader

EDGCUMBE ARMS
COMBAT TEN

Dade speedloader

Most competitive activities carry within them the seeds of trivialization—which are not long in germinating. Such was certainly the case with police revolver competition, which was inaugurated on a nationwide basis in the USA in around 1960, in an ambiance of enthusiasm for the practical benefits to be reaped. Study seminars for firearms instructors from across the continent were held in conjunction with the first several championships: the idea was to develop and disseminate the techniques that would help police officers to use their service revolvers—like the Smith & Wesson Model 64 (bottom right)—more effectively.

PETER WEST'S "EXCELSIOR"

Country of origin: Great Britain
Type: Revolver
Calibre: .38 Special
Capacity: 6
Action: Selective double action
Operation: Crane mounted

cylinder swings leftward out of frame for loading and unloading; hand ejection
Construction: Steel
Barrel length: 6in (152mm)
Length overall: 11.5in (292mm)
Weight (empty): 56oz (1588g)
Sights: Square post foresight and notch backsight with 3-dot system on Aristocrat rib. Backsight click adjustable for windage and elevation. Individually adjustable 3-range elevation cams
Comments: Police competition revolver built on Smith & Wesson Model 586 with Douglas barrel. Barrel 1in (25mm) diameter at muzzle.

PETER WEST'S "SOUVERAIN"

Country of origin: Great Britain
Type: Revolver
Calibre: .38 Special
Capacity: 6
Action: Selective double action
Operation: Crane mounted cylinder swings leftward out of frame for loading and unloading; hand ejection
Construction: Steel
Barrel length: 6in (152mm)
Length overall: 11.25in (286mm)
Weight (empty): 57oz (1616g)

Sights: Square post foresight; notch backsight click adjustable for windage and elevation. Foresight has individually adjustable elevation cams for three ranges. Three-dot quick acquisition system
Comments: A sophisticated police competition revolver made from a Smith & Wesson Model 586 with a Douglas barrel, Aristocrat rib and sights and Pachmayr grips. Detent in top of crane for forward alignment; barrel 1in (25mm) diameter at muzzle.

The worthy aspirations outlined above did not last for long. Within a decade, the line was dominated by competition specials like Peter West's "Excelsior" (top left) and "Souverain" (top right), which were barely man-portable and for which the shooting techniques did not altogether down-translate to service revolvers.

Ron Power, Austin Behlert and Fred Sadowski were among the pioneers of the competition special in the USA. Pip Watts built the first one in

Britain, and Peter West, builder of the pair shown here, is currently the foremost British maker. Nowadays, these guns all run much to a pattern: Douglas Premium barrels rifled for wadcutters; Aristocrat rib-mounted sights, with the backsight mounted high enough to accommodate a point of aim at the chin while dropping bullets into the chest, and a three-position cam adjustment for changing the elevation at each of three distances.

The most popular gun for the treatment is the Smith & Wesson, either on the K or the more recent and slightly larger L frame—although Sadowski specialized in building on Colt Pythons, and Jim Clark, among others, has built some fine competition guns on Ruger Security Sixes.

The popularity of the Smith & Wesson is due both to the low cost of the basic unit (thanks primarily to extreme efficiency in manufacture) and to its excellent mechanical design, which makes the mechanism comparatively straightforward

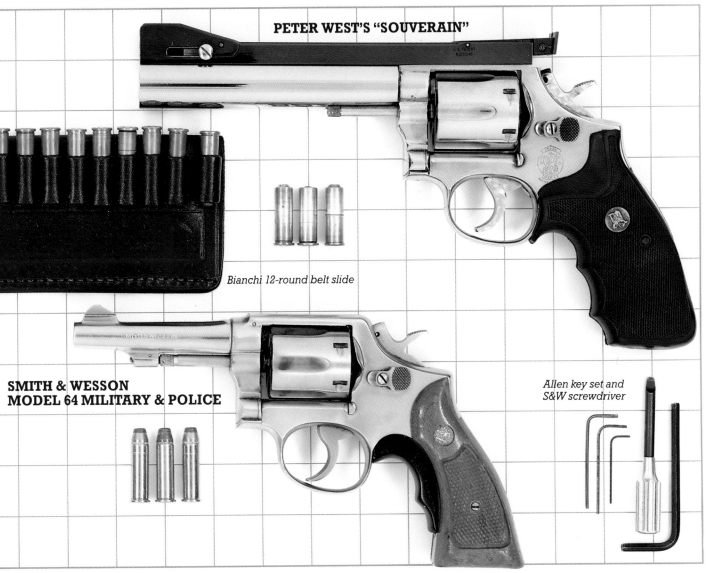

PETER WEST'S "SOUVERAIN"

Bianchi 12-round belt slide

**SMITH & WESSON
MODEL 64 MILITARY & POLICE**

*Allen key set and
S&W screwdriver*

to work on. The crucial adjustments of cylinder timing and trigger return are easy to effect on the Smith & Wesson, while the double engagement on double action gives a longer hammer throw, which allows a somewhat softer mainspring to be used.

SMITH & WESSON MODEL 64 MILITARY & POLICE

Country of origin: USA
Type: Revolver
Calibre: .38 Special
Capacity: 6
Action: Selective double action
Operation: Crane mounted cylinder swings out of frame to left for loading and unloading; hand ejection
Construction: All stainless steel except for hammer and trigger, which are chrome plated
Barrel length: 4in (102mm)
Length overall: 8.75in (222mm)
Weight (empty): 32oz (907g)
Sights: Square ramp foresight and square notch backsight, milled integrally into barrel and frame respectively; non-adjustable
Comments: Introduced in 1981, this is the stainless steel version of

the Model 10 Military & Police that dates from 1902. The gun shown has a Tyler T-Grip adaptor, but is otherwise unmodified

---

When a gun like the Smith & Wesson Model 64 is reworked for police revolver competition, the forward lockup may be remounted under the new barrel, but more often it is deleted and a sprung detent is built into the top of the crane. Alignment, headspace and endplay are all checked, but the heart of the job is the action work designed to bring the weight of the double action pull down from about 15lb (6.8kg) ex-factory to about 6lb (2.7kg)—and that perfectly smooth and even. Usually, the single action function is suppressed, since most competitors shoot double action exclusively, and eliminating the single action bent allows the geometry of the top of the trigger and the foot of the hammer to be modified to enhance the quality of the double action.

EDGCUMBE ARMS COMBAT TEN

Country of origin: Great Britain
Type: Revolver
Calibre: .38 Special
Capacity: 6
Action: Double action only
Operation: Crane mounted cylinder swings out of frame to left for loading and unloading; hand ejection
Construction: Steel
Barrel length: 4in (102mm)
Length overall: 9.3in (263mm)
Weight (empty): 40oz (1134g)
Sights: Standard integral square notch backsight. Square ramp foresight milled into barrel between integral protective ribs
Comments: A custom service revolver built on a Smith & Wesson Model 10, Douglas barrel and Hogue grips. Edgcumbe roller bearing action was subsequently replaced with a reworked standard action. Crane detent replaces forward lockup.

A kind of halfway house between the rusticity of the service revolver and the grotesque oversophistication of the competition specials is

the customised beltgun exemplified by the Edgcumbe Arms Combat Ten (bottom left). The barrel comes from the same Douglas blank as the competition guns, and the action work is similar, except that the mainspring is left full strength and the trigger return spring near full strength, so as to ensure optimum reliability. The integrally machined foresight and protective rails are a stylistic feature of this gun.

Edgcumbe is now defunct, but Peter West, Adrian Cook, Shield and Majex in Great Britain, and a host of fine smiths in the USA, do work of this kind, for the customised beltgun is much in demand. Just as the competition specials were illustrating what magic quality gunsmithing could create, factory quality control became sufficiently erratic that reliability and performance could no longer be taken for granted. Sheer prudence dictated that a gun intended to save lives should be attended to by a custom pistol-smith before going into service.

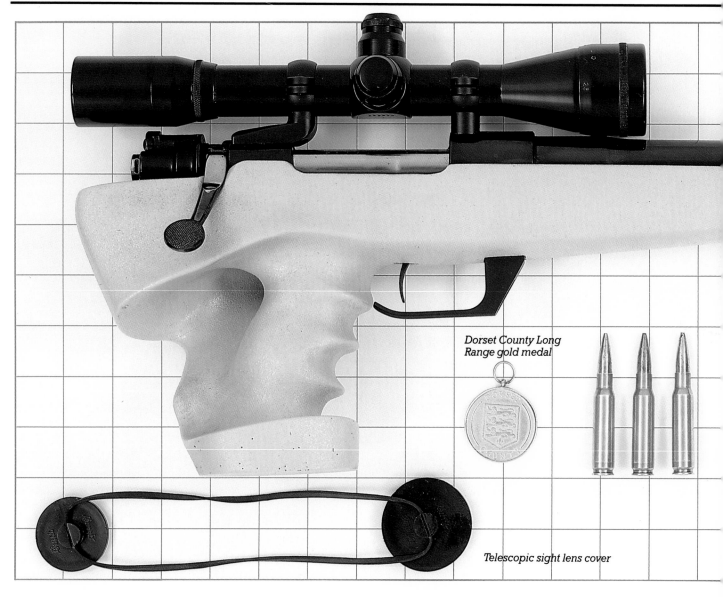

Dorset County Long Range gold medal

Telescopic sight lens cover

That a conflict can develop between shooting when viewed as a search for precision, and the same sport when viewed as a quest for physical skill, is something that we have several times remarked. It arose quite clearly with Bench Rest Rifle and with UIT Fullbore and Smallbore Rifle, and occurs in all sections of the sport as the equipment becomes more and more specialised.

The trivialisation of equipment—building to the rules—is an inevitable feature of any equipment sport. And at some point, a faction will arise claiming that it has all become plain silly. Rarely, however, will the factions coalesce more quickly nor the conflict be as unpleasant as it was with British Long Range Pistol Shooting.

The founder of Long Range Pistol was Gillie Howe, a much-decorated colour segeant of Royal Marines who, the story goes, used to while away the time on often-tedious NATO postings above the

Arctic Circle by plinking across the tundra with his issue Browning High Power. The temptation was to shoot at things further and further away, and he became quite fascinated by the question of long range handgun marksmanship.

Back at home port, and trying to raise money for the Royal Marines Pistol Team, the idea occurred to run a fund-raising long range pistol shoot. It took awhile for approval to filter back down the system, but Howe's match was eventually held at East Holme, Dorset, on 25 September, 1971, and eighty-seven competitors took part. A re-run the following year attracted 128 entries, and in 1973, the meeting was extended over two days. Howe left the Corps at the end of 1978, and opened a gunshop at Southbourne, near Bournemouth.

Pure accuracy is scarcely a question that fails to interest Howe. He was, after all, co-designer with Ken Pratley of

the Kengil Free Pistol, a manually operated single shot with a sliding breech block (like that of an automatic pistol) which was winning everything in 1980, ousting Pip Watts' Clansman and Dalesman bolt actions from the record book. This must have been particularly satsfying in that Watts was the high priest of engineering to the rules, and the antipathy between him and Howe was legendary.

The four Long Range pistols illustrated here and overleaf were designed and built by Andy Wooldridge of Shield Firearms, who trained with the late Pip Watts, and carries on the master's tradition of engineering to the brink of the rules in his indefatigable search for the last possible shaving of precision.

SHIELD LONG RANGE FREE PISTOL

Country of origin: Great Britain
Type: Pistol

Calibre: 7.62mm NATO (.308 Winchester)
Capacity: 1 round
Action: Mauser turnbolt action single shot pistol
Operation: Lifting bolt handle unlocks forward locking bolt and cocks striker
Construction: All steel. Carbon fibre/glass fibre stock. Built on Mauser 98K action with Douglas barrel and Shield trigger unit.
Barrel length: 12in (305mm)
Length overall: 20.25in (54mm)
Weight (empty): 10.27lb (4.66kg)
Sights: Burris 7-power telescope in custom mounts
Comments: Set up for ILRPSA Free Pistol "A" competition

The bolt gun is a Mauser-actioned 7.62 NATO single shot, with a Shield set trigger. Wooldridge beefed up the mainspring and reduced firing pin travel, thus shortening the lock time by about 25 per cent. The stock is synthetic; the muzzle brake is more for the benefit of the scope than that of the shooter. The gun was built for the ILRPSA's (International Long Range Pistol Shooters'

SHIELD LONG RANGE FREE PISTOL

Brass plaque in the form of the Shield Firearms trademark

SHIELD NEW SERVICE LONG RANGE POCKET PISTOL

Association's) Free Pistol "A" classification which is fired at 200 and 300 metres, 12 shots in 12 minutes at each distance, including two sighters. Wooldridge's load consists of a 168gr Sierra Match King ahead of 35 grains of Reloder 7 which, he says, should hold 3 inches at 200 metres.

Barrel length is restricted to 12in (305mm) and grip circumference to 10in (254mm). There is no weight restriction, but the tendency lately has been to hold to 4.5lb (2.04kg), which is the limit for the "Production Free Pistol" category.

A Free Pistol is a Free Pistol, and the Shield's stiffest competition these days is from George Swenson's phenomenally accurate Swing, another rifle-derived bolt action. The engineering principles upon which the Swing is based are Bench Rest proved. The ultra-stiff receiver uses a four-lug forward locking bolt with a lock time of 1.24 milliseconds. In 7.62 NATO

calibre it uses a 12in (305mm) Schultz & Larsen barrel rifled one turn in 12in. Swenson builds the pistols on his left hand single shot action so that the bolt may be opened without disturbing the right hand's grip.

With selected loads and fired with the butt rested, in usual Long Range fashion, the Swing is said to post dependable 0.5 minute-of-angle groups, and to be capable of 0.25 minute under perfect conditions. That is superb accuracy for a pistol, and no-one would contend that guns like this ought to be useful for much else. They are not, after all, meant to be pocket pistols.

SHIELD NEW SERVICE LONG RANGE POCKET PISTOL

Country of origin: Great Britain
Type: Revolver
Calibre: .45 Colt
Capacity: 6 rounds
Action: Selective double action

Operation: Retracting thumblatch on left of frame frees crane mounted cylinder to swing out for loading or unloading. Simultaneous hand ejection.
Construction: All steel. Glass fibre/carbon fibre stocks
Barrel length: 3.55in (90mm)
Length overall: 9.5in (241mm)
Weight (empty): 4.5lb (2.04kg)
Sights: .140in post foresight in Parker-Hale tunnel; Beeman backsight with 1.16in notch. 7in radius.
Comments: Set up for ILRPSA Pocket Pistol competition. Built on Colt New Service.

The other gun illustrated *is* a pocket pistol, however. It started as a Colt New Service (one of the largest revolvers made) that Wooldridge found in a bin at Edgcumbe Arms (Watts' firm) and subsequently modified to the limits permitted by ILRPSA "Pocket Pistol" rules. It has a barrel of 3.55in (90mm) with a maximum grip circumference of 10in (254mm), with no wrist support. The trigger is set to release at 2.2lb (1kg). According to the

rules, the sights may not overhang either the muzzle or the wrist joint. The foresight here is a .140in post in a Parker-Hale tunnel; the backsight is a modified Beeman with a 1/16in notch on a 7in radius, giving the same picture as the All Comers' gun.

The barrel is made from a Douglas blank with a 1-in-16in rifling. The massive underlug gives some forward inertia to resist recoil, in the interests of recovery rather than comfort, since the course of fire calls for five shots in 30 seconds, fired twice at 100 metres. Two sighters are allowed beforehand.

Wooldridge uses 7.5gr of Vihtavuori N310 behind a 185gr Sierra match hollow point, with CCI 300 primers. On a still day it will group into 3 inches. A .357 would be a better choice, Wooldridge says; the .45 Colt was just what came to hand. It may be interesting, but if this is a pocket pistol, Howe would contend, then the rules are wrong.

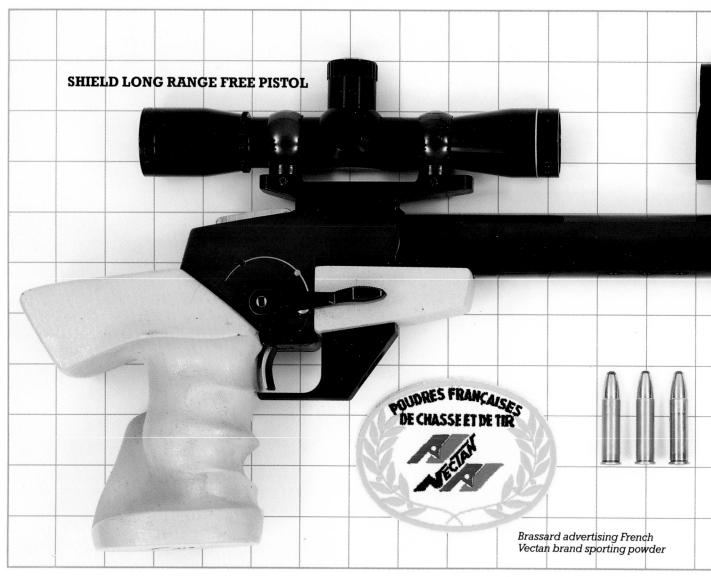

SHIELD LONG RANGE FREE PISTOL

Brassard advertising French Vectan brand sporting powder

The International Long Range Pistol Shooters' Association (ILRPSA), founded in 1976, took over a fairly well elaborated corpus of rules. The sport had been growing on an ad-hoc basis for half a decade, and the first national championships had taken place the year before.

Since then, further and welcome categories have been added, taking aboard, notably, .45 ACP pistols and muzzle loading revolvers. Long Range Service Pistol is still the only category that requires a "using" gun—in this instance, an as-issued Browning High Power. The other categories have mostly been customised to perdition.

SHIELD LONG RANGE FREE PISTOL

Country of origin: Great Britain
Type: Pistol
Calibre: .357 Magnum
Capacity: 1 round
Action: Single shot falling block
Operation: Lifting sidelever lowers sliding breechblock, activates extractor and cocks internal hammer. New round is introduced by hand.
Construction: All steel. Glass fibre/carbon fibre stock.
Barrel length: 10in (254mm)
Length overall: 15.25in (387mm)
Weight (empty): 8.37lb (3.8kg)
Sights: Leupold M8 4-power extended eye relief telescope on custom mount.
Comments: Set up for ILRPSA Free Pistol "B" competition. Designed and built by Andy Wooldridge of Shield.

SHIELD RUGER LONG RANGE ALL COMERS' REVOLVER

Country of origin: Great Britain
Type: Revolver
Calibre: .357 Magnum
Capacity: 6 rounds
Action: Single action revolver
Operation: Gate loading, rod ejection. Hammer must be manually cocked for each shot.
Construction: All steel. Receiver and most action components investment cast.
Barrel length: 9in (229mm)
Length overall: 15in (380mm)
Weight (empty): 5.47lb (2.48kg)
Sights: .140in blade foresight in Parker-Hale tunnel with custom adaptor block and extended sunshade. Beeman backsight on 3.5in extension with custom backplate and 3.32in x .085in notch.
Comments: Set up for ILRPSA All Comers' competition. Built by Andy Wooldridge on a .30 Carbine Ruger New Model Blackhawk.

The guns shown fall in Free Pistol "B" and All Comers' categories. Free Pistol "B" differs from "A" only as to cartridge. The latter admits full-power rifle cartridges, with all their ballistic advantages, while the former is restricted to recognised pistol cartridges for which commercial ammunition is readily available, the round not to exceed 1.75in (44mm) overall length. This will probably be modified in due course to accommodate the recently introduced .357 Maximum. Maximums are currently being shot and tolerated as being within the spirit if not the letter of the rules. Wildcat cartridges are out.

The pistol (above left) is chambered for .357 Magnum, loaded to maximum allowable l.o.a. with 180-grain Speer .358 rifle bullets ahead of 16.5 grains of H4227 with CCI Bench Rest primers. It will hold 4.5in at 200 metres. The gun is a massive falling block designed and built by Andy Wooldridge of Shield Gunmakers. It is sidelever operated and is fired by an internal hammer operating on a 47° arc. The trigger engages a free-floating sear, and is adjustable between 1 and 2.5lb let-off weight. The rules admit any safe trigger weight, and releases in the vicinity of 1lb seem to be preferred.

A maximum barrel length of 12in (305mm) is permitted (measured from the breechface). The grip circumference is subject to the usual ILRPSA 10in (254mm) rule, measured with a wire loop. Only the butt of the pistol may contact the rest. As a result, all British Long Range pistols have perfectly flat butts of ten inches circumference.

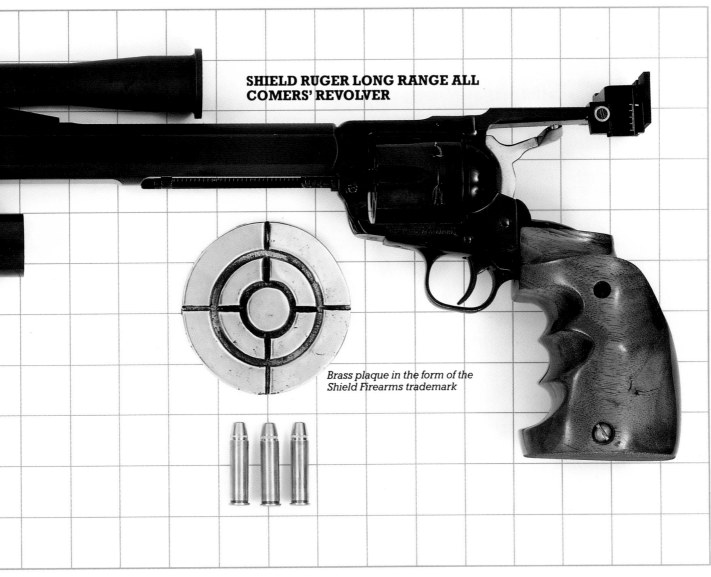

SHIELD RUGER LONG RANGE ALL COMERS' REVOLVER

Brass plaque in the form of the Shield Firearms trademark

As might be imagined, bench technique is even more critical than it is for Bench Rest Rifle.

The revolver (above right) is for All Comers' category, shot at 100, 200 and 300 metres. The 100-metre stage consists of two sets of 5 shots in 30 seconds, with two sighters beforehand, while the 200 and 300 metre stages each call for twelve shots in twelve minutes, two sighters included.

The gun is a Ruger Blackhawk, rechambered from .30 M1 Carbine and rebarrelled with a Douglas Premium 1¼in o.d. blank machined square, of .357in bore diameter with a 1-in-10in twist. The .30 Carbine was chosen because its cylinder is slightly longer than that of a .357 Blackhawk, thus permitting a slightly longer (0.1in) loaded round. When the .357 Maximum is legalised, it will doubtless become the calibre of choice.

Wooldridge loads 16 grains of H4227 behind a 180-grain Sierra Silhouetter and CCI 550 primers for 300 metres, 15

grains for 200 metres and 12.5 grains of Blue Dot for 100 metres. These are comparitively mild loads, he says, chosen to avoid excessive wear on the forcing cone. Higher velocities would minimise wind drift, but would unfortunately ruin the barrel too quickly.

The gun has been fitted with a wider hand to take up slack and tighten the lock up. Chamber/barrel alignment has been trued, the gun retimed and the trigger adjusted for a 2.2lb (1kg) release.

The foresight is a Parker-Hale tunnel mounted on an adaptor block with an extended sunshield (in case Bisley ever has sunshine coinciding with a Long Range shoot). The foresight element is a .140in post which matches a Shield 1 x 1½in backsight plate with a notch 3.32in wide by .085in deep. The backsight itself is a Beeman Unit extended 3.5in (89mm) rearward for a sight radius of 15in (381mm). The Beeman is an airgun sight—happily robust enough to take the pounding

that Long Range pistols generate, and is the unit of choice because of its very wide range of adjustments necessitated by the parabolic trajectory described by airgun pellets.

All Comers' was the original Long Range event, intended for biggish revolvers, out of the box. That promptly went by the board when Pip Watts introduced his Dalesman, a bolt action built on the Mannlicher action with a five-shot rotary magazine. The overall cartridge length rule has nursed the event back towards the initial intent somewhat. The rules now require either a revolver or semi-automatic pistol, and big Shield wheelguns rule.

In the United States, guns of comparable sophistication are used in Metallic Silhouette competition in "unlimited" class. But there are several important distinctions. One, of course, is that most Metallic Silhouette competition is in the "production" and "modified production" categories that

permit the relatively impecunious or non-specialist competitor still to take part in such events with a chance of success.

Second, the accuracy requirement in Long Range is much more severe. British Long Range matches are won with minimum groups from braced positions on paper targets. A one foot group at 200 yards will get you nowhere. But it is all you really need on Silhouettes. Of course, you may have to produce it standing, using iron sights and firing a load that will sledge over half a hundredweight of steel ram at the end of its trajectory. Alternatively, one shoots sitting, prone or supine, but without any form of artificial support for the gun.

"Unlimited" class caters for the engineering freaks; it is by reserving the rest of the sport for shooters that the International Handgun Metallic Silhouette Association has managed to enrol 40,000 registered competitors into its lists.

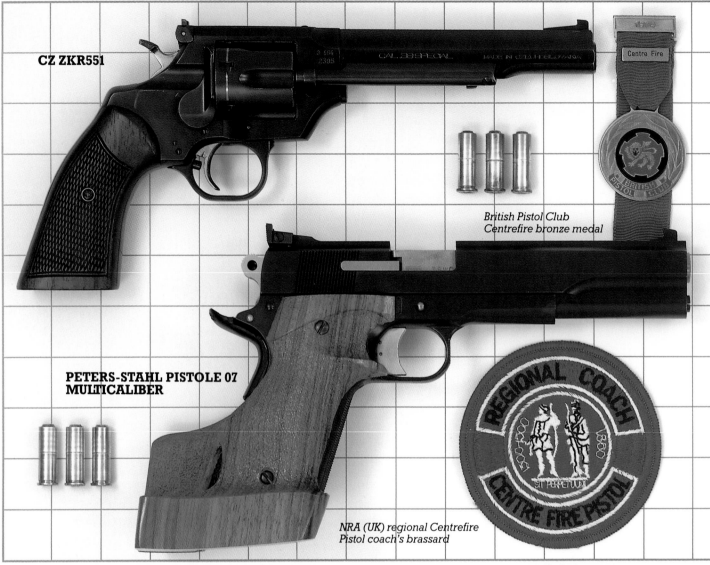

CZ ZKR551

PETERS-STAHL PISTOLE 07 MULTICALIBER

British Pistol Club
Centrefire bronze medal

NRA (UK) regional Centrefire
Pistol coach's brassard

The revolver, by the mid-1950s, was on the way out as the centrefire choice for 3-gun American National Match Course competition. Two-thirds of the course consisted of 5-shot sets under time pressure (20 seconds, then 10 seconds) and all shooting was with one hand, unassisted. A revolver shooter had his work cut out even before the advent of the alibi rule, which allowed reshoots in the event of a malfunction. That sealed it. A seemingly trivial rule effectively disbarred a whole category of weapon, probably inadvertently.

If the cylinder gun is no longer viable for the 2700 course, it remains a very vigorous contender in UIT Centrefire, where only one shot per exposure of the target is required. The course consists of 30 shots slowfire precision at the International ring target, followed by 30 shots duelling at a rectangular vestige of the old International silhouette. The latter stage, which the UIT now prefers to

call "Rapid", was shot according to French duelling rules. The target faces round for three seconds, during which the shooter must lift the pistol from a 45° depressed position and fire one shot. The target then disappears for seven seconds, and the shooter lowers his arm to the ready position. The seven-second interval allows ample time for cocking a revolver.

Up until about 1950, the course was generally undertaken with the Luger pistol. From the mid-1950s, American .38 revolvers largely displaced the Luger and were seriously disputed only by Russian revolvers.

CZ ZKR551

Country of origin: Czechoslovakia
Type: Revolver
Calibre: .38 Special
Capacity: 6
Action: Single action only
Operation: Solid frame, gate loading, rod ejection. Gate on right of frame rocks rearward, locking action and freeing cylinder to rotate clockwise. Cases are

manually ejected by a sprung rod ejector mounted offset under the barrel, as on the 1873 Colt
Construction: All steel
Barrel length: 5.9375in (151mm)
Length overall: 11.625in (295mm)
Weight (empty): 37oz (1049g)
Sights: Square post foresight; square notch backsight click adjustable for windage and elevation
Comments: An elegant gun, very satisfying to use and a highly effective match contender.

The Soviet revolvers were probably made on a semi-custom basis. Not so the Czech ZKR551 (upper left), which enjoyed a considerable export market. Introduced in 1957, the ZKR551 is a six-shot, single action, gate loading, rod ejecting target revolver in .38 Special calibre, conceived from the outset for one specific event. Distinguished by a very low bore line and a fast lock time, it is an elegant, impeccably built gun. Aside from the fact that replacement stocks are needed to avoid grip slippage in recoil, it has no vices.

PETERS-STAHL PISTOLE 07 MULTICALIBER

Country of origin: West Germany
Type: Self-loading pistol
Calibre: .45 ACP, .38 Super, 9mm Parabellum, .38 Special Wadcutter
Capacity: 7+1 in .45; 5 rounds in .38 Spl.
Action: Single action
Operation: Recoil operated. Blowback for .38 Spl.; cam-operated locked breech for other three calibres
Construction: All steel; early production built on Caspian Arms 1911 receivers. Hammer-forged barrels with polygonal form rifling
Barrel length: 6in (152mm)
Length overall: 9.5in (241mm)
Weight (empty): 43oz (1219g) in .45
Sights: Square format. Interchangeable post foresight; backsight click adjustable for windage and elevation
Comments: Calibres interchange by swapping barrel and magazine. Same breechblock and recoil spring used throughout. Base of recoil spring guide rod carries locking cams on upper surface. .38 unit is superbly accurate. Introduced 1986.

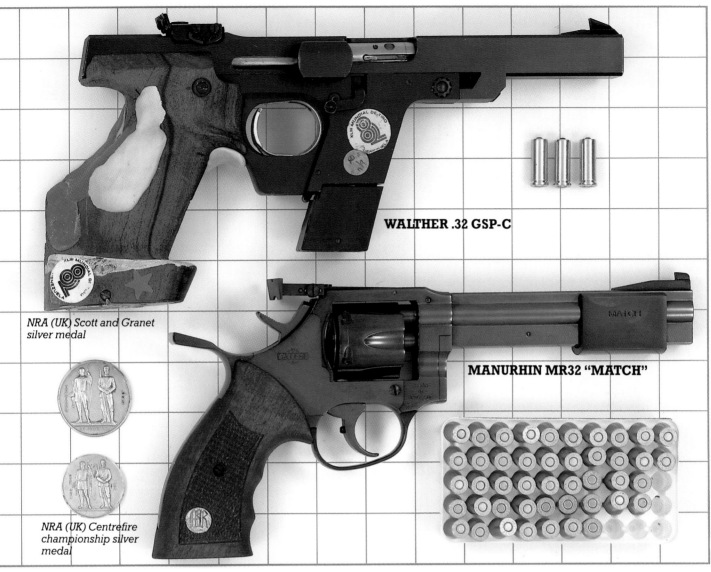

WALTHER .32 GSP-C

NRA (UK) Scott and Granet silver medal

NRA (UK) Centrefire championship silver medal

MANURHIN MR32 "MATCH"

Automatics normally have a lower bore line still, better balance, softer recoil and less disturbance on discharge. Consequently, .38 selfloaders were preferred by many shooters. The Peters-Stahl Multical (lower left) is typical of the genre: a 5-shot blowback, built on a Colt 1911 frame and chambered for .38 Spl. wadcutter only. Superbly accurate, it is thought by some to be more powerful than necessary. So to another rule change.

UIT Centrefire rules permit any calibre from 7.62 to 9.65 mm (.30-.38 calibre). But rather than scoring normally, the practice in recent years has been to plug gauge all impacts to .38 calibre. Therefore, shooters who insist on using the larger calibres get all the disadvantages of increased recoil, but are deprived of the compensating advantage of a broader hole in the target.

WALTHER .32 GSP-C

Country of origin: West Germany
Type: Self-loading pistol

Calibre: .32 S&W Long Wadcutter
Capacity: 5
Action: Single action
Operation: Recoil operated, unlocked breech, blowback operation
Construction: Machined steel barrel, receiver and bolt. Die cast aluminium frame. Hand detachable firing unit (trigger and hammer assembly) made of pressings
Barrel length: 4.25in (108mm)
Length overall: 11.5in (292mm)
Weight (empty): 45.5oz (1290g)
Sights: Interchangeable post foresight; square notch backsight click adjustable for windage and elevation
Comments: Available as a 3-calibre kit with conversions to .22LR or .22 Short for Standard Pistol, Standard Handgun, Ladies' Match and Rapid Fire Pistol.

The scoring rule can be seen as a backdoor effort to force shooters to give up "realistic" handguns in favour of guns like the Walther GSP32 (upper right). The GSP, in fact, was introduced in .22LR and .22 Short, for the Standard Pistol and Rapid Fire events, in 1968; the .32 S&W Long centrefire version came later. A brilliant design in every respect, the GSP has been one of the most competitively successful and probably most profitable target weapons ever made. The forward mounting of the magazine gave it a distinctive silhouette and solved a lot of design problems, but made overall length a critical dimension. In order for it to fit inside the referee's box and still carry enough barrel to reassure shooters (who are used to a long barrel on a target pistol), the heel support has to be cut short, thus sacrificing some stability of hold. A glance at the Bowler Olympic grips on the Peters-Stahl Multicaliber will make the point.

MANURHIN MR32 "MATCH"

Country of origin: France
Type: Revolver
Calibre: .32 S&W Long
Capacity: 6
Action: Single action only
Operation: Manual hand ejection; crane-mounted cylinder swings to left. S&W-type thumblatch clears locks at the rear of the cylinder and at the ejector rod tip
Construction: All steel
Barrel length: 5.9375in (151mm)
Length overall: 11in (279mm)
Weight (empty): 42oz (1191g) (with barrel weight)
Sights: Square notch rear; interchangeable square post foresight; backsight adjustable for windage and elevation
Comments: Designed especially for the UIT Centrefire match; superlative quality. Barrel weight is linearly adjustable.

For those who are happy enough to shoot .22 events with a .22 pistol, but prefer a gun for centrefire, the recently introduced Manurhin MR32 Match (lower right) was most welcome. Based on the .357 MR73, the .32 Match is single action only. The distinctive tang permits precise hand placement on the backstrap— a chronic problem with target revolvers. All the money is in the metalwork; the stocks on this gun are meant to be thrown away and replaced.

111

SMITH & WESSON MODEL 14 K38 MASTERPIECE

HKS speedloader

COLT PYTHON

Dade speedloader

Metropolitan Police range record medal

SMITH & WESSON MODEL 14 K38 MASTERPIECE

Country of origin: USA
Type: Revolver
Calibre: .38 Special
Capacity: 6
Action: Selective double action (also available single action only)
Operation: Manual hand ejection; crane mounted cylinder swings to left. Thumblatch on left of frame pushes forward to clear locks at rear of cylinder and tip of ejector rod, releasing cylinder to swing out
Construction: All steel
Barrel length: 6in (152mm); 8.375in (213mm) also available
Length overall: 11.125in (283mm) with 6in (152mm) barrel
Weight (empty): 38.5oz (1091g) with 6in (152mm) barrel
Sights: Square post foresight; square notch backsight click adjustable for windage and elevation
Comments: The K38 was probably the most popular target revolver ever made; its discontinuance in 1982 was greeted with universal incredulity.

The Smith & Wesson K38 (upper left) is probably the most successful target revolver of all time. Part of its long-running success was due to the emergence of nationwide police pistol competition in the USA just as revolvers were fading from the scene in National Match Course events. The K38 made the transition from favourite for the one to favourite for the other. Its only serious competitor, during the sport's initial decade (the 1960s), was the Colt Python (lower left).

COLT PYTHON

Country of origin: USA
Type: Revolver
Calibre: .357 Magnum
Capacity: 6
Action: Selective double action
Operation: Manual hand ejection; crane mounted cylinder swings to left. Thumblatch on left of frame pulls rearward to release cylinder. Rear locking only
Construction: All steel; stainless steel optional
Barrel length: 6in (152mm); 2.5in (63.5mm), 4in (102mm) and 8in (203mm) also available
Length overall: 11.5in (292mm) with 6in (152mm) barrel

Weight (empty): 43.5oz (1233g) with 6in (152mm) barrel
Sights: Square ramp foresight, pinned to barrel rib. Square notch backsight click adjustable for windage and elevation
Comments: Advertised as "The world's finest revolver." It is not, but it is very good nonetheless.

The Python's advantages were muzzle heaviness and greater overall weight, both of which made it hang more steadily on target. However, it cost nearly twice as much as the S&W. There was obviously an opportunity here, and the Smith K, whose frame and action could be salvaged cheaply from clapped-out service revolvers, became the basis of a new generation of rebarrelled and finely tuned competition guns, usually with very light double-action triggers, cam-adjustable sights for the three standard distances, and weighing in excess of 50 ounces (1415g).

Colt's E-frame lies halfway in size between Smith & Wesson's K and N frames, and by the late

1970s, S&W had visualized a critical gap in their otherwise plethoric line precisely at this point. There were several incentives. The big N-frame, designed for .44 and .45 calibres, was more in the way of beef and bulk than the .357 really needed. The K, on the other hand, was proving too frail. Police departments were trading up from .38 Special to .357 Magnum, in search of more dependable stopping power, and moreover were using Magnum loads in training in place of underloaded .38 wadcutters. The Models 19 and 66 were fine for the occasional cylinder of full loads, but a steady diet of Magnums resulted in swollen stop notches, frozen gas checks, stalled cylinders mistiming and general looseness. If law enforcement magnumania persisted, S&W's longstanding stranglehold on the police market was jeopardized. Also, there was the chance to recapture business lost to the custom shops, by undercutting them.

SMITH & WESSON MODEL 686

Austrian Jetloader

RUGER GP-100

Bianchi 12-round belt slide

HKS speedloader

US National Police Pistol Championships brassard

SMITH & WESSON MODEL 686 DISTINGUISHED COMBAT MAGNUM

Country of origin: USA
Type: Revolver
Calibre: .357 Magnum
Capacity: 6
Action: Selective double action
Operation: Manual hand ejection; crane mounted cylinder swings to left. Thumblatch on left of frame pushes forward to clear locks at rear of cylinder and tip of ejector rod, releasing cylinder so that it can swing out
Construction: All stainless steel. Model 586 in carbon steel also available
Barrel length: 6in (152mm) shown; 4in (102mm) also available
Length overall: 11.5in (292mm) with 6in (152mm) barrel
Weight (empty): 46oz (1304g) with 6in (152mm) barrel
Sights: Square ramp foresight with red plastic insert; square notch backsight click adjustable for windage and elevation
Comments: Built on S&W's new L-frame, intended to be strong enough for a steady diet of magnum loads. But, like all .357 revolvers, it works equally as well with any .38 Special load.

The stainless Model 686 (upper right) and its blued steel counterpart, the 586, both introduced in 1981, were Python size, Python strength and Python shaped, at almost precisely half the price. The new L-frame, as it was designated, has proved a tremendous success.

The L, in essence, is a slightly magnified K—some of the action components interchange—and uses, with only slight modification, the mechanism and format that Smith & Wesson introduced in 1899 on the .38 Military & Police; the forward locking lug, at the end of the ejector rod, was added in 1902. It is an elegant, nicely engineered action.

RUGER GP-100

Country of origin: USA
Type: Revolver
Calibre: .357 Magnum
Capacity: 6
Action: Selective double action
Operation: Manual hand ejection. Thumblatch on left of frame pushes

inward to clear locks at rear of cylinder and front of crane, releasing cylinder to swing out
Construction: All steel; action strips out of underside of solid frame; no sideplate
Barrel length: 4in (102mm) shown; 6in (152mm) also available
Length overall: 9.3in (236mm) with 4in (102mm) barrel
Weight (empty): 40.5oz (1148g) with 4in (102mm) barrel
Sights: Interchangeable square ramp foresight. Square notch backsight click adjustable for windage and elevation
Comments: Introduced in 1986, the GP-100 is intended to be the first of a new generation of Ruger double action revolvers that will replace the earlier designs. The GP-100 approximates Colt's E and I frames and S&W's L frame.

The only American manufacturer of comparable quality who can match price with Smith & Wesson is Sturm, Ruger & Co. of Southport, Connecticut. For the past decade, Ruger have been giving Smith & Wesson hard running in both official and civilian markets worldwide.

The introduction of the GP-100 (lower right) in 1986 consolidated Ruger's position as S&W's primary competition, able to match models and features nearly all the way across the range. And it was no coincidence that the GP-100 was another Python clone: the same barrel profile, the same frame size, the same heft, and so on.

The basic layout is that of the smaller Service Six, but the GP-100 incorporates improvements in the mechanism and in the disposition of metal, some original and some previously tried and proven in the mighty Redhawk .44 Magnum, introduced in 1979. It is an impressive gun and a worthy competitor for the L-frame.

British rules restrict competitors to one speedloader. The speedloaders (from left) are the Dade, the HKS and the Austrian Jetloader. The HKS can be used with wadcutters but the others really need round-nose or spire-point projectiles.

STERLING MARK VII PISTOL

HECKLER & KOCH VP-70

A sidearm is meant for constant wear and reactive use. In the latter application, it needs the balance and agility of a good bird gun to enable it to be brought to bear and to deliver a hit on the target within fractions of a second. In the former application, it must be light and compact enough to disappear from mind when holstered, lest it should seem a burden to the man who has to carry it.

The three guns shown here adhere to neither of these criteria: they are, rather, the most recent manifestations of the longlived urge to make the pistol over-perform. This proclivity goes back at least to the time of the horse-pistol, when detachable stocks were fitted in an attempt to create ersatz carbines. In the first place, all such attempts contradict the purpose of the pistol; in the second place, they simply do not work. The advantage gained by fitting a stock—which is intended to give greater support and stability and thereby enhance accuracy—is altogether nullified by the effect on the sights, which require a 20-inch (508mm) eye relief. A flip-over aperture would take care of this, but over some 300 years, only Sterling (see below) seem to have though of it.

HECKLER & KOCH VP-70

Country of origin: West Germany
Type: Pistol/Carbine
Calibre: 9mm Parabellum
Capacity: 18 + 1
Action: Semi-automatic; unlocked breech; blowback operated. Striker-fired, with a double-action-only trigger mechanism
Operation: Single shots only, with double action on each shot, as a pistol; optional 3-round bursts with stock fitted
Construction: Steel subframe; polycarbonate receiver
Barrel length: 4.6in (117mm)
Length overall: 8in (203mm); 21.5in (546mm) with stock
Weight (empty): 2.125lb (0.96kg); 3.44lb (1.56kg) with stock
Sights: Shadowbox foresight with polished side-ribs; square notch backsight, drift adjustable for windage

Comments: Bulky; extremely high cyclic rate on burst; trigger too heavy. Few have been made.

The Heckler & Koch VP-70 (bottom left) was introduced in 1978 and, so far as is known, is still in production, although few can have been made. The VP-70 was probably inspired by the selective-fire Stechkin of similar format, which was issued to non-commissioned officers and vehicle crews of the Red Army during the 1960s.

The VP-70 is a blowback 9mm Parabellum with a heavy slide and a heavy recoil spring to avoid premature opening. It carries a twin-stack 18-round magazine and seems to function fairly well. Extensive use of polymers in the receiver keeps the overall weight (without the stock) down to 2.125lb (0.96kg), which means that the VP-70 could serve as a rather voluminous holster pistol were it not for the trigger, which is double action for each shot and so heavy as to make useful accuracy out of the question in the absence of the detachable stock (bottom right).

With the stock in place (but not otherwise) one has the option, via the thumblever selector, of single shots or 3-round bursts. Cyclic rate is very high: the three cases are spat out over the ejection port almost simultaneously. Impacts are normally on a steep diagonal. The buttplate is hinged and the stock is hollowed so that the pistol will fit inside. The plastic plank can be worn on the belt—which rather makes our point about this whole category of weapon.

BERETTA MODEL 93R

Country of origin: Italy
Type: Pistol/Carbine
Calibre: 9mm Parabellum
Capacity: 15 + 1; 20-round magazine interchanges
Action: Semi-automatic; locked breech; recoil operated. Three-round bursts optional.
Operation: P38-type tipping locking block, one wing of which on each side locks into vertical mortises in the inner slide sidewalls

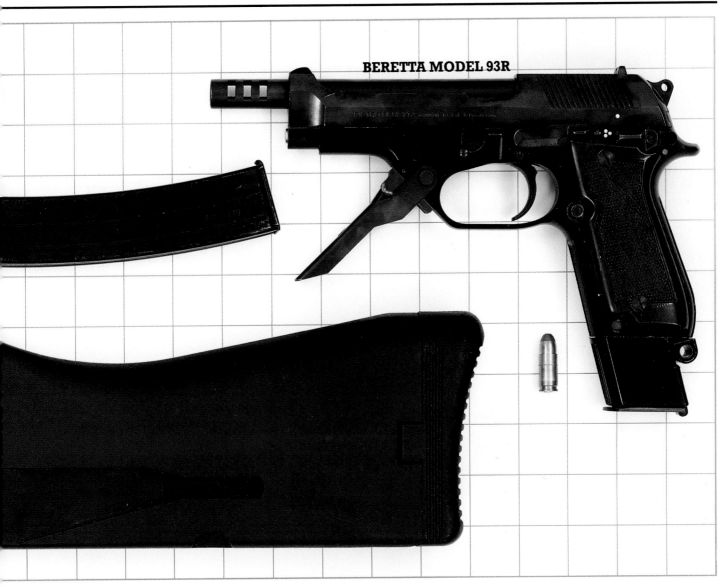

BERETTA MODEL 93R

Construction: Steel slide and barrel assemblies; aluminium alloy frame
Barrel length: 6.1in (155mm)
Length overall: 9.5in (241mm); 23.6in (599mm) with stock
Weight (empty): 2.44lb (1.11kg)
Sights: Square ramp foresight; square notch backsight
Comments: Dangerous to bystanders.

The Beretta Model 93R (top right) takes a folding steel skeleton stock (not shown) which is not as supportive as the stock of the Heckler & Koch VP-70, but is certainly better than nothing. The shooter puts his left thumb through the front of the over-sized trigger guard, with his fingers round the fold-down foregrip. There is a choice of single shots or 3-round bursts, with or without the stock fitted.

The Model 93R succeeded the Model 1951A, which was selective fire (semi- or fully-automatic) and had a larger, wooden foregrip but no buttstock. The 1951A was said to have been designed for

government close protection services—which was reason enough to avoid the company of important Italians! We found the gun to be controllable, on fully-automatic, in either the vertical or the lateral plane, but not in both at once. The lack of a buttstock also made it difficult to point.

The Model 93R was obviously developed to overcome or mitigate the 1951A's short-comings. The three-shot burst limiter and skeleton stock are both meant to enable the shooter to contain the shots on target, or at least to direct and control them to better effect. But getting from carry mode to aim is still an extended procedure, and if one is going to that much trouble one could as well use a carbine. Alternatively, a pistol would be much faster into action. The time spent setting up a 93R would be better spent seeking cover.

STERLING MARK VII PISTOL

Country of origin: Great Britain

Type: Pistol
Calibre: 9mm Parabellum
Capacity: 10-round magazine supplied; 20- and 34-round magazines available
Action: Semi-automatic; unlocked breech; recoil operated
Operation: Fires from closed bolt; pressure in bore uses cartridge case to force breechblock rearward
Construction: All steel; tubular receiver
Barrel length: 4in (102mm)
Length overall: 14.75in (375mm)
Weight (empty): 5.5lb (2.5kg)
Sights: Square post foresight; flip-over square notch or aperture backsight
Comments: An interesting weapon with a buttstock; uninteresting without one.

With its extended receiver and side-mounted magazine, the Sterling Mark VII (top left) reminds one of a Borchardt with handlebars—and is resolutely unholsterable. The 4in (102mm) barrel makes one wonder if it is really worthwhile; the frank answer is that it is not, unless one adds the optional plastic buttstock (not shown) to

convert the piece to a straightforward carbine. Curiously, the folding stock made for the Sterling Mark IV and Mark VI is not available on the Mark VII, although its flip-over aperture backsight seems to indicate that the use of a stock was envisioned from the outset.

In our view, the shooter will do best to decide from the outset whether he needs a pistol or a carbine, and to arm himself accordingly. It is difficult to foresee a situation in which one of the hybrids shown here would be a wise choice. That said, however, they do present an interesting challenge to markmanship: the development of the skills and techniques necessary to get optimum performance from them can be a fascinating and altogether worthwhile undertaking. Using these weapons over standard pistol and carbine courses will give the shooter an interesting benchmark for evaluating the merits and demerits of each of these types.

HUNTING
SHOTGUNS

Norman Cooper

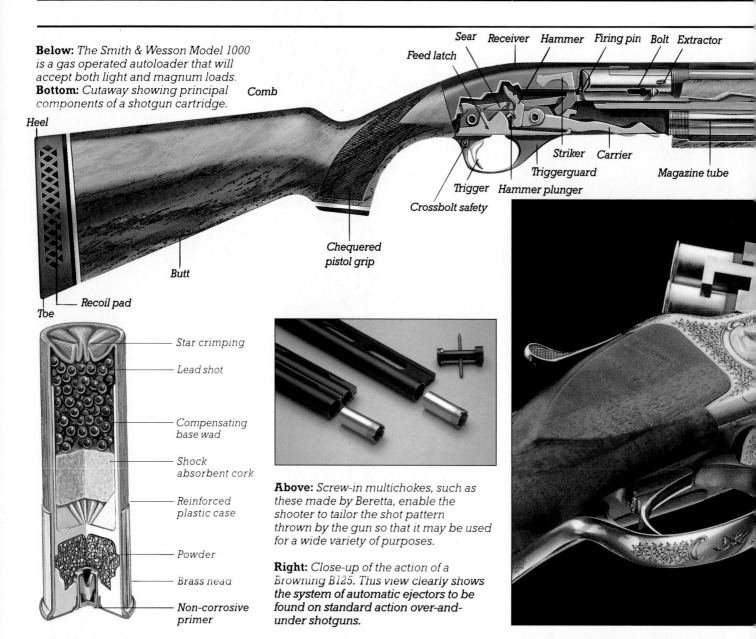

Below: *The Smith & Wesson Model 1000 is a gas operated autoloader that will accept both light and magnum loads.*
Bottom: *Cutaway showing principal components of a shotgun cartridge.*

Comb

Sear Receiver Hammer Firing pin Bolt Extractor

Feed latch

Striker Carrier

Triggerguard

Magazine tube

Trigger Hammer plunger

Crossbolt safety

Chequered pistol grip

Heel

Butt

Recoil pad

Toe

Star crimping

Lead shot

Compensating base wad

Shock absorbent cork

Reinforced plastic case

Powder

Brass head

Non-corrosive primer

Above: *Screw-in multichokes, such as these made by Beretta, enable the shooter to tailor the shot pattern thrown by the gun so that it may be used for a wide variety of purposes.*

Right: *Close-up of the action of a Browning B125. This view clearly shows the system of automatic ejectors to be found on standard action over-and-under shotguns.*

We know that our primitive ancestors killed fresh meat for their cave-dwelling families, for we have the bones of small and large mammals found in those very caves to prove it. It is probable that many of the kills were made with the aid of stones and, later, slings. The coming of bows and arrows—the longbow, famous in English history and legend, and the crossbow, which was more popular on the continent of Europe — led to larger game's being taken by arrow or bolt, but it was uncommon for small game to be so killed.

Even after the coming of the gun and the gunpowder to use with it (for until then there was no *gun* powder as such, the lethal formula being restricted to fireworks and the like), the taking of birds in flight was accomplished by the hawk, in the case of the gentry, and by the net by common folk, the latter kills no doubt being clandestine and illegal in the great majority of cases. Hawks were greatly treasured by their owners and good ones commanded high prices: it is recorded that in the reign of King James I of England, one Sir Thomas Monson gave £1,000 ($1,600) for a pair of goshawks. Given the value of money then and now, that was probably a greater sum than the £30,000 ($48,000) which a pair of best London guns will cost today.

The early guns were used to shoot at game that was motionless or nearly so, both on land and water. The shooter would conceal himself in an appropriate way: for the killing of wildfowl, shooters often employed what we would now call hides or blinds, constructed on the edges of rivers, lakes or meres. In 1645, Sir Edmund Bedingfeld wrote to Lord Bath, seeking his aid for redress against "such persons as daily do shoot in handguns in rivers and pits so as there is no fowl that do remain in the country. A man disposed to have a flight with hawks may seek ten miles ere he find one couple of fowls to fly at, where in all years past there should have been found in the same places five hundred couple of fowls". Sir Edmund goes on to say that the Clerk of the Peace in Norfolk (for it was in that most famous of shooting counties that he wrote) had in his book only 18 persons licensed "for to shoot in guns", whereas "I think that there are not less than three score that daily do exercise and practise shooting at fowl with their guns". And in a final note, Lord Bath is told that "if this be not remedied, you, with all the rest of the nobility may put forth your hawks to breed and to keep no more". I have rendered this in modern English, but the state of affairs it relates might perhaps have its counterpart even today.

Thus, firearms were used for the killing of quarry by the middle of the 17th century. At that time and for many years after, the fowling pieces, as they were known, were mainly of foreign origin, the majority coming from France and Germany. The locks were by this time flintlocks, and both these countries were noted for the rapidity of ignition and reliability of their locks. It was with the aid of a Nuremberg gun that, in 1726, one George Markland revolutionized the shooting of game when he shot a flying pheasant.

Gun Dogs

Markland was not only what we today would call a field sportsman; he was also a poet, and he recorded the event for posterity in a poem entitled "Pteryplegia or the Art of Shooting Flying". He was also one of the earliest "dog men", for there is a copy of this book inscribed by the author in his own hand, as follows: "This book is dedicated to 'Tracie' the spaniel, who did first spring birds to sportsmen and to his obliged and humble servant, the author". All this took place in the county of Berkshire and, as far as we know, it is the earliest record of a gun dog being used—which is not to say that there were no other gun dogs of the same period. However, it is from George Mark-

Action bar — Ventilated rib — Gas port — Bead

Barrel — Choke tube

Fore-end — Cylinder — Piston

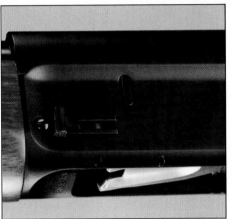

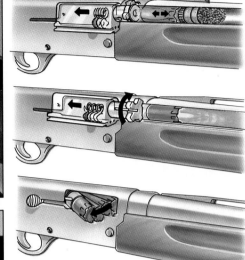

Above: *The firing sequence of a Browning recoil-operated autoloading shotgun. As the shot is fired the barrel and rotary bolt recoil backwards (top) compressing the breechblock spring. The spring drives the breechblock backwards (centre), unlocking the rotary bolt and ejecting the shell (bottom).*
Left and above left: *Close-up of the magazine cut-off and method of loading.*

land's reference to Tracie "springing" birds that we derived the name for a type of dog that is in widespread use today, for the same purpose as it was more than 250 years ago. Markland's gun was a single-barrelled one, but by the last quarter of the 18th century we had double-barrelled ones. Also, by that time, certain English makers had begun to achieve a great reputation for guns which were not only the equal of foreign arms but in some respects superior, notably in their weight, the English guns being lighter than those of their European competitors. Some makers turned out guns of such high quality and efficiency that their names became famous wherever shooting men gathered. The flintlock gun had by this time reached the peak of its perfection, with rollers on the moving parts, so-called rainproof pans and the fastest of lock times.

Perhaps the man who epitomized the gunmakers of this period was Joseph Manton, whose guns were of such fame and quality that by the early part of the 19th century he was able to ask, and get, 70 guineas (£73.50; $120) for one of his sporting guns, a sum possibly equivalent to more than 200 times that figure today. He was acknowledged to be the greatest expert on guns and shooting of his day and perhaps one of the greatest of all time. Manton

also made improvements in the actual shot which the shooter poured down the barrel of his muzzleloader. Unhappily, he died a poor man in 1835: like some of his illustrious competitors, he was better at designing and making guns than holding on to money. The same could be said of some of the other people involved with the art of shooting flying. No less a figure than Charles Eley, a name still famous today, lost a lot of money in making the very earliest cartridges for easier loading of the muzzleloader. Some time later, while working on his famous copper caps for percussion guns, Eley was killed by the explosion of the fulminate of mercury with which he was working in his Bond Street central London factory. The firm of Eley then moved their factory to Edmonton, then a desolate marshland area to the north of London but conveniently near the long-established gunpowder mill at Waltham Abbey in rural Essex.

By this time the percussion system had superseded the flintlock for both military and sporting weapons. It offered many advantages to both, for it was more portable, reliable and virtually weatherproof. By the middle of the 19th century, it had become almost universal, although there were still many flintlocks in use. Game was still shot, as it had been for the past century or more,

by walking the moors and fields and putting up game en route, or, in the more open areas of Britain, with the aid of pointing or setting dogs. These indicated the presence of game by "pointing" or "setting" it, halting in their progress in front of the shooter until he came up to the spot where the dog was pointing and then moved in to flush the game and shoot it as it sped away. At this time, the spaniels—both those which would "spring" their game and the cockers, whose speciality was the finding and flushing of woodcock in cover—pointers and setters had it all to themselves in the shooting field. It was not until 1840 that a ship put into Poole, Dorset, carrying a dog known as the St John (from its place of origin in Newfoundland) which, when crossed with a pointer, produced the first of our modern retrievers, now so universally used in the field.

Woodlands were shot in much the same way as more open ground, by walking. The mainstay of shooting in Britain was undoubtedly the partridge, a native grey bird. There are many 19th-century prints and paintings that show shooters in tall hats, with buskins or high gaiters up to their knees, walking through fields of stubble, grass or root crops, with a covey of partridges getting up in front of them to be shot with muzzle-loading guns. Bags were not as large as they

WOODCOCK SHOOTING.

Top left: *An early photograph of Sir Everard Doyle and friend preparing to set out for a day's shooting—a sport once confined almost exclusively to Britain's landed aristocracy.*

Left: *An engraving made in 1810 of woodcock shooting. The top hatted hunter is armed with a flintlock which with its slow lock time would have made wing shooting an extremely challenging sport.*

later became, but it is recorded that, in 1802, the Earl of Clermont shot 51 couple of woodcock before three o'clock in the afternoon on a late December day, on the estate of Lord Farnham in Ireland, using a pair of French double guns. A good day at partridges might produce from 20 to 50 brace. It was relatively uncommon for a day's pheasant shooting to exceed that number, and often the bag would be smaller. Grouse were shot either by walking them up or over dogs, while wildfowl were shot either on passage or by decoying them to ponds or waterways. There were in existence what were known as "bank guns", large and heavy fowling pieces, often of large calibre, such as 8, 6, 4 and even 2 bore. These were fired from the tops of the large dykes or "banks" which channelled water across the low-lying Fenlands of East Anglia.

We do not know who introduced grouse driving, nor precisely where it was first attempted—but we do know that by about 1840 it was not uncommon for guns to be concealed behind low walls or in natural pits on some moors, to which the birds would be driven. Bags at first were small by the standards of some 30 years later. By 1850 several moors had laid out "natural" cover for the driving of grouse, but the construction of what our Victorian ancestors

called "batteries", which we know as "butts", came later.

Two things helped to bring about a vast increase in the amount of grouse driving: the development of the railways, which made the North of England and Scotland much more accessible, and the realization that driving the grouse increased not only the amount of shooting but also the numbers of grouse. This is because the grouse is a strongly territorial bird: the old birds drive away the younger and more prolific breeding birds, so that eventually any given area will have fewer grouse upon it. Also, when shooting walked-up grouse, the first to rise are always the old birds in a covey, so it is almost always the younger birds, which rise later, that are shot. In contrast, when grouse are driven it is almost always the old birds which are first over the butts; thus, a higher proportion of these are shot, leading to greater breeding success in the following year.

The advent of grouse driving and the better moor management which resulted led to a vast increase in the number of grouse on nearly all moors (although grouse can be cyclical in number, because of disease and other factors). Bags began to be numbered in thousands per year, or even per day, where before a bag of 100

was considered good. Grouse, which have never been reared artificially, were then found in numbers which today can hardly be believed. The advent of the breech-loading gun, and later the hammerless ejector gun, came in time to turn this to great advantage not only for shooting but also for the economy of those parts of Britain where the birds flourished.

By the turn of the century, the grouse had established itself as the premier game bird of Britain for many people—and one man had established a record that will never be excelled. On 30 August 1888, Lord Walsingham killed 1,070 grouse to his own gun on his own Blubberhouses Moor, Yorkshire. Starting at about 5 am and continuing until 7 pm, two teams of beaters drove the moor (not a large one, by grouse moor standards) alternately in opposite directions through its narrowest part, which is roughly in the centre. Three black-powder guns were used, with two loaders. Legend had it that Lord Walsingham was so far from fatigued that he afterwards played cards until the early hours of the next morning. The story also relates that the feat was provoked by an acquaintance who had dared to suggest that because Blubberhouses was a little moor, there could not be many birds on it.

Above: *A moment's repose during a shooting picnic of 1896. This was a "golden age" of hunting when social etiquette and codes of sportsmanship came to the fore.*

Right: *Edward VII pheasant shooting, his loader standing by. Royal patronage of the shooting sports during the latter part of the nineteenth century did much to enhance their social standing.*

Lord Walshingham was acknowledged to be one of the finest shots in an age of fine shots. Alas, although his ancestors had been landowners in Norfolk for about 700 years, his income did not compare with some of his illustrious contemporary shots and by the end of the Edwardian period most of his assets had to be sold: the cost of keeping up with the shooting and social set of the late Victorian and Edwardian periods demanded not only that you were a first-rate shot but also that you had a very deep pocket. This was the era of perhaps the greatest amount of shooting ever done, not only in Britain but overseas. A number of British shots travelled extensively for their sport, for just as the railways had opened up the remoter parts of Britain, so the coming of the fast steam ship had made it easier to travel the world. At the same time, the territories of the British Empire had increased, so that large numbers of Britons were stationed in areas where shooting could be had for little or nothing. "Shooting leave" was part of the colonialist's job, whether one was a soldier or a civilian.

The big game shooting was superb, not only for royalty, viceroys and other notables, but also for the man of modest income. We are concerned here with the shotgun, and the chances for this arm, too, were some-thing to marvel at, both in variety and quantity: duck in Egypt and Kashmir, by the thousands at morning flight; sandgrouse coming in to waterholes in Africa and India, in similar numbers; ducks and geese in almost every river and lake in India in the cold weather; snipe in the "jheels" or flooded paddy fields of Eastern India; peafowl, jungle fowl and pigeons on the edges of the jungles which covered a great deal of India and Burma. Shooting camps at Christmas were part of the lifestyle of many of those stationed in India.

Shooting in the USA

The gun trade was able to take advantage of this upsurge in the sport of shooting. At the same time, the population of the USA was expanding at a remarkable rate. It is perhaps true to say that in the USA the emphasis was less on shooting as a sport but rather more on it as a way of providing food, not only for the shooters' families but also for the millions who were pouring into the United States from all over the world. The immigrants initially settled in the eastern States, but settlers pushed ever westward too. They needed firearms, as did the gunners who provided a cheap source of food in the shape of large and small game for market. Many of these used shotguns which had been exported from Britain, although their rifles were largely produced in the USA.

So much game was slaughtered in the USA during this period that one bird at least was rendered extinct. The passenger pigeon, flocks of which had, in the mid-19th century, darkened the skies for hours on end during their annual migration from north to south of the USA, were so reduced in numbers by mass killing, mainly by shooting, that the last survivor of the species died in captivity early in the 20th century. The commercial hunting of ducks and geese along the eastern seaboard and in areas along their main migration routes, the "flyways" from Canada and the northern states at the onset of winter, also reduced the numbers of some species to danger level. This led to restrictions not only on the length of shooting seasons but also on daily bag limits for virtually every quarry species in the United States, and to a lesser extent in Canada. Such restrictions are still applied, and by careful conservation, control and the encouragement of managed breeding areas, many birds and animals which, 60 years ago, were in danger of going the way of the passenger pigeon, now have thriving populations.

Above: *During the heyday of hunting at the end of the nineteenth century, gunmakers such as Watson & Hancock produced the fine shotguns and rifles favoured by European sportsmen.*

Left: *As large game grew increasingly rare in Europe, gun and dog were used to hunt smaller beasts. In France hare shooting became particularly popular.*

Right: *"Duck Hunters on the Hoboken Marshes", painted in 1849 by William Ranney, presents a familiar scene of wildfowlers in stealthy pursuit of their quarry out on the water.*

Further consideration of shooting in the USA is given at the end of this introduction.

In Britain, and to a lesser extent in continental Europe, the same threat to quarry species did not exist. The great estates remained virtually intact; farming methods favoured the successful breeding of pheasants and partridges in the wild; rabbits flourished everywhere; and marshes were largely undrained, providing great duck shooting sport. Improved moor management meant grouse by the tens of thousands. In the bogs of Ireland, Wales and some parts of Scotland there were even professional snipe shots, while the rhododendron coverts in the west of Ireland, parts of Wales and the West Country were the home of large numbers of woodcock.

Although the vast shoots were largely the sporting grounds of the wealthy, there were plenty of farms and smaller estates where shooting could be had for what now seems an incredibly small sum of money. Below the high-water mark, the foreshores were open to that intrepid breed of shooters, the wildfowlers. Armed not only with a gun but with a knowledge of local geography, winds, weather and above all the tides, they could have sport indeed in the winter months when the conditions were right, even if they earned all they got the

hard way, with blank mornings and evenings to make up for the occasions when it all came right.

The shoulder gunner had his sport, and so did the punt gunner, that loner among sportsmen. In the period between about 1870 and 1914, there were gunning punts to be seen on almost every suitable estuary and tidal river in Britain. In England, from Berwick-on-Tweed in the eastern border region around the coast to the southern shore of the Solway Firth in the west, punt gunners were numbered in hundreds at one time. In 1887, no fewer than 70 mustered in that famous Essex wild-fowling river, the Blackwater, for a flock shoot at Brent geese. Around 700 birds were killed in a coordinated effort on the flocks of several thousand geese which were then in the river, which at that point is almost one mile wide. Firing between 1-2lb (0.45-1.9kg) of shot and loaded with several ounces of coarse-grained black powder, the big punt guns were largely the medium by which numbers of professional puntsmen earned a somewhat precarious winter livelihood, in England and in several of the estuaries (mainly on the west coasts) of Scotland and Ireland. Drowning was an occupational hazard, for with their shallow draft and perhaps no more than 5-6in (13-15cm) of freeboard

punts were easily swamped in anything of a sea. In spite of much talk of huge bags, the average per shot fired was seldom higher than single figures over a season.

In addition to the professional puntsmen, there were many enthusiastic amateur practitioners of this most arduous form of shooting. As the 20th century began, many big-bore guns for the pursuit of wildfowl were in use: 10-bores, 8-bores, 6-bores (these were nearly all surviving muzzleloaders) and even 4-bores were built by gunmakers.

Pheasant and Partridge

Meantime, game shooting went from strength to strength, for this was the age of the introduction of pheasant rearing and, to a lesser extent, the rearing of grey partridges. The large estates of East Anglia, where the climate, terrain and farming methods so suited wild game, reared thousands of pheasants annually. One such, at Elveden on the borders of Norfolk and Suffolk, was owned by a famous shot from India, Maharajah Duleep Singh. He turned it into a magnificent shoot which, when it was sold after his death to Lord Iveagh, continued in even greater fame as one of the best shoots in England. Before 1914, it was not unknown for 20,000 pheasants to be reared in a sea-

son at Elveden. At another famous East Anglian estate, Euston, there began the system of picking up partridge eggs from wild nests, putting them under bantam hens and then replacing the eggs in the nest of the wild bird just as they hatched; the partridge hen having meanwhile been fooled by dummy wooden eggs which were placed in the nest when her eggs were taken. This drastically reduced egg losses from predators in the wild, and led to even more partridges over the guns in the autumn. It became known as the "Euston system" and was widely copied.

The gunmakers of the time vied with each other to produce not only the best guns but to sell them to the practitioners of this splendid shooting. The hammerless ejector was by now almost universal on the great shoots, although at least one famous shot, the then Prince of Wales, later King George V, shot with hammer ejector guns until his death in 1936. The famous London makers made singles, pairs and even triples, for on the very big days each shooter employed two loaders and three guns. Bags then were numbered in hundreds, sometimes in thousands. The record bag of pheasants in Britain was shot at Beaconsfield, Buckinghamshire, in December 1913, when seven guns killed 3,937 pheasants.

Less than two years later, in wartime, the record bag of grouse was shot at Littledale and Abbeystead Moor, Lancashire, when eight guns killed 2,929 grouse. In 1905, 1,671 partridges were shot by eight guns at Lord Leicester's Holkham estate in Norfolk; the record stood until 1953, when it was beaten by some 400 birds at Rothwell, Lincolnshire.

It is no coincidence that nearly all the bag records, not only for game but also for wildfowl, date from the period between 1900 and 1920, the odd exceptions being those for ptarmigan and black game. The former was set on 25 August 1866, when *one gun* shot 122 birds in Ross-shire, Scotland. The latter record was set in 1860, on an unknown date and to an unknown number of guns, on Cannock Chase, Staffordshire. The number killed was 252, which sounds incredible to anyone who has known Cannock Chase at any time during the past 50 years. But there were red grouse and black game in Pembrokeshire until the middle of the last century, and a few red grouse in South Shropshire as late as the 1950s. The Welsh record bag of grouse, of more than 1,500 birds, was shot in North Wales only some 75 years ago.

It was not only in Britain that vast numbers of game were found, for in many parts of Europe the nature of the terrain, the huge estates and the agricultural methods meant that the populations of game, particularly partridges and pheasants, flourished as never before or since. The plains of Eastern Europe provided (and still do, on a smaller scale) tremendous shooting: in Hungary, on 12 November 1910, nine guns shot 6,381 pheasants. Hungary exported partridge eggs to Britain for many years, until World War II ended the trade, and these were used to augment British stocks. (In the USA the grey partridge is known as the Hungarian partridge, often abbreviated to "Hun".) The marshes of Poland provided hordes of wildfowl. The British General Sir Adrian Carton de Wiart, VC, lived there in 1924-39 as the guest of Prince Charles Radziwill, whose estate in the Pripet Marshes ran to 500,000 acres (202,350 ha). Over 15 years, the General shot more than 20,000 duck to his own gun, beside numerous other quarry. More recent shooting practices in Europe are considered later in this introduction.

World War I caused a major upheaval in shooting and the making of guns in Britain. Very many shooting men fell on the battlefields, as did many gamekeepers. The manufacture of guns ceased while many of their makers produced military weapons or

Above and below: *To take a crossing bird the gun must first pick up the target's trajectory, swing through it, and fire. The amount of lead given depends on the* angle at which the bird is crossing and its speed. Follow-through is vital, most shots being missed because the swing is stopped as the trigger is pulled.

Above: *A handsome yellow labrador returning to the gun with a downed mallard. Gundogs have a crucial role to play in the field, finding, flushing and retrieving game—especially from water.*

Right: *In a butt on a grouse moor a gun prepares to take a bird while his loader stands ready. Driven grouse are fast flying unpredictable birds, capable of challenging the most experienced shots.*

components for the same. With the coming of peace, shooting got off to a slow start, but by the early 1920s the sport had recovered a good deal of its former character. However, the deaths of many of the heirs to the large estates and the increase in taxation, particularly death duties, led inevitably to the break-up of many of the great establishments that had made possible Victorian and Edwardian shooting on the grand scale. Good shooting could still be had, farming continued along much the same lines as pre-1914, with the horse as the main source of power, hay made much later than modern silage, corn cut with a binder, and stubble fields often left all winter to be ploughed in the spring. Thus, the partridge and rabbit flourished, while the wildfowler still had the complete freedom of coastal marsh and estuary. Good rough shooting could be rented for 6d (2½p; 4¢) an acre (0.4 ha); indeed, much of it could be had merely for the asking and the delivery of a brace of birds to the farmer at the end of the day. It was still considered that 1,000 acres (405 ha) was as much as a gamekeeper could look after well, and the big estates often employed as many as 10 gamekeepers or more, for even a head gamekeeper in those days was rarely paid more than £3 ($5) per week.

During the slump in farming which lasted from 1925 to around 1936, when agriculture began to revive somewhat, many farms were run on a "dog and stick" basis, reverting to the most basic methods. This paid very little, but also cost very little. It was not good for farming but was, in some ways ideal for shooting: plenty of wild corners, seeding weeds giving good nesting cover and, above all, thousands of rabbits.

Guns continued to be made by the thousands in Birmingham, but the output of the London makers was numbered in hundreds, not all of which were made wholly in the capital. Some were made "in the white", as it was called, in Birmingham and were then engraved, finished and proved in London. Birmingham makers varied from the large companies, such as Webley & Scott, Midland Gun Company, Birmingham Small Arms Company (always known by their initials of BSA) and W.W. Greener, all of whom made a gun completely "in house", to smaller companies and family businesses. The latter might buy action bodies and barrel tubes from foundries specializing in them and then do all the necessary work in workshops which had often remained unchanged since the mid-19th century. Guns by the hundreds were exported each year to the Commonwealth countries and

several companies produced guns especially for this Empire trade. Greener's actually called one of their models the "Empire"; it was a simplified version of the boxlock action that, as they said, could be used with little skilled maintenance and repaired, if need be, with little skilled knowledge—an essential requirement if the nearest gunsmith was several hundred miles away.

The London makers vied with each other to extol the virtues of their products, the overall tendency being to lighter guns than in the pre-1914 era. Churchill probably began the trend with his famous "Twenty Five", a gun with 25in (635mm) barrels and a narrow rib which subsequently became known, as it still is, as the "Churchill rib". Up to this time, barrels had generally been 28in (711mm) in length or more, but although the vast majority of barrels continued to be made in lengths of more than 25in (635mm), there are still those who prefer short barrels and several makers still produce them.

By 1938, shooting and gunmaking in Britain had recovered much of the ground lost through World War I, and in that year Birmingham alone turned out about 20,000 guns, with smaller numbers being made elsewhere. But in 1939 war came again, and once more the sport had to suffer. As in

1914-18, the trade turned to making weapons and parts for military use. Some small companies suffered loss by bombing, and when peace came in 1945 shooting was at a low ebb indeed. Penal taxation led to the large estates once more diminishing in size; wage increases meant that one gamekeeper had to try to do the work formerly done by two or three; and there was no food available to rear pheasants or duck or to sustain them later on.

By contrast, farming enjoyed an extremely prosperous time. Often, a farmer was able to keep a shoot going on his own land, or several farmers would combine and put their land into a communal shoot. Soon, the general public had more money and more leisure time in which to spend it, and participant sports, including shooting, became increasingly appealing. The motor car became almost universal and shooters thought little of driving several hundred miles for their sport. This led to great pressure on the areas where free shooting was available, notably the foreshores and coastal marshes, and by the 1960s all these were controlled in some way or other and the days of free access were gone for ever. Olders shooters resented this, yet could see no alternative if the marshes were not to be overshot.

Sadly, the same era saw the end of the vast majority of the British gun trade. Some firms did not survive the war, others folded in the years following it. By the 1960s, three of the four large makers mentioned above had gone, and by the 1980s Britain's last surviving quantity maker, Webley & Scott, had also ceased to make shotguns, the company now making only air guns. Many London makers had closed, amalgamated or retained their names purely as a marketing device. The equivalent situation in the USA and Europe is discussed below.

The Current Situation

What is the position today, in the late 1980s? There is an increasing interest in shooting of all kinds. Pheasant shooting is supported by a large national rearing programme, ranging from large shoots rearing thousands to a group of friends who own or rent some land and turn down a few dozen birds. The virtual demise of the wild grey partridge as a result of farming methods totally unsuited to its wellbeing has to some extent been compensated for by increased rearing of the red-legged variety—although this could be at risk as a result of EEC legislation, drawn up by bureaucrats who may never have seen a partridge in the wild. The grouse generally is in decline and much time and money is being spent to find out why. Drainage of many wetlands has affected the numbers of wildfowl far more than shooting pressures, while waders such as snipe have also suffered from habitat destruction.

Increasingly, shooting is being let by the day and by the bird—and providing that the sport is of good quality, I see nothing wrong in that. For the cream of the sport, driven grouse shooting, increasing demand and reduced numbers of birds has meant that the cost has escalated beyond all reason. In contrast, the far greater numbers of pheasants and partridges now being reared has resulted in this kind of shooting remaining good value for money. Such shooting is to be had all over Britain and even abroad, where in recent years even the Communist countries (or some of them) have realized that their game stocks are a saleable asset with which to earn foreign currency.

The regrettable shrinking of the British gun trade has been offset by a vast increase in the number of foreign guns marketed, many with the game shot and rough shooter in mind and some even for the specialist wildfowler. The London "carriage trade", although small in numbers, still flourishes, but for the vast

Above: *A typical American hunting scene: one man, his dog, and a downed bird. The gun, less typically, is a Finnish Valmet; the receiver also accepts double rifle or combination shotgun/rifle barrels.*

Left: *The American hunter is not inhibited by social convention from using magazine-fed shotguns. Here a Benelli Super 90 allows the shooter fast reloads when tackling a bird going away.*

majority of shooters, a good foreign gun has replaced the English one of their fathers and grandfathers—unless they prefer to spend perhaps an even larger sum of money on a second-hand English gun.

The Great Divide

Working guns, like any tool, normally evolve to the task and in this respect it is instructive to contrast the types of shooting, and the types of gun used for it, in Britain and the United States. Briefly, in the UK the game comes to the gun while in the US, the gun goes to the game.

The American sportsman shoots an occasional bird; his English counterpart harvests a feathered crop. The American restricted by tight bag limits, simply has no concept of the volume of shooting that the Englishman takes for granted. If the American has less sport, he also works a lot harder for it. The techniques of wildfowling are similar, but the approach to upland game is quite different. Even on commercial game farms—a recent phenomenon in the US—the birds are walked up, with or without the aid of pointers. The English "rough shooter" walks up birds, but the vast majority of game is driven over the guns. And on a good day, the shooting will be

quite brisk. The American, in brief, walks much but shoots little; the Englishman shoots prodigiously, walks only from the Land Rover to the butts, and, with any luck, someone else will carry his gun for him.

The ideal gun for English conditions would be slightly on the heavy side, to swing well. The volume of shooting would put a premium on magazine capacity and recoil absorption. The Remington 1100, in a word. The American, who is lucky to average a shot every 500 yards (457m) of the great trek, would be well equipped with a light double, easy to carry and quick to mount on a rising bird. As we all know, it has actually worked out precisely the other way round. The reasons for this are social and historical.

In Britain, as in most of Europe, game is property, and hunting, from medieval times, has been a prerogative first of the aristocracy and then of the gentry. The peasantry poached if they dared. America emphatically repudiated this tradition. Game was a public resource and even private land, unless posted to the contrary, was open to shooting in season. Bag limits were adjusted to ensure that the resource was equally shared; landowners fared no better than anyone else. In Britain, wingshooting was developed to an art form

during a period of rising upper and upper middle class affluence; it reached its peak during the apogee of empire. The daily bag, on great estates, would run to thousands, and a dedicated wingshot, like the Earl de Grey, would down half a million birds in a lifetime's sport.

The shotgun, in hands like these, became a magic wand. The firepower problem was overcome by using braces and trebles of matched guns, with loaders handing them forward. With the birds overhead, the shooting was incredibly fast. A deft-handling gun was essential, and the recoil problem was overcome with light loads, for ranges were short. The aristocracy set the style; the gentry emulated and the common folk never got a glimpse, unless they were gamekeepers. They used boxlocks; the gentry used sidelocks. Even today, magazine-fed shotguns are not permitted on many shoots, while over-unders are still sometimes looked at askance. Such is the power of snobbery.

The American was locked into no such syndrome. He had no loader behind him, and when a covey rose, he might need a third or fourth shot to down a wounded bird. His shots would mostly be going away, in which case heavier loads and a

Above: *Part of the "feathered crop" of grouse garnered during a day's shooting in the UK. In the great days of the British Empire, the daily bag on a large estate might run into thousands.*

Left: *Taking a pheasant high overhead during a day's rough shooting in England. Such birds will be walked up, but more commonly shooting in the UK involves game being driven over the guns.*

recoil-absorbing gun were called for. His incoming shots would either be decoyed duck, in which case heavy loads were the order of the day, or else they would be dove coming to feed, in which case the action would be fast and the shots frustratingly difficult; in such circumstances four or five in reserve would not be surplus to requirement.

Finally the American had no inbuilt social inhibitions against mechanical development, nor was there an operational taboo against repeating mechanisms. American sport tended to be a solitary enterprise; in Britain it was a social occasion. The evolution, or lack thereof, in each country had a logic, but it was not the logic that a superficially objective appraisal might have anticipated. The exception to the general scheme of things is wildfowling. Ducks are ducks and mud is mud. There is little social cachet in skulking pre-dawn on the foreshore, with the weather its foulest when shooting is best. Then, the Englishman is likely to use a self-loader, and apologises to no one. But he is a different species of sportsman, whereas his American counterpart may be out after partridge or pheasant the next day, and as often as not taking along with him the same gun, if not perhaps the same dog.

Apart from a tendency to stack the barrels one atop the other, some would contend, sporting shotguns have not radically changed across the centuries. Indeed, the optimum balance and stock dimensions for semi-instinctive wingshooting were worked out in flintlock days, and subsequent ignition systems have merely been "dropped into the design", as one might put it.

INTERARMCO REPRODUCTION PERCUSSION SINGLE MUZZLE-LOADING SHOTGUN

Country of origin: Italy
Type: Percussion
Calibre: 12 gauge
Capacity: 1
Action: Percussion
Operation: Muzzle loading
Construction: Steel
Barrel length: 34.5in (876mm)
Length overall: 51in (1295mm)
Weight (empty): 7lb (3.18kg)
Sights: Brass bead.

An original flintlock sporting gun would be too valuable to shoot. So would a "best" percussion piece, as far as that goes, but here the reproduction-mongers have come to our rescue. Italian and Spanish makers currently offer both single- and double-barrelled percussion guns of acceptable quality, such as the Italian single by Interarmco (bottom), which is patterned after an original by the great Scottish gunmaker Alexander Henry. The shot flask and cap box are necessary accoutrements, as would be a powder flask and plenty of cloth or tow wadding to be used to keep the shot in place atop the powder.

The percussion system, a vast improvement upon the flintlock which preceded it, lasted only a relatively short time, from about 1836 until the first breechloaders, in pin-fire, rim fire and centre fire, came on to the market about 30 years later. By the 1880s, muzzleloaders had ceased to be made except for certain colonial markets. For many years, the indigenous inhabitants of certain areas were forbidden to possess breechloading guns, and percussion muzzleloaders were being exported to Africa from both Birmingham and Liège as late as the 1930s.

HILL DOUBLE 10 BORE

Country of origin: Great Britain
Type: External hammer breechloader
Calibre: 10 gauge
Capacity: 2
Action: Drop down
Operation: Manual
Construction: Damascus or twist barrels; steel action
Barrel length: 31.25in (794mm)
Length overall: 47.25in (1200mm)
Weight (empty): 9.69lb (4.4kg)
Sights: Brass bead.

The double-trigger side-by-side Hill shotgun (centre) is a prime example of a fairly early breechloading wildfowling gun of the black powder era, before the development, or widespread popularity, of inside-hammer mechanisms.

Proved only for black powder, it is capable of projecting 2oz (57g) of shot, more than the average modern 10-bore nitro powder cartridge: the slight extra chore of having to load one's own cartridges is more than compensated for by the pleasant and yet effective way in which it shoots 2oz (57g) of shot ahead of 4 drams (15ml) of black powder. The larger calibre guns handle larger shot, which helps with the longer ranges at which wildfowl are often required to be shot if one is to take advantage of what may be rare opportunities at wild geese or high-flying ducks. The rubber recoil pad on the gun shown is a modern replacement for a much older one that had crumbled away. The 10-bore cartridges shown are loaded with 2oz (57g) of No 3 shot: shot sizes such as No 1 or No 3 stack better in the larger cartridge cases than they do even in the 12-bore cartridge case.

The gun shown can be dated with reasonable accuracy, since it has rebounding locks,

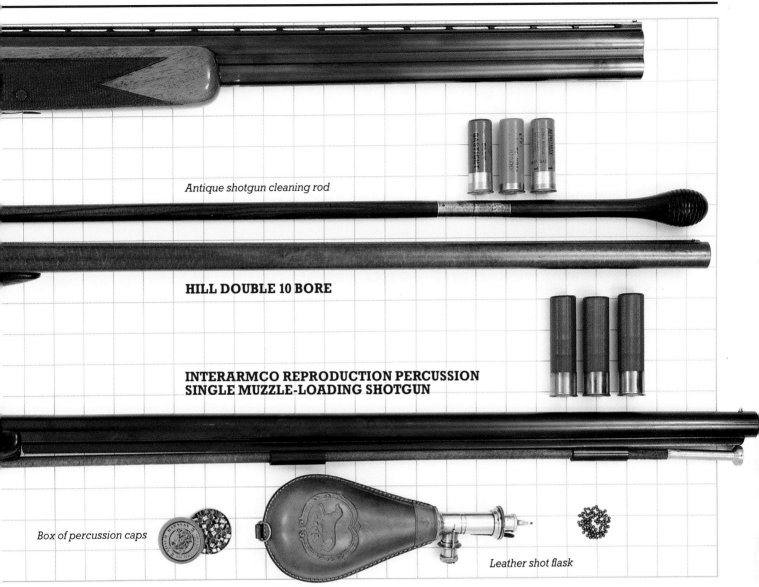

Antique shotgun cleaning rod

HILL DOUBLE 10 BORE

INTERARMCO REPRODUCTION PERCUSSION
SINGLE MUZZLE-LOADING SHOTGUN

Box of percussion caps

Leather shot flask

Above: *Barrel manufacture at the factory of W.W. Greener, one of the great 19th Century gunmakers.*

which were not common until the early 1870s, and yet still has a side nail for securing the fore end, which is a direct survival from the muzzleloader. By about 1875, the side nail had given way to the snap-on catch fore end—so this gun can be dated between 1870 and 1875. It was proved in Birmingham, where there were then three listed gunmakers named Hill.

BROWNING SPECIAL SKEET

Country of origin: Belgium
Type: Over and under
Calibre: 12 gauge
Capacity: 2
Action: Drop down
Operation: Top lever opening
Construction: Steel
Barrel length: 26.5in (673mm)
Length overall: 43.5in (1105mm)
Weight (empty): 7.5lb (3.4kg)
Sights: Brass bead.

Side-by-sides are so elegant and efficient that there seemed little real reason to give the barrels a quarter turn, although London gunsmiths would provide them in that form for the occasional eccentric customer. The real popularity of the stacked-barrel scattergun, which nowadays has become overwhelming, dates from John M. Browning's design of the early 1920s, which is still in manufacture and is still one of the world's most prestigious factory-built guns.

The gun shown (top) is a Special Skeet Model made by FN of Belgium, chiefly for the North American market, in the 1950s and 1960s. It is marked "Browning Arms Co.", with the St. Louis and Montreal addresses. The scroll engraving pattern differs from the border engraving of acanthus leaves which characterized the guns exported to Britain; these also lacked the engraved bust of John Moses Browning which appeared underneath the action of the American guns. The stock has a half pistol grip rather than the full pistol grip now almost universal on over-and-unders.

Most skeet guns of this period had barrels which were marked "Skeet 1" and "Skeet 2", the chokes differing slightly: one usually bearing around five points of choke or improved cylinder, and the other around eight or nine points, quarter choke. The theory behind this was that you shot the slightly tighter-choked barrel at the outgoing target, leaving the more open barrel to deal with the incomer. Since most guns by this time had selective single-trigger actions, the shooter could choose which way round to fire them.

Like all Browning skeet guns of its period, the gun shown has about four points of choke in each barrel; so, in fact, the selection of barrel makes no difference. Over the 25 years or so since this gun was made, skeet guns have tended to be made with no choke at all in the barrels; in fact, even "trumpet choking" has been seen, whereby the barrels actually open out at the muzzles to give the widest possible spread to the shot pattern.

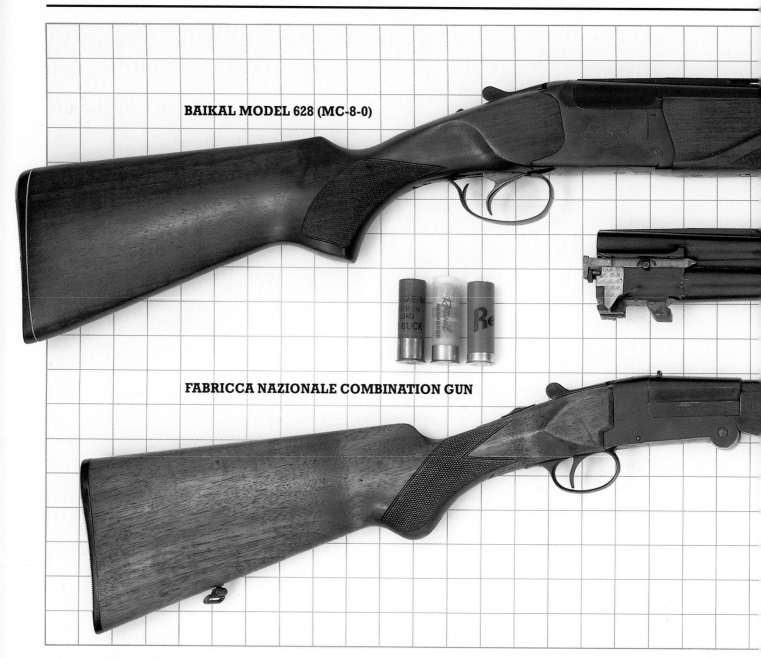

BAIKAL MODEL 628 (MC-8-0)

FABRICCA NAZIONALE COMBINATION GUN

Just as Lord Acton saw history as the chronicle of liberal democracy's triumphal ascendance, so do most students of firearms look on their development as a linearly progressive search for firepower. But in neither case is this the only vantage point; as far as firearms go, it is one of several that make sense. However, if one puts oneself in the position of a 16th-century arquebusier who has just discharged his firelock, one can readily understand why increased firepower was an early priority. There were various attempted solutions—lockplates on rails, Roman candle loads, and so forth—but the simplest and most reliable was to double one's effectiveness by adding another barrel. Experimentation did not stop there, of course; early pole-mounted hand cannon with sheaves of barrels survive.

Lots of barrels, however, create lots of problems; among them, weight, bulk, inaccuracy and expense. It is difficult enough to regulate two or three barrels to shoot to the same point of aim, and with even more barrels one loses the handling qualities that a sporting gun needs. One occasionally sees break-open shotguns with three or four barrels, but these are for the most part curiosity pieces—gunmakers' whims—rather than guns for use. German shooters are quite fond of three-barrelled combination guns, called "drillings", but in these days, when more than two shots are required, one generally has recourse to a repeating mechanism.

Fortunately, there are many circumstances in which two shots suffice, and others in which the advantages of a double outweigh the advantages of a magazine repeater. Examples of the former include wildfowling, where more than a two-shot capacity is illegal in many jurisdictions, and trap shooting, where, under international rules, only two shots are allowed—by which time the target is pretty well out of range in any case.

The same might be said for most game shooting, for there is rarely a legitimate target for a third shot—but it is as a trap gun that the double, and particularly the over-under, really excels. In trap shooting, although the departure angle may vary, the targets are always moving away and travelling at a prescribed speed. Therefore, the choke in each barrel may be optimized for the shot. Magazine repeaters may change barrels, or offer various choke inserts for a single barrel, but only the double offers a different choke for each shot.

The double is the most sophisticated of sporting guns—and often the most expensive and the most open to snobbery as well. But it also has applications at the other end of the scale, for a well-chosen double is the most useful and most versatile of working guns—as the two examples shown here demonstrate.

BAIKAL MODEL 628 (MC-8-0)

Country of origin: Soviet Union
Type: Shotgun
Calibre: 12 gauge
Capacity: 2
Action: Boxlock over-under
Operation: Toplever disengages single under lug; ejector; single selective trigger; automatic thumblever safety
Construction: All steel; chrome-lined bores
Barrel length: 28in (711mm)

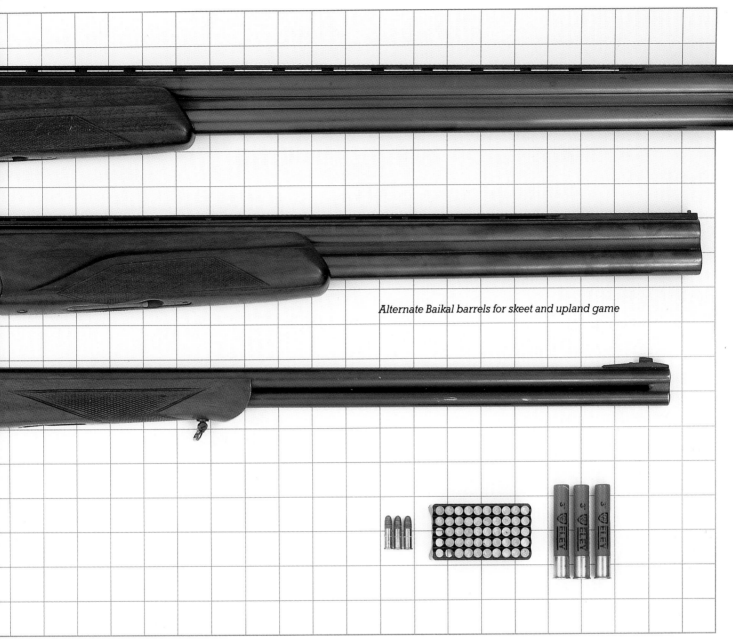

Alternate Baikal barrels for skeet and upland game

barrel set is shown mounted; 26in (660mm) spare barrel set is shown below the gun
Length overall: 43in (1092mm) as shown
Weight (empty): 7lb (3.2kg); spare barrel set weighs 4lb (1.8kg)
Sights: Brass bead on sighting rib
Comments: An excellent gun and, at current prices, outstanding value for money.

The Russian Baikal Model 628 12-bore (top) is shown with two sets of barrels. The longer set, shown mounted, is more tightly bored and is used for trap and wildfowling, while the shorter, more open set (shown below gun) serves for skeet and upland game. So far as is known, rifle barrels are not available for the Baikal. This is a pity, for they would extend this supremely functional gun's utility still further. As it is, slug or buckshot make it quite a viable proposition for medium game.

The Soviets are obsessively close-mouthed about arms production. Thus, little is known about the Baikal that cannot be seen in the photograph here—except that the Soviets export these guns in vast quantities to be sold at a price (presumably subsidized) that makes it difficult to justify not buying one. Quality varies from gun to gun, but it is always better than that of cheap European guns of the same type. The bores are chrome-plated, as is usual with Russian small arms, and the mechanisms have no conspicuous vices. We rate these guns highly.

FABRICCA NAZIONALE COMBINATION GUN

Country of origin: Italy
Type: Over and Under combination gun
Calibre: .410 gauge 3-inch in upper barrel; .22 LR in lower barrel
Capacity: 2 (1 round for each barrel)
Action: Hinged barrel breakopen over-under
Operation: Thumblever releases barrels to pivot down and to move on around to folded position if desired; selective single trigger; non-ejector
Construction: All steel
Barrel length: 24.5in (622mm)
Length overall: 41in (1041mm)
Weight (empty): 6.2lb (2.81kg)
Sights: Square post foresight; notch rearsight
Comments: A solid and robust example of an eminently functional gun.

We have stated that we would like a set of rifle barrels for the Baikal; equally desirable is a set of combination barrels like those on the Fabricca Nazionale Combination Gun (bottom). Cheap and of Italian manufacture, the Fabricca Nazionale is nevertheless a solid, workmanlike and extremely useful sort of gun. Chambered for 3-inch .410 gauge shotshells in the upper barrel and .22 rimfire in the lower, it is much used by trappers, farmers, ornithologists and those who might need an easily-packed survival gun. The outsize hinge allows it to fold up on itself for easy stowage.

The chambering makes the gun ideal for shooting rats and most garden pests, but rather too light for crows, foxes or marauding dogs, for which a 20-bore/.22 Hornet combination would be better. The US firm of Savage does not offer the Hornet, but they will combine .222, .223, .30-30 or .22 Magnum with a 20-bore. No doubt someone has a Hornet option in mind, for this supremely functional type of working gun is manufactured in almost every country.

GREENER GP SHOTGUN

Country of origin: Great Britain
Type: Shotgun
Calibre: 12-gauge
Capacity: 1
Action: Martini-type tipping block
Operation: Lowering lever ejects round from chamber and cocks striker
Construction: All steel
Barrel length: 32in (813mm)
Length overall: 48.5in (1232mm)
Weight (empty): 6.84lb (3.1kg)
Sights: Bead foresight
Comments: An extremely robust gun. "GP" is said to stand for "general purpose". Note the thumblever safety on the side of the receiver. Greener have long since ceased trading, but Webley, who purchased Greener's, still manufacture the gun on a small scale, while Squires Bingham, gunmakers situated in the Philippines, are also said to be making it.

The most vital attributes of a working gun, whether it is a military weapon or otherwise, are robustness and reliability.

Taking these as criteria, few guns can excel the nearly-indestructible Martini, a fact that explains both its widespread popularity and the multitude of applications to which it has been put in the century or more since its adoption into British service in the early 1870s.

Besides being the service rifle of the line, it has been offered as a shotgun—as seen here in the Greener GP (top)—riot gun, line-thrower, harpoon gun, clinker gun (for shooting vitreous residue from the walls of furnaces) and target gun. There have doubtless been other applications as well.

The Martini-Henry's service adoption was a result of the success of the Prussian Dreyse needle-gun in the Schleswig-Holstein Campaign of 1864. The Dreyse was fragile and spat gas badly, but despite these formidable shortcomings it clearly outclassed the Danish muzzleloaders that were

Above: *W.W. Greener, whose firm made the 12-gauge shotgun shown (top).*

ranged against it. Thus, every army in Europe began the search for a breechloader.

Great Britain adopted the Snider conversion which, by insetting a laterally swinging

breechblock, transformed the muzzleloading Enfield Pattern 53 into a breechloading cartridge gun. But the Snider-Enfield was never more than a stopgap, and in October 1866 the British Army began testing no fewer than 104 possible replacements. The winner was a boxy tipping-block design by Friedrich von Martini of Switzerland—essentially a refinement of an earlier design by Henry O. Peabody of Boston. Peabody's rifle was quite successful on its own account and was purchased by Canada, Denmark, France, Romania, Switzerland and Turkey.

The conspicuous difference between the Peabody and the Martini was that the former had a large, outside-mounted hammer while the latter was striker-fired, powered by a coil spring within the breechblock. This was a mechanical novelty that attracted vociferous criticism. More serious defects, however, were a chronically poor trigger, poor mechanical

GREENER GP SHOTGUN

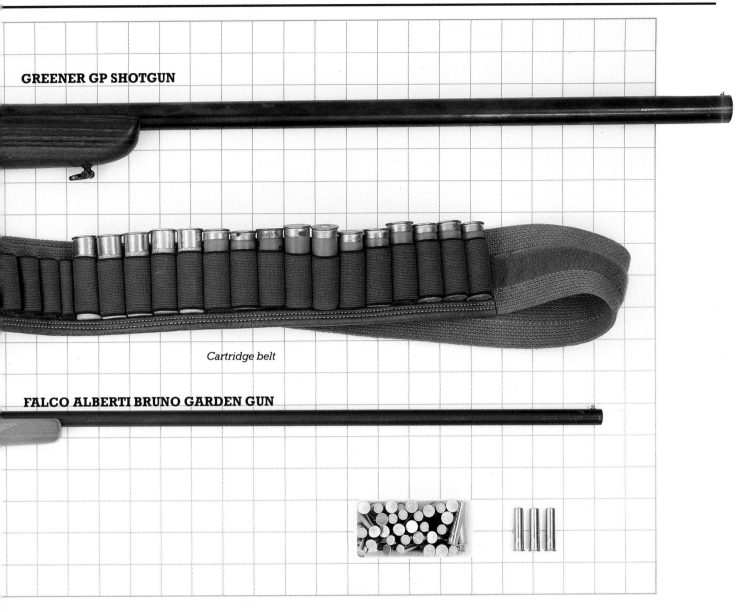

Cartridge belt

FALCO ALBERTI BRUNO GARDEN GUN

leverage which extending the lever arm did little to rectify, and the fact that the gun would fire on closing if grit got into the mechanism (although this final point was rectified in due course of time).

The Martini gave severe problems during the Egyptian campaign of 1882, the root cause of these, however, being the fragile rolled-brass cartridge, riveted to an iron head. The subsequent changeover to a solid-drawn cartridge, along with a few engineering changes, made a fine gun of it: the Martini gave sterling service during the Zulu Wars and in extended campaigns on the Indian frontier—although it was never pitted against a European army.

As the Martini's military career waned with the development of magazine-fed repeating rifles, many thousands were smoothbored for use by farmers in vermin control. The firm of W.W. Greener, who had acquired manufacturing rights,

made them afresh as shotguns, like the 12-gauge example shown here. Meanwhile, BSA used the Martini action in a splendid series of .22in target rifles which, at the last report, were still in manufacture.

Greener also produced a range of police shotguns on the Martini action, and these saw wide use both in Great Britain and in the colonies, particularly in Hong Kong and Singapore. One model, used by the Egyptian police, was chambered in 13-gauge to preclude its use, if misappropriated, with commercial ammunition. Another version used a three-pronged firing pin, the two outer prongs falling into an annular groove in the special casehead of the ammunition which was used.

The Martini is deservedly part of the myth of Empire, and as such was celebrated in both prose and verse by Rudyard Kipling, who, speaking through the mouth of a veteran in his

"Barrack-Room Ballads", urged proper care of weapons on the recruit: "When 'arf of your bullets fly wide in the ditch,/Don't call your Martini a cross-eyed old bitch;/She's human as you are—you treat her as sich,/An' she'll fight for the young British soldier." Its ruggedness is such that it will remain in use as a working gun in a variety of roles for many years to come.

FALCO ALBERTI BRUNO GARDEN GUN

Country of origin: Italy
Type: Shotgun
Calibre: 9mm rimfire
Capacity: 1
Action: Single action, exposed hammer gun
Operation: The spur ahead of the trigger guard presses rearward to release the barrel to hinge open. The hammer must be thumb-cocked to fire
Construction: All steel
Barrel length: 27.625in (702mm)
Length overall: 40.5in (1029mm) (with stock cut down)

Weight (empty): 2.94lb (1.33kg)
Sights: Brass bead foresight
Comments: A crudely-finished gun, but entirely sound mechanically; it locks up tightly and has a reasonable trigger.

The little 9mm Falco Alberti Bruno garden gun (bottom) is not so much indestructible, like the Martini, as it is basic. There is little to go wrong—and although it may be no good for smashing down doors, it does the same job for the allotment holder or kitchen-gardener that the Greener GP does for the farmer. The 9mm rimfire shells put little strain on the mechanism and pose little in the way of a public hazard, but they will do very well for small vermin at close range.

The gun folds over on itself for ease of transport, and the ludicrously long barrel is fitted solely for the purpose of qualifying it as a shotgun under British law—otherwise it would be about 12in (305mm) shorter.

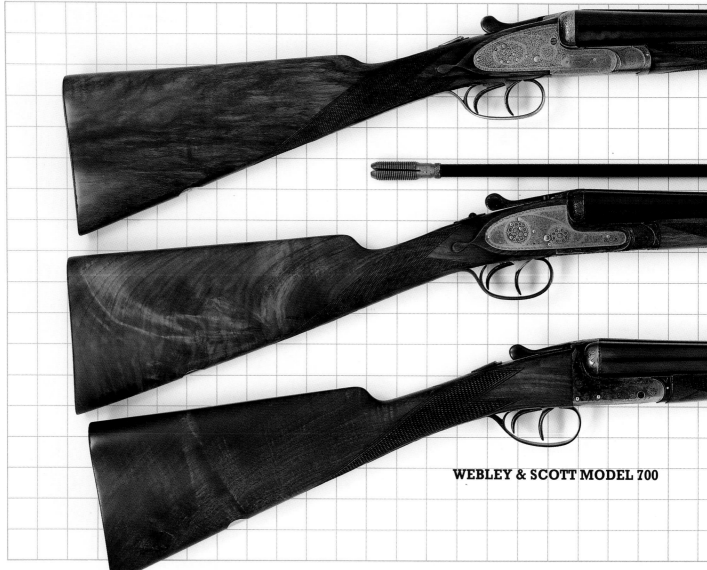

WEBLEY & SCOTT MODEL 700

The side-by-side is so much *the* British shotgun that, even today, it is regarded as bad form on some shoots to arrive with an over-under—while a "mechanical repeater" would be unthinkable. However, snobbery does not make one rich, and few indeed can afford a London best gun. The guns shown here are examples of what British gentlemen actually shoot.

THOMAS WILD SIDELOCK EJECTOR

Country of origin: Great Britain
Type: Double barrelled shotgun
Calibre: 12 gauge
Capacity: 2
Action: Break open; sidelock; ejector; double trigger
Operation: Toplever operated
Construction: Steel
Barrel length: 27in (686mm)
Length overall: 44.5in (1130mm)
Weight (empty): 6.38lb (2.89kg)
Sights: Brass bead.

First is a typical example of a good quality sporting gun by

Thomas Wild (top), a well known Birmingham maker. Made as one of a pair in 1955, it bears what was then Wild's address, 17-18 Whittall Street, Birmingham, then in the centre of the gunmaking quarter. It is one of the streets that the reconstruction of the city centre in the 1960s left empty of gunmakers; only a handful now remain in Birmingham, and some of these have been driven out to the suburbs. The writer bought this gun in 1958, after a long search for an English sidelock gun with 2.75in (70mm) chambers—the vast majority in those days had 2.5in (63.5mm) chambers—at a price he could afford.

The gun is light, yet so well balanced that shooting even 1.125oz (32g) loads from it does not produce any unacceptable recoil. It has been used for every kind of shooting, from geese on the famous marshes of the Wash in Lincolnshire, via snipe, woodcock and duck in the wilder places of West Wales, to the cream of all shooting, driven grouse in the North

of England and in Scotland. Like all good guns that one uses for years, it has become an old friend, associated with much pleasure and some superb days of sport. So great is my affection, that the fact that it is now worth perhaps 30 times what it cost me would not persuade me to sell it!

AYA No. 1

Country of origin: Spain
Type: Double barrelled shotgun
Calibre: 20 gauge
Capacity: 2
Action: Breakopen sidelock with assisted opening mechanism; ejector; double trigger
Operation: Toplever operated
Construction: Steel
Barrel length: 27in (686mm)
Length overall: 44in (1118mm)
Weight (empty): 6lb (2.72kg)
Sights: Gold bead.

Hand finished guns, even by provincial makers, are very expensive these days. For quite some decades, however, more work for the money could be bought in Spain, and it

occurred to some to teach the Spaniards to work to British style and standards. In the 1950s, the directors of a company known as Anglo-Spanish Imports, then based in Ipswich, Suffolk, approached the leading gunmakers of Eibar, Northern Spain, asking them to make guns for the British market. The guns were to be virtual copies of British models. Probably, neither side in the arrangement foresaw the success the venture would have over the next 30 years.

Before that time, the Spanish guns exported to Britain had tended to be the types made for the Spanish home market and elsewhere in Western Europe: rather heavy, often fitted with sling swivels, and, at the lower end of the market, roughly finished and with metal softer than it should have been. If fact, much like the cheap Belgian guns that were marketed in Britain before World War II at prices that Birmingham could not match. That has changed over the past 20 years. Now, even at the cheaper end of the

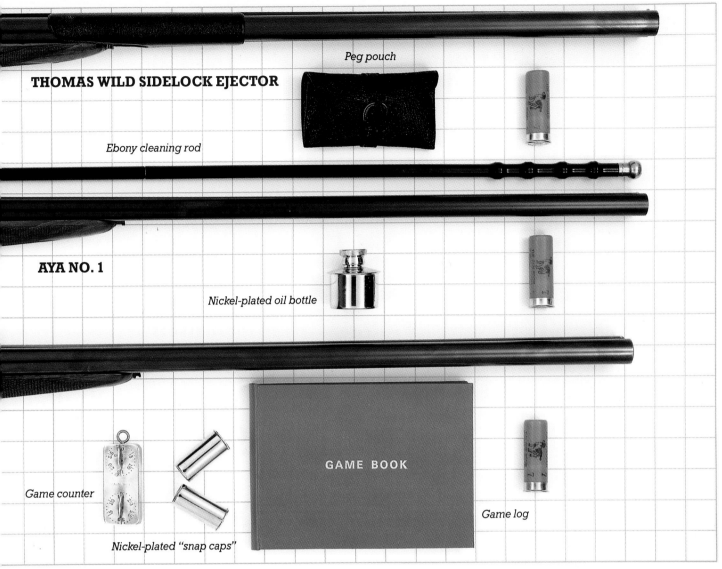

THOMAS WILD SIDELOCK EJECTOR

Peg pouch

Ebony cleaning rod

AYA NO. 1

Nickel-plated oil bottle

Game counter

GAME BOOK

Nickel-plated "snap caps"

Game log

price range, Spanish guns have shaken off the poor reputation once attached to them by some British shooters and by certain sections of the gun trade.

AyA now export to Britain a large selection of guns, ranging from a boxlock non-ejector with a trigger plate action, through several boxlock ejectors and an inexpensive (for what it is) sidelock ejector, to the gun at the top of their normal range, the No. 1 model sidelock ejector (centre). With an assisted opening system fitted, it can be made in more than one calibre if required, and is available at a price around one-quarter that of the same type of British-made gun. That is one reason why more AyA guns are sold in Britain than any other make of comparable type.

WEBLEY & SCOTT MODEL 700

Country of origin: Great Britain
Type: Double barrelled shotgun
Calibre: 12 gauge
Capacity: 2

Action: Break open; boxlock; ejector; double trigger
Operation: Manual; toplever operated
Construction: Steel
Barrel length: 26in (660mm)
Length overall: 43in (1092mm)
Weight (empty): 6.31lb (2.86kg)
Sights: Brass bead.

The other approach to making good guns affordable was to follow Colonel Colt's example and machine more precisely, so that less handwork was required. This is more or less what Webley tried to do.

The firm of Webley & Scott Ltd. has existed in Birmingham for many years, having been formed around the turn of the century by the amalgamation of two then well known companies: P. Webley and W. & C. Scott. Although the company also made sidelocks—one of their plainer grades was advertised at £39.00 ($58.00) in 1939—they were best known for the production of boxlocks. (They were also general engineers, with a large factory in the

Handsworth district of Birmingham.) Large numbers of guns were produced on an action in which the forward lump of the barrels showed through the action body—a method not commonly used by other makers of boxlock guns.

When production was resumed after World War II, demand exceeded supply. Delivery delays thwarted potential customers, so this period coincided with the beginning of Spanish imports and the first of what became a flood of imported over-under guns. Webley & Scott took over W.W. Greener, the only other Birmingham maker producing a gun completely "in house", in 1966, but this did not seem to help what were by now falling sales. A brief attempt to build an over-under on a Beretta action and barrels was a failure, and by the early 1980s the controlling company had hived off gunmaking to former employees of Webley & Scott Ltd., forming a new company with an old name, W. & C. Scott Ltd. Now, under the ownership

of Holland & Holland, boxlocks are produced in three grades under the W. & C. Scott name. The Webley Model (bottom), in a version known as the Kinmount, is now the cheapest British double gun on the market, at a 1987 price of just under £2,000 (around $3,000). A boxlock is also produced under the Holland & Holland name—and this will leave the buyer with no change from £5,000 (around $7,500)!

Clearly, the English cannot afford to shoot English guns, or at least very few of them can. The reason for this is that, due to legislative restrictions, there is not enough of a domestic market to support a machine-made gun. The carriage trade, handwork sector is simply the only one left and it is devoted to quality rather than innovation. The result is that a best London gun, though magnificent, looks more antique by the year. And even these guns depend for the most part upon the export market. The Englishman, meanwhile, shoots the best gun he can afford.

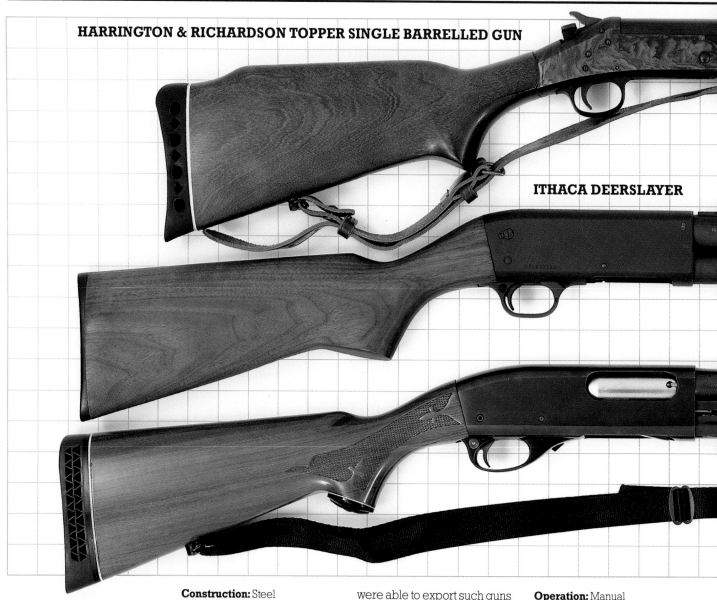

ITHACA DEERSLAYER

Ubiquity and case capacity enable the 12-bore shell to be offered in a vast array of loadings, from blank to solid slug, including along the way distress flares, rubber balls, stun loads, birdshot, buckshot, hypodermic projectiles and even high-explosive and incendiary. Some of these are hard to come by, but enough of them are to hand to make the 12-bore the most versatile and useful working gun one can possess. Other guns are nice; a 12-bore is often essential.

HARRINGTON & RICHARDSON TOPPER SINGLE BARRELLED GUN

Country of origin: USA
Type: Single barrel, outside hammer
Calibre: 12 gauge
Capacity: 1
Action: Break open
Operation: Thumb cocking; transfer bar from hammer to striker. Plunger depresses to unlock barrel.

Construction: Steel
Barrel length: 24.5in (622mm) (Buck model)
Length overall: 39.5in (968mm)
Weight (empty): 5.625lb (2.55kg)
Sights: Brass bead standard; rear sight and blade fore sight on Buck model.

In its most basic form, the all-round working 12-bore, fit for anything from rats to bear, is a break-open single shot with sling, recoil pad and rifle sights, like the Harrington & Richardson Topper (top). Pumps give more fire-power but at three or four times the price, which explains the historical popularity of the single shot, particularly in the USA, where they were part and parcel of every small farm, regarded as almost as much of a tool as an axe or a spade. In Britain, they were often the guns favoured by the small farmer or smallholder.

Their prime advantage was, of course, price, for they could be made almost entirely by machine—and often were. For this reason, American makers

were able to export such guns to Britain, in competition with the products of Birmingham, before 1914 and again between the two World Wars. One such maker was Harrington & Richardson: I have seen several of their guns bearing British black powder proof marks, showing that they came into Britain very early in this century. They continued to be imported until around 1985, when the very high cost of dollar imports as the pound reached an all-time low made them too expensive to compete with Italian and Spanish guns of the same type. In today's affluent society, the market for such guns has, in any case, diminished greatly, most people preferring the more versatile double or repeater.

ITHACA DEERSLAYER

Country of origin: USA
Type: Slide-action ("Pump action")
Calibre: 12 gauge
Capacity: 5 (or 8 with magazine extension)
Action: Conventional receiver but with bottom ejection

Operation: Manual
Construction: Steel
Barrel length: 24.25in (616mm)
Length overall: 44in (1118mm)
Weight (empty): 6.75lb (3.06kg)
Sights: Rear leaf; front ramp and day-glow bead.

A nearly ideal working gun, if one could afford it, was the Ithaca Model 37, shown here in the Deerslayer version (centre), an immensely robust, reliable and easy-handling pump gun.

The Ithaca Gun Co. of Ithaca, New York State, was established in 1880 and in more than 100 years has produced almost every kind of shotgun and, in World War II, a variety of military weapons for the US Government. However, they are best known for their trap guns and slide-action shotguns. In 1911 they produced a single barrelled gun designed specially for trapshooting; it was succeeded in 1922 by an improved model which continued in production for many years. The examples I have seen were of high quality,

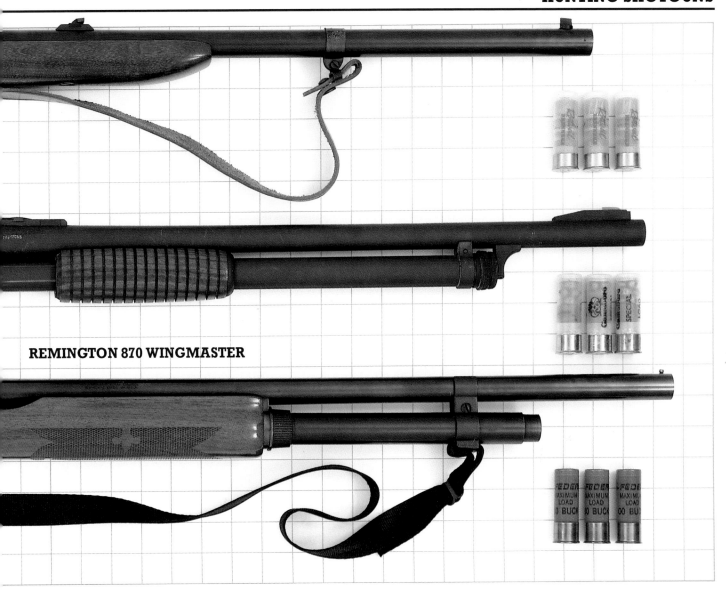

REMINGTON 870 WINGMASTER

with good wood and fine engraving.

In 1937, Ithaca introduced a slide-action gun, the Model 37 Featherlight, which was destined to become a classic. As its name implied, it was at least one pound (.45kg) lighter than any of its competitors—and this was the result of good design, not the use of alloys. Unlike other guns of its type, which used side ejection, the Model 37 used a bottom ejection system for spent cartridges. This gave three benefits: it prevented rain or snow getting into the action when the gun was carried normally; in the event of a burst cartridge, any brass fragments or burnt powder grains were deflected downward, away from the shooter's face; and it suited the left-handed shooter admirably, for he had no spent cases flying past his face, as he did with side ejection.

The Model 37 has been made in 12, 16 and 20 gauge and in many formats: trap, riot guns and, in the version shown here, the Deerslayer, equipped with rifle type sights and a cylinder barrel designed to shoot slug loads for deer. Because of the bottom ejection, the receiver on this shotgun is shorter than is usual on most slide-action or pump guns, and this factor gives the Ithaca Deerslayer its lighter weight and better balance.

REMINGTON 870 WINGMASTER

Country of origin: USA
Type: Slide-action
Calibre: 12 gauge (also available in 20, 28 and .410 gauges)
Capacity: 5 (extension magazines up to 8 shots available)
Action: Slide, or pump (Remington themselves call the 870 a pump gun)
Operation: Manual
Construction: Steel
Barrel length: 25in (635mm); also in lengths from 18in (457mm) to 30in (762mm)
Length overall: 45.5in (1156mm); others from 40.5in (1029mm) to 50.5in (1283mm)
Weight (empty): 7.5lb (3.4kg); others from 6lb (2.72kg) upward
Sights: Brass bead (varies with some models).

In terms of sheer popularity, however, the Ithaca cannot compare with the Remington Model 870 (bottom). Introduced in 1950 to replace the Model 31, the 870 was an instant success and has consolidated its position over almost 40 years. Made in almost every kind of model from the 18in (457mm) barrelled Police Model to the 30in (762mm) barrelled 3in (76mm) Magnum, and in four gauges, with versions now fitted with the internally threaded "Rem" choke system, it has become the most popular pump gun ever, with sales of more than four million. With a strong action, with double action bars, and walnut stocks and fore ends (except on the Police and Special Purpose models), all models are now fitted with recoil pads in 12 and 20 gauge.

An annoying shortcoming, whereby a cartridge which was not pushed fully into the magazine might slip the retainer to be pushed back into the receiver, tying up the mechanism, has recently been rectified. Normally, the barrel

needed to be removed to reduce the jam, whereas in a Smith & Wesson or Winchester, the round could simply be pumped through. Remington's adoption of this feature has returned them to the lead.

Although pump guns are still very popular on both the trap and skeet fields in the USA, it is some years since I saw anyone shooting a pump action competitively in Britain. The introduction of ISU Skeet, with its gun-down start position and fast, simultaneous doubles, means that the pump gun is really a non-starter for skeet in Britain. For wildfowl in the USA and game shooting within the EEC, all pumps and selfloaders must be fitted with a plug limiting their capacity to three cartridges. The relatively new sport of Practical Shotgun has revived interest in the pump, especially when, like the Wingmaster shown here, it is fitted with an extension magazine. Although it is more expensive than most, the Model 870 has the advantage in quality and durability over its cheaper rivals.

TARGET
SHOTGUNS

Norman Cooper

Front sight   Ventilated rib

Muzzle   Barrels   Forearm   Forearm release mechanism

We do not know when men first began to shoot at artificial targets, but it happened before firearms came into common use and involved, of course, bows and arrows. In our youth we all read of the legendary exploits of Robin Hood and his ability to split a willow wand with an arrow. Although we have no concrete evidence of this, we do know that shooting at a popinjay was common in medieval times. The popinjay was a brightly-coloured facsimile of a bird, suspended at the top of a tall pole. One shot at it with a bow, and it is quite possible that in a wind the popinjay might move and thus introduce a little variety into the sport.

So important was the efficient use of a bow considered that football was banned lest it interfere with young men's archery practice. It was the custom in certain parts of Britain, and also on the Continent, to hold annual events at which men from a particular area were expected to attend and show that their bows and arrows were in good condition and fit for use. Of course, at these gatherings there were competitions in which all were expected to participate. In Scotland these were known as Wappenshaws or "weapon shows", and the term persisted long after the bow had been superseded by the gun. In fact, in my early clay shooting days, some clubs still called their annual Christmas shoot a Wappenshaw.

Although early firearms were undoubtedly used to shoot at some kind of artificial target, this generally involved muskets and early rifles, with perhaps an occasional shot with a smoothbore gun loaded with small shot. Until the invention and subsequent improvement of the flintlock gun, it was virtually impossible to shoot at any kind of moving target, the earlier matchlock system being too slow in ignition to allow for accurate shooting at anything other than a fixed mark. With the coming of the flintlock gun, it not only became possible to shoot at moving targets, but also to do so with considerable accuracy. By the end of the first quarter of the 19th century, the flintlock had been refined to a gun not only of beauty but also of extreme efficiency by the standards of the day, and many thousands of head of game were shot each year with the aid of the flintlock system.

However, the flintlock's days began to be numbered as the result of the invention of the percussion lock, credited to a Scottish clergyman, Alexander Forsyth, who took out a patent in 1807 for his new lock, which used a mixture of mercury fulminate and potassium chlorate as a detonating agent. By the time Forsyth died in 1843, the percussion system was in widespread use, although he had been treated quite shabbily by some of the military authorities whom he had tried to interest in the potentially important military application of his invention.

The percussion system made possible even more accurate and faster shooting, but although Great Britain teemed with game of all kinds, shooting was largely confined to the autumn and winter months. Some shooters, understandably, sought a kind of shooting which could be done in the months when game was not shot. They had a suitable quarry near to hand, for in the days before root crops were developed and only breeding cattle could be over-wintered, the commonest source of fresh meat was the pigeons which were bred for the purpose in dovecotes and pigeon lofts throughout the land. A smaller breed than the wild wood pigeon, these were more akin to the stock dove, often known as the blue rock, whose fast, agile flight was well known to the shooters of the day. Although we do not know exactly when men began to shoot at them competitively, the first clubs to take part in the sport were certainly established by the middle of the 19th century.

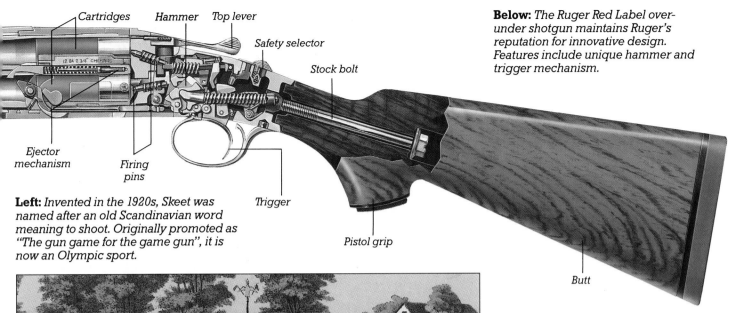

Cartridges   Hammer   Top lever

Safety selector

Stock bolt

Ejector mechanism

Firing pins

Trigger

Pistol grip

Butt

Left: *Invented in the 1920s, Skeet was named after an old Scandinavian word meaning to shoot. Originally promoted as "The gun game for the game gun", it is now an Olympic sport.*

Below: *The Ruger Red Label over-under shotgun maintains Ruger's reputation for innovative design. Features include unique hammer and trigger mechanism.*

Left: *"Pape-Gaye" or popinjay shooting as practised in 19th century Belgium. These original "high birds" were among the earliest known artificial targets, dating back to the Middle Ages.*

Below: *"Scent bottle" percussion lock, patented by Scottish clergyman Alexander Forsyth, offered faster and more reliable ignition than the flintlock.*

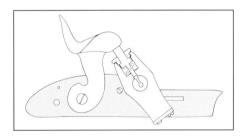

One of the first, if not the first, of these pigeon shooting clubs was established at the Old Hats public house at Ealing, in those days a village some miles outside London. The name Old Hats, which was applied both to the public house and to the shooting ground, derived from the fact that the pigeons were placed under old hats, which were pulled away with cords to release the birds. Another famous venue was soon established at the Red House at Battersea, a little closer to central London, Both venues were the scene of much shooting and much betting — and betting remained a feature after the hats were replaced by rather more sophisticated means of releasing the birds.

These were metal boxes, soon to be called traps, which could be collapsed by means of a string or lever. The pigeon was placed in the trap and, when the shooter called, a man pulled the string or lever (and what better name for him than a trapper?), the trap collapsed and the pigeon flew off, to be shot by the shooter standing ready. Traps were first used at Hornsea Wood House, north of London, and in a short time the sport had spread to many other venues. Before long, it came to be regulated by sets of rules, notably those published by two very famous venues, the London Gun Club

and the Hurlingham Club, both in the London area. The last set of rules governing the sport of live pigeon shooting in Great Britain was published by the Hurlingham Club in 1901. Many of these rules remain in force today, substantially unchanged, to govern the successors to live pigeon shooting. In countries where live pigeon shooting from traps is still legal, these rules have hardly changed at all, nor has the practice of gambling large sums of money on the outcome. One of the rules was, and is, that the pigeon had to drop inside a circular boundary fence around the shooting area. If it fell outside the fence, it failed to score, even if it was dead. Even today, it is possible to recognize a live pigeon shooter even when he shoots clays, for he will nearly always use his second barrel, just to make sure!

Specialized Equipment

The rules were strict, whether they concerned the pigeons, as fair birds, the shooters or even the trappers, for it was not unkown for trappers, for a consideration, to place the bird in the trap in such a way that it became an easier or a more difficult target, or secretly to pull out a few flight feathers to ensure that the bird's flight was erratic.

Remarkable scores were achieved in the last two decades of the 19th century: the celebrated shot, Captain A.H. Bogardus scored 99 out of 100 pigeons as early as 1880, and over the next 20 years several scores of 100 out of 100 were recorded.

Specialized equipment was soon developed. By this time the breechloading gun had superseded the muzzleloading percussion gun (although there were many shooters who, even after the advent of the breechloader, continued to use the muzzleloaders with which they had grown up.) The early rules allowed for 1.25oz (35g) of shot to be loaded into cartridges used in the sport, and many shot flasks still in existence today are so marked. When the breechloader was used the heavier load required a heavier gun with a longer chamber than most game guns, and such guns were called "pigeon guns". Later, when live pigeon shooting from traps was forbidden by law in Great Britain, such longer-chambered, heavier, 12-bore guns continued to be made, principally for wildfowling, and they were then usually known as "demi-magnums".

Among the places where live pigeon shooting became immensely popular abroad was Monte Carlo, the site, in its heyday in Victorian and Edwardian times,

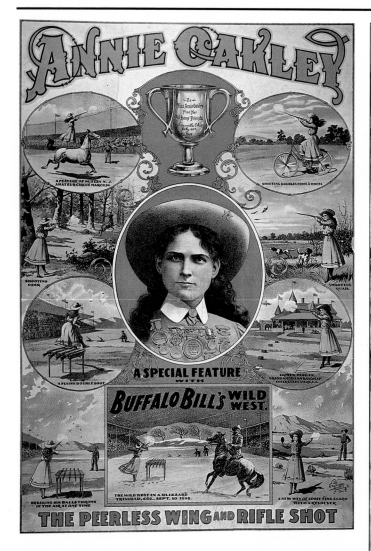

Above: *A poster advertising Annie Oakley's exploits with Buffalo Bill's Wild West Show. It is not generally realised that Annie was an accomplished clay shot and gave exhibitions throughout the USA and Europe.*

of many famous matches. The gambling on the matches complemented the action in the famous Casino, and huge sums were won and lost at both venues. The ground at Monte Carlo was believed to favour the pigeons: certainly, the shooting was regarded as very difficult, for many matches were shot over only a few birds, and if you could kill, for example, 12 pigeons out of 12 released, you had probably won the match. Live pigeon shooting continued in the Principality of Monaco until the 1950s. It was widely believed that it was the late Princess Grace's influence that had it stopped, just as it was believed in Great Britain that it was the influence of Queen Alexandra which led to legislation outlawing the sport in Britain in 1921.

Live pigeon competition still takes place in several countries; I can immediately think of Spain, Portugal, Egypt, Mexico and San Remo, and there may well be others. Where traps are used, the rules remain much the same and large sums can still be won and lost. Matches may consist of no more than 8 or 10 birds, and averages of 90 per cent or so are achieved. Pigeons which are not killed often fly straight back to their loft, which is seldom more than about half a mile away, and then are caught up again when the next day's shooting takes place.

Marker men placed with flags well beyond the boundary fence signal whether the bird has dropped dead inside or outside the fence. Perhaps surprisingly to the modern day clay shots, whose use of the over-and-under gun is almost universal, many live pigeon trap shooters use side-by-side guns.

Glass Targets

Long before live trap shooting became illegal in Great Britain, thought had been given to shooting at inanimate moving targets, the very first of which were glass balls. At first they were of plain glass, but later coloured ones were used; some were even filled with small feathers which fluttered down when the glass was broken. I have in my possession a beautiful blue ball of this kind, bearing the famous name of W.W. Greener and the firm's London and Birmingham addresses. This will have been made before 1880, for glass balls and the machines to throw them began to be used as early as 1870. Some of the machines were simple, rather like the Roman ballista in miniature; others were more complicated and were capable of throwing the balls over different trajectories and even throwing two at a time.

By their very nature, the glass balls were

not very difficult to hit, for they lost velocity quite quickly, and it was around 1880 that an American named Ligowski is believed to have made the first of what we now call clay pigeons or clay targets. Legend has it that he got the idea of producing a skimming object by watching boys throwing flat stones across water, as most of us have done in our youth. Be that as it may, the first clay targets were made of just that: clay, baked in brick kilns. Many of the early ones had a tongue or lip on the rim which helped to position the target on the arm of the trap (as it was already called). The brick targets were very hard and various makers experimented with different mixtures in an attempt to achieve a better target. In the 1880s there was a law suit between two London gunmakers, the one alleging that the other had infringed the appellant's sole right to use the words "clay pigeons", in that the defendant's targets were not made of clay at all, but a mixture of ash and tar! The judge ruled that as everyone understood what was meant by clay pigeons, the fact that the defendant's targets were not actually made of clay was of no legal significance.

The British have been said to be a great nation of "clubbers" and, true to form, the first mention of a clay pigeon club occurred

Above: *An advertisement for the 1907 Monte Carlo Grand Prix winning Smokeless Diamond Powder. Its reputation for being "marvellously quick" was a sure-fire copyline in days when slow burning black powder was still widely used.*

Left: *Ladies enjoying live pigeon shooting at Monte Carlo. Spent cartridges litter the firing point while feathers surround the traps. A dog stands ready to pick up. Live shooting was outlawed in Britain in 1921 but continued into the 1950s in Monaco where huge sums were wagered on the results.*

in England in 1884, when one was formed at Botley, in Hampshire. From early pictures of the throwers used, it seems that they were not very different from those listed in the gunsmiths' catalogues in the 1930s and even later, although perhaps our Victorian ancestors might have difficulty recognizing the large automatic traps in use on some grounds today. The clays were certainly similar by this time to modern ones.

A governing body was soon formed to regulate the new sport in Britain. Initially, it was named the Inanimate Bird Shooting Association, but by the turn of the century it had become the Clay Bird Shooting Association and had already drawn up and published a set of rules. Naturally enough, since the only type of competition they had for comparison was the then legal live pigeon shooting from traps, these rules governed only what we would now call Down-the-Line shooting, which took its name from the fact the shooters stood in a line of fire and each shot in turn, so that the shooting went "Down-the-Line". In America, where the sport had also caught on, they retained the name Trap Shooting, and both names continue to be used.

This was an era of great matches and large audiences for both shotgun and rifle competitions. Just as large crowds

turned out to watch the rifle shooting at Wimbledon and later Bisley, so they did to watch the celebrated clay shots of the day, some of whom had started as shooters of glass balls. It was the many marathon matches that really drew the crowds. There were famous exhibition shooters whose exploits were widely reported. Among them were two of exceptional skill and fame: W.F. "Doc" Carver and Captain Adam H. Bogardus. Both had started match shooting with glass balls, Carver having won a match with a Mr. Scott by only two balls, breaking 9,737 to Scott's 9,735 — and this out of 9,950 balls shot by each man! We have no way of knowing just how difficult the targets were, but just imagine the sheer physical feat of firing that number of shots in rapid succession! Captain Bogardus was of similar physical toughness, for in 1879 he had shot at glass balls non-stop for over seven hours, his final score being 5,500 broken with only 356 missed. By the time that clay targets became widely used, Bogardus and Carver were considered the best in the world. When they shot a match in the early 1890s, Carver had the better of it, breaking 2,227 against Bogardus's score of 2,103 out of 2,500 birds each. The one lady shot that most people have heard of, Annie Oakley, also became a very good clay shot

and gave exhibitions both in the USA and on her tours of Great Britain.

Bear in mind that all this early shooting was done with black powder and very often with heavy loads of shot, for although the early rules laid down maximum charges of shot for competition shooting, the shooters could make their own rules for exhibitions and demonstrations. Bogardus, for example, was quite often known to use a 10-bore for marathon shoots and, when he did so, made use of 1.5oz (43g) of shot and 4 drams (7g) of black powder. I have such a 10-bore, made in about 1875, and I have shot it with just that load, in fact with a heavier shot charge: great fun, but I certainly would not want to face shooting at several thousand targets with such a load.

The sport continued to grow in the period up to World War I, becoming popular not only in Great Britain and America but in many countries in Europe. With the advent of the War, shooting for sport virtually ceased, but after 1919 clay shooting got under way again, although still only in the version which had followed the lines of earlier live trap shooting.

The guns used were almost all of the side-by-side variety, and because shooting took place from 16 yards (15m) behind the trap (and at longer distances for what were

Above: *Taking a down-the-line target at a county shoot. Still the most popular clay shooting discipline in Britain, DTL presents targets going away at different angles from a trap set 16 yards in front of the firing line. Two shots are allowed at each clay and after five clays, shooters move "down the line".*

Right: *Clay shooting from the back of a boat adds enjoyment to a leisurely cruise; a turbulent sea can present the shooter with new challenges.*

known as "handicap by distance" events) they nearly all carried a good ideal of choke in both barrels. Although shot charges tended to be lighter than the 1.35oz (35g) used by the live pigeon shooters, they were usually heavier than most game shots used, 1.125oz (32g) of shot being the norm. This, coupled with the fact that it was quite common to shoot 100 targets or more in the course of a day, meant that the guns used were generally heavier than game guns, which in any case were usually open bored and, in that respect, less suitable for trap shooting. In fact, many of the guns used were those which their owners or previous owners had used for live pigeon shooting. In America, the slide action or pump gun was already in use on the line, and a few of the relatively new semi-automatic guns also were making an appearance. Also, because of the one-shot-only rule, several single-barrel trap guns were marketed, including some of exceptional quality.

In addition to clay pigeon competitions, there were a number of shooting schools in Britain, at which such targets were thrown to simulate as far as possible the flight of game birds and thus provide practice for the game shot. Because so much of the game shooting in the UK consisted of driven birds, especially pheasants, there were constructed special towers upon which traps could be placed, sometimes at different levels, to give the high, fast targets demanded by the game shot. These towers could be from around 50-120 feet (15-36m) in height, but there were very few really high ones, since the cost involved was a severe deterrent to their erection and use. In America, where game was seldom if ever driven in the same way, such towers were unknown.

But apart from impromptu matches between friends at these "sporting" clays, there was as yet nothing for the man who wanted to shoot clays with the same gun that he used for game or rough shooting. However, in the middle of the first decade after the Great War, this situation was to change, leading to a form of clay target shooting that soon became very popular. The idea originated with a Massachusetts kennel owner named C.E. Davies, who installed two traps at different heights on opposite sides of a circle roughly 40 yards (37m) in diameter, around the perimeter of which he and his friends walked, shooting at targets released from the traps in turn. The targets were constant, but by changing firing points the shooters varied the angles, and because the ranges at which the targets were shot were never more than 40 yards (37m), and usually nearer 30 yards (27m) or even less, the guns used were the same ones with which they shot game birds and animals.

Skeet Shooting

The story goes that the original circle soon had to be reduced to a semi-circle in consequence of Davies' neighbours building a chicken run in the beaten zone, thus preventing the full circle from being used. But the shooting positions remained around the rim of the semi-circle. Be that as it may, the new kind of shooting soon began to catch on, especially when many shooters realized that they did not have to buy a special Trap gun to compete. Promoted under the slogan "The gun game for the game gun", rules were drawn up, and in the mid 1920s an American shooting magazine offered a 100-dollar prize for the best name for this new sport. The prize was won by Mrs Gertrude Hurlbutt of Montana, who sent in the name "Skeet", from an old Scandinavian word which simply meant "Shoot". This name quickly came into common use and remains so today. The name and the sport crossed the Atlantic in the late 1920s, and Skeet is believed to

Above: *Taking a high tower target in ISU skeet with a Miroku 3800. The trap is set 3m from the ground in the high tower and targets are thrown 65m.*

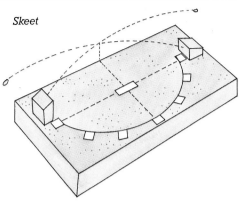

Skeet

Above: *Skeet is shot on a semi-circular layout with clays thrown from high and low towers situated on each side. A round of ISU skeet consists of 25 targets taken from eight stations. Singles and doubles are thrown and one shot per target is allowed.*

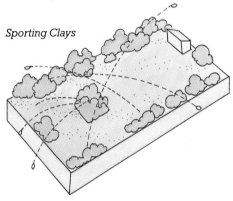

Sporting Clays

Above: *Sporting is a British clay discipline which attempts to recreate the challenge and unpredictability of game shooting. Traps are often hidden behind cover and clays are thrown which simulate a variety of game.*

and these were quickly snapped up. One or two companies began to make clay targets again, among them Britain's oldest ammunition company, Eley, then known as I.C.I. Kynoch, Ltd., who had a plant for making clay targets in Bedfordshire.

By the 1960s, increased leisure time and income, plus a tendency towards parti-cipant sports, saw an upsurge in clay shooting on both sides of the Atlantic. In Britain, the two original versions of the sport showed a steady increase in support, but perhaps the biggest growth occurred in what was now known as "Sporting" shooting. Although a national championship for this kind of shooting had been held in pre-War days, by the 1960s it had grown, first, to a two-day event and then later to three days; by the 1980s, four days were needed to accommodate the entries, which often numbered over 1,000. Another hugely popular shoot, also with four-figure entries, is the annual Game Fair Championship, held each July in conjunction with the Game Fair, at sites all over Britain. In less than 30 years, this event has grown from two days to three, and it attracts many shooters who perhaps would not enter any other national event. There are many other such shoots held all over Britain from March until October, and many of them count their entries in hundreds, from the almost profes-sional clay shot to the man who just wants to have a go with his game gun, and it is often this class of shot who is the backbone of the hundreds of smaller events up and down the country. In the 1960s, Winchester began a franchise operation in the USA, aimed at setting up all over the States shooting grounds to which people could go and, on paying a fee, shoot either Skeet or Trap. There were other facilities provided, such as food, drink and ample parking arrange-ments. With a great number of shooters and vast areas of land, this kind of operation presents no real difficulty in the United States, but it is much more difficult in Great Britain. Nevertheless, a number of com-mercial grounds were established in the UK in the 1960s and 1970s. Some simply provided instruction and practice, but others offered such facilities as catering and a comfortable clubhouse. In the mean-time, the numbers of those taking part in clay shooting continued to grow, for although Great Britain has game shooting in greater abundance than perhaps almost any other country in the world, coupled with a greater variety, there is still not enough to go round for every one who wants to shoot. Indeed on a day's rough shooting, one would be lucky to fire more than half a dozen shots.

By contrast, one can go to a clay shoot and, if one desires, fire anything from 50 to 150 cartridges a day. If ownership of a gun means that it should be fired, then this kind of shooting is just what is needed. So much so that the mid-1980s has seen a tremendous upsurge in the number of commercial shooting grounds established in Great Britain, ranging from small operations active on a fortnightly basis to grounds open five or six days a week. Some of these offer a wide range of shooting, plus a bar or restaurant on the premises or

have first been shot in Britain at the Waltham Abbey Gun Club in Essex, which had been established prior to 1914.

The late 1920s also marked another mile-stone in the story of clay shooting in Britain, for in 1928 the controlling body of the sport changed its name to the Clay Pigeon Shoot-ing Association; the CPSA celebrates its Diamond Jubilee in 1988. In the next 11 years, clay shooting continued to grow in Britain, but at nothing like the speed at which it grew in the USA, where already the national Trapshooting events drew entries of several hundreds. In 1939, World War II effectively put a stop to clay pigeon shooting in Britain, except in the Royal Air Force, where some of the top pre-War clay shots became instructors for thousands of airgunners who learned to shoot at moving aircraft with the aid of shotguns and clay targets, the principles of swing and lead being the same for both kinds of shooting. As it was another two years before America came into the War, the sport continued there until 1942, when it had to cease.

From 1946 onwards, very slowly, the sport got under way again, although cartridges in Britain were still in short supply, most being of "utility" type with a plain paper case and rolled turnover. There were supplies of ex-RAF Trapshooting cartridges available

locally. There are now also hotels that offer clay pigeon shooting weekends, with a layout either in the hotel grounds or adjacent to them, with one or more qualified instructors, and an inclusive tariff which provides first class accommodation plus a good deal of shooting tailored to the experienced shot as well as the beginner.

Business Entertainment

Many businesses are now arranging clay shooting for their clients, as a change from rounds of golf, race days and similar types of business entertainment. This kind of shooting will usually involve one of the bigger grounds. There are also companies that will arrange shooting at a stately mansion or some similar venue, in a package deal including food and drink, the provision of guns if required, and, of course, instruction for those who need it. This kind of shooting is invariably of the "sporting" variety, which can easily be set up on a temporary basis: not only are Skeet and Trap much more specialized, but also they both require a permanent facility. There are still many grounds simply providing instruction or practice under supervision. These often supplement their income by holding open competitions, as

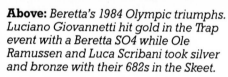

Above: *Beretta's 1984 Olympic triumphs. Luciano Giovannetti hit gold in the Trap event with a Beretta SO4 while Ole Ramussen and Luca Scribani took silver and bronze with their 682s in the Skeet.*

Left: *Olympic Trap has five firing points with three voice-actuated traps placed 15 metres in front of each one. A clay may be thrown from any trap and two shots are allowed at each target.*

Right: *Mohamed Khorshed of Egypt shooting Olympic Skeet. The gun is held at the hip and only mounted when the target is thrown—up to 3 seconds after the shooter has called it.*

do many of the hundreds of clubs which operate all over the British Isles, ranging in size from less than 20 members to several hundred, and in facilities from a couple of traps in a field to sophisticated layouts for several shooting disciplines.

Two of these disciplines have long been Olympic sports. First came Olympic Trap or Trench, as it was known originally, which has been included in the Olympic Games for more than 30 years; then came International Skeet, introduced into the Games in 1968. The United Kingdom has won a gold medal for the Trap event, but a Skeet medal has so far eluded British shooters. World Championships are held in other disciplines and in some of these Britain has won several gold medals, notably in Sporting events, which present severe difficulties when it comes to setting up a common standard for the Olympic Games.

Today, clay pigeon shooting or clay target shooting flourishes. The latter term has been introduced in some cases to distinguish one national governing body from another. For example, the governing body in England has, since 1928, been called the Clay Pigeon Shooting Association; the Welsh national body was formerly known as the Welsh CPSA but is now called the Welsh Clay Target Shooting

Association; and we now also have governing bodies for Scotland, Ulster, Jersey and, the latest, the Manx CPSA. All the smaller bodies mentioned have memberships of a few hundred or even less, but in the summer of 1987, *the* Clay Pigeon Shooting Association had a membership in excess of 17,000. Needless to say, many members of the smaller bodies also belong to the English Association, in order to take part in the very much larger national events which that body controls.

In America there are two domestic governing bodies: the American Trapshooting Association, or ATA, and the National Skeet Shooting Association of America, or NSSA. Rather strangely, these control only the home disciplines of Trap and American Skeet, while all international disciplines are controlled by the National Rifle Association, always known by its initials, NRA. The domestic disciplines in America are much less difficult than the international ones, which may account for the comparatively few American shooters of world class in relation to the tens of thousands of sportsmen who shoot clay targets in the USA.

Likewise, in Britain, there are disciplines which are not shot outside the UK, and these are controlled by the CPSA or the

other home controlling bodies. International disciplines are controlled internationally by overall bodies based outside the UK, and within the UK by an International Board of the CPSA.

The two main disciplines in both Great Britain and the USA are somewhat similar. The layouts for Down-the-Line shooting in the UK and Trapshooting in the USA closely resemble each other in dimensions. The main difference is in the scoring: the Americans permit only one shot, whereas in Britain two barrels may be fired at a target if required, a kill with the first barrel counting three points and with the second barrel only two points. This has the effect of reducing the number of ties in competition, where several men may break 100 out of 100 but some may need the second barrel for one or two of the targets. Double rise shooting is a variation on this type of shooting, two targets being released simultaneously.

Domestic Skeet in Britain is shot from the seven perimeter stations only, whereas American Skeet uses Station 8. Targets only have to travel 55 yards (50m) and the shooters' gun position is optional, many people starting with the gun already in the shoulder. Release of the targets is made immediately the shooter calls. One result is

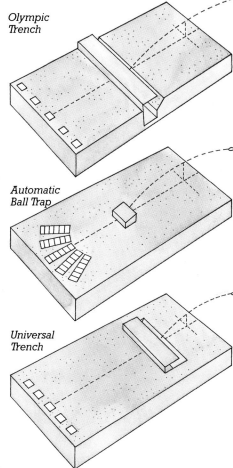

Olympic Trench

Automatic Ball Trap

Universal Trench

Above: *Olympic Trench requires five firing points each with three traps. A clay may be thrown from any trap and two shots are permitted. ABT is similar, but clays are thrown at unpredictable angles and elevations from a single trap, while Universal Trench employs five traps to increase the variety.*

that scores of several hundred without a miss have long been common in the US, and shooters are working towards that point in Britain, where 250 straight kills have already been shot.

Olympic Events

If we move on to the Olympic form of clay shooting, the oldest, Olympic Trap, is shot from five positions on a common axis. In front of each position are three traps, each set to throw a target at a different height and angle. The traps are remotely controlled and are totally unpredictable, so that the clay may emerge from any one of the three, and it is an extremely fast bird, travelling up to 80 metres (87 yds) from the trap. Two shots may be fired and the score is the same whichever barrel actually breaks the clay. Gun position is optional, but all shooters seem to have the gun in the shoulder prior to calling for the target, and it is the sound of the shooter's voice which actuates each trap.

Olympic Skeet (or ISU Skeet as it is often known, the international controlling body being the International Shooting Union) requires a faster target, which has to travel 65 yards (59m); a "gun down" position, the gun butt having to be at hip level; shooting

from Station 8; and, above all, the difference that targets are released at a random time scale after the shooter calls, varying from immediate release to a delay of up to three seconds — which can seen a very long time when you are waiting! International events in both these types of shooting are always shot over 200 targets, and even now there are very few shooters who have managed a possible score.

There are two further international forms of shooting that have achieved a certain degree of popularity, particularly on the continent of Europe. Both have rules similar to those for Olympic Trap, but Automatic Ball Trap uses only one trap while Universal Trench uses five. Because of this, they are both very much easier and cheaper to install than Olympic Trap, which accounts for their popularity. Olympic Trap requires the installation of fifteen automatic traps — three for each of the five firing points (shown in the diagram at top right).

Sporting shooting is immensely popular in Great Britain. It can consist of almost any kind of layout which the organizers care to put on or have facilities for. The larger competitions may use as many as ten stands, which will bear various names but which will usually have a high tower, from which "driven pheasants" may be thrown; a

lower tower for "partridges"; a sharply rising target, the "springing teal"; and often a trap which will bowl a special clay target along the ground, the "bolting rabbit". Other names may reflect the ingenuity of the organizers and may be called by almost any name that has the required game shooting connotation.

The most difficult form of Sporting shooting has reached international status; the first World Championships were shot in Britain in 1978, and they have taken place in various countries every year since. This is called FITASC Sporting, after the initials of the controlling body. As many as ten "parcours", or stands, are used, each with three traps, throwing no less than five different types and sizes of targets at different angles and at high speeds. The targets are thrown when the referee sees that the shooter is ready, and the gun must be away from the shoulder until the target appears. By common consent, this is the most difficult form of clay shooting: a shooter who can break 150 or better out of the 200 targets in an international competition is very good indeed. Britain has won more medals in this type of international shooting than any other nation, including both individual and team gold medals in world events.

The smallest following for any type of shooting in the clay world is enjoyed by what is known as ZZ shooting. This originated in Monte Carlo after the banning of live bird trap shooting, and its rules closely follow those of the earlier sport. Using expensive special targets, whose flight is unpredictable, it is costly both to install and to shoot and has only a handful of supporters in Britain.

What of the future? I predict a continued growth of the sport in Britain, providing that shooters can fight off the efforts of zealots who seek to put even more restrictions on the possession and use of shotguns under the fatuous guise of controlling the misuse of guns by criminals. In America, there is a growing interest in Sporting Shooting, and several British competitors and officials have been to the US to asist in setting up Sporting layouts. I would like to see only international disciplines shot — after all, we do not play two kinds of soccer. But old habits and the wish for huge scores die hard with some people. By and large, clay shots everywhere are straight, helpful to beginners and fun to be with — so why not join them?

Practical Shotgunning

The clay pigeon disciplines each test the wingshooter's skills: Trap involves going-away shots; Skeet emphasises crossing shots; Sporting throws everything. Clay pigeon then is a target shooting sport based on the shotgun's rôle as a tool for harvesting wildfowl and game birds. Practical Shotgun is a target competition based on the shotgun's other primary rôle: as a fighting implement.

Shotgun completed the Practical Shooting trilogy: it was inevitable that it would follow Practical Pistol and Practical Rifle, but no one knew quite what form it would take, or how it would be scored (or the targets patched). Its first competitive airing was in the spring of 1979, when Nigel Hinton's Milton Small Arms Club in Kent offered a shotgun stage as an adjunct to an open Practical Rifle match. Thenceforth, the shotgun sideshow became a familiar feature of rifle competitions and the following year Peter Sarony included a shotgunner (along with a sniper and two riflemen) in the main team event at the 1980 Practical Rifle National Championships. The real father of the sport, though, was Peter Eliot, a former British Army close combat instructor (who had taught the shotgun to the Royal Ulster Constabulary) and who was then a member of the Essex Police support unit. He was appointed chairman of the UK Practical Shotgun Commission early in 1981.

Eliot is a master tactician, and it is thanks to him that Shotgun is the most realistic of the Practical disciplines. A Practical Shotgun competition is tremendously exhilarating, stressful and exciting. Its practitioners are devoted to the sport, and a very high proportion of them are police officers. The first British Championship took place in November of 1981, following a Southern Area Championship the previous summer. The first European Championship was in 1987.

A typical Practical Shotgun match will comprise several standard exercises, a bush run, a jungle alley, a house clearance and a man v. man. These are all terms of craft. The standard exercises are tests of basic skills, and will typically involve fire from various positions (standing, kneeling, prone, barricade) as well as hip shooting, ambidextrous and fire with movement.

Bush runs and jungle alleys are field courses involving movement across several hundred metres of terrain, often laced with tunnels, scramble nets, routes through the treetops or along streams, and obstacles of various sorts. Some courses are semi-alpine, some semi-aquatic and most require a reasonable degree of physical fitness. The crucial difference is that bush runs are pure speed events, while jungle alleys are tactically scored. A master at fire with movement will win a bush run. He will take all targets on a dead run. A jungle alley requires a wholly different approach.

The shooter's target score will be modified by bonus points for use of cover and penalty points for tactical violations; targets will be well concealed and there will be a generous deployment of trip wires and booby traps, all of which demand very careful observation of every scrap of terrain from the ground immediately underfoot,

out to the limits of effective range. One is still against the clock though; the jungle alley is the essence of Practical Shotgun.

Varied Competitions

House clearances are also tactically scored, and differ from the jungle alley in their setting, which will be in or among buildings. Ranges are comparatively short and targets will not be that hard to locate. Nor are trip wires commonly used. The crucial factors are use of cover and the ability to evaluate sometimes complex situations at a glance, distinguishing hostiles from penalty targets and taking out the former in correct sequence. Highly developed ambidextrous skills are also at a premium, since all shots from left of cover must be taken from the left shoulder.

Man v. man, as the name implies, is a knockout competition, usually involving a little running, a bit of shooting and a good deal of reloading. A fast, positive reload is the key to this one.

Most major competitions will also incorporate a night stage, a slug stage and fire from vehicles. Practical Shotgun, more than most sports, calls on the total man. It requires fitness, the mastery of a wide range of shooting and gunhandling skills, and total mental

Above: *Practical puts a premium on quick thinking. Here, the UK national ladies champion, Madelaine Padmore, uses a field expedient while firing through a barricade aperture.*

Left: *Agility is vital in a sport that routes competitors through tunnels, over walls, and up nets. Here former national champion, Ray Edmonson, engages targets from an awkward perch.*

involvement. The latter includes enhanced powers of observation and fast decision making. One leaves a match with a great sense of accomplishment.

Though paper targets are sometimes used, particularly indoors where, at the distances involved, there would be a danger of rebounding shot, most Practical Shotgun stages are conducted against steel plates of headbox, half-silhouette and silhouette size, calculated to drop from a solidly placed pattern of buck out to about 45 metres. Paper targets are scored for the highest scoring single hit. Ammunition is tightly specified, and will be either birdshot, buckshot or slug, depending on application. Course design is carefully planned with a view to terrain and the danger zone, and buck will only be used against an adequate natural backstop. The fact that LG (equivalent to American 00 buck) has a maximum range of nearly 800 metres (compared to about 200 metres for birdshot) is constantly borne in mind.

Some of us are nostalgic for early days, when Practical was a pump gun game. A well-used pump is quite elegant: there is a skill involved which is nice to watch. These days, it is all autoloaders and efficiency. But that is now. At the first Southern Area Championship, 60 per cent of the competitors used Mossberg 500s, while most of the rest used Remington 870s. There were three gas-operated 1100s, each of which jammed, and it was awhile before automatics overcame the stigma of unreliability. The writing was on the wall, though. Jams notwithstanding, those guns placed 2nd, 8th and 10th.

Nowadays, the guns that win in the UK are the Franchi SPAS 12 and the Remington 1100, the former of which is renowned for its reliability in all circumstances. Its front-heaviness makes it a bit slow mounting, but recoil is extraordinarily soft and the gun tracks extremely well. The 1100, normally used with a Choate pistol-grip stock, is lighter and more agile, and is perfectly reliable providing that it is cleaned every 250 rounds.

US Events

Practical Shotgun in the US is still not as doctrinally or administratively coherent as it is in the UK. But they do shoot enough to break 1100s at an impressive pace. The gun was engineered to shoot forever with light, clay target loads, giving a couple of lifetimes of goose shooting into the bargain. But a relentless diet of buck and slug overloads the system. There are several ways

round. Remington make a heavier-framed 1100 for the 3-inch magnum shell; modified for the standard 12 bore, it gives all the longevity you could hope for. A 20-bore on the standard 12-bore frame, tightly choked so as to maximize energy on the target, also has adherents. The Benelli inertial operated semi-auto enjoys a popularity in the US that it never managed to acquire in Britain. The SPAS 12, on the other hand, is usually dismissed as too portly to cope with. Optical sights such as the Aimpoint are currently much in favour with Practical Shotgunners Stateside.

There are several forms of shoot. Shotguns are much used in 2nd Chance type matches, that involve clearing targets off a table top. Buck is used on skittles, while a slug stage involves sledging over massive steel cutouts in the silhouette of a Soviet battle tank. Both the US Practical Shooting Association and *Soldier of Fortune* magazine hold competitions similar in format to those in Britain. But so far, these have been three-gun events (rifle, pistol and shotgun), with the scattergun having yet to emerge as the sporting tool of a distinct and freestanding competitive discipline. However, we should be surprised if that situation is not rectified by the time this book appears on the bookshelves.

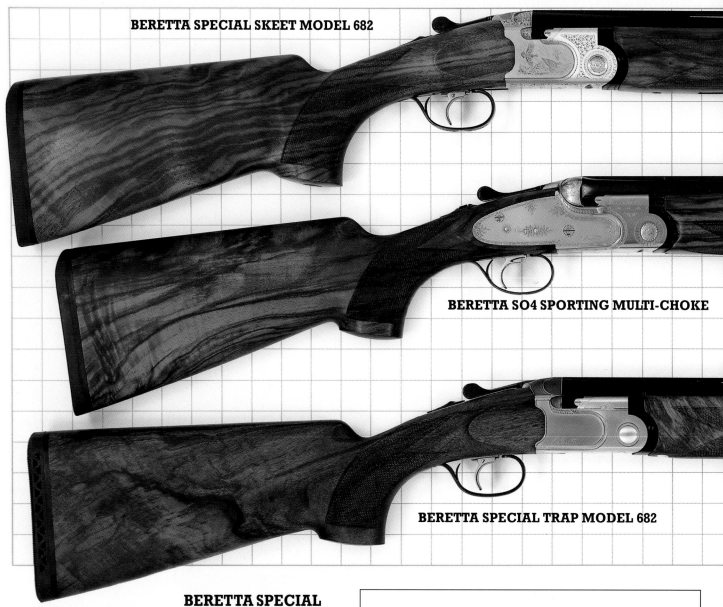

BERETTA SPECIAL SKEET MODEL 682

BERETTA SO4 SPORTING MULTI-CHOKE

BERETTA SPECIAL TRAP MODEL 682

BERETTA SPECIAL SKEET MODEL 682

Country of origin: Italy
Type: Over and Under
Calibre: 12 gauge
Capacity: 2
Action: Standard
Operation: Drop down
Construction: Steel
Barrel length: 28in (711mm) nominal
Length overall: 45.25in (1149mm)
Weight (empty): 7.8lb (3.54kg)
Sights: Day glow type front bead.

It would be unusual indeed if a Beretta should fail to please anyone shopping for an over-under, for their quality is probably unsurpassed in a production gun and the range of choice, when it comes to design for application, is intimidatory. Beretta currently offer no fewer than nineteen 12-bore sporting guns on the UK market, along with ten trap guns and several skeet models.

As well as being one of the world's largest firearms manufacturers, they are also the world's oldest industrial concern. Traditionally, they have claimed an unbroken line of descent in gunmaking from 1680, but records have been discovered relating to one Bartolomeo Beretta (1490-1567), a master barrel-maker of Brescia. The firm is still in the control of the Beretta family.

It is the advent of the multi-choke which largely explains the relative lack of specialized skeet guns in Beretta's otherwise plethoric line. Currently, they make only two: the Skeet Model 682 (top), and the up-market SO4 sidelock at four times the price. But the skeet, sporting and game configurations are close enough together that the non-specialist can very easily screw two cylinder bore inserts into the muzzle and have a very effective substitute skeet gun.

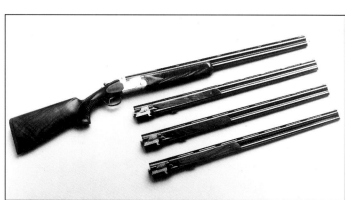

Above: *A Beretta 4-barrel skeet set featuring (from top to bottom) 12, 20, 28 and .410 gauge barrels. Beretta over-unders are world renowned.*

BERETTA SO4 SPORTING MULTI-CHOKE

Country of origin: Italy
Type: Over and Under
Calibre: 12 gauge
Capacity: 2
Action: Sidelock
Operation: Drop down
Construction: Steel
Barrel length: 28in (711mm) with internally threaded multi-choke system
Length overall: 46.75in (1187mm)
Weight (empty): 7.75lb (3.52kg)
Sights: Day glow type front bead.

The elegant sidelock (centre), while it will do excellent work afield, is actually one of a comparatively new breed of competition gun, and is now the biggest seller among competition models in the UK. Not so long ago, the game of Sporting Clays was shot with a

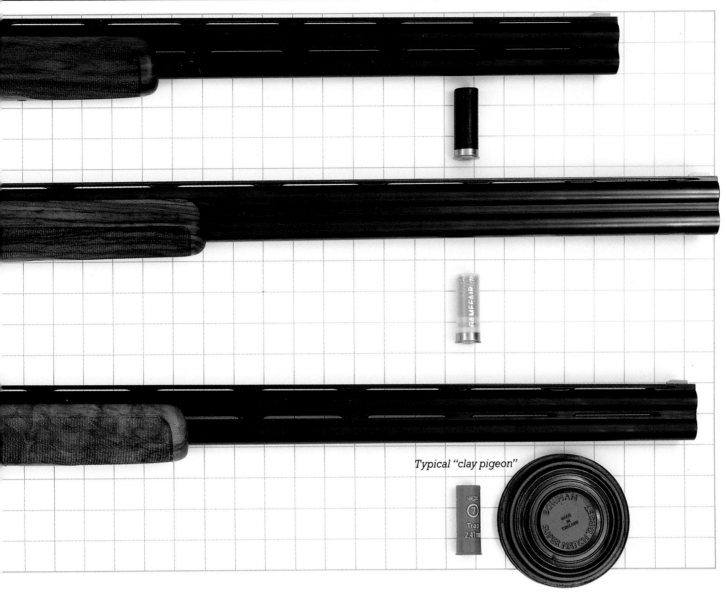

Typical "clay pigeon"

variety of guns, most of them skeet guns, field guns or even trap guns from which maybe some of the choke had been bored out.

Sporting Clays, as a discipline, evolved directly from the shooting schools that date back to the turn of the century. The game shots of that time were in the habit of using these schools for practice for their game shooting, or as "pipe-openers". By the late 1920s, competitions began to be organized and continued apace until 1939. After World War II, the sporting shooting began to increase once more and by the early 1970s such events as the British Open Sporting Championship and the Game Fair Championship were attracting entries in the hundreds, while more local events were expanding along similar lines. Gunmakers realized that what was wanted was a gun bored neither so open as a skeet gun nor as tightly choked as a trap gun. And so the sporting gun was

born, initially with fixed borings of ¼ and ½ choke, or ¼ and ¾, but for several years past in multi-choke models also.

BERETTA SPECIAL TRAP MODEL 682

Country of origin: Italy
Type: Over and Under
Calibre: 12 gauge
Capacity: 2
Action: Standard
Operation: Drop down
Construction: Steel
Barrel length: 30in (762mm)
Length overall: 47in (1194mm)
Weight (empty): 8lb (3.63kg)
Sights: Day glow type front bead.

Trap is a rather different sport, and the Trap Model 682 (bottom) is one of ten such guns currently listed. Trap shooting or, as it was commonly known in Britain, Down-the-Line shooting (a name that is still used for the most common form of the particular kind of trap shooting shot in the UK, certainly until very recent years, when perhaps sporting shooting has

begun to overtake it in sheer numbers of entries) is the oldest form of competitive clay shooting, both in the UK and in the USA.

It evolved directly from the 19th-century sport of shooting live pigeons released from traps, a sport which had in its turn evolved from the practice of putting live pigeons (from specially bred strains, based on the smaller varieties of wild pigeons) under old top hats, which were then pulled away with cords to release the birds. The gun (for they were shot at by one man at a time) then fired at the bird, which was either "killed" or "lost". By the last decade or so of the 19th century, this sport had spread over almost the whole of Europe and special guns had begun to be made for it.

These were often known as "pigeon guns" and were generally heavier than game guns, for the shot loads allowed for trap shooting were usually 1.25oz (35.5g) and the extra weight of the gun counteracted

the extra recoil produced by these loads. When live pigeon shooting from traps was banned both in Britain and the USA, it gave a great boost to the sport of shooting at clay targets which had, in fact, started as early as the 1880s.

The pigeon or trap guns were for many years side-by-side guns, although some special single-barrelled trap guns were made in the United States in the 1920s and 1930s, while the advent of the semi-automatic and the pump gun meant that a good many of these were seen on the trap layouts, particularly in the United States.

The resurgence of the sport after World War II coincided with the growth in popularity of the over-under gun, and now almost every maker of note produces a special trap gun, some in several models. These are different in conformation from every other variety of over-under, and are really only suited to the specialized sport for which they are made.

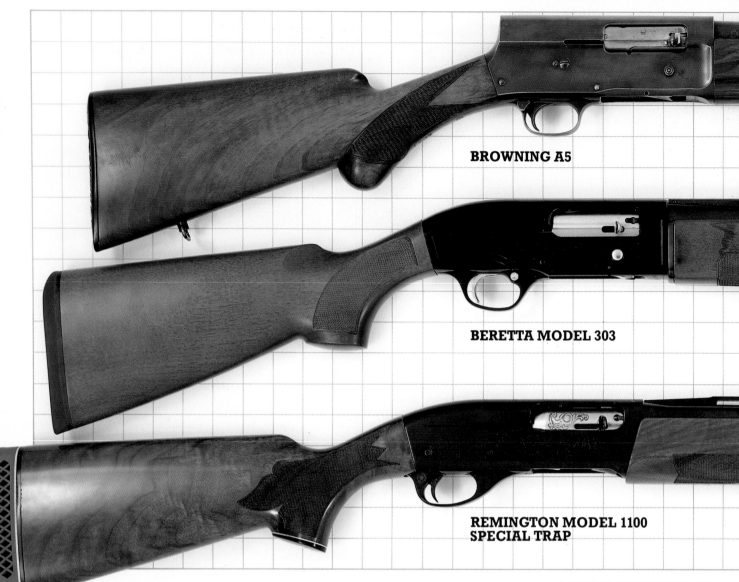

BROWNING A5

BERETTA MODEL 303

**REMINGTON MODEL 1100
SPECIAL TRAP**

BROWNING A5

Country of origin: Belgium
Type: Self-loading shotgun
Calibre: 12 gauge; it has also been made in 16 gauge, and in 20 gauge under licence in the USA
Capacity: 5
Action: Long recoil; locked breech
Operation: Barrel recoils full length of receiver; bolt is retained at rear until the barrel has returned fully forward and is then released to follow
Construction: Steel
Barrel length: 24.75in (629mm) (as shown, with Cutts Compensator)
Length overall: 44.5in (1130mm)
Weight (empty): 8.6lb (3.9kg)
Sights: Brass bead

One suspects that John Browning invented the automatic shotgun—the Browning A5 is shown (top)—for the same reason that the man climbed the mountain: because it was there. But once he had done so, and proved that it worked reliably, it seemed to be just what a lot of people wanted. Patented in 1900, it was, until the advent of the Remington Model 1100 more than 50 years later, the largest selling gun in the world.

Browning originally offered the design to the Winchester Repeating Arms Co., New Haven, Connecticut, as he had done with many previous designs. This time, however, he wanted a royalty arrangement rather than a single, fixed payment for the manufacturing rights. He and Winchester could not agree, so Browning went off to Belgium to arrange for manufacture of the gun by Fabrique Nationale d'Armes de Guerre, one of the few firms with the resources to make such a gun. Production began in 1903, and the A5 became one of the classic guns of modern times: over the next 80 years it was made in millions. Its famous square-backed receiver could be seen in gun shops all over the world and its long-recoil action was copied by almost every rival gunmaking factory. On firing, the barrel and bolt recoil, locked together, the full length of the receiver. The barrel then returns forward alone, ejecting the spent shell, whereupon the bolt follows, loading a fresh round out of the magazine and into the chamber.

The A5 was heavy, but it was also solid and reliable, and it could be adjusted to suit different loads. It was made in almost every style or format: magnum, police models, riot guns, barrels with and without ribs. Before World War II, and for some time after it, if one saw a semi-automatic shotgun on the line at a clay shoot, one could bet that it was a Browning of this kind. It was issued to British troops in Malaya during the troubles of the 1950s, proving its worth in the jungle when loaded with buckshot. It was made under licence in the USA by Remington, as their Model 11, from 1905 until production by Remington ceased in 1948. It has been so closely copied in Japan that one can hardly tell the copy from the real thing.

REMINGTON MODEL 1100 SPECIAL TRAP

Country of origin: USA
Type: Self-loading shotgun
Calibre: 12 gauge
Capacity: 3
Action: Gas operated self-loading
Operation: Piston and return spring; vertically tipping locking block locks bolt to receiver
Construction: Steel
Barrel length: 30in (762mm)
Length overall: 52in (1321mm)
Weight (empty): 8.25lb (3.74kg)
Sights: Brass front bead

The Browning A5 is still in production and still going strong. In recent years, however, it has been eclipsed by a more recent classic, the gas operated Remington 1100 (bottom), shown here in its Special Trap guise, with long barrel, ventilated rib and rubber recoil pad—the latter a belt-and-braces measure, in that the 1100 is one of the softest recoiling guns ever made. It is also extremely reliable, although European trap shooters favour an over-under

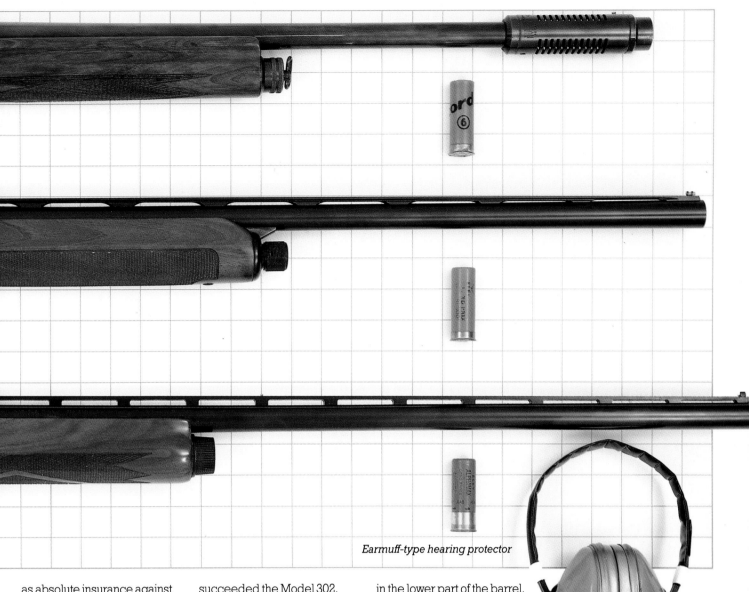

Earmuff-type hearing protector

as absolute insurance against the possibility of a feed or ejection jam—something that the American trap shooter, who only engages single target, need not trouble himself over. Until very recently, in fact, some very fine single-shot American trap guns were being made by Ithaca and others.

BERETTA MODEL 303

Country of origin: Italy
Type: Self-loading shotgun
Calibre: 12 gauge; also made in 20 gauge
Capacity: 4
Action: Gas operated; self-loading
Operation: Gas piston and return spring; tipping block on top of bolt locks into roof of barrel extension
Construction: Aluminium alloy receiver; other parts steel
Barrel length: 28in (711mm)
Length overall: 45.25in (1149mm)
Weight (empty): 7.25lb (3.29kg)
Sights: Day glow front bead.

One of the most impressive and successful of the new generation of self-loading shotguns is the gas operated Beretta Model 303 (centre). The 303

succeeded the Model 302, which in turn followed the 301. It is one of the more handsome guns of its kind, and has proved over the past 20 years to be reliable, with a capability of accommodating almost any cartridges without adjustment.

As in all gas operated guns of this type, gases generated by the firing of the cartridge are tapped off through a vent in the lower part of the barrel, whence they impinge upon the head of a piston, connected by a rod to the action, which is driven rearwards, withdrawing and ejecting the spent cartridge on its way. When it reaches the rearmost part of its travel, the return spring takes over, pushing the bolt forward again, picking up the new cartridge and feeding it into the breech.

Unlike the Remington 1100, which has its manual safety bolt at the rear of the trigger guard, the Beretta Model 303 has its gold-plated safety in the front of the guard. Its trigger is also gold-plated, although in the writer's experience this gold-plating, which is nothing new, wears off fairly rapidly. Weighing 7.25lb (3.29kg) in 12 gauge, as shown here, and 6.25lb (2.83kg) in 20 gauge, the gun is available in field, magnum, multi-choke and sporting versions. The multi-choke models are supplied with three chokes, although more are available.

Left: *Luciano Giovanetti, gold medal winner at the 1984 Los Angeles Olympics, with his Beretta S04 over-and-under trap gun.*

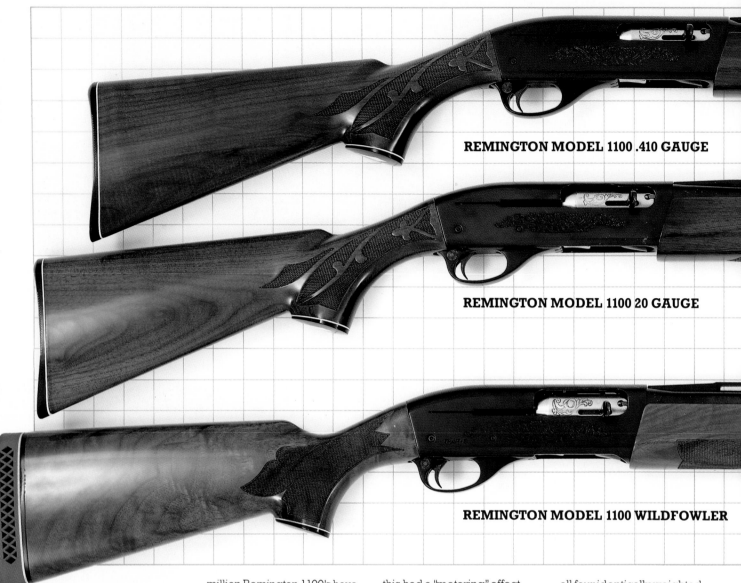

REMINGTON MODEL 1100 .410 GAUGE

REMINGTON MODEL 1100 20 GAUGE

REMINGTON MODEL 1100 WILDFOWLER

REMINGTON MODEL 1100

Country of origin: USA
Type: Self-loading shotgun
Calibre: 12 gauge; 20 gauge; 28 gauge; .410 gauge
Capacity: 3 rounds in most models; extended magazines are available
Action: Gas operated self-loading
Operation: Piston and return spring; vertically tipping locking block locks bolt to receiver
Construction: Steel
Barrel length: From 20in (508mm) to 32in (813mm)
Length overall: As illustrated, from 46in (1168mm) to 50.75in (1289mm)
Weight (empty): From 6lb (2.72kg) to 8lb (3.63kg), depending on format
Sights: Brass front bead.

For the past 20 years, since its introduction, the Remington Model 1100 has consistently outsold all other self-loading shotguns, both in the United States and in most other countries as well. At the time of writing (1987), well over three

million Remington 1100's have been built, a production figure which now exceeds even that of John Moses Browning's original Model A5 which has, except for the World Wars, been in continuous production at Fabrique Nationale, Belgium, since 1903. From 1903 to 1948, the Browning was also manufactured by Remington for the American market.

The quite amazing popularity of the Remington 1100 must surely indicate that it incorporates, in something of an overwhelming manner, those qualities that people desire in a repeating shotgun. Those qualities are, of course, durability, reliability, simplicity and balance. The 1100 has all these; it has also the reputation of being very soft in recoil.

The Model 1100 was designed by Robert P. Kelly and a team of Remington engineers, and was distinguished by its piston, which surrounded the magazine tube and which was impaled by two rather long and narrow gas ports. By design,

this had a "metering" effect which delivered a reasonably uniform impulse over a wide range of cartridge pressures, thus ensuring functional reliability (without adjustment) whatever the load used. An ancillary advantage of the system was that it permitted the use of extended magazines; most competing shotguns mounted the gas port and piston squarely in front of a three-shot magazine.

Capitalizing on a good thing, Remington offer the Model 1100 in four gauges—12 gauge; 20 gauge; 28 gauge; .410 gauge—and in a host of formats, guises and configurations: goose guns, quail guns, skeet guns, trap guns, deer guns, riot guns, youth guns, plain and fancy, as well as straight-grip stocks, folding stocks, Monte Carlo stocks, and mirror-image actions for left-handers.

The Remington Model 1100's shown in the two upper positions in the photograph are skeet guns in .410 gauge (top) and 20 gauge (centre). Another pair, in 28 gauge and 12 gauge,

all four identically weighted and balanced, would make a complete set for American skeet shooting. Trap guns, used for going-away targets rather than crossing shots, have barrels about 4in (102mm) longer and more tightly choked, and also have somewhat different stock measurements.

Even in Great Britain, where self-loaders are not altogether "socially acceptable", several well-known clay shots have made themselves more than respected with Model 1100's, while in the United States it is the gun of choice. Evidence of this was first seen in 1969, when both the US Army and the US Air Force sent official teams to contest the British UIT Skeet Championship; at least three-quarters of the members of these contingents used Remington 1100's.

The remaining gun (bottom) in the photograph is a Model 1100 wildfowler, with a 30in (762mm) full-choked barrel chambered for 3in (76.2mm) shells. Apart from its chamber

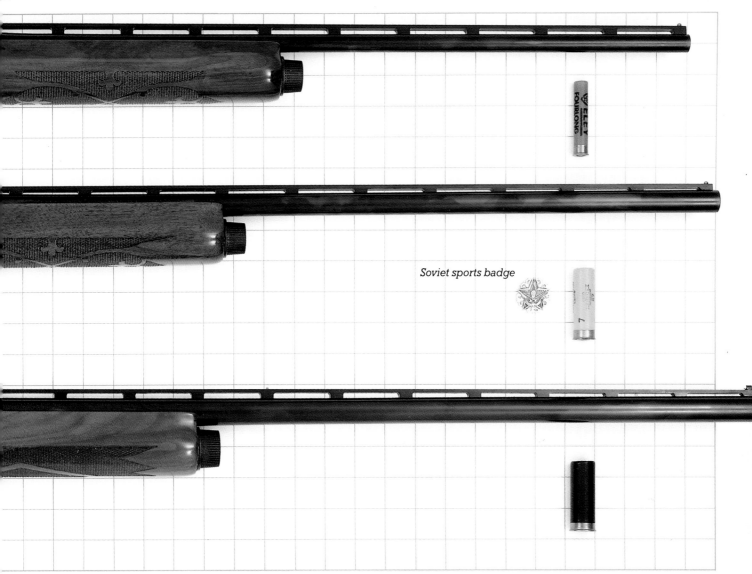

Soviet sports badge

length, it is nearly identical to the Remington 1100 trap model shown on the previous spread (bottom). It is overwhelmingly popular in the United States, where the rules allow only one shot at the target.

Most forms of trap shot in Great Britain, however, allow two shots. Hence the popularity in the UK of the over-under, since on a fast-receding target it is thought desirable for the second shot, if needed, to be from a more tightly choked barrel than the first.

Jim Carmichael, the respected Shooting Editor of *Outdoor Life*, once wrote: "Anyone who can shoot well, will probably shoot better with an 1100." That may be pushing the absolute truth a little, but many 1100 users no doubt believe it—and many people went to the 1100 because they *did* shoot better with one.

Right: *Olympic skeet shooting, Los Angeles, 1984. Skeet guns usually have shorter barrels than trap guns.*

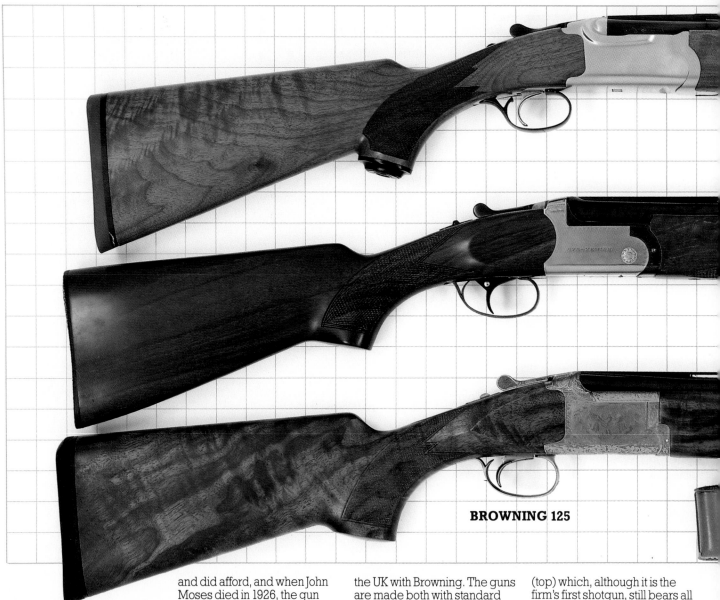

BROWNING 125

BROWNING 125

Country of origin: Belgium
Type: Over and under
Calibre: 12 gauge
Capacity: 2
Action: Standard
Operation: Drop down
Construction: Steel
Barrel length: 28in (71mm)
Length overall: 45.5in (1156mm)
Weight (empty): 7.69lb (3.49kg)
Sights: Pearl bead.

When, in the early 1920s, John Moses Browning designed his first over-and-under gun—a Browning 125 is shown (bottom) —he probably did not realize how much influence he would have on the shooting habits of the world. Although some of the very famous London gunmakers had produced over-and-unders even before World War I, it was the famous factory at Liège, Belgium, known by its first two initials as FN, which enabled the over-under to be made at a price that many people could

and did afford, and when John Moses died in 1926, the gun was in production as the last design evolved by the most inventive man in the history of firearms.

By the 1930s these guns were selling in the USA in substantial numbers. In 1939 a Browning over-under was listed at a price of £19 19s 0d (£19.95) in Britain, and I have seen several of these pre-1939 guns in use to this day. The dollar price would have been in the region of $85 for the plain standard gun. In the immediate post-War years, an over-and-under gun almost invariably meant a Browning, although my first such gun was made by Savage and sold in Britain in 1939 for £10 10s 0d (£10.50) in non-ejector form, a variety which FN never made as a Browning design, theirs all being ejectors.

At present, Liège makes only the more expensive grades of Browning, the lower-priced ones being made in Japan by B.C. Miroku, who share a marketing operation in

the UK with Browning. The guns are made both with standard barrels and with internally threaded variable chokes, which Browning called the Invector system. At the very top of the market, the highest-grade Brownings will cost around £8,000; at the bottom of the range around £1,000. Variations are made for all the clay shooting disciplines and for field use.

RUGER RED LABEL

Country of origin: USA
Type: Over and under
Calibre: 12 gauge
Capacity: 2
Action: Standard
Operation: Drop down
Construction: Steel (gun shown with brushed stainless steel action)
Barrel length: 26in (660mm)
Length overall: 43in (1092mm)
Weight (empty): 7.5lb (3.4kg)
Sights: Gold bead.

Rivalling the traditional Browning for popularity in the USA is Ruger's elegant and recently-introduced Red Label

(top) which, although it is the firm's first shotgun, still bears all the hallmarks of this famous inventor of guns and his team. Sturm, Ruger had been producing rifles and pistols for many years before turning their attention to shotguns, and their first was an over-and-under 20 bore, a very popular gun in the USA. Within about five years, the 12 bore was added to their range, along the same lines as the 20 bore. Both guns come in several barrel lengths and degrees of choke boring and are offered in both blued actions and brushed stainless steel actions. There are no visible screws or pins on the actions which, although devoid of any engraving, still manage to look very handsome. Both the 20 bore (blue finish only) and 12 bore (stainless steel action) are available in two barrel lengths, 26in (660mm) and 28in (711mm), and two Field choke borings plus a Skeet gun, and are chambered for 3in (76mm) cartridges. The guns are fitted with a hammer interrupter which is only lifted clear of the

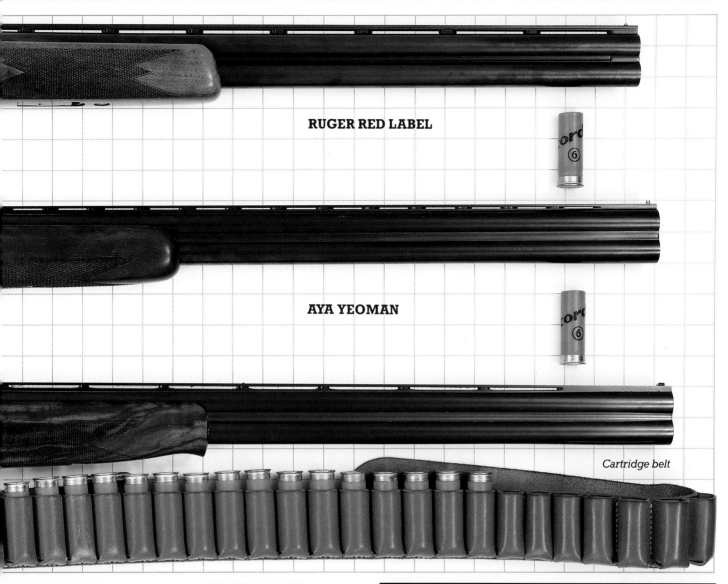

RUGER RED LABEL

AYA YEOMAN

Cartridge belt

hammers by a deliberate pull of the trigger, a valuable safety device similar in its effect to the intercepting safety sears found on most quality sidelock guns and some high-quality boxlocks.

The automatic safety catch incorporates the barrel selector, which pivots from one side to the other and, unlike any other over-and-under, indicates the barrel to be fired first by the unmistakable letters "B" and "T", for bottom and top, rather than the letters "U" and "O" or other symbols which may be more ambiguous. Although the guns weigh 7lb (3.18kg) in 20 bore and 7.5lb (3.4kg) in 12 bore, they handle extremely well and do not feel as heavy as they are. Finish is excellent, the American walnut woodwork being unusually handsome for its kind, and although the guns are not at the cheaper end of the market, they appear to be very good value for money. In 1986, both the 20 bore (introduced in 1977) and the 12 bore (1982) were priced at around $800 (£540) in the USA.

AYA YEOMAN

Country of origin: Spain
Type: Over and Under
Calibre: 12 gauge
Capacity: 2
Action: Standard
Operation: Drop down
Construction: Steel
Barrel length: 28in (711mm)
Length overall: 44.5in (1130mm)
Weight (empty): 7.25lb (3.29kg)
Sights: Brass bead.

One of the firms seeking to serve the lower end of the quality shotgun market is AyA of Spain, whose move to a larger and extremely modern factory in 1986 gave them enough of a boost in efficiency to consider cutting prices. They had, in fact, made over-under guns for some years, but in the higher-priced range, producing guns that were near-identical to the famous Merkel shotguns of Suhl—an excellent recommendation.

The new gun (centre) was called the Yeoman after the company's value-for-money side-by-side which, for 15

years, had made good running in Britain as a sound and well-finished gun, albeit on the plain side.

There are two models, one with standard barrels bored ½ and full chokes and the other a multi-choke version, with three internally threaded choke tubes supplied with the gun and others available at extra cost. The selector for the selective single trigger is a button on the actual trigger rather than the more conventional one fitted to the top strap. A free or non-auto safety catch is fitted as

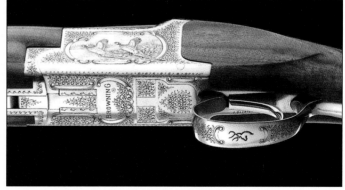

Above: *An example of the fine English scroll engraving on the barrel vane and fences of a Browning 125*

standard, but an automatic one can be fitted at slight extra cost. The gun is aimed at the clay shooting market rather than the game shot and, in the early days from the launch date, demand is proving greater than supply. Thus, deliveries may be somewhat delayed, but this was to be expected and the position will undoubtedly improve with time.

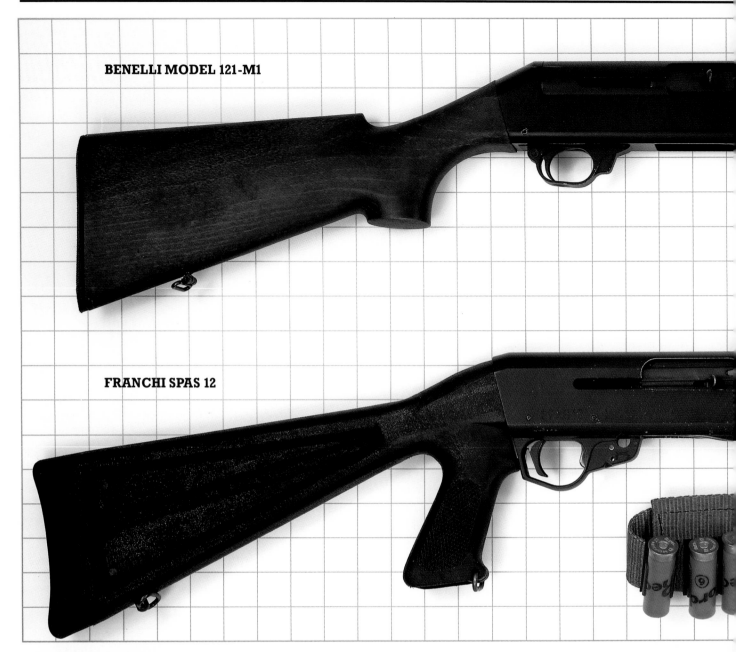

BENELLI MODEL 121-M1

FRANCHI SPAS 12

The term "riding shotgun" has passed into the American vernacular as a description of the position of the front-seat passenger in a vehicle. It stems, no doubt, from the practice of the stagecoach companies of the Old West in putting a scattergun guard alongside the driver for bullion runs. However, the Royal Mail coaches of 18th-century England carried a blunderbuss-armed guard in the same position. If the subject were fully researched, it would probably be found that the shotgun's combat role goes back even farther—to the "deck sweepers" of close naval combat.

From the trenches of World War I to MacArthur's island-hopping campaign of World War II, and thence to the jungles of Malaya, the smoothbore weapon has continued to prove itself in close-quarter combat. So much so, in fact, that it could conceivably replace the rifle as the primary individual weapon of the infantryman. The US Army has desired an individual area-fire capability for some time, and one of the Joint Services Small Arms Program's current projects concerns the development of what is variously referred to as a MIWS or a CAW—translating to "multi-purpose individual weapon" and "close assault weapon" respectively. The current prototypes are box-fed shotguns using high-velocity tungsten alloy buckshot or flechette loads, which are said to be effective to a range of 150 yds (137m).

While the armed forces and industry concoct a new generation of hardware, the capabilities and techniques for using what we already possess have been defined and redefined through sport. Practical Shotgun was developed in Britain, where the first National Championships took place in 1981, and the sport has since been taken up in other countries.

Two of the leading Italian contenders in the Practical Shotgun field are shown here. The only non-Italian gun widely used in top-level competition is the Remington Model 1100.

BENELLI MODEL 121-M1

Country of origin: Italy
Type: Shotgun
Calibre: 12 gauge
Capacity: 7
Action: Self-loading; recoil operated; inertial unlocking
Operation: Inertial piece in bolt assembly moves forward 0.1in (2.54mm) during recoil to unlock bolt head
Construction: Aluminium lower receiver; other parts steel
Barrel length: 20in (508mm)
Length overall: 39.75in (1010mm)
Weight (empty): 7.2lb (3.27kg)
Sights: Ramp foresight; notch rearsight
Comments: Elegant, reliable, and of sophisticated design. Difficult to unload.

The Benelli Model 121 (top) is an elegant weapon, beautifully styled and technically radical. The use of upper and lower receiver assemblies, which slide apart on disassembly, makes maintenance easy, while the locking system confuses even engineers. Basically, the Model 121 is recoil operated, but with a static barrel. The bolt is cammed out of engagement by an inertial piece. That this works is undeniable, but the cyclic speed is such as to suggest semi-blowback operation.

The professional shooter

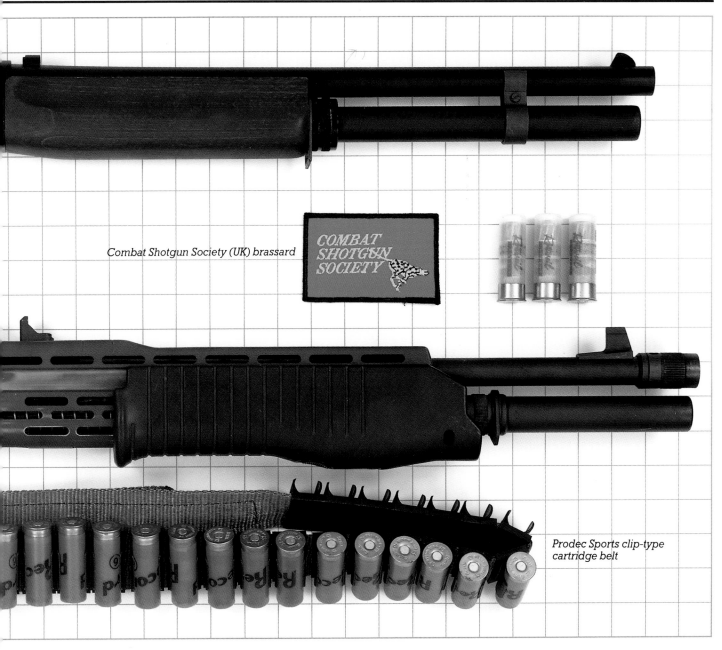

Combat Shotgun Society (UK) brassard

Prodec Sports clip-type cartridge belt

John Satterwhite is said to be able to empty his Benelli in less than one second, finishing with eight ejected hulls in the air at once. While this is, for most of us, of strictly academic interest, it is the speed-of-fire aspect that has made modified Benellis the first choice in the United States for shotgun skittles matches. The modifications consist of porting and muzzle brakes and weights, all calculated to diminish muzzle lift, allowing the gun's potential rate of fire to be deployed in a lateral sweep along the tabletop. Most Benelli aficionados say that they can deliver five shots per second when everything goes right.

The lack of a gas assembly makes the gun defter and more agile in handling than are most shotguns with extended magazines. Indeed, its only known vices are its somewhat brisk recoil and the fact that it is

difficult to unload. Early versions, practically speaking, had to be shot empty. Later ones can be hand-cycled to unload, but it is still a chore.

FRANCHI SPAS 12

Country of origin: Italy
Type: Shotgun
Calibre: 12 gauge
Capacity: 8
Action: Gas operated self-loader or manual pump repeater
Operation: Conventional, save that pushbutton in fore-end allows it to be snapped backwards, closing gas port and converting to pump operation. The gun has two manual safeties; a rotary lever for transport and a Garand-type "fast action" safety in front of the trigger guard
Construction: Aluminium receiver; other parts steel
Barrel length: 21.5in (546mm)
Length overall: 41in (1041mm)
Weight (empty): 9.6lb (4.35kg)
Sights: Square post foresight; large aperture backsight mounted on barrel

Comments: Heavy and extremely reliable; it can be used with many special purpose munitions.

The Franchi SPAS 12 (bottom) in some respects counterpoints the Benelli. Where the latter is agile and easy to handle, the SPAS is ponderously muzzle-heavy and slow to mount. Whereas the Benelli has the reputation (which it has earned) of kicking hard, the SPAS is the softest of 12-bores and is, despite the ferocious cosmetics, used for clay pigeon shooting by rheumatoid arthritics who would not otherwise be medically allowed to shoot.

The cosmetics of the SPAS are mostly functional. The pistol grip may be a matter of fashion, but the massive front end derives from the fact that the gun is dual-function pump action or gas-operated self-

loading. An inset pushbutton latch in the fore-end allows it to be clicked rearward, closing the gas system for manual operation. Experienced users may go to pump operation in the case of malfunction, but the purpose of it is to allow the gun to be used as a manual repeater with special low-pressure ammunition which would not cycle it as a self-loader. Examples are gas munitions, plastic pellet "stinger" shot, baton rounds, high explosive and flares.

The SPAS normally comes with a folding metal stock with a pivoting "shepherd's crook" that hooks under the forearm, permitting the gun to be shot one-handed from the hip quite handily. The gun shown here has a moulded Choate replacement stock, minus the hook.

The SPAS has been criticised for its complexity, which will initially baffle the untrained.

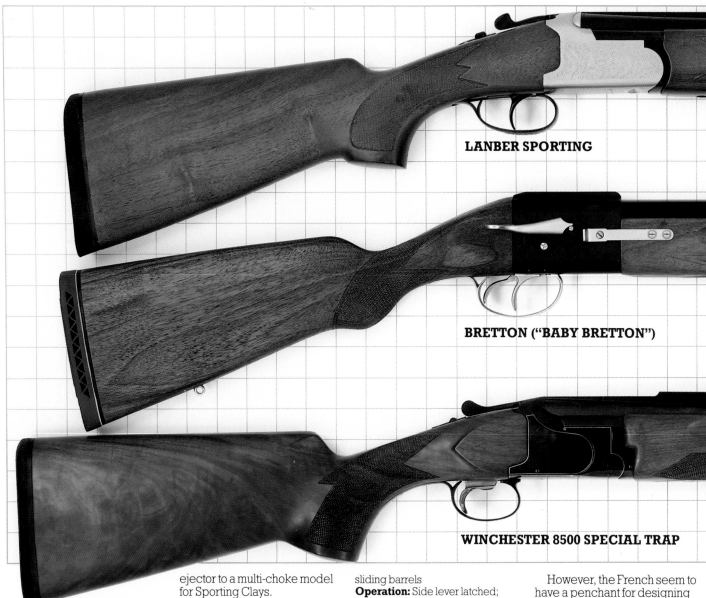

LANBER SPORTING

BRETTON ("BABY BRETTON")

WINCHESTER 8500 SPECIAL TRAP

LANBER SPORTING

Country of origin: Spain
Type: Over and Under
Calibre: 12 gauge
Capacity: 2
Action: Standard
Operation: Drop down
Construction: Steel
Barrel length: 28in (711mm)
Length overall: 44.5in (1130mm)
Weight (empty): 7.25lb (3.29kg)
Sights: Brass bead

The ubiquitous over-under format comes at all levels of sophistication from rustic to exquisite, passing through the category of "sound but unexciting"—a label that well describes the Lanber (top). Built by Spain's largest maker of over-unders, it has the reputation in the United Kingdom of being a good gun for the money. Currently, that money is £450 for the most expensive of six models in the line, which ranges from a basic non-

ejector to a multi-choke model for Sporting Clays.

A feature of the guns is that, apart from the 3in (76mm) Magnum model, the field models have rather more open boring than some others at the inexpensive end of the market, where half- and full-choke seems to be the norm. The multi-choke models come with five different chokes and a hefty spanner to assist in screwing or unscrewing them. The engraving, although done by machine, is at least respectable, and spare parts are readily available if needed. In persevering only with a 12-gauge gun, with minor variations, Lanber Armas S.A., to give them their full title, have secured a niche in the British market which must give their agents great satisfaction.

BRETTON ("BABY BRETTON")

Country of origin: France
Type: Over and Under
Calibre: 12 gauge
Capacity: 2
Action: Original and unique

sliding barrels
Operation: Side lever latched; barrels slide to open
Construction: Steel and alloy
Barrel length: 27.75in (705mm)
Length overall: 45in (1143mm)
Weight (empty): 5.125lb (2.32kg)
Sights: Front bead

The bizarre, featherweight Bretton (centre) is more of a latter-day garden gun. (Note that the gun shown here lacks its muzzle-locking collar). The French, frankly, have never succeeded in building a shotgun which achieved any volume sales outside France, and it is to be doubted whether they have exported more than a handful of shotguns over the past 80 years, unless it was to their former colonial empire. And although many guns sold in France itself in the past bore French names and addresses, on closer examination they were revealed to have been made in Liège, for sale by a retailer in Paris or some other large French city. There were even some German-made guns which bore similar names.

However, the French seem to have a penchant for designing guns which are unusual and, judged by conventional designs, perhaps even outlandish. In the post-War era, particularly in the 1950s and 1960s, determined efforts were made to sell the Darne gun, a sliding breech side-by-side, in Great Britain. It was extremely well made and handsome—although the technical claims made for it were more apparent in theory than in practice—but never succeeded in selling more than a handful outside France. The company which made it ceased trading some years ago.

The Bretton, which is often called the "Baby Bretton", falls into much the same category. It is an unusual design, in which the barrels, having been unlocked from the action by means of a large lever on the right side of the action, slide forward to open the gun. As this is done, the spent cartridge case is ejected, although not very forcibly. The barrels, which can be fitted with

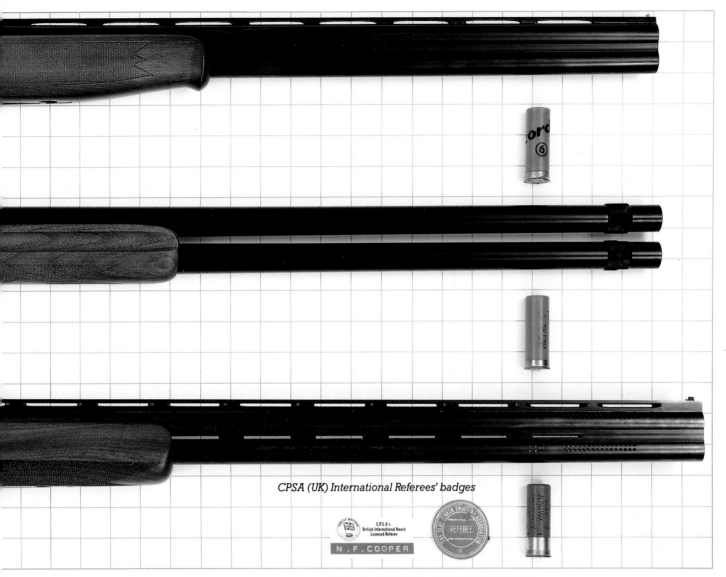

CPSA (UK) International Referees' badges

C.P.S.A.'s
British International Board
Licensed Referee

REFEREE

N. F. COOPER

variable chokes, are secured together only at the breech and at the muzzles, the latter by means of a detachable twin collar (not shown in the photograph). It has two triggers. Its chief "claim to fame" is its extraordinary lightness, but as might be expected, except with very light loads the recoil is considerably above that from heavier guns. I suspect that, like the Darne, it will disappear from the sporting scene.

WINCHESTER 8500 SPECIAL TRAP

Country of origin: Japan
Type: Over and Under
Calibre: 12 gauge
Capacity: 2
Action: Standard
Operation: Drop down
Construction: Steel
Barrel length: 30in (762mm)
Length overall: 50.75in (1289mm)
Weight (empty): 8.3lb (3.8kg)
Sights: Pearl bead.

Quite at the other end of the spectrum from the Bretton is

the splendid Winchester 8500 Special Trap (bottom).

With the modern pattern of huge conglomerate companies, it is perhaps not surprising that the giants of ammunition production in the United States, Winchester and Remington, long ago came into the maw of the two largest chemical companies in America, Du Pont and Olin Industries, the former owning Remington and the latter Winchester.

Above: *A Pazelli International clay target machine; this version can hold 200 individual targets*

Remington has retained the manufacture of its ammunition, shotguns and other firearms within the United States, but Olin, on the other hand, has for several years past transferred the making of shotguns to a Japanese subsidiary. Nikko

Arms had formerly exported guns to the United Kingdom under three names: its own, Shadow and Winchester; and I suspect that it was arranged later that Nikko would market only under the Winchester name.

The range of models includes several over-unders, among them the 8500 Special Trap shown here. It is of quite distinctive appearance, with a plain black action, high trap rib and ventilated mid-rib. An unusual note is that the bottom barrel is "ported"; that is, it has a series of small round holes running along the barrel for some 4in (102mm) from around 3in (76mm) from the muzzle. The theory behind this is that the gases, or some portion of them, are vented before they leave the muzzle, thus helping to reduce muzzle "flip" and assisting in keeping the gun on target for the second shot. The method has been used before, mainly by means of venting right at the end of the barrels, but "porting" is claimed to be more effective and less noisy.

BLACK POWDER & VINTAGE FIREARMS

Richard Munday (Introduction) and Bill Curtis

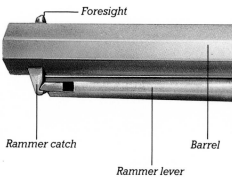

Foresight

Rammer catch

Rammer lever

Barrel

Below: *The French Lock. Cocking action rotates the tumbler, compresses the leaf spring and engages the sear. Pressure on trigger releases cock and flint which falls striking sparks on the frizzen.*

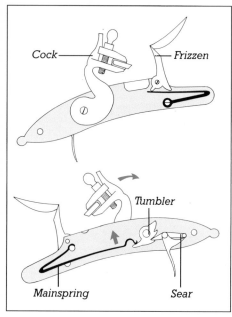

Cock

Frizzen

Tumbler

Mainspring

Sear

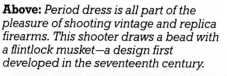

W hen a British international rifle team returned to England in 1877, the squad's adjutant described their weapons as "relics of a bygone age". They had just been defeated by the Americans in what the latter, with a developing flair for publicity, had proclaimed to be the "Championship of the World" at Creedmoor, on Long Island. Long range "Match Rifle" shooting of the kind with which Creedmoor and its British equivalent Wimbledon were synonymous was a somewhat esoteric Anglo-American speciality, but it was an intense and highly prestigious domain of ballistic experimentation, and lessons were drawn from the fact that the British had lost with muzzleloaders, whilst the victorious Americans had proved the merits of the breechloader.

A return match was held, 108 years later—and the British were still using muzzleloaders: original .461 Gibbs-Metfords from the period of that earlier Creedmoor match. In an experimental revival of the long range black powder meetings the British muzzleloaders had already beaten a Canadian breechloading team at Bisley in 1984, despite various other concessions that the Canadians had made to technical modernity. With a touch of eminently British priggery, the home team

Above: *Period dress is all part of the pleasure of shooting vintage and replica firearms. This shooter draws a bead with a flintlock musket—a design first developed in the seventeenth century.*

Below: *Major Edson Warner of Canada competing with his Martini action breech loader. Target barrels and modern sights may be controversial but the performance of such "old timers" remains impressive.*

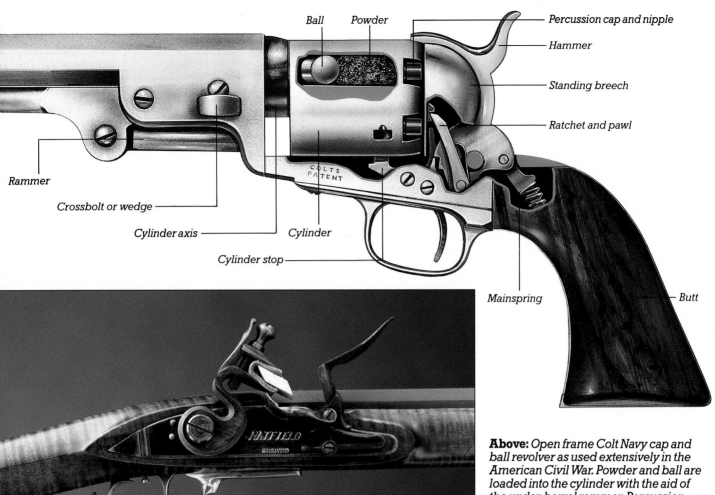

Ball   Powder   Percussion cap and nipple

Hammer

Standing breech

Ratchet and pawl

Rammer

Crossbolt or wedge

Cylinder axis

Cylinder

Cylinder stop

Mainspring

Butt

Above: *Open frame Colt Navy cap and ball revolver as used extensively in the American Civil War. Powder and ball are loaded into the cylinder with the aid of the under-barrel rammer. Percussion caps are then attached to each nipple.*

Left: *A Hatfield flintlock squirrel rifle. These full-stocked hunting rifles typically carried octagonal barrels, hair triggers, scrolled trigger guards and were normally .45 calibre or smaller.*

disdained such innovations as mixed nitro and black powder backing copper gas-checked bullets, and 20th-century target sights; instead, they kept strictly to the "spirit of the original", the concept which has become the benchmark of present-day competition with historical weapons.

Considerations of Marksmanship

Charges of 90 to 106 grains (5.8gm to 6.9gm) of Treble Strength No 6 black powder, individually pre-measured to keep load tolerances within one grain (.0648gm) —which Sir Henry Halford had observed, in 1888, could make a difference of 10in (25.4cm) in point of impact at 1,000 yards (914.4m)—were slipped down the old, much-vaunted shallow-grooved Metford rifling, and topped with a thin patch of hard glazed card. Atop that, in turn, a long cylindro-conical lead bullet, hardened with tin and antimony and wrapped in a paper patch wound anti-clockwise for clockwise rifling, was then seated. Within a preferred weight range of 530-560 grains (34.3-36.3gm), the bullets had also been pre-weighed to keep batch tolerances down to one grain (.0648gm).

Beyond the technical precision of preparing a muzzleloader for thousand-yard shooting, were all the standard long range marksmanship considerations of relative humidity, air temperatures and pressures, and the enhanced wind-doping problems of that big, comparatively slow projectile. Lateral wind corrections for the Gibbs-Metford are reckoned to average one-and-a-third times that for a modern 7.62mm target rifle, but the old steeply-diving cannon shell is much more susceptible to head and tail winds at extreme distances.

The Gibbs-Metfords with which the British beat the Canadians in 1984 and with which they faced the Americans in 1985 were still in premium condition, gems of the gunmaker's art, and the apogee of muzzleloading weaponry. But it all availed the British nothing: the Americans won again. And like Colonel Peel, the British adjutant in 1877, members of the 1985 British team were heard muttering afterwards about the merits of going over to breechloaders — perhaps to some Farquharson or Edge falling-block of suitable Imperial pedigree, or maybe even (it was contemplated, with a touch of *fin de siècle* despondency) to the Americans' own Sharps-Borchardt.

As the British tried to prove again to the Americans that the sun had never really set on the muzzleloaders of Imperial Wimbledon, it appeared that little had changed over the past century. And, indeed, defining the "end" of the muzzleloading era, let alone that of the much broader category of black powder weaponry in general, is a very tricky business. The time-span which separates the assault rifle from the flintlock is a relatively short one; and firearms are durable items, which often pass through many hands and generations, and from those who can afford new technology to those who cannot. Whether even nowadays relics of the black powder era can properly be described as obsolete, probably depends on the area of the globe one is discussing, and the current availability there of the Kalashnikov.

Certainly there is a substantial overlap between the regular, working use of black powder guns and the modern, historically-inspired black powder revival. Bill Curtis, rifle secretary of the Muzzle Loaders' Association of Great Britain, started black powder shooting in 1950 when he found muzzleloading shotguns and their myriad of period accessories gathering dust in Australian gunshops. Turner Kirkland, who introduced the first production modern black powder "replica"—a "Kentucky" rifle

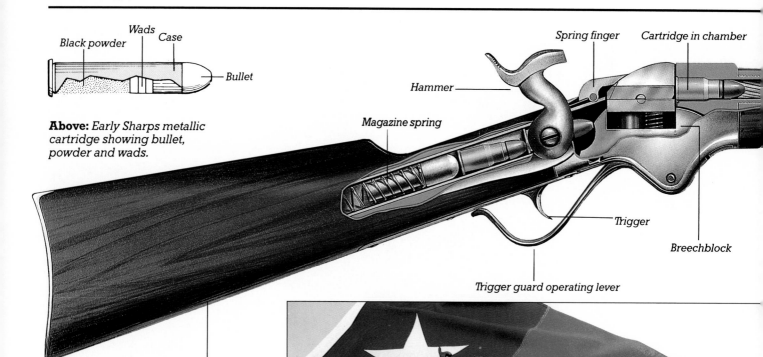

Black powder　Wads　Case

Bullet

Above: *Early Sharps metallic cartridge showing bullet, powder and wads.*

Magazine spring

Hammer

Spring finger　Cartridge in chamber

Trigger

Breechblock

Trigger guard operating lever

Butt

Above: *The 1860 Spencer tubular magazine rifle. The lever action chambered and ejected the rimfire round, but the hammer had to be cocked by hand.*

Right: *Top quality replicas for the modern black powder shooter: Gallager carbine, Sharps long range and sporting rifles, Sharps carbine, Berdan rifle, and the Pennsylvania rifle.*

Far right: *"First Snow" painted in 1855 by Arthur F. Tait, a romanticized scene of buckskinners hunting deer with full-stocked rifles that latter day mountain-men emulate at their annual "rendezvous".*

—to the USA in 1955, entered the firearms world with a worn-out 1849 .31 Colt Pocket Model purchased in 1932 for 75¢. Val Forgett, often described as the "father of modern black powder shooting", who first introduced Italian-made replica percussion revolvers to the USA and who was subsequently knighted for his services to the gun industry of the Val Trompia, had himself started black powder shooting at the age of eight. When Forgett brought out his Navy Colt replicas in 1958, prices of the originals were picking up with the approach of the American Civil War centennials, but until a few years previously they were readily available for $50-$75.

Elmer Keith, the "father of the .44 Magnum", had started his splendid six-gunning career with an old Navy Colt; and in some backwoods areas of America, flintlocks were still working guns at least into the 1930s. In that same decade in Europe, several manufacturers were still producing pinfire cartridges, and the shotgun market to this day includes a rich mix of vintage weapons. Early central-fire hammer shotguns from the 1860s and 1870s, with Damascus barrels pitted way out of their original black powder proof and never proved for nitro powders, still see working use on English farms.

Entering the domain of the early cartridge firearms, past and present are inextricably intertwined. The Historical Breechloading Smallarms Association defines the "Classic" period as that half century of rich mechanical invention between the general introduction of breechloaders and World War I: and the sporting firearms of today and the modern shooting sports themselves are in a substantial measure the product of that fifty-year period.

Enduring Technology

The favourite weapon of today's Practical Pistol shooter, the Colt .45 Automatic, was introduced in its first variant to the US Army in 1911; the Smith & Wesson .44 Magnum and the sleek-lined Colt Python are both built on frames and actions essentially dating from the 1890s. On target rifle ranges, the most commonly favoured bolt action is still based on that of the 1898 Mauser of Hohenzollern Germany, whilst smallbore shooters still use the Martini action that British troops carried at Isandhlwana and Rorke's Drift. The modern double sidelock ejector "best" shotgun is still that of the Classic period, and virtually indistinguishable inside or out from its

predecessor built at the end of the reign of Queen Victoria.

It could be claimed that modern shooters are still armed with the technology of the last century, and that black powder shooting itself never really died out. The most one can speak of is a gradually emerging appreciation of earlier firearms as historical artifacts; and if one had to name one origin for the renaissance of their use, it would probably be with the formation of the National Muzzle Loading Rifle Association in the United States.

In February 1931, Red Ferris and Oscar Seth had gathered 67 competitors for a muzzleloading rifle match in western Ohio; not long afterwards, Boss Johnson and Pop Neighbert brought muzzleloaders together for another shoot, over the border in Indiana, at the little hamlet of Friendship. The two groups united to form the NMLRA in 1935, and in due course the Association built up a 175-point range on a 92-acre (37ha) site at Friendship.

American muzzleloaders now congregate at Friendship for a two-day turkey shoot in the autumn, and for the six days of the US Championship, which end annually on Labor Day (in early September). The Championships include some 70 events and 14 aggregates, of which the most

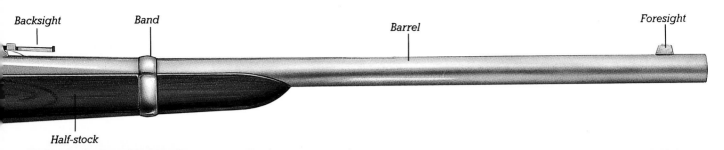

Backsight   *Band*   *Barrel*   *Foresight*

Half-stock

prestigious is the four-part National Championship. This is composed of a 25-yard (22.86m) offhand match, 50-yard (45.72m) benchrest matches in open sight and any-iron-sight categories, and a 100-yard (91.44m) benchrest shoot—distances all within the capabilities of the patched-ball long rifle famous in American frontier romance.

Recreating History

Two elements may be discerned in the black powder historical revivalism which began at Friendship: an interest in the technical history of firearms and marksmanship, and the desire to recreate an "historical period". At the beginning of the 1950s, the separate development of these two themes was illustrated by the formation of the Muzzle Loaders' Association of Great Britain, and the North-South Skirmish Association in the United States.

The North-South Skirmish Association emerged from a confrontation between a team of latter-day Confederates and a platoon dressed in the uniforms of the Civil War Union army, at the Berwyn Rod & Gun Club in May 1950. The Confederates proceeded to wipe out a 25-yard (22.86m) balloon array faster than the Bluebellies,

and beat them also on a 50-yard (45.72m) conventional target shoot. Since then, the N-SSA has grown to include contingents of some 150 recreated Civil War regiments, and, as well as regional matches, hosts national events every spring and autumn at Fort Shenandoah, Virginia. The nationals include both individual and team shooting events, the latter still often on frangible targets, which offer a ready display of the state of the "battle". The N-SSA also includes events for cannon, which always seem to attract black powder shooters.

With the approach of the Civil War centennials, interest in recreated skirmishes burgeoned. Soon, imported Zouave Remingtons abounded, and there were more reproduction Confederate revolvers on the American market than the Confederacy ever possessed. But there were also more Harper's Ferry flintlock pistols than Harper's Ferry Arsenal turned out, and more Patersons and Walkers than Sam Colt could ever sell, for the historical revivalism spread out across the frontiers of American history.

There were a host of other local centennials to celebrate—like that of Union City, Tennessee, which Turner Kirkland of Dixie Gun Works marked by touching off a cannon and blowing the windows out of the

Obion County courthouse—and then there was the up-coming American Bicentennial. The Brigade of the American Revolution and various other "1776" groups were formed, and in Pennsylvania, a "tactical musket" competition was developed, in which rival teams in period uniform performed a 200-yard (182.8m) march-down to a drummer's time, halting to fire volleys along the way at silhouettes of 18th-century soldiers, before the final 30-yard (27.2m) bayonet charge into the targets. On the East Coast still earlier colonial times were remembered by a new St. Marie Cittie Militia, and on the West Coast by a Renaissance/Reformation group in the Conquistadores' California; whilst more modern types out in the desert wanted to re-fight the Indian Wars, and re-formed US Cavalry units began gathering annually at Tucson and Fort Huachuca, Arizona.

Meantime, latter-day mountain men had been springing up all over the place, and the annual "rendezvous" of the frontier fur trapper has become the modern buck-skinner's jamboree, with muzzleloading shooting competitions ranging from splitting bullets on axe blades to chopping logs with musket balls. In the mid-1970s, the National Rifle Association of America started hosting

a yearly rendezvous at Santa Fé, and there are a number of specialist groups devoted to the practice, like the American Mountain Men from California, and the Montana-based National Association of Primitive Riflemen.

Elements of Pageantry

Whilst period costume is often preferred, if not obligatory, at many American muzzleloaders' rendezvous, it is generally not acceptable at meetings of the Muzzle Loaders' Association of Great Britain. If the advent of the N-SSA serves to mark the growth of the pageant approach to muzzleloading, the history of MLAGB since its formation in 1952 illustrates the development of black powder shooting as a manifestation of "serious" academic study of firearms history. At least that is how the British, ever fond of making a virtue out of perceived necessity, often regard it. In the subtle historical theatre of English society on Bisley Camp, conscious anachronism might seem to come too close to satire: in order to gain acceptance and respectability with the ultra-conservative British National Rifle Association, MLAGB sought to minimize the eccentricities of their profile. Such eccentricities might be deemed to include

pistol shooting, which was a highly dubious interest in the eyes of some members of the NRA's old guard, and MLAGB in fact only permitted pistol competition at Bisley when they were more securely established in the late 1960s. MLAGB concentrated on shooting the .577 Enfield of the NRA's own early Volunteer history, and attracted a great deal of interest and expertise from collectors of vintage weaponry.

The contrast between New World black powder fancy-dress and Old World sobriety is, of course, not clear cut. Britain has its own Civil War revivalists (though the Sealed Knot is only secondarily interested in actual musket shooting), and Sussex mountain men have been known to rendez-vous in the improbable setting of the South Downs. The United States, on the other hand, holds 13 out of 18 world championship titles in black powder shooting, as Val Forgett, Chairman of their international shooting team as well as having been an active member of the North-South Skirmish Association, points out. Yet it is, none-theless, in Europe that black powder shooting as a modern international sport was established, and Britain, with the oldest national black powder association in the Old World, has played a leading rôle in its development.

France started shooting black powder at the end of the 1950s, and a quarter-century ago the first Entente Cordiale match was held, an annual event hosted alternately in England and France ever since. It was from the Entente Cordiale that the concept of a wider international black powder meeting was mooted, and in 1971 muzzleloaders from both sides of the Atlantic gathered at Vaudoy-en-Brie to establish the Muzzle Loading Associations' International Committee. The first international Black Powder Olympics were held in Madrid the following year, and annually thereafter the scale of the meeting grew. When the US first partici-pated in 1976, there were 16 nations shoot-ing, and by the time the Americans played host at Quantico in 1980, there were 20.

National Shooting Traditions

The nine individual and team events which today constitute the international programme for musket and muzzleloading rifle competition are no more than the common factors which enable a much richer variety of national shooting traditions to be brought together. The percussion events, for instance, are divided simply by calibre at 100 metres (109.36 yds), to segregate the large bore military rifles from

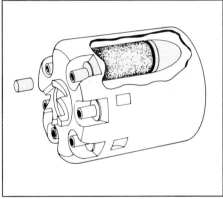

Above: *A modern reproduction matchlock at the moment of ignition. These guns have very slow lock times making a steady hold and follow-through vital to accurate performance.*

Left: *On the Gallery range at Bisley one competitor fires his percussion revolver while another reloads. In modern competition, replica guns are permitted providing that they are "within the spirit of the original".*

Right: *Extracting maximum accuracy from a black powder revolver demands great dedication. Awkward balance, fine trigger blades, indistinct sights and slow lock times make high scores hard to build. Hence the common practice of scoring the best ten from 13 shots.*

Above: *A cutaway cylinder from a six shot percussion revolver showing a chamber charged with powder and bullet and nipples ready for capping.*

the .45 calibre "small-bore" target weapons —but the latter include both the long range rifles that have been revived for Creedmoor-style shooting and the offhand rifles of the continental European *Schützen* tradition.

Schützen, which was the ancestor of today's UIT rifle shooting, just as long range shooting set the pattern for the modern matches of the British and American National Rifle Associations, has begun a revival on both sides of the Atlantic. In the USA, where the North American Schuetzen Bund was the first national rifle organization, with some 130,000 members before World War I, the pedigree of Alpine shooting is strong; but even in Britain, where it never took root, the appeal of the beer and black powder of a *Schützenfest* has proven irresistible. MLAGB organized a *Fest* in 1986, the final shoot-offs of which were held on the traditional, carefully hand-painted pictorial targets.

The international flintlock matches—rifle at 100 metres (109.36 yds), smoothbore musket at 50 metres (54.68 yds)—likewise bring together hardware from different traditions, and miss out individual specialities, like the British rapid fire course for the Brown Bess: ten shots in a hot, smoky ten minutes. The international programme does, however, include a matchlock event,

introduced in 1977 at the behest of the Japanese, for whom the match-fired weapon was the naturally available black powder gun. Whilst matchlocks remained in general use in the Orient until the mid-19th century, they were going out of fashion in Europe two centuries earlier: but the replica manufacturers have come to the European shooters' rescue. The revival still has a long way to go, however, if modern matchlock shooting is to reach the scale of the great international competitions of the 16th century—like the six-week Zürich *Freischiessen* of 1504, which drew on competitors from Cologne to Venice.

The international pistol programme includes individual events for smoothbore flintlock pistols and for rifled single-shot percussion pistols, and individual and team matches for percussion revolvers, all at 25 metres (27.34 yds). Once again, individual national specialities open up the variety of competition much wider: in Britain, the Crimea Cup includes a stern 10-yard (9.144 m) test of rapid thumb-cocking or trigger-cocking skills in a series of five shots in ten seconds; whilst out at 100 yards (91.44 m), those using percussion revolvers shoot a long range match of five-shot strings which must be completed within thirty seconds.

Muzzleloading pistoleers have also experimented with the electronic target apparatus of the British Duelling Federation, which measures the speed and accuracy of an exchange of shots in a confrontation between a pair of duellists at 25 metres (27.34 yds), on Regency-style silhouettes representing the two opponents. Such a competition puts a premium on the shooter's nerve, especially with a flintlock, where a smooth follow-through is essential to stay on target between the flash in the pan and the ignition of the main charge.

Speed of Ignition

It was speed of ignition which distinguished the flintlocks of the great gunmakers, with their patent breeches and refined actions, and which today separates the best quality target replicas from the mere "look-alikes". Speed of discharge is of the essence for the pistol shooter, with his unsteady hold, and perhaps still more so for the shotgunner, where live quarry would instinctively "duck the flash". On the clay pigeon layouts of modern international muzzleloading competition, the slower ignition of the less-distinguished flintlock shotguns is compensated by stationing the flint shooters only five metres (5.47 yds)

from the trap, as opposed to eight metres (8.75 yds) for percussion shotgunners. The international muzzleloading clay courses are derived from Down-The-Line, but guns of the pre-choke era could also do well on Skeet or on Sporting layouts.

In the game field itself, the only half-significant disadvantage of the muzzle-loader, compared with the modern shotgun, is its slowness of reloading. And whereas the target rifle or pistol shooter can spread out his multitude of accoutre-ments on the firing line, the game shooter must carry them all with him: shot flask, powder flask, thick felt wads with greased edges, thin card top wads with vent holes, nipple key, spare nipples, pricker for cleaning the same, percussion caps and cap dispenser (or spare flints), and a powder measure for safer reloading.

"Who has not been put off his shooting", asked H. A. Leveson, recalling mid-19th-century shooting parties in 1868, "by having to wait while some nervous, fidgety old gentleman hunts in a dozen pockets?" With practised, deft hands, loading time of a double could be got down to half a minute, but over-hastiness might easily lead to charging one barrel twice or sparking off the new load on a scrap of smouldering tow in the bore. The answer, of course, is for the sportsman to have servants to load for him. Lord Walsingham, one of the greatest game shots of the 19th century, could keep up a prodigious rate of fire with his retinue loading three muzzleloading guns—but even then, there could be perils. On one partridge drive, a spark apparently caught the transfer of powder from one loader's flask to another, and Walsingham and his entire party disappeared in a cloud of smoke. Lord Walsingham was subsequently persuaded to go over to breechloaders; but to the end of his days, when modern, choked, fluid-steel-barrelled hammerless ejectors had become the norm on the great estates, Walsingham still prefered the cylinder-bored damascus-barrelled ham-mer guns of the early cartridge era. His shooting with them is enduring proof of their capabilities: on 30 August 1888, he used four of them to drop 1,070 grouse with 1,510 cartridges.

In some areas of game shooting, like wildfowling with punt guns, black powder has always retained its position; but its really big come-back has been in the hunting of deer and other larger-sized game in the United States. The .58 calibre Civil War rifles beloved of the North-South Skirmish Association, driving a 500-grain (32.4gm) Minié bullet at 1,000 feet per second (305 mps), have all the power necessary to sledge over the heavy iron silhouette of a javelina or a ram in *Siluetas Metalicas*, or to take any living game on the American continent. And likewise, in recent years bull moose have fallen to the Brown Bess.

Black Powder Hunting

That said, black powder hunting demands very considerable stalking skills for close, precise shot placement: for neither round ball nor elongated bullet will mushroom or deliver shock like modern high velocity rounds, and unless the spine of a deer-sized animal is hit, the quarry will commonly run for upwards of 50 yards (45 m) before dropping to a muzzleloader. Round ball is often favoured for varminting, offering higher velocity and therefore flatter trajectory to reach out to smaller game targets, whilst elongated bullets—either the original skirted Minié or the new solid-based Maxi—are generally preferred for their improved sectional density (and therefore better penetration and down-range ballistics) on larger animals.

From Turner Kirkland's introduction of his first "squirrel rifle", made by Dumoulin in Belgium back in 1955, the American replica

Above: *Andy Courtney's flintlock sawback duelling pistol achieves ignition, shrouding the target in a blue haze. Shot at 50 metres, flintlock pistol events allow 13 shots to be fired with the best 10 to count.*

Left: *Smoke fills the air of the Century range at Bisley as competitors test their black powder pistols at 100 yards. Fired from the seated position, or from a trench, with the butt supported on sandbags, in skilled hands these guns give impressive accuracy.*

Right: *Even high tower pheasants are well within killing range of black powder muzzleloading shotguns. It is only when it comes to reloading that these fine guns show their age, as without a retinue of loaders, birds must be taken strictly two at a time.*

industry flourished with the production of all sorts of black powder hunting rifles. Perhaps the most famous type is the "Hawken," which is available today in widely varying degrees of authenticity and at an even wider range of prices.

"Spirit of the original" is a more elastic term in the hunting field than on the target range of international competition: fast 1:48in twist barrels and modern sights are common, whilst some hunters even mount telescopics, in states where they are permitted. Of the various legal advantages which shooters of muzzleloaders have enjoyed in the USA and Europe (but not in Britain), compared with modern firearms enthusiasts, the special black powder hunting season offered in the majority of the United States has been the most significant. It might, indeed, be said that the biggest market interest in black powder revivalism is only peripherally motivated by historical appreciation of black powder weaponry, and that its real drive has been the opportunity to bag a second deer in one year.

If the world's largest muzzleloading market was promoted by the favour of the law, the revival of interest in the early cartridge firearms of the Classic era emerged in defiance of legal adversity.

Draft proposals for a new firearms law in Britain in 1973 which would, *inter alia*, have threatened the collection of vintage weapons, inspired a reaction from keen arms historians, shooters and collectors, who came together to defend the British smallarms heritage. From their "Ad Hoc Committee" emerged the Historical Breechloading Smallarms Association, which now meets monthly as a learned society at the Imperial War Museum. HBSA held range days as an active shooting organization, and in 1979 introduced its competitions into the great annual British pistol meeting at Bisley.

Testing Forgotten Skills

Aided by the availability of period weapons on loan at the firing point, the Classic events grew rapidly at the National Pistol Association meetings. Historical verisimilitude is their keynote: from their location on the home range of Victorian and Edwardian target shooting, to the recreated period targets upon which they are shot, to the courses of fire themselves: drawn from actual Bisley competitions before World War I. The Bisley Gallery ranges do not now afford quite the variety of moving target possibilities which they offered in their

heyday, but the Classic matches are still able to test a number of almost forgotten skills: like single-handed double-action rapid fire with a .45 calibre service revolver.

HBSA is as interested in rifle as it is in pistol shooting history, and its members revived a selection of longarm competitions for the 1986 commemorative shoot of Bisley's South London Rifle Club, categorized into percussion, "Victorian" and "Edwardian" weapon-entry classes. The "mad minute" — the frenetic display of bolt-action firepower of 1914 fame — has reappeared at Bisley; and so too in recent times has volley firing, which was introduced in a Classic-inspired event hosted by modern Practical Rifle shooters.

Armistice Day 1918 marks the end of the HBSA's Classic period; beyond it, a post-Classic period through to 1945 has been outlined. The Vintage Arms Association (a less rigorously academic British shooting group) already carries its "vintage" through to 1933; and in Italy, a quasi-historical rifle competition has emerged, for which the only parameters are military obsolescence and a non-selfloading action. But World War I does mark a watershed in the history of the shooting sports, and nowhere can this be seen more clearly than in the form of shooting carried on at Bisley in Britain.

INDIA PATTERN BROWN BESS MUSKET

SPORTING SHOTGUN BY SAMUEL
AND CHARLES SMITH OF LONDON

Even when their technology became obsolete, the use of the muzzleloading gun and rifle never quite ceased. Small numbers of enthusiastic nostalgics, and larger numbers of practical but impecunious shotgunners, found them to be both cheap and effective. Indeed, among the punt gunners the muzzleloader reigned supreme and was only slightly edged aside by the expensive and complicated breechloader.

Thus, when the modern muzzleloading revival began, there was already a tradition in the use of guns a century or more old. The founding members of the Muzzle Loaders' Association of Great Britain, in 1952, were all experienced black powder users. For the most part, they had been using shotguns, both flintlock and percussion cap, and two examples of these—a 16-gauge sporting shotgun made around 1815 by Theophilus Richards of Birmingham, and a 12-gauge shotgun dating from around 1858 and made by Samuel and Charles Smith of London—are shown here, along with a fine specimen of the legendary British Army Brown Bess flint-lock musket.

INDIA PATTERN BROWN BESS MUSKET

Country of origin: Great Britain
Type: Smoothbore flintlock military musket
Calibre: .753in
Capacity: 1
Action: Flintlock
Operation: Muzzleloader
Construction: Iron barrel; walnut stock; brass mounts
Barrel length: 38.625in (981mm)
Length overall: 54.25in (1378mm)
Weight (empty): 9.875lb (4.48kg)
Sights: No backsight; bayonet stud acts as front sight
Comments: The standard infantry musket of the Napoleonic Wars, with a rate of fire of four rounds per minute and accuracy estimated at the ability to hit a figure target at 75yds (69m). The musket illustrated carries the Tower Ordnance Store Keeper's Stamp for 1800 and is marked on the butt plate tang "2 BWA", indicating that it was issued to the Bridge Ward Association of the City of London Volunteer Forces (the Alderman of Bridge Ward at that time being Sir William Curtis).

The Brown Bess musket (top) shown here is the 3rd Model, or India Pattern, which was used from the 1790s onward, throughout the Wars of the French Revolution and the Napoleonic Wars.

Its 38.625in (981mm) barrel of .753in (19mm) calibre orginally took an undersized ball contained in a paper cartridge with 165 grains (10.7g) of black powder, some of which was also to be used for priming the lock. Modern shooters use closer-fitting bullets and rather less powder to produce acceptable target accuracy at 50m (55yds).

SPORTING SHOTGUN BY THEOPHILUS RICHARDS OF BIRMINGHAM

Country of origin: Great Britain
Type: Single-barrelled shotgun
Calibre: 16 gauge
Capacity: 1
Action: Flintlock
Operation: Muzzleloader
Construction: The twist barrel is manufactured from horse shoe nails and is so marked "Stubs Twisted". It is octagonal at the breech, becoming 16-sided and then round after a baluster turn. The gun has a walnut stock and iron mounts.
Barrel length: 29.625in (752mm)
Length overall: 46.25in (1175mm)
Weight (empty): 6.56lb (2.98kg)
Sights: Front silver foresight barleycorn
Comments: The example shown bears Birmingham post-1813 proof marks and was made c1815.

SPORTING SHOTGUN BY SAMUEL AND CHARLES SMITH OF LONDON

Country of origin: Great Britain
Type: Double-barrelled shotgun
Calibre: 12 gauge
Capacity: 2
Action: Percussion cap
Operation: Muzzleloader
Construction: Double iron Damascus barrels; walnut stock; iron mounts
Barrel length: 29.25in (743mm)
Length overall: 45.875in (1165mm)
Weight (empty): 6.625lb (3.005kg)
Sights: Silver bead foresight
Comments: The example shown is one of a pair made for the Chaworth Musters family of Nottinghamshire around 1858.

The shotguns shown here are a 16-bore flintlock single-barrelled game gun (centre) by Theophilus Richards (uncle of the celebrated William Westley Richards), made in Birmingham around the year 1815, and a 12-bore percussion cap double-barrelled game gun (bottom), weighing only around 6.5lb (2.95kg), by the leading London gunmaking brothers Samuel and Charles Smith, dating from c1858.

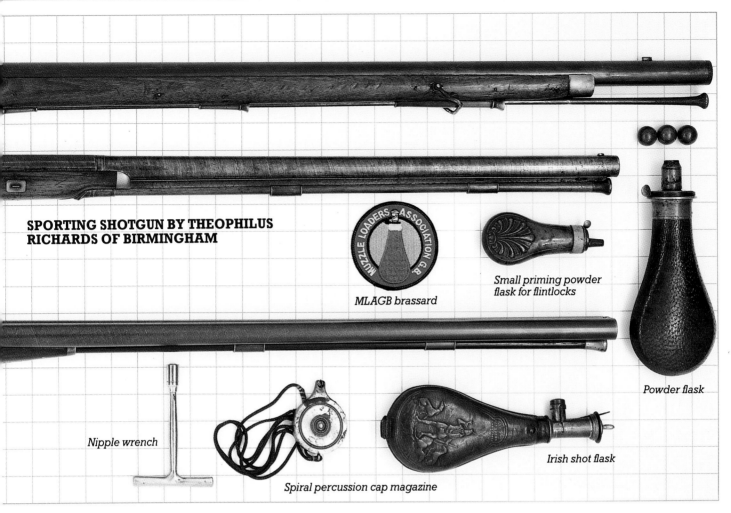

**SPORTING SHOTGUN BY THEOPHILUS
RICHARDS OF BIRMINGHAM**

MLAGB brassard

*Small priming powder
flask for flintlocks*

Powder flask

Nipple wrench

Spiral percussion cap magazine

Irish shot flask

In use, these game guns take a load very similar to that found inside the modern shotgun cartridge, but using about 70 grains (4.5g) of black powder. The early pioneers of modern muzzleloading reported fairly frequently that they were welcomed at clay pigeon shoots and were treated with amused tolerance until they showed that they could shoot just as well as the breech-loaders—at which point the amused tolerance gave way to a certain resentment and to comments about smoke and unregulated shot loads.

The shooter requires certain accessories to use such guns, and some are illustrated here. First, and usually essential, are the powder and shot flasks, although it is possible to carry prepared loads in small containers. The drawback inherent in this is the necessity to continue carrying the containers when they are empty. Wads are usually carried loose in the pocket.

Right: *Muzzleloading shotguns may look anachronistic to some, but they shoot as well as breechloaders.*

Percussion caps may be carried loose, also, but are more often carried in some form of dispenser which will allow them to be placed straight onto the nipples

without the necessity of fumbling for them. Flintlock guns require fine grain powder for priming, and this is usually carried in a small separate flask. As can be seen from the

cloth patch illustrated here, the Muzzle Loaders' Association of Great Britain adopted the powder flask as their emblem on the foundation of their organization in 1952.

Partly because of the restrictive firearms licensing laws of the United Kingdom, there was an early interest in the muzzleloading rifle among modern British shooters. With its antique status, the muzzleloading rifle needed no licence, and it used the same black powder as the then unrestricted shotgun. Bullets, of course, were not usually available from any other source than the shooter's own mould and lead pot.

In those halcyon days, few muzzleloading enthusiasts took very much notice of the legal requirement that, once the decision was taken to shoot the antique weapon, it should be registered. After all, once registered, it was sometimes almost impossible to de-register it for resale as an antique: many police forces made this process very difficult, although not all were so unreasonable.

In the early 1950s, the pioneers of the Muzzle Loaders' Association of Great Britain, who had been surreptitiously banging away (quite illegally) in various fields and farms with muzzleloading rifles, decided to organize more formal meetings, initially at Bisley and afterwards at other military ranges. This growing formality led in time to the enthusiasts' nationwide organization of today and, in 1971, to the foundation by Britain and France of the international governing body that now includes 22 countries.

The standard rifle of the British muzzleloader has always been one or another version of the Enfield military rifle in .577in calibre—and this in spite of the quite widespread survival of the classic English 16-bore stalking rifle, also known as the "ounce rifle" from the weight of its projectile. Enfields survived in vast numbers, thanks to the Volunteer Movement of 1859 and to the encouragement given during the 19th century to rifle shooting by the state and by the National Rifle Association.

In the 1860s, a number of very specialized long-range rifles were built for the minority of shooters interested in target shooting as a pure sport. These scarce precision rifles are in great demand today, and this is reflected in the prices they now command. They are bought for use and, in the hands of experts, astonish modern shooters by their amazing precision at all distances out to 1,000yds (914m). Although they are shot on modern targets and cannot quite compete with the latest in modern technology, they can nevertheless produce scores which are close to those of today's target rifles.

Among the elite of target rifles also are those from an earlier period, that of the Regency and of the small, highly specialized rifle clubs founded as a result of the French Wars, and the contemporary "invasion scares" of around 1800. These rifles are extremely rare today, commanding such high prices that they feature only to a limited extent in modern competitions. The military Baker rifle (which had emerged as the winner in a competition held at Woolwich Arsenal in 1800 to select an arm for an Experimental Corps of Riflemen) from which many of them evolved is more common, but its slow rifling twist, of one turn in 10ft (3m), and its large charge, although effective on the field of battle, cannot compete with the target-shooting derivatives using a spiral of one turn in 30in (0.76m) and sophisticated sights.

LONG-RANGE TARGET RIFLE BY GEORGE GIBBS OF BRISTOL

Country of origin: Great Britain
Type: Long-range target rifle
Calibre: .461in
Capacity: 1
Action: Percussion cap
Operation: Muzzleloader
Construction: Steel barrel; walnut stock; iron mounts
Barrel length: 36in (914mm)
Length overall: 51.75in (1314mm)
Weight (empty): 9.8lb (4.45kg)
Sights: Long tang-mounted rear sight vernier adjustable for elevation only; variable aperture front sight with wind gauge adjustment and cross-levelling spirit level
Comments: A false muzzle is used for ease of loading and to protect the rifling. The rifling is Metford's pattern with shallow grooves and a gaining twist: the rifle carries the Metford Barrel Licence Patent Serial No 45. Such rifles are intended for accurate shooting to 1,000yds (914m) with a heavy 550-grain (36g), hardened, cylindro-conoidal, paper-patched bullet and charge of 90 grains (6g) of powder.

The Metford Rifle (top), made by George Gibbs of Bristol about the year 1866, represents one of the last words in

LONG-RANGE TARGET RIFLE BY GEORGE GIBBS OF BRISTOL

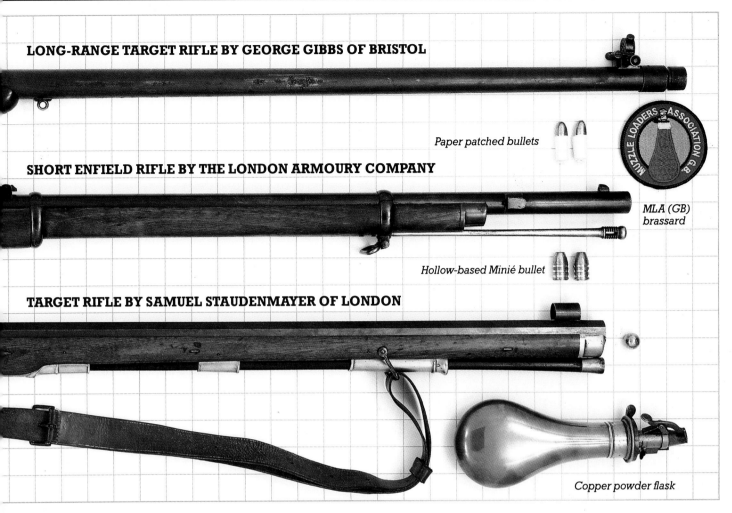

Paper patched bullets

SHORT ENFIELD RIFLE BY THE LONDON ARMOURY COMPANY

MLA (GB) brassard

Hollow-based Minié bullet

TARGET RIFLE BY SAMUEL STAUDENMAYER OF LONDON

Copper powder flask

precision long-range shooting. Note the false muzzle for extra care in loading and cleaning; the long tang-mounted rear sight with its vernier adjustment; and the windage-adjustable foresight with its levelling bubble and provision for different sight elements. The calibre of this model is .461in (11.7mm): its bullet, a hardened, cylindrical, paper-patched slug of 550 grains (36g) was driven by 90 grains (6g) of the finest quality black powder available at the time. In this connection, it should be noted that modern powder is not as good as the powder made in the heyday of the manufacture of these celebrated rifles.

SHORT ENFIELD RIFLE BY THE LONDON ARMOURY COMPANY

Country of origin: Great Britain
Type: Pattern 1861 Enfield Short Rifle
Calibre: .577in
Capacity: 1
Action: Percussion cap
Operation: Muzzleloader
Construction: Iron barrel; five-groove rifling; 48in (1219mm) spiral

Barrel length: 33in (838mm)
Length overall: 48.5in (1232mm)
Weight (empty): 8.72lb (3.96kg)
Sights: Barleycorn front sight; rear sight adjustable for elevation only from 100yds (91m) to 1,250yds (1143m)
Comments: These Short Enfield rifles represented the final attempt to stay in business of the London Armoury Company who, having lost the government contract for the Pattern 1853 Long Enfield, went out of business shortly afterwards. The example shown was used in the Ashburton Match which was shot at Wimbledon in 1866.

The typical Enfield Short Rifle, Pattern 1861 shown here (centre) is a Volunteer Model made by the celebrated London Armoury Company in 1865. The example shown is known to have been used in the Ashburton Match at Wimbledon in 1866.

TARGET RIFLE BY SAMUEL STAUDENMAYER OF LONDON

Country of origin: Great Britain
Type: Target rifle
Calibre: .615in
Capacity: 1
Action: Flintlock

Operation: Muzzleloader
Construction: Iron barrel, octagonal and stocked to the muzzle, with no provision for a bayonet; walnut stock; brass mounts on the Baker military pattern; wooden ramrod
Barrel length: 30in (762mm)
Length overall: 45.5in (1156mm)
Weight (empty): 8.875lb (4.03kg)
Sights: Front sight is a plain blade protected by sun shade; first rear sight is a barrel-mounted notch with leaves for 100, 200 and 300yds (91, 183 and 274m), which can be located anywhere along the barrel by sliding it along grooves cut the length of the barrel on either side of the top flat; second rear sight is a tang-mounted aperture sight adjustable for windage and elevation.
Comments: This is the type of target rifle that would have been used by such Regency-period organizations as the Duke of Cumberland's Sharpshooters, the Robin Hood Riflemen or the Acrotomentarian Society of Riflemen, to name but three.

This rare and valuable Regency-period Target Rifle (bottom) was made in London by the celebrated Samuel Staudenmayer about the year 1805. Its bore is based on that of the Baker rifle, but it carries the fast twist and superior sights of the true target rifle.

The Baker rifle, adopted in 1800 to arm the newly raised 95th Regiment, was the first rifle to see widespread issue in the British Army, and also one of the most battle tested.

Designed by Whitechapel gunmaker Ezekiel Baker, it was a 20-bore (.625″) weighing 9lb (4.1kg), and was rifled with seven grooves that made only ¼-revolution in the length of the 30in (762mm) barrel. This extremely slow twist was probably chosen so as to ease the task of loading the closely-fitted, patched bullet, particularly when the bore was fouled. The drawback was that accuracy deteriorated badly at ranges beyond 200 yds (183m).

Volunteers preferred rifles of the Baker pattern by makers such as Staudenmayer, with a steeper twist such as ¾-turn or even a full turn.

Shown with each of the arms illustrated here are the appropriate bullets, while below the bottom gun is a high-precision powder flask especially designed for use with such rifles. The cloth badge of the Muzzle Loaders' Association of Great Britain, the pioneer British muzzleloading organization, founded in 1952, is also shown.

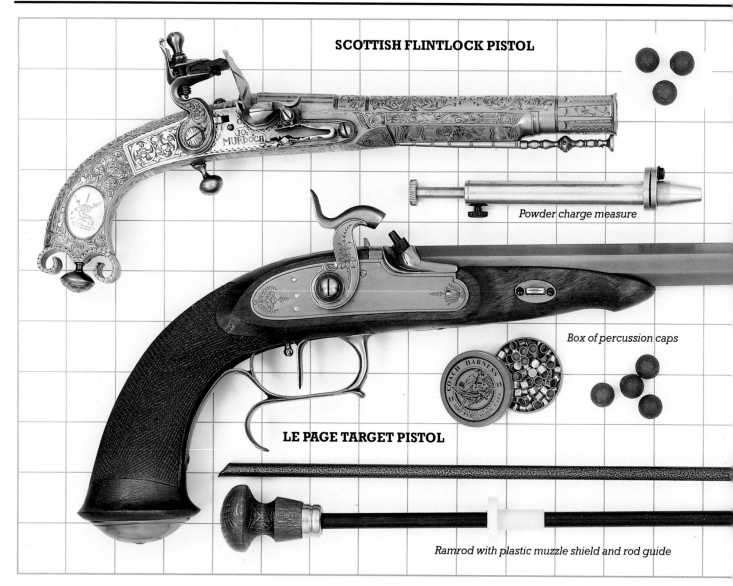

SCOTTISH FLINTLOCK PISTOL

Powder charge measure

Box of percussion caps

LE PAGE TARGET PISTOL

Ramrod with plastic muzzle shield and rod guide

REMINGTON NEW MODEL ARMY PERCUSSION REVOLVER BY UBERTI

Country of origin: Italy
Type: Percussion revolver
Calibre: .44in
Capacity: 6
Action: Percussion; single-action mechanism
Operation: Rammer-loaded from front of cylinder, usually with the use of prepared paper cartridges
Construction: Iron or steel, with brass trigger guard
Barrel length: 8in (203mm)
Length overall: 13.75in (349mm)
Weight (empty): 44oz (1247g)
Sights: Post foresight; notch backsight in topstrap groove
Comments: This is a replica of the strongest and one of the most reliable service revolvers of the American Civil War of the 1860s, during which some 130,000 of these arms saw service.

COLT MODEL 1860 ARMY PERCUSSION REVOLVER BY ARMI SAN MARCO

Country of origin: Italy
Type: Percussion revolver
Calibre: .44in
Capacity: 6
Action: Percussion; single-action mechanism
Operation: Rammer-loaded from front of cylinder, usually with the use of prepared paper cartridges
Construction: Iron or steel, with brass trigger guard and frontstrap
Barrel length: 8in (203mm)
Length overall: 13.75in (349mm)
Weight (empty): 44oz (1247g)
Sights: Brass blade foresight; a notch on the nose of the hammer serves as a backsight
Comments: This is a replica of the foremost revolver of the American Civil War, during which the Union government purchased 127,156 units. Total production of this arm in the period 1860 to c1873 amounted to some 200,500 units.

Although there had been a replica revolver class in international black-powder shooting from the earliest days, no other replicas were allowed until the sport's international governing body, the MLAIC, decided in 1981 to bring in replica classes for all disciplines. Manufacturers were quick to produce a range of very high quality arms to meet the ensuing demand. The two Italian-made percussion revolvers illustrated on the right—the Remington New Model Army (top right) and the Colt Model 1860 Army (bottom right)—are among the most popular of their kind.

As the modern interest in original black-powder arms increased, particularly in the United States, demand for such weapons outstripped supply and, with prices of originals soaring, manufacturers perceived a new market. There had always been a strong collector interest in the Colt models, and this forced up the prices of good originals and made shooters increasingly nervous of marring the finishes or otherwise damaging valuable items. Thus the first of the replicas arrived on the market in the late 1950s in the form of the Navy Colt. Since then, the production of replicas of every type of antique firearm has become very big business.

Other than in the revolver types, replicas were slow to arrive on the scene in the United Kingdom, partly because of the innate conservatism of British shooters and partly because of a relatively plentiful supply of good shooting originals. British firearms laws treat replicas as being no different from modern arms, and this too depressed demand for them.

LE PAGE TARGET PISTOL BY PEDERSOLI

Country of origin: Italy
Type: Percussion pistol
Calibre: .44in
Capacity: 1
Action: Percussion, with set trigger
Operation: Muzzleloading
Construction: Iron or steel
Barrel length: 9.75in (248mm)
Length overall: 16.25in (413mm)
Weight (empty): 38oz (1077g)
Sights: Post foresight; notch backsight
Comments: A rather plain reproduction of adequate quality; it shoots quite well.

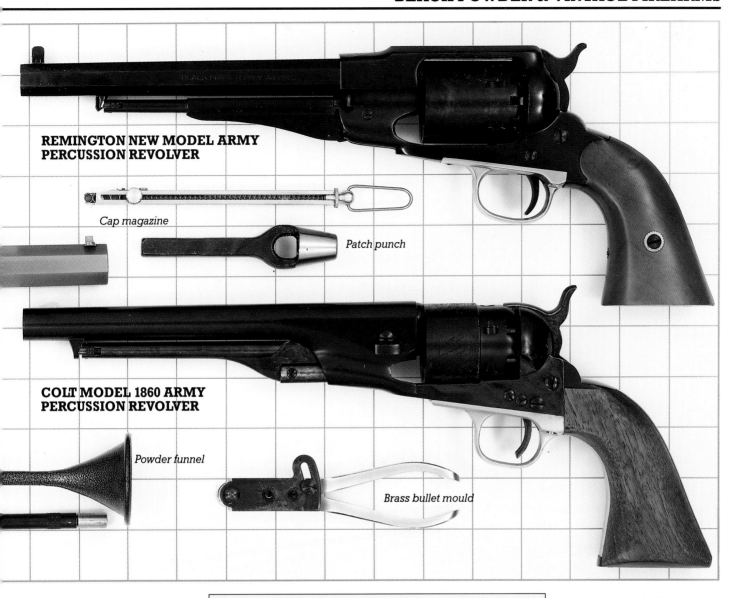

**REMINGTON NEW MODEL ARMY
PERCUSSION REVOLVER**

Cap magazine

Patch punch

**COLT MODEL 1860 ARMY
PERCUSSION REVOLVER**

Powder funnel

Brass bullet mould

The Le Page Target Pistol (bottom left) made by Pedersoli of Italy is a typical example of a modern target pistol replica. It is a copy of an arm typical of its place and period, of the type made by Le Page, the foremost of Parisian gunmakers, in the period c1840-70. Although of good quality, it is scarcely up to Le Page's standards.

SCOTTISH FLINTLOCK PISTOL BY UBERTI

Country of origin: Italy
Type: Flintlock pistol
Calibre: .60in
Capacity: 1
Action: Flintlock
Operation: Muzzleloading
Construction: All steel
Barrel length: 7.75in (197mm)
Length overall: 11.75in (298mm)
Weight (empty): 24oz (680g)
Sights: None
Comments: Production of the highly distinctive pistols of this type, which remained a part of Highland dress until 1850, was centred on the village of Doune near Stirling. Murdoch, whose

Above: *Samuel Colt of Hartford, Connecticut; a man of restless ambition and natural mechanical aptitude, he patented a revolver as early as 1835.*

name appears on the lockplate of this modern reproduction, was one of the foremost Doune craftsmen.

The Scottish Flintlock Pistol (top left) illustrates another aspect of modern replica making. It is a copy of a Scottish all-metal flintlock pistol of the late 18th century. These highly attractive arms were retained for full-dress decorative purposes with Highland dress until quite recent times. Although they were perfectly functional, it is doubtful if they were much used after the 18th century: the modern copies are made as collectors' items rather than for use.

No muzzleloading arm can function without its accessories, and a range of such artifacts is illustrated here. They include a long loading tube to deposit the powder charge right into the breech; a loading and cleaning rod; a bullet mould (for the revolvers on the right); a wad punch; a bar percussion cap dispenser; a powder measure; and a tin of percussion caps.

*Nipple wrench
(with spare nipple in place)*

Although the British muzzleloading enthusiast was noted for his preference for military and target rifles of the types used by his own ancestors, there remained a significant minority of black-powder shooters who were attracted by the kinds of arms used by the pioneers on the American frontier as they pushed its boundaries ever westwards. This interest, in Europe, was undoubtedly fuelled by the very many publications, originating in the United States but readily available overseas, that catered to the very large home market of black-powder enthusiasts.

The considerable rarity in the United Kingdom and elsewhere of rifles of original manufacture from the America of the 18th and 19th centuries led to European enthusiasts being forced to have recourse to replicas. Such arms tend to fall into two categories: factory-made guns, usually originating in Italy or Spain, and guns in which a variable—but usually considerable—amount of handwork has been involved. In the latter category, this may mean a piece which is wholly handmade by an enthusiast who possesses the skill and knowledge to accomplish such

a feat, or a kit-built gun, which involves little more expertise in its assembly than that which is possessed by the average household do-it-yourself enthusiast.

KENTUCKY (PENNSYLVANIA) FLINTLOCK RIFLE BY PALMETTO ARMOURY

Country of origin: Italy
Type: Flintlock rifle
Calibre: .45in
Capacity: 1
Action: Flintlock
Operation: The powder is measured into the bore and then the ball, surrounded by a lubricated patch, is pushed home on to the charge with a ramrod. Fine priming powder for ignition is poured into the pan beneath the frizzen
Construction: Iron or steel barrel and lock; brass furniture
Barrel length: 40.5in (1029mm)
Length overall: 57.5in (1460mm)
Weight (empty): 7.6lb (3.46kg)
Sights: Blade foresight; "buckhorn" notch open backsight
Comments: The gun illustrated here is a modern reproduction of mediocre quality, the stock being especially unsatisfactory.

The first two of the three rifles illustrated on this spread are examples of the two broad

categories into which the American muzzleloading sporting rifle falls. The so-called Kentucky Rifle (top) is probably better described as the Pennsylvania Rifle. Rifles of this type feature a long barrel of very small bore, usually around .400in (10.2mm) to .450in (11.4mm), and are said to be of legendary accuracy, as well as being very economical in terms of powder and lead. However, their range is limited: they are not really of much use beyond about 80yds (73m)—which was, of course, an adequate distance in the wooded country of colonial America for which the original arms of this type were made.

"HAWKEN" PERCUSSION RIFLE BY ARDESA

Country of origin: Spain
Type: Single-shot percussion rifle
Calibre: .54in
Capacity: 1
Action: Percussion lock
Operation: Muzzleloading
Construction: Steel or iron, with brass furniture
Barrel length: 32in (813mm)
Length overall: 49in (1245mm)
Weight (empty): 9.28lb (4.21kg)
Sights: Brass blade foresight; open notch backsight with elevation adjustment ladder
Comments: This is a reproduction

of a percussion rifle characteristic of those used by mountain men and plains' hunters on the American frontier in the period around 1830-60.

During the earlier part of the 19th century, as exploration opened up the plains' areas of mid-western America and larger game was encountered in consequence, it became necessary to enhance the power of rifles by increasing both their bore size and their powder charges. The generic term for the percussion rifle of this type was "Hawken", after the brothers of that name who are said to have specialized in producing them. Because of the additional barrel weight, it was no longer possible to retain the very long barrels of the earlier American rifles—as may be seen in the characteristic Hawken-style rifle shown here (centre).

CREEDMOOR MATCH RIGBY-TYPE PERCUSSION RIFLE BY INTERMARCO S.A.

Country of origin: Spain
Type: Percussion rifle
Calibre: .45in
Capacity: 1
Action: Percussion

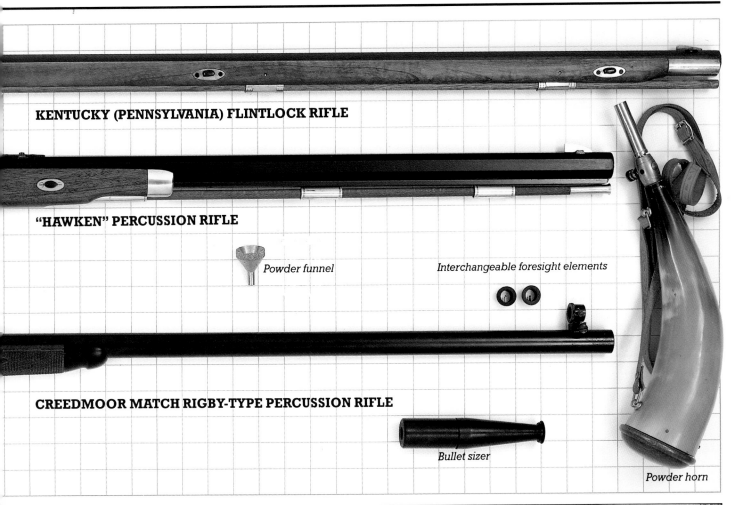

KENTUCKY (PENNSYLVANIA) FLINTLOCK RIFLE

"HAWKEN" PERCUSSION RIFLE

Powder funnel

Interchangeable foresight elements

CREEDMOOR MATCH RIGBY-TYPE PERCUSSION RIFLE

Bullet sizer

Powder horn

Operation: Muzzleloading
Construction: Steel
Barrel length: 32.5in (825mm)
Length overall: 49in (1245mm)
Weight (empty): 8.19lb (3.7kg)
Sights: Shaded foresight with three interchangeable elements; tang-mounted aperture backsight (shown here folded part way forward), micrometer adjustable
Comments: A modern reproduction of good quality of an arm typical of the long-range target rifles of the 1870s, which were soon

to be outmoded by breechloading rifles of similar format.

The superior quality of the best British-made long-range target rifles, and their success in the hands of modern shooters, led inevitably to the production of copies by replica makers. The Spanish-made Creedmoor Match Rigby-type Percussion Rifle illustrated here (bottom) is

an example of what is thought of as a rifle in the British style. The barrel of this example is some 4in (102mm) shorter than would normally be expected in a long-range rifle of this kind—although it is perfectly adequate for shooting at 100m (109yds), the range at which the vast majority of rifles of this type might be expected to be used. The advent on the black-powder scene of such English-

Above: *A contemporary engraving of the international rifle match held at Creedmoor in 1876. The rivalry between competing countries at such events was intense.*

style rifles, including the Enfield, as well as German Schützen rifles, marked a clear break with the American concept of the replica arm.

**PEDERSOLI BROWN
BESS FLINTLOCK MUSKET**

PEDERSOLI
BROWN BESS
FLINTLOCK MUSKET

Country of origin: Italy
Type: Flintlock musket
Calibre: .75in
Capacity: 1
Action: Flintlock
Operation: Muzzleloading,
usually with the use of prepared
paper cartridges
Construction: Iron, with brass
furniture
Barrel length: 42in (1067mm)
Length overall: 58.5in (1486mm)
Weight (empty): 9.44oz (4.28kg)
Sights: Blade foresight; no
backsight
Comments: The Brown Bess was
the musket of the line in the British
army for close on 130 years. The
example shown here (centre) is a
modern reproduction of a militia-
pattern Brown Bess musket of the
kind made by Grice in 1762. The
iron ramrod and forward ferrule are
taken from the Short Land Pattern
musket of 1768.

Although the early days of the
modern muzzleloading
shooting era saw an almost
exclusive use of the rifle for
target work, the smoothbore
musket first appeared in
competition in 1958 with the
introduction of the Brown Bess

Cup, which called for the firing
of 10 shots in 10 minutes at a
distance of 75yds (69m). The
demand for such arms for
competition work remained
limited, but a new interest was
growing in the field of historical
re-creation, which led to the
formation of various regimental
display organizations and also
a number of societies, led by
The Sealed Knot, dedicated to
the re-creation of the English
Civil War of the 17th century.

Many of the people
concerned in these organizations constructed their own
muskets, for firing blanks, but
the demand for arms was such
that many had to make do with
historically out-of-period
muskets of 18th-century type,
like the reproduction Brown
Bess musket shown here
(centre). This model was easily
available, mainly because of
the growing demand in the
United States of America, as the
bicentenary of the American
War of Independence
approached, for muskets of
that period.

HEGE MATCHLOCK
MUSKET

Country of origin: Switzerland
Type: Matchlock musket
Calibre: .63in
Capacity: 1

HEGE MATCHLOCK MUSKET

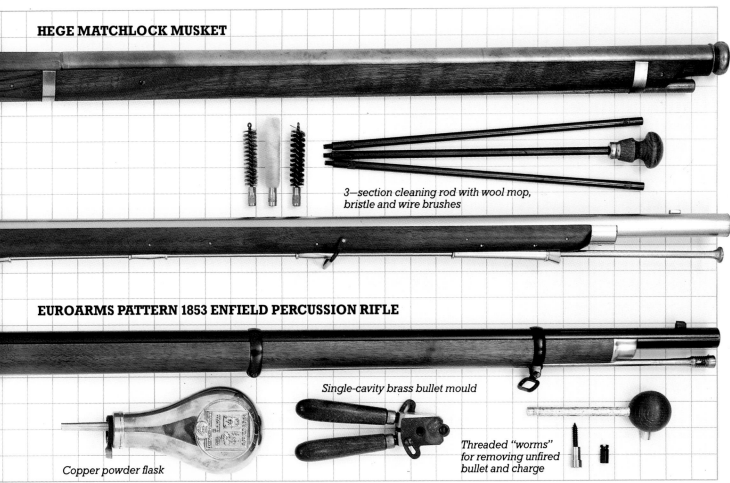

3—section cleaning rod with wool mop, bristle and wire brushes

EUROARMS PATTERN 1853 ENFIELD PERCUSSION RIFLE

Single-cavity brass bullet mould

Copper powder flask

Threaded "worms" for removing unfired bullet and charge

Action: Reverse serpentine, with the match holder held away from the pan by spring pressure
Operation: Muzzleloading: pressure on the underlever (trigger) pushes the match holder down into the pan
Construction: Iron
Barrel length: 42.75in (1086mm)
Length overall: 58in (1473mm)
Weight (empty): 11lb-plus (4.99kg-plus)
Sights: Blade foresight; crude notch backsight
Comments: This is a modern reproduction of the typical military arquebus of the 16th and 17th century. Powder charges for such an arm were normally carried pre-measured in individual vials, while the arm was discharged from a forked rest (not shown here).

The production in modern times of matchlock muskets, aside from the home-made ones built by members of the British society known as The Sealed Knot and similar historical re-creation groups, came about as a result of the involvement of the Japanese in international muzzleloading competitions from 1976. The Japanese shooters claimed that in their own country they were

Left: *Test firing a replica of a 17th century Swiss Luntenschloss matchlock.*

only permitted to use the traditional matchlock types of Japan, and that they must therefore be permitted to introduce a matchlock class. This claim was granted, and this created a demand for all types of authentic matchlock replicas: the Swiss-made matchlock musket of early 17th century European type illustrated here (top) is a typical example. Such weapons also meet the requirements of the English Civil War re-creation societies for authentic muskets.

EUROARMS PATTERN 1853 ENFIELD PERCUSSION RIFLE

Country of origin: Italy
Type: Percussion rifle
Calibre: .577in
Capacity: 1
Action: Percussion
Operation: Muzzleloading, usually with the use of prepared paper cartridges
Construction: Steel or iron, with brass trigger guard and fore-end tip
Barrel length: 38.5in (978mm)
Length overall: 55.25in (1403mm)
Weight (empty): 9.94oz (4.51kg)
Sights: Post foresight; notch backsight with elevation ladder
Comments: Issued just in time for the Crimean War of the mid-19th century, the Pattern 1853 Enfield was perhaps the best rifle of its

type. It was used by both sides in the American Civil War, when it won wide respect.

The demand for replicas of 19th-century rifles was slow to materialize in the United Kingdom, because of the comparatively large availability of good shooting originals, and also because of a lack of interest in American-style shooting. In the 1970s, however, there was perceived to be a substantial market for the Enfield series of rifles in the United States, created by the populous American Civil War re-creation societies, who not only needed the rifles for parade use but also shot them competitively.

The greatest original production in the Enfield series was of the Pattern 1853 Infantry Rifle-Musket, also known as the Long Enfield or the Three-Band Enfield. The example of a modern replica shown here (bottom) is made in Italy for Euroarms of the USA, but perhaps the most famous name in the field is that of the British firm of Parker-Hale of Birmingham, who responded to the demand with a splendid series which now constitutes a major aspect of British muzzleloading rifle meetings.

WEBLEY WG TARGET MODEL REVOLVER

WEBLEY MARK I REVOLVER

"The sun," it used to be said, "never sets on the British Empire": and throughout that diverse agglomeration of real estate Webley revolvers kept the peace, rolled back frontiers and generally alleviated the white man's burden. Back in Britain, they ensured that an Englishman's home was his castle—defensible as such. For more than a century, the Birmingham firm of P. Webley & Son, later Webley & Scott, maintained a handgun dynasty worthy of an imperial age.

WEBLEY MARK I REVOLVER

Country of origin: Great Britain
Type: Revolver
Calibre: .455in
Capacity: 6
Action: Selective double action
Operation: Hinged-frame, break-open, automatic-ejection revolver
Construction: All steel
Barrel length: 4in (102mm)
Length overall: 9.375in (238mm)
Weight (empty): 35oz (992g)
Sights: Blade foresight;

square-bottomed V-notch backsight machined in stirrup latch; non-adjustable
Comments: The first of a distinguished dynasty.

Webley's preeminence was assured when their Mark I .455 revolver (bottom left) was adopted for service use in 1887 to replace the controversial and unpopular Enfield Model 1882. The Webley was compact, robust, reliable, easy handling and very fast to reload. The basic excellence of the design was such that the four succeeding Marks involved changes of detail rather than substance.

The Mark I is distinguished by its light hammer, the recoil shoulder at the top of the backstrap, and the lack of a horseshoe-type cylinder retainer. However, its definitive feature is the recoil shield, which was machined integrally with the frame. On the Mark I* and later Marks, the recoil shield was a hardened steel plate screwed to the standing

breech, a modification that significantly simplified manufacture of the receiver. Note the holster guide ahead of the cylinder.

WEBLEY WG TARGET MODEL REVOLVER

Country of origin: Great Britain
Type: Revolver
Calibre: .450in
Capacity: 6
Action: Selective double action
Operation: Hinged-frame, break-open revolver with automatic simultaneous ejection. Thumblever on left of frame releases barrel to hinge open
Construction: All iron or steel
Barrel length: 7.5in (190.5mm)
Length overall: 13.25in (337mm)
Weight (empty): 42oz (1191g)
Sights: Nickel-silver blade foresight; U-notch backsight drift adjustable for windage. Backsight leaf is laterally dovetailed to the crossbar of the barrel latch.
Comments: Perhaps the finest revolver ever built.

Most specialists regard the Webley WG Model (top left),

introduced in 1888, as the finest production revolver ever made. The WG went through several evolutions and was eventually replaced after World War II by the WS Model, which used the same frame and mechanism as the Mark VI service model.

The WG was made in "service" and "target" versions, the latter dominating pistol competitions for several years while the former was often purchased by officers as a personal sidearm. No revolver ever made possesses a finer trigger action.

The WG introduced the famous Webley stirrup latch, with the thumblever on the left of the frame. When the horseshoe cylinder retainer was introduced, the WG was fitted with that also. Unlike the government revolver, the Webley WG had a sideplate on the left of the receiver, which permitted access to the mechanism, and also had a trigger guard that was an integral part of the receiver forging.

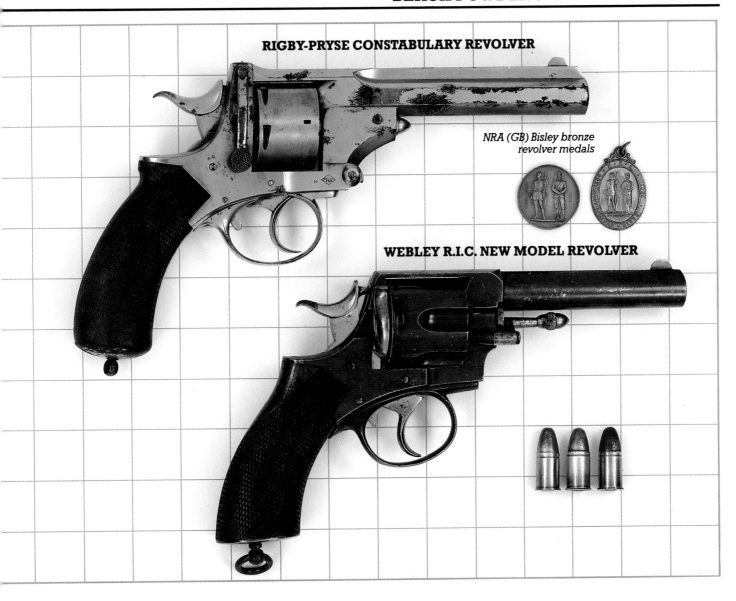

RIGBY-PRYSE CONSTABULARY REVOLVER

NRA (GB) Bisley bronze revolver medals

WEBLEY R.I.C. NEW MODEL REVOLVER

RIGBY-PRYSE CONSTABULARY REVOLVER

Country of origin: Great Britain
Type: Revolver
Calibre: .450in
Capacity: 6
Action: Selective double action
Operation: Hinged frame; automatic simultaneous ejection. Hammer rebounds to safe carry position; ejector star does not trip when fully extended
Construction: All iron or steel
Barrel length: 5.5in (140mm)
Length overall: 10.375in (264mm)
Weight (empty): 34oz (964g)
Sights: Blade foresight; V-notch backsight milled in topstrap extension; non-adjustable
Comments: The example shown here was probably manufactured by Webley for the trade; in this instance, for J. Rigby and Co. of London and Dublin.

Pryse-type revolvers, like the Constabulary model shown (top right), were called after the designer, Charles Pryse the Younger, and enjoyed wide popularity during the latter half

of the 19th century. They were manufactured, presumably under licence, by a number of firms in Britain, Belgium and, perhaps, elsewhere. Field Marshal Lord Roberts is known to have carried one made by Thomas Horsley of York and Doncaster.

Pryse revolvers are easily identified by the distinctive pair of vertically mounted locking levers, one on either side of the gun, which are pinched in at the bottom to allow the barrel and cylinder to hinge down. The end of the topstrap fitted into a slot in the top of the standing breech, where it was secured by a cylindrical lug entering from either side. This was a strong and successful system—hence its popularity. Curiously, it is not mentioned in Pryse's 1876 patent, which relates to aspects of the internal mechanism. The Pryse revolver shown on this spread was made, probably by Webley, to be marketed by the firm of J. Rigby and Co. of London and Dublin.

WEBLEY R.I.C. NEW MODEL REVOLVER

Country of origin: Great Britain
Type: Revolver
Calibre: .476in
Capacity: 6
Action: Selective double action
Operation: Solid frame, gate loading, rod ejection; ejector rod, mounted on swivel, carries within cylinder axis when not in use
Construction: All iron or steel
Barrel length: 4.5in (114mm)
Length overall: 9.625in (244mm)
Weight (empty): 30oz (850.5g)
Sights: Square profile blade foresight; V-notch backsight milled in topstrap; non-adjustable
Comments: After the Smith & Wesson M&P and the Colt OP, this was perhaps the most successful police revolver ever made. It has an exquisite action.

More popular, no doubt, than the Pryse revolver, was Webley's famed R.I.C. Model (bottom right), which was introduced in 1867. The Royal Irish Constabulary, formed in the following year, promptly adopted it—hence the

designation. The R.I.C. remained in production into the 20th century, probably until 1914, when the Webley plant was fully devoted to war production. Over the years, the mechanism evolved; a host of variations will be encountered, chambered for .442, .450, .455/.476, .455/.450, .430, .44 WCF and .45 Colt with barrels as long as 7in (178mm). The Metropolitan Police, along with many British county forces, adopted a 2.5-inch (63.5mm)—barrelled version, and, in one form or another, the R.I.C. saw service with police units in Australia and South Africa as well.

The R.I.C. was a solid-frame, gate-loading, rod-ejection, selective double action revolver. For its calibre, it was surprisingly light and agile. Pull weights of R.I.C. revolvers are usually heavier than those of Webley WG models, but the smoothness of the trigger action is superb, succeeding in putting almost all more modern revolvers to shame.

LUGER (MAUSER PARABELLUM) SELF-LOADING PISTOL

COLT MODEL 1911 SELF-LOADING PISTOL

Bisley Pistol '79 gold medal

The introduction of Classic as a major shooting discipline in the United Kingdom has resurrected a rich heritage of long-forgotten courses of fire, as well as encouraging some wonderful old guns to reappear from out of cupboards up and down the country. The four guns shown here are typical of the elegant sidearms of times past that have lately found a fresh competitive vocation.

LUGER (MAUSER PARABELLUM) SELF-LOADING PISTOL

Country of origin: Germany
Type: Self-loading pistol
Calibre: 7.62mm Parabellum (.30in Luger)
Capacity: 8
Action: Single action; striker cocked automatically for each shot
Operation: Short recoil toggle link action; barrel and upper receiver recoil rearward until ramp faces "break" the toggle linkage
Construction: All steel
Barrel length: 6in (152mm)
Length overall: 10.6in (269mm)
Weight (empty): 33oz (936g)
Sights: Pyramid foresight post and U-notch backsight; foresight is drift adjustable for windage
Comments: The example shown is from the first post-World War II commercial production for the US market, with the Mauser crest on the middle link and the American eagle on the receiver ring. It is a sidearm of very fine quality.

The Luger, shown here in Mauser Parabellum form (top left), is perhaps the most famous, and certainly one of the most beautiful, handguns ever produced. Introduced in 1900, it was still in service (notably in Portugal, Switzerland and Angola) three-quarters of a century later. Its most extensive use came during World War I, when it was the German service pistol About 2,500,000 Lugers of all sorts are thought to have been built. There were four basic models: 1900, 1906, 1908 and 1929, the last-named a Swiss variation manufactured at Waffenfabrik Bern.

The example shown here was made at Mauser in the late 1960s. It incorporates the grip safety of the 1906 Model (the service P08 did not have one) along with the straight frontstrap of the 1929 Model. It is in the Swiss standard 7.62mm calibre, whereas German service pistols were 9mm.

The Luger was muzzle light, jam prone and dirt sensitive—but it pointed instinctively and was extremely accurate.

COLT SINGLE ACTION ARMY REVOLVER

Country of origin: USA
Type: Revolver
Calibre: .45in Colt
Capacity: 6
Action: Single action
Operation: Solid-frame, single-action, gate-loading, rod-ejection revolver
Construction: All steel; colour case-hardened receiver
Barrel length: 5.5in (140mm)
Length overall: 10.875in (276mm)
Weight (empty): 37oz (1049g)
Sights: Square profile blade foresight; square notch groove backsight machined in topstrap
Comments: An example of post-World War II commercial production of the 1873-vintage classic revolver.

The Colt Single Action Army revolver (bottom right) shares with the Luger the honour of being one of the most glamorous and celebrated sidearms ever produced. If machines can have charisma, these two have it: they have grace, flair, style and personality. Both were, by all rights, obsolescent when introduced, yet both have inspired loyalty and admiration for a century or thereabouts.

The Colt had the misfortune to miss out on wars. Adopted in 1873, its only combat use was in the Indian Wars, although some were reissued for service in the Philippines early in the 20th century, when its replacement, the .38in Colt New Army revolver, proved underpowered.

The 1873 Colt is better known as a civilian sidearm than it is for its service with the US Cavalry. Known as the "Peacemaker" in .45 calibre, and as the "Frontier Model" in .44-40, the Single Action Colt was the great equalizer, the gun that made the Old West a

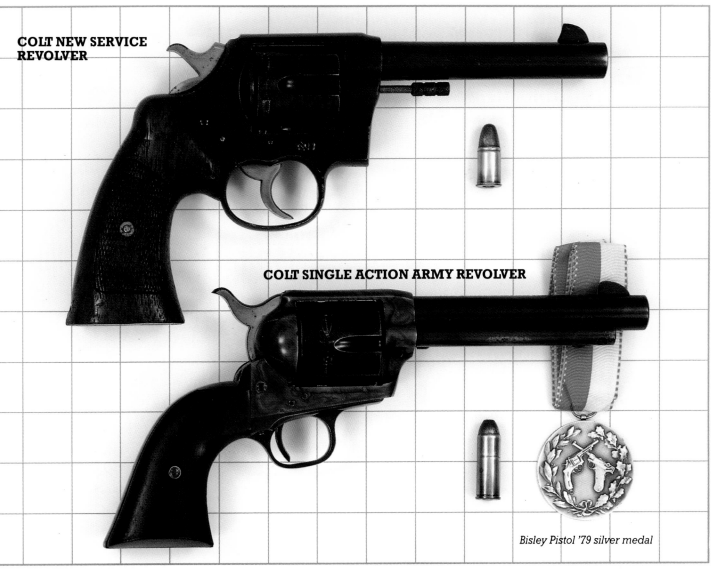

COLT NEW SERVICE REVOLVER

COLT SINGLE ACTION ARMY REVOLVER

Bisley Pistol '79 silver medal

much safer and more tranquil place than is popularly imagined nowadays.

The "Model P", as the factory called it, was always superbly built. It feels wonderful in the hand: its grip, balance and poise are splendid. Its faults are a surfeit of screws that tend to work loose and a couple of fragile springs that are prone to breakage.

COLT NEW SERVICE REVOLVER

Country of origin: USA
Type: Revolver
Calibre: .455in
Capacity: 6
Action: Selective double action
Operation: Crane-mounted cylinder swings out of frame to left; simultaneous hand-ejection
Construction: All steel
Barrel length: 5.5in (140mm)
Length overall: 10.8in (274mm)
Weight (empty): 40oz (1134g)
Sights: Blade foresight; notch backsight milled in topstrap; non-adjustable
Comments: The example shown is one of many supplied to British forces during World War I.

The double action Colt New Service revolver (top right) was a stopgap effort that was militarily adopted in 1909 after the .38 Colt New Army revolver had proved a battlefield wimp in Cuba and the Philippines. The US Army knew by that time that it needed a self-loading pistol, but it had not yet tested one that was sufficiently reliable.

World War I saw the wheelgun's revenge, as tens of thousands of New Service revolvers, chambered for .45 ACP and re-adopted as the Model 1917, saw service in the trenches. In .455in, it was issued as well to British and Canadian forces, and was for many years the sidearm of the Royal Canadian Mounted Police.

The action of the Colt New Service was too stiff, the trigger reach too long and the grip atrocious (the example shown here has replacement grips, but they are nearly as bad as those of the original). It has been unkindly described as "an ape's gun".

COLT MODEL 1911 SELF-LOADING PISTOL

Country of origin: USA
Type: Self-loading pistol
Calibre: .45 ACP
Capacity: 7 + 1
Action: Single action; outside hammer cocked by recoil for each shot
Operation: Short recoil; locked breech. The breech end of the barrel is link mounted and swings downward to release the slide to recoil back alone
Construction: All steel
Barrel length: 5in (127mm)
Length overall: 8.6in (218mm)
Weight (empty): 39oz (1106g)
Sights: Blade foresight; U-notch backsight drift-adjustable for windage
Comments: With only slight modification, this was the standard US service pistol for 74 years and, in the view of many, is still the best.

The Colt Model 1911 (bottom left) was the gun that, as remarked above, the US Army was looking for in the first decade of the 20th century. John Browning spent some ten

years in perfecting the design: when he was ready, the gun thundered through a 6,000-round test firing with no malfunctions or breakages.

The Model 1911 is distinguished from the later (post-World War I) Model 1911A1 by its flat backstrap, long trigger, short tang and the lack of half-moon cuts in the frame just to the rear of the trigger. Although recently replaced as the standard US service pistol, the Model 1911 is still at the height of its popularity, and has tremendous sporting vocation. It is also the handgun of choice for tens of thousands of police officers and private citizens who feel that its combination of stopping power, firepower, reliability and portability cannot be bettered. On the score of portability, Colt offer four miniaturized versions: Combat Commander (steel), Commander (aluminium frame), and the Officers' Model (in either steel or aluminium). Old soldiers never die—and the Model 1911 is young still.

GLOSSARY

ACP Automatic Colt Pistol.

Action The mechanism of a firearm involved in presenting the cartridge for firing and in ejecting the spent case and introducing a fresh cartridge.

Aperture sights A type of iron sights (q.v.) in which the backsight takes the form of a small hole or aperture. Also called a "peep sight".

ATA Amateur Trapshooting Association, incorporated in Delaware; the governing body for trapshooting in the US.

Automatic A firearm which continues firing for as long as the trigger remains depressed or until the magazine or belt containing extra ammunition runs empty. A machine gun.

Automatic ejection A system predominantly used on breakopen revolvers on which, as the barrel is tipped down, the ejector is automatically activated to clear the chambers. See "hand ejection" and "rod ejection".

Automatic revolver A rare type of revolver, of which the Webley Fosbery and the Union are the best known examples, that uses the recoil energy of cartridge discharge to rotate the cylinder and cock the hammer for each succeeding shot.

Back action lock A lock, normally carrying an outside hammer, on which the V-type mainspring is mounted to the rear of, rather than to the front of, the cock or hammer.

Backstrap The rear of the two gripstraps on a handgun, which lies under the heel of the hand when a firing grip is taken.

Ball A military term for standard, full jacketed ammunition.

Ballistic coefficient The ratio of a bullet's sectional density (q.v.) to a co-efficient of form, which reflects its aerodynamic qualities. The ballistic coefficient is an indicator of a bullet's ability to retain its velocity over distance and permits a calculation of trajectory.

Ballistics The science of cartridge discharge and the bullet's flight, divided into four distinct phases. Internal ballistics concerns ignition, combustion and the bullet's travel from the chamber to the muzzle. Intermediate ballistics concerns the bullet's emergence into the atmosphere and the effects of muzzle turbulence, blast and flash. External ballistics, the original science of gunnery, concerns the bullet's flight from muzzle to target, while terminal ballistics concerns the interaction between bullet and target. In the case of travel through flesh, this is known as wound ballistics.

Bar Also called action bar: the portion of the receiver of a breakopen gun that extends forward of the standing breech, which carries the pivot and against which the barrel flats seat.

Barrel A cylindrical part of a firearm through the bore (q.v.) of which the shot is fired. The barrel serves the purposes of imparting direction and velocity to the projectile or projectiles.

Barrel time See "bore time".

Battery The disposition of the parts of a firearm when the breech is locked up, ready for firing.

Battery cup A type of priming assembly generally used in shotshells, in which the primer cup and anvil are supported by an outer cup.

Bedding The manner in which the barrelled action of a rifle is fitted to the stock.

Belted Said of a cartridge case which has a raised circumferential ridge, or "belt", immediately ahead of the extractor groove. Headspace (q.v.) is against the forward edge of the belt.

Bench rest A solidly constructed table and seat used for testing a rifle or pistol's grouping ability. A shooting sport in which firearms are shot for group rather than for a points score, and in which the shooting is done from a solidly constructed bench.

Berdan primed A centrefire cartridge, the anvil of which is an integral part of the brass of the case itself, with two or more flash holes disposed around it. Named for the designer, Col. Hiram Berdan, an American officer of the 19th century.

Birdshot Shotgun pellets of comparatively small diameter, meant to be used on birds in flight and small game such as rabbit and squirrel. See "buckshot".

Black powder See "gunpowder".

Blowback Also called "unlocked breech". Said of a self-loading or automatic firearm whose breechblock and barrel are not mechanically locked together when in battery or at the moment of firing. Used in comparatively low-powered weapons, in which the inertia of the breechblock, and casewall adhesion against the chamber, are sufficient to retard opening until breech pressures have fallen to a safe level.

Bolt A form of breechblock, usually cylindrical in cross section, that operates on a prolongation of the bore axis, and is withdrawn over a distance greater than the length of the cartridge, to expose the chamber. Lends itself well to magazine feeding. On a revolver, the cylinder stop (q.v.).

Bolt action A firearm that uses a mobile breechblock acting along a linear extension of the bore axis, and hand operated either on a pull-push basis, or on a turnbolt basis.

Bore The calibre of a shotgun. See "gauge". The interior of a gun barrel.

Bore diameter The diameter of the inside of the barrel (q.v.) after boring but before rifling. The land diameter (q.v.).

Bore gauge A device for measuring the inside diameter of a gun barrel.

Bore scope An optical device for inspecting the interior surface of a gun barrel.

Bore time The period of time between ignition of the powder charge and the projectile's quitting the muzzle. Also called "barrel time". See "lock time".

Bottle necked Said of a cartridge whose projectile diameter is substantially less than the body diameter of the case. Such a case affords adequate powder capacity and is necked down as required to grip the projectile.

Boxer primed A centrefire cartridge, the primer assembly of which contains a separate anvil, whose feet lie to either side of a central flash hole (q.v.). Named for the designer, Col. Edward Mounier Boxer, a British officer of the 19th century.

Boxlock A firearm—normally a double-barrelled shotgun or rifle—on which the firing mechanisms are housed in recesses in the rear of the receiver. See "sidelock".

Breech plug A threaded plug, often incorporating the tang, that closes the breech end of the barrel of most muzzleloading firearms.

Breechblock The part that seals the rear of the chamber and supports the casehead when the cartridge is fired. Breechloading firearms are classified according to the type of breechblock employed, and the mechanical means of locking it into place for firing and displacing it for reloading.

Breechloader A firearm which is loaded from the rear. The firing chamber will normally be machined into the rear end of the barrel, but may be (as, for example, is the case with revolvers) a separate piece aligned with the barrel for firing.

Buckshot A term for the larger sizes of shotgun pellets, useful against fox and feral dogs, and in an anti-personnel role, but not usually humane on deer.

Bullet The projectile of a rifle or pistol. Common and journalistic practice often uses bullet and cartridge as synonymous terms. This is never correct. The bullet is the projectile only; the cartridge is the assembly of case, primer, powder and bullet.

Bullpup A shoulder gun in which the receiver is located well back in the stock, so much so that the cheek is alongside the breech on firing.

Burst fire Said of a firearm the mechanism of which is fitted with a ratchet escapement device that permits a predetermined number of shots (usually 3) to be fired each time the trigger is pressed. See "selective fire".

Buttstock Or butt. That portion of the stock (q.v.) that enables the firearm to be braced against the shoulder and cheek for firing.

Calibre The diameter, nominal diameter, or designation of a bore, projectile or cartridge, normally expressed in hundredths of an inch or thousandths of an inch, or in millimeters, though shotgun calibre is usually expressed in a system based on fractions of a pound (e.g., 12 bore). Also used as a measure of length in multiples of bullet or bore diameter.

Cannelure A circumferential groove or indentation round a bullet or cartridge case.

Capping breechloader A type of early breechloader circa 1860, which was fired by a standard percussion cap which was placed on an external nipple or chimney after the breech had been closed.

Carbine A small rifle, shorter, lighter and handier than a full size rifle.

Cartridge A round of ammunition consisting, in modern times, of case, primer, powder and projectile (either single or multiple). In ancient times the cartridge (from the French *"cartouche"*) consisted of the powder and ball in a paper packet, with the percussion cap or priming powder separate.

Case The metallic body of a cartridge (q.v.), made usually of brass but sometimes of steel, aluminium, copper or plastic. Normally, the primer or primer assembly fits into the base of the case, the bullet is crimped into the forward end and the powder charge is contained within.

Case mouth The forward edge of a metallic cartridge case, the inside diameter of which normally corresponds to the bore diameter (q.v.) of the firearm and into which the projectile is seated.

Casehead The base of a cartridge case.

Caseless A type of experimental cartridge that does not use a cartridge case, and consists normally of a projectile attached to or embedded in a block of propellent.

Cast off Displacement of the butt to the right of the bore axis. This positions the aiming eye, when the gun is brought to the right shoulder, with the line of sight.

Cast on Displacement of the butt to the left of the bore axis. Positions the eye in the line of sight when the gun is fired from the left shoulder.

Centrefire A cartridge in which the primer or primer assembly is seated in a pocket or recess in the centre of the base of the case. A firearm which uses centrefire cartridges.

Chamber The part of a firearm that contains the cartridge when it is fired.

Charger A device, normally of pressed metal, which holds a group of cartridges for easy and virtually simultaneous loading into the magazine of a firearm.

Choke A barely discernible constriction near the muzzle of a shotgun that has the function and effect of regulating pattern density, as measured by the percentage of pellets that would be contained in a 30" circle at 40 yards. Choke classifications are: cylinder bore (40%), improved cylinder (50%), quarter choke (55%), half choke (60%), three-quarter choke (65%), full choke (70%).

Chronograph A device, usually electrical, for measuring bullet velocity.

Clip A device, normally of pressed steel, which holds a group of cartridges and which is inserted into the magazine, along with the cartridges it contains, in order to reload the gun.

Cock A pivoted piece, normally spring activated, that holds the match, pyrites or flint on a matchlock, wheellock or flintlock mechanism; often called the "dog" in Mediterranean countries.

CPSA Clay Pigeon Shooting Association, headquartered at Buckhurst Hill, Essex; the governing body for the clay sports in the UK.

Crane The pivoting member on which the cylinder is mounted on a revolver, the cylinder of which swings out for loading. Also called the "yoke".

Crown The form of the muzzle where the bore emerges, normally chamfered or recessed.

Cylinder stop On a revolver, the part, normally spring activated and housed in the floor of the frame, which engages in the cylinder stop notch (also called "bolt cut") arresting the cylinder's rotation and locking it so that the chamber to be fired is locked in alignment with the barrel.

Delayed blowback Also called "retarded blowback" and "hesitation locked". Said of a self-loading or automatic firearm whose breechblock and barrel are not positively locked together, but which incorporates a mechanism which causes the breechblock to operate against an initial mechanical disadvantage, thus delaying its opening.

Direct delivery Said of a gas operated firearm if the gas bled from the barrel via the port is piped back to the receiver where it acts directly on the bolt carrier.

Discipline A competitive shooting sport, conducted according to a recognised set of rules.

Double A firearm, normally a shotgun or rifle, with two barrels in parallel, disposed either laterally (side-by-side) or vertically (over-under or juxtaposed). Usually, a separate lock will service each barrel, so that if one lock should fail, the other barrel will still fire.

Double action A revolver or pistol on which a long pull-through on the trigger will rock the hammer back against the mainspring and release it at the top of its travel to fire the shot. On a revolver, subsequent shots may be fired the same way; on a pistol, the slide will normally cock the hammer after the first shot so that subsequent shots are taken with just a light pressure on the trigger.

Drachm An apothecary measure sometimes used for indicating black powder loads in older texts. Equivalent to 60 grains weight and *not* equivalent to a dram, with which it is sometimes confused. See "dram".

Dram A unit of measure equivalent to 27.34 grains. Not the same as a drachm.

Drilling A three-barrelled break-open gun, typically with a rifle barrel mounted centrally beneath side-by-side shotgun barrels, though all possible combinations and dispositions will be encountered. Popular in Germany and Austria for "battu" shooting. From the German *drei*, for "three".

Ejector A part whose function is to throw a spent case clear of the gun.

Ejector star On a revolver, the collective ejector, operating through the cylinder axis which, when activated, clears all chambers at once. The ratchet is normally machined as part of the ejector star.

Elevation Vertical disparity in a bullet's flight, due to errors in range estimation or what have you. See "windage".

Extractor A part, normally hook- or crescent-shaped, which withdraws a spent case from the chamber.

Face The front surface of the standing breech on a breakopen shotgun—the surface that supports the base of the cartridge. A worn gun with looseness or space at the breech is said to be "off the face".

Falling block An action type in which the breechblock, usually lever operated, moves vertically (or nearly so) in internal receiver mortises. A very strong, compact and usually elegant action.

Firearm A lethal, barrelled weapon which uses the pressure of combustion-generated gases to propel a projectile or group of projectiles.

Firing pin In a hammer-fired gun, that part which physically impacts the primer to detonate it. N.B., a striker fired gun does not have a firing pin. See "striker".

Flash hider A device, usually consisting of linear slots or prongs, fitted to the muzzles of some firearms, designed to break up and minimize muzzle flash (q.v.).

Flintlock A system widely used in the 17th-19th centuries in which ignition is achieved by striking a flint against an upright steel face called the frizzen. The resultant sparks ignite the priming powder in the pan, which burn through the touch hole to ignite the main charge in the barrel.

FMJ Full metal jacket, referring to a bullet.

Forcing cone The angles or chamfer slightly enlarging the breech end of a revolver barrel meant to accommodate very slight instances of chamber misalignment and guide the bullet into the bore.

Fore-end The portion of a gun or rifle stock located ahead of the receiver, which is normally gripped by the left hand.

FPS Feet per second.

Frame The receiver (q.v.) of a revolver or pistol.

Frame window The opening in a revolver frame in which the cylinder rotates.

Freebore The distance between the front of the bearing surface of the chambered bullet and the beginning of the rifling. Zero freebore gives best accuracy.

Frizzen The vertical iron face of a flintlock gun against which the flint strikes to produce sparks. Usually formed as a vertical extension of the pan cover.

Front locking Said of a bolt action gun which has locking lugs on the front of the bolt which engage in corresponding mortises either in the front of the receiver or in the rear of the barrel, or in an intermediate sleeve or collar between the two, and immediately behind the chamber.

Frontstrap The forward of the two gripstraps on a handgun, that falls underneath the fingers when a firing grip is taken.

Gain twist A system of rifling, popular in the late 19th century, which commenced with almost straight rifling near the breech, becoming progressively steeper as it approached the muzzle. Gain twist was meant to enable lead bullets to be driven at greater velocities without stripping in the rifling, than would have been possible otherwise.

Gas operated Said of a self-loading or automatic firearm which uses combustion gases, tapped via a port along the barrel, to impulse a piston that cycles the action. Gas operated systems are classified as long stroke, short stroke or direct delivery (q.v.).

Gas retarded Said of a firearm if gas bled from the bore is used, not to cycle the action but to delay its opening by acting to hold the breech closed. See "delayed blowback".

Gate loading A type of revolver on which one of the recoil shields (q.v.) is notched or relieved so that a cartridge may be introduced into a chamber aligned with it. A small hinged "gate" closes this loading port when not in use.

Gauge The calibre of a shotgun, usually expressed in fractions of a pound. British: "bore", as in "12 bore", "20 bore", etc. The bore diameter of a 12 gauge gun would correspond to the diameter of a spherical lead ball weighing 1/12lb. In like fashion, a bore-diameter lead ball for a 4-bore would weight ¼lb, for an 8-bore ⅛lb, and so forth. The lone escapee of this archaic system is the .410 gauge, with a bore diameter of .410"; a 12 gauge measures about .729" cylinder bore.

Grain An avoirdupois unit of measurement used for expressing the weight of cartridge components. There are 7,000 grains to the pound; one grain = 0.002285 ounce or 64.79891 milligrammes.

Groove The spiral cut produced by a rifling cutter.

Groove diameter In a rifled barrel with an even number of grooves, the diameter of the inside of the barrel as measured from the bottom of one groove to the bottom of the groove opposite.

Gun In common parlance, any firearm. In British usage, a shotgun, but not a rifle or handgun. In military usage, field artillery, coastal artillery, naval artillery or aircraft cannon, but not small arms of any type.

Gunpowder Also called black powder, the standard propellant for firearms from their introduction in the early 14th century until the late 19th century when black powder was quickly superceded by smokeless powder (q.v.).

Hammer The part, powered by the mainspring, that is driven round its axis of rotation, and drives the firing pin into the base of the chambered cartridge. The firing pin may or may not be part of the hammer. See "firing pin" and "striker".

Hammer spur The thumbpiece on the top rear of the hammer that enables it to be drawn to full cock.

Hammerless Said of a firearm, particularly a shotgun, without visible, external hammers. Most such guns are in fact hammer fired, but use internal hammers.

Hand Part of a revolver mechanism which, attached to and activated by either the hammer or trigger, engages the ratchet and causes the cylinder to rotate.

Hand ejection A system most often used on swingout cylinder revolvers, in which the

ejector rod is pushed rearward by hand in order to clear the chambers. See "automatic ejection" and "rod ejection".
Handgun A firearm intended to be aimed and fired in the hand or hands, without being braced against the shoulder and cheek. A catch-all term for any pistol or revolver.
Hangfire A cartridge which discharges after a delay. Dangerous.
HBSA Historical Breechloading Small Arms Association, based at the Imperial War Museum, London. A scholarly association and collaterally, the governing body for the Classic events.
Headspace The distance between the face of the breechblock in battery and the point at which the cartridge case abuts against the chamber, normally the front surface of either the rim, belt, shoulder or mouth.
Heeled bullet An early type of revolver bullet which had a reduced diameter heel which seated in the mouth of the cartridge case.
Hinged frame A breakopen gun, that hinges open for loading or disassembly.
HK Heckler & Koch, of Oberndorf am Neckar, West Germany.
Hollow point A bullet with a hollow in the nose, designed to mushroom on impact.

IHMSA International Handgun Metallic Silhouette Association, the governing body of the sport.
ILRPSA International Long Range Pistol Shooters' Association, founded 1976. The governing body for Long Range Pistol Shooting in the UK.
IMR Improved Military Rifle, a DuPont trade name for its line of single base, tubular powders.
IPSC International Practical Shooting Confederation, the world governing body for the Practical Shooting sports, founded in 1976 at a conference in Columbia, Missouri, and currently headquartered in Brussels, Belgium.
Iron sights A sighting system consisting normally of a foresight and backsight not containing glass or reflective elements, magnifying or not.
ISU International Shooting Union. See "UIT".

Jacket The skin or covering of a composite bullet, usually made of copper, gilding metal, cupro-nickel or mild steel. The core, inside the jacket, is normally of a lead alloy. The jacket is hard enough to hold rifling at velocities that would strip a lead bullet.

Land diameter In a rifled barrel with an even number of grooves, the diameter as measured from land to land (q.v.). Bore diameter (q.v.). See also "groove diameter" and "land to groove diameter".
Land to groove diameter In a rifled barrel with an odd number of grooves, the distance from the bottom of a groove to the top of the land opposite. Special equipment is required to measure bore diameter in such a barrel.
Lands The upstanding ridges of metal left between the grooves when a barrel is rifled. The lands bite into the bullet, causing it to spin in flight, thus imparting gyrostatic stability and preventing it from tumbling end over end.
LC Long Colt.
Lead The forward allowance required to hit a moving target, most commonly a bird in flight.
Length of pull The distance from the centre of the buttplate to the face of the trigger.
Lever action A firearm that uses a breechblock that is operated by a downward rotational action on a sidelever or underlever. The motion of the breechblock may be linear, vertical, axial, tipping or otherwise.
Lock The ignition mechanism of a firearm, e.g. matchlock, wheellock, flintlock, miquelet lock, percussion lock, sidelock, boxlock, back action lock, etc., (qq.v.).
Lock time The period of time between the sear's releasing the hammer or striker and the firing pin or hammer nose's impacting the primer. See "bore time".
Locked breech Said of a self-loading or automatic firearm whose breechblock and barrel are mechanically locked together when in battery and at the moment of firing.
Lockplate The flat metal plate on which the mechanism or lock (q.v.) of early firearms is mounted.
Long recoil A recoil operated firearm in which the barrel and breechblock are locked together for the full distance of travel, after which the barrel returns forward while the breechblock is retained rearward. When the barrel has fully returned, the breechblock is released to fly forward, chambering a fresh cartridge in the process.
Long stroke Said of a gas operated firearm if the piston is attached to the bolt and accompanies it during the full length of the operating cycle.
LR Long Rifle: designation of the most popular variety of .22 rimfire cartridge, universally used in pistols as well as rifles.

Machine carbine A submachine gun (q.v.).
Machine pistol In Continental parlance, a submachine gun. Sometimes applied to a pistol, with or without a buttstock attachment, capable of fully automatic fire.
Machine rest A mechanical test unit in which a gun in mounted for group testing.
Magazine The part of a firearm containing the reserve ammunition supply, and out of which cartridges are mechanically fed to the chamber for firing.
Magnum A term borrowed from the vintner's trade to designate a cartridge that is notably powerful.
Mainspring The spring, in a firearm, which powers the hammer or striker.
Matchlock An early ignition system in which a smouldering "match"—usually a nitrate-soaked cord—was applied directly to the priming powder in the flashpan to ignite it to burn through the touch hole and ignite the main charge.
Mauser type Said of a bolt action rifle containing many of the design elements of the Model 1898 Mauser, notably twin forward locking lugs, an integral double column magazine and often a collar-mounted external extractor and fixed ejector.
Mid-range trajectory Refers to the maximum height above line of sight which the bullet will reach in flight, with the gun sighted to strike point of aim at a given distance.
Minute of angle The unit of measurement for sight adjustments; a unit of angular measurement equal to 1/60th of one degree, subtending 1.047" per hundred yards. Roughly speaking, an inch at a hundred yards, two inches at two hundred, and so forth.
Miquelet lock A type of flintlock popular in Spain and Italy, characterized by its external mainspring and a laterally acting sear that protrudes through the lockplate to engage the forward edge of the cock (or "dog", as it was commonly called). Very reliable, but hard on flints.
Misfire A cartridge which fails to discharge.
MLAGB Muzzle Loaders' Association of Great Britain. Governing body for black powder shooting.
Monoblock construction A production method for double barrelled shotguns whereby the breech end of the barrels, including the lumps, are machined from a single block of steel, with the tubes sleeved in.
Musket A smoothbore military shoulder gun intended to fire a single projectile, normally a round ball of nearly bore diameter.
Muzzle brake A device fitted to or machined into the muzzle of a firearm and intended to reduce recoil and muzzle flip by redirecting the combustion gases.
Muzzle energy The energy of the projectile, measured near the muzzle. May be calculated (for any distance for which figures are known) by multiplying the square of the velocity in feet per second by the weight of the bullet in grains, and dividing by 450,240, to yield energy in foot pounds.
Muzzle loader A firearm that loads from the front end: the end of the barrel (muzzle) or, in the case of revolvers, the front of the cylinder.
Muzzle velocity The speed of the bullet, measured in feet per second or metres per second, a short distance from the muzzle.

Neck The constricted forward section of a bottle-necked cartridge case—the portion that grips the bullet.
Neck (v.) To alter the diameter of the neck of a cartridge case so as to change its calibre. Thus, the .25-06 is the .30-06 necked down to .25 calibre, while the .35 Whelen is the .30-06 necked out to .35 calibre.
Neck size (v.) To prepare a cartridge case for reloading by using a die to return the neck to the correct size to hold the bullet but without resizing the body of the case, which is called "full length resizing".
Needle fire A transitional ignition type in which the firing pin took the form of a "needle" which was driven forward through the base of the cartridge, through the powder charge, until it impacted the primer, which was affixed to the base of the bullet.
NMC National Match Course: the traditional US National Championship pistol course administered by the NRA of America. Also called the 2700 Course after the maximum possible score.
NRA National Rifle Association (of America, founded 1871) or (of Great Britain, founded 1860), a governing body of various shooting sports in each country.
NSRA National Small-bore Rifle Association (UK). Governing body for small-bore (rimfire) target shooting in the UK.
NSSA National Skeet Shooting Association, the governing body for Skeet in the US.

Offhand A prescribed firing position. With pistol: standing, with the pistol held in one hand, unsupported. With rifle: standing, without support.
Ogive The curved portion of a bullet between the bearing surface and the tip.
Open frame Said of a revolver frame which has no topstrap.
Open sights A sighting system consisting of a post or bead foresight and a notch, V or groove backsight, or any comparable arrangement not using globes, tunnels or apertures.
Over-under A double barrelled gun on which the two barrels are mounted one above the other.

+P A designation applied to certain American cartridges loaded to higher-than-standard pressures. Not safe in all guns of that calibre. Use only in guns that are +P approved by the manufacturer.
Paradox gun A predominantly smoothbore gun, usually of 10 or 12 bore, with the forward few inches of the barrel rifled, designed to use either a shot load or solid projectiles effectively, popular in Africa in the mid-19th century.
Pattern The disposition of shots or shotgun pellets in a vertical plane at the target. The percentage of shotgun pellets in a load that fall within a 30" circle at 40 yards. See "choke".
Pepperbox A type of early percussion revolver with a barrel cluster rather like a long cylinder, (but with no single, separate barrel) and with a bar type hammer striking from above. Normally double action only. Popular during the early and mid-19th century.
Pinfire A metallic cartridge in which the primer is normally contained, cup upward, in a base wad (see "wad") and which is discharged by the blow of the hammer, falling at 90° to the axis of the cartridge, which drives a protruding pin into the primer. A gun which takes cartridges of this type.
Pistol A handgun. In normal usage, the term "pistol" refers to any handgun except revolvers, and includes self-loaders, manual repeaters, single-shots, double or multi-barrelled pistols and freak types such as belt buckle pistols, cutlass pistols and so forth. It is unusual, but not incorrect, to apply the term to revolvers: British military nomenclature always classified revolvers as a type of pistol.
Pitch Also called twist. The rate at which rifling (q.v.) turns, measured in calibres, inches or centimetres. A typical pitch would be one turn in 14 inches.
Point blank A range near enough so that the target can be hit without having to take elevation adjustments to compensate for bullet drop.
Port pressure In a gas operated (q.v.) firearm, the peak pressure over the gas port; determines port diameter.
PPC Practical Pistol Course. The former FBI qualification course which forms the basis of the US and British Police Pistol competitions—PP2 in Britain.
Primer The part of the cartridge that ignites the propellant powder. In a metallic cartridge, the primer is part of the assembly, but earlier ignition systems used various types of separate and external primers. A modern primer consists essentially of the cup, anvil and pellet, the latter usually a lead styphnate based compound, though mercury fulminate was previously used.
Primer pocket The counterbore in the centre of the base of a centrefire cartridge in which the primer assembly is seated.
Proof The testing of firearms for their ability to withstand safely the pressure of cartridge discharge. In most European countries, proof is a statutory obligation and testing is done at designated proof houses (q.v.). In the United States and Switzerland, proof is non-statutory and is conducted by the manufacturer.
Proof house A designated laboratory for conducting pressure tests of firearms.
Proof load A cartridge for testing purposes only, loaded to higher than standard pressures and intended to burst weapons that do not incorporate a stipulated margin of strength.
Proof mark A mark or symbol stamped or engraved on a firearm to indicate that it has successfully been proof tested. In the absense of better particulars, proof marks are often valuable in helping identify and date a firearm, as well as providing information on patterns of trade. Proof marks are only those relating to proof and should not be confused with inspection and other marks applied by the manufacturer, the military or other administrative customers.
Pump action A firearm that employs a breechblock that is operated by linear manual pressure, normally on a mobile fore-end, though variants with mobile pistol grips or handgrips exist. The breechblock will normally act linearly but may act rotationally. Also called "slide action" and, colloquially, "trombone action".

Ramrod A rod, normally of wood or iron, used for loading a muzzleloading firearm, and normally stored in a groove underneath the barrel.
Rear locking Said of a bolt action gun on which the locking lugs are toward the rear of the bolt and which lock into the receiver behind the magazine well.
Rebated head Said of a cartridge of which the head diameter is less than body diameter, measured just ahead of the extractor groove. Such a case will headspace (q.v.) either against the shoulder or casemouth. Rebated head cartridges are intended to function in a firearm whose breechblock or bolt face was orginally designed for a smaller case.
Receiver The principal structural component of a firearm. The buttstock is attached to the back of the receiver, the barrel and fore-end to the front, and the action operates within it. Called the "frame" on a revolver or pistol.
Receiver bridge On a bolt action weapon, the portion of the receiver that normally extends over the top of the bolt just ahead of the bolt handle. If this part does not extend over the top of the bolt, it is referred to as a "split bridge".
Receiver ring The forward end of the receiver of a bolt action gun, into which the barrel is screwed.
Recoil lug A lug or face, normally on the underside or rear of a receiver that transfers the forces of recoil from the barrel/receiver group to the stock.
Recoil operated Said of a self loading or automatic firearm operated by mobile components—the barrel and breechblock—which recoil rearward in reaction to the projectile, which is being propelled forward. See "short recoil" and "long recoil".
Recoil shield On a revolver, the face of the standing breech and particularly the cheek to either side that prevents the chambered rounds from falling out of the cylinder.
Recoil spring On an automatic or semi-automatic firearm, the large spring that returns the breechblock to battery. Not the mainspring (q.v.).
Repeater A firearm containing reserve ammunition which may be discharged, shot after shot, until the reserve is exhausted, as opposed to a single shot firearm, for which the reserve ammunition is usually carried in a belt, pocket or pouch worn by the shooter.
Revolver A repeating handgun that carries its cartridges in a cylinder that is drilled linearly with chambers that are disposed round a common central axis. Each chamber contains a cartridge, and is rotated into alignment with the barrel for firing. See "pistol", "cylinder" and "chamber".
Rifle A shoulder gun intended to fire a solid or composite projectile of bore diameter, and having a rifled barrel designed to impart a spin to the projectile. See "musket", "shotgun" and "carbine".
Rifling A series of sprial grooves cut or formed into the interior of a barrel. The upstanding ridges of metal between the grooves are termed lands (q.v.).
Rimfire A metallic cartridge in which the priming compound is deposited centrifugally in the hollow rim of the case round its entire circumference. The firing pin crushes the rim against the rear face of the barrel, which serves as an anvil for the purpose.
Rimless Said of a cartridge of which the base diameter and body diameter are the same. Such a case will normally have an extraction groove machined round it, yielding a "rim" of body diameter. A rimless case will headspace (q.v.) against the case mouth, if straight walled, or against the shoulder if bottlenecked.
Rimmed Said of a cartridge whose base diameter is greater than its body diameter, measured just ahead of the rim. Such a cartridge headspaces (q.v.) against the rim, which also serves for extraction.
Rod ejection A system primarily used on solid frame revolvers, in which ejection is accomplished by rotating the cylinder so that each chamber in turn aligns with the ejector rod mounted under the barrel, and with the loading gate, out through which the spent case may be pushed.
Rolling block An action type in which the breechblock is mounted on a stout transverse pivot and rolls backward to expose the chamber.
Round A unit of ammunition consisting of the primer, case, propellant and bullet. A cartridge (q.v.).

S&W Smith & Wesson, of Springfield, Massachusetts.
Sabot A heavy cup wad, usually of plastic, which itself takes the rifling and falls away ahead of the muzzle; permits a small calibre projectile to be used in a larger calibre gun or rifle, often at extreme velocities. From the French *sabot*, or "wooden shoe".
Safety A mechanical device intended to prevent accidental discharge; may be either manually operated at will, such as a thumblever or crossbolt, or an automatic safety such as a firing pin block or magazine disconnector, or indeed something between the two, such as a grip safety.
Sear The piece—either part of the trigger or an intermediate piece—that holds the hammer or striker at full cock. Pressure on the trigger (q.v.) causes the sear to release the hammer or striker to fly forward and fire the shot.
Sear surface Those surfaces of the trigger, sear, hammer or striker involved in holding the mechanism at full cock, or releasing it to fire the shot.
Sectional density The weight of a bullet in pounds, divided by the square of its diameter in inches. For a given calibre, the longer the bullet, the heavier it will be, the greater its sectional density, the better it will retain its velocity over distance.
Selective fire Said of a firearm capable of either semi- or full automatic fire, or

GLOSSARY

semi-automatic or burst fire, or all three. Most selective fire weapons have a selector switch or lever; some have separate triggers for each mode while others fire semi-auto on short pulls and automatic on a long pull of the same trigger.

Self loader A firearm which harnesses the energy of cartridge discharge to extract and eject the spent case and to load a fresh cartridge into the chamber. Also called semi-automatic or, sometimes, automatic, (qq.v.).

Semi-automatic Self loader (q.v.).

Semi-wadcutter A type of revolver bullet with a flat nose of nearly bore diameter, and a sharp shoulder ahead of the bearing surface, also called "Keith type" after the designer, Elmer Keith.

Short recoil A recoil operated firearm in which the barrel and breechblock are locked together through a short distance of travel, whereupon the two are uncoupled, the barrel is arrested and the breechblock continues rearward, extracting the spent case from the chamber. Most self-loading pistols are of short recoil operation. See "recoil operated" and "long recoil".

Short stroke Said of a gas operated firearm if the piston operates over only a short distance and impulses the bolt and bolt carrier rearward. Also called "tappet operated".

Shot A pellet of a shotgun cartridge; alternatively, all of the pellets or the pattern of the pellets from a shotgun cartridge. The effect or the noise or the incident of a cartridge being fired. The person who shoots.

Shotgun A smoothbore shoulder gun intended for the most part to fire shells containing a number of small round pellets, the size of which varies according to the application. A load of birdshot would typically contain some 300 pellets, while a buckshot load, used at close range on deer, fox or boar, would consist of only 12 pellets, each of .33" diameter. Shotguns may also fire single projectiles of bore diameter (rifled slugs) or a wide variety of specialist ammunition.

Shoulder gun A firearm meant to be fired supported by the shoulder and cheek, as opposed to a handgun. A catch-all term for any rifle, shotgun or combination gun.

Side-by-side A double-barrelled gun on which the two barrels are mounted one beside the other, i.e., in a horizontal plane.

Sidelock A firearm—normally a double-barrelled shotgun or rifle—on which the lockwork is mounted on detachable lockplates which are mortised into the stock on either side, just to the rear of the receiver. They are more expensive than boxlocks (q.v.), hence enjoy more status.

SIG Schweizerische Industrie-Gesellschaft, of Neuhausen am Rheinfall, Switzerland.

Sighting in Test firing a firearm so as to adjust the sights to produce impacts on point of aim at a given distance.

Silencer A sound moderator (q.v.).

Single action A revolver or pistol on which the hammer must be cocked before the first shot may be fired. On single action revolvers, the hammer must be drawn to full cock for each shot; on pistols, the slide will automatically recock the hammer for the second and subsequent shots. See "double action".

Single shot A firearm containing only the shot to be fired, and which must be reloaded with a fresh cartridge externally carried, each time a shot is to be fired. See "repeater".

Sleeving The practice of cutting a damaged barrel off several inches ahead of the breech, and fitting a new tube.

Small arm A firearm capable of being carried and used by one man, as opposed to crew-served weapons.

Smokeless powder A form of nitrocellulose-based propellant which replaced gunpowder (q.v.) in small arms cartridges at the end of the 19th century. Smokeless powder was first produced by the French chemist Paul Vieille in 1884 by gelatinising nitrocellulose with ether-alcohol. Smokeless powder is classified as single based or double based depending on whether the nitrocellulose is used with a nitroglycerine additive.

Smoothbore A firearm, such as a musket or shotgun, which is not rifled. A shotgun.

Snaphaunce An early type of flintlock (q.v.) in which the frizzen (q.v.) and the pan cover were separate parts.

Snub A revolver with a short, or "snub nosed" barrel, that is to say a 2in barrel on small framed revolvers and 2.5 to 3.5in barrels on larger frame sizes.

Soft point A jacketed bullet with exposed lead at the tip, designed to mushroom on impact.

Solid A heavily jacketed bullet designed for deep penetration on heavy game, without deforming.

Solid frame Said of a revolver on which the frame window (q.v.) is broached through a solid piece; that is to say that the construction is neither breakopen nor open framed (qq.v.). Most swingout cylinder revolvers have solid frames.

Sound moderator A device attached to the muzzle of a firearm, and sometimes sleeving the barrel and parts of the breech as well, intended to attenuate the noise of cartridge discharge by containing the expanding gases until they have slowed to subsonic levels.

Speedloader A device that carries revolver cartridges in circular pattern, enabling a revolver to be reloaded in a single gesture.

Spitzer A type of sharply pointed rifle bullet introduced in military service at the end of the 19th century, and whose improved aerodynamic and wounding qualities quickly made obsolete the jacketed round-nose projectiles then in use. From the German *spitze* meaning "point".

Springfield The US government small arms manufacturing facility, Springfield Armory, at Springfield, Massachusetts. A firearm designed or manufactured there, particularly the Model 1873 or Model 1903 rifles.

Standing breech The receiver face that supports the casehead when the chambered cartridge is fired in certain types of firearm, notably revolvers and break-open shotguns and rifles.

Stock The part of a firearm that facilitates its being held for firing, notably the butt, fore-end, pistol grip, handguard, etc.

Striker In a gun that does not have a hammer, the part that impacts the primer to detonate it. A striker is itself powered by the mainspring, and operates linearly; a hammer operates rotationally. See "firing pin" and "hammer".

Submachine gun A fully automatic or selective fire weapon of pistol calibre.

Tappet operated See "short stroke".

Tipping block An action type in which the breechblock, usually lever operated, is hinged at the back and tips down at the front to expose the chamber.

Tipping bolt Said of a bolt type breechblock which tips to lock. Normally a square face on the rear underside of the bolt will lock against a corresponding face on the receiver.

Top strap Part of a revolver frame extending over the top of the cylinder and connecting the top of the standing breech with the forward portion of the frame into which the barrel is screwed.

Trajectory The arc described by a projectile from the muzzle to its point of impact.

Transitional revolver An early type of percussion revolver with a pepperbox (q.v.) action but with a single, rifled barrel.

Trigger A part which, when pressed, releases the hammer or striker to fire the gun.

Trigger bar On a self-loading pistol, or any other firearm in which the trigger is at some distance from the sear, an intermediate piece connecting the two parts. Sometimes called a drawbar, especially on double action pistols with pivoting triggers.

Trigger reach The distance, on a handgun, from the point on the backstrap which would be covered by the web of the hand, to the point of finger contact on the trigger.

Tumbler A shaped block attached to the pivot of the cock of a flintlock or similar gun, operating inside the lockplate. The mainspring normally bears on the tumbler, which also carries the bents, or cocking notches as well.

Twist The rate at which rifling causes the bullet to rotate. See "pitch".

UIT The *Union International de Tir*, an international governing body for shooting sports, recognised by the International Olympic Committee. Founded in 1907 and headquartered in Paris until 1945. Subsequently removed to Wiesbaden, West Germany as one of the spoils of peace, and currently headquartered in Munich. Sometimes known as the International Shooting Union, or ISU.

Unlocked breech See "blowback" and "delayed blowback".

Vierling A shoulder gun with four barrels, usually mixed, rifle and shotgun. From the German, *vier*, for "four". See "drilling".

Wad The material (fibre, plastic, cloth, leather or whatever) between the powder charge and the projectile or shot charge. In a roll-crimped case, a card wad is used to contain the shot in the case, while a base wad is normally used to locate the primer in a pinfire (q.v.) case.

Wadcutter A pistol bullet of cylindrical form with a flat point of bore diameter, designed to cut a clean hole in a paper target.

WCF Winchester Center Fire.

Web The wall of brass between the casehead and the combustion chamber or case body.

Wheel lock An early ignition system in which a serrated steel wheel was spun against iron pyrites contained in a clamp in order to generate sparks to ignite the priming charge. Quite fast and reliable, but expensive, hence rarely used for military small arms.

Wildcat A cartridge not commercially manufactured. Normally one formed by necking and reprofiling a standard case to yield a ballistically advantageous result.

Windage The lateral deflection in a bullet's flight, due to wind drift, the earth's rotation, sighting error or whatever. See "elevation". Archaic: the leakage of propellant gases past the bullet or shot charge in the bore.

Worm A corkscrew-like attachment on a ramrod (q.v.) used for withdrawing an unfired or misfired charge.

Yoke See "crane".

Zero Short for "zero sight adjustment", meaning that the gun is correctly sighted to hit the desired point of impact at a given range with a given load, in the absence of wind. Any adjustments for wind, therefore, will be counted out from the zero setting. If either the range or the load are changed, then the zero itself will have to be changed.

BIBLIOGRAPHY

Ackley, Parker O, *Handbook for Shooters and Reloaders*, Salt Lake City, Utah, 1962.
Akehurst, Richard, *Game Guns & Rifles: Percussion to Hammerless Ejector in Britain*, London, 1969. Reprint, 1985.
Anon. (A Traveller), *The Art of Duelling*, London, 1836. Reprint Richmond, Surrey, 1971.
Anon. (NRA of America), *NRA Practical Shooting Rules (Provisional)*, Washington, 1982.
Anon. (Union Internationale de Tir), *Special Technical Rules for Free Pistol, Air Pistol, Rapid Fire Pistol, Sport Pistol and Center Fire Pistol, Standard Pistol*, Munich, 1986.
Anon. (Muzzle Loading Association of Great Britain), *Rules, Regulations and National Competitions Rules and Details*, Newport Pagnell, Buckinghamshire, 1986.
Anon. (Union Internationale de Tir), *Special Technical Rules for Smallbore Free Rifle, Smallbore Standard Rifle, Air Rifle, Bigbore Free Rifle, Bigbore Standard Rifle*, Munich, 1986.
Anon., *Panorama of the Volunteer Rifleman's Exercises*, London, 1860. Reprint Wembley, Middlesex, 1984.
Anon. (Sélection du Reader's Digest), *Les Armes Françaises à Travers les Ages*, Paris, 1972.
Anon. (Thompson/Center Arms Co.), *Shooting Black Powder Guns*, Rochester, New Hampshire, 1983.
Anon. (Clay Pigeon Shooting Association), *CPSA Year Book and Averages*, Buckhurst Hill, Essex, (various years).
Anon. (International Practical Shooting Confederation), *IPSC Shooting Principles and Rules, 7th Edition*, Stoke-on-Trent, Staffordshire, 1986.
Anon. (Scottish Shooting Council), *The Scottish Shooting Council Handbook*, Edinburgh, 1984.
Anon. (Police Athletic Association), *Rifle & Pistol Championships, Bisley*, Liverpool, annual.
Anon. (Speer, Inc.), *Speer Reloading Manual No. 10 for Rifle and Pistol*, Lewiston, Idaho, 1979; 4th printing, 1982.
Anon. (US Army Marksmanship Training Unit), *Pistol Marksmanship Manual*, Fort Benning, Georgia, 1969.
Anon. (NRA of America), *American Handguns & Their Makers*, Washington, 1981.
Anon., *Fabrique Nationale d'Armes de Guerre, 1889-1964*, Liège, 1965.
Antal, Dr Laslo, *Competitive Pistol Shooting*, Wakefield, West Yorkshire, 1983.
Antal, Dr Laslo, *The Target Gun Book of UIT Pistol Shooting*, Droitwich, Worcestershire, 1985.
Arnold, Dave, *Shoot a Handgun: A Manual for South African Men and Women on How to Shoot a Handgun, 2nd Edition*, Johannesburg, 1982.
Askins, Charles, *The Pistol Shooter's Book*, New York, 1962.
Atkinson, John A., *The British Duelling Pistol*, London, 1978.
Ayoob, Massad F., *Hit the White Part*, Concord, New Hampshire, 1982.

Bady, Donald B., *Colt Automatic Pistols*, Alhambra, California, 1956; revised edition, 1973.
Bailey, D. W., *British Military Longarms*, 1715-1865, London, 1986.
Barker, A. J. and John Walter, *Russian Infantry Weapons of World War 2*, London, 1971.
Barnes, Frank C., *Cartridges of the World, 5th Edition*, Northbrook, Illinois, 1985.
Barnes, Duncan et al, *The History of Winchester Firearms, 1866-1980, 5th Edition*, Tulsa, Oklahoma, 1980. Previous editions 1966 and 1975, George Watrous et al.
Bearse, Ray, *Sporting Arms of the World*, New York, 1977.
Beaufroy, Captain Henry, *Scloppetaria: or Considerations on the Nature and Use of Rifled Barrel Guns, with Reference to their Forming the Basis of a Permanent System of National Defence, Agreeable to the Genius of the Country*, London, 1808. Reprint Richmond, Surrey, 1971. First published anonymously, signed "A Corporal of Riflemen".
Beaumont, Richard, *Purdey's: The Guns and the Family*, Pombret, Vermont, 1984.
Beckett, Ian F. W., *Riflemen Form: A Study of the Rifle Volunteer Movement, 1859-1908*, Aldershot, Hampshire, 1982.
Belford, James N. and Jack Dunlap, *The Mauser Self-Loading Pistol*, Alhambra, California, 1969.
Berger, R. J. *Know Your Broomhandle Mausers*, Southport, Connecticut, 1985.
Blackmore, Howard L., *Royal Sporting Guns at Windsor*, London, 1968.
Blair, Claude (ed), *Pollard's History of Firearms*, Feltham, Middlesex, 1983.
Blair, Wes, *The Complete Book of Target Shooting*, Harrisburg, Pennsylvania, 1984.
Blatt, Art, *Gun Digest Book of Trap & Skeet Shooting: A Guide to the Clay Target Sports*, Northfield, Illinois, 1984.
Bock, G. and W. Weigel, *Handbuch der Faustfeuerwaffen*, Melsungen, Germany, 1968.
Boothroyd, Geoffrey, *Guns Through the Ages*, New York, 1961.
Boothroyd, Geoffrey, *Gun Collecting*, London 1961. Reprint, 1987.
Boothroyd, Geoffrey, *The Handgun*, New York, 1970.
Boothroyd, Geoffrey, *The Shotgun: History and Development*, London, 1986.
Bornecque, Major, *Armement Portatif*, Paris, 1897.
Braverman, Shelley (ed), *The Firearms Encyclopedia*, Athens, New York, 1959.
Breathed, John W., Jr. and Joseph J. Schroeder, Jr., *System Mauser: A Pictorial History of the Model 1896 Self-Loading Pistol*, Chicago, 1967.
Burrard, Major Sir Gerald, *The Identification of Firearms & Forensic Ballistics*, London, 1951.
Burrard, Major Sir Gerald, *The Modern Shotgun*, 3 Volumes. London, 1961. First published 1931-32.
Busch, Ted, *Commercial Shooting Ranges*, Minneapolis, Minnesota, 1982.
Butler, David F., *The American Shotgun*, Middlefield, Connecticut, 1973.
Buxton, Warren H., *The P.38 Pistol*, 2 vols, Los Alamos, New Mexico, 1978 & 1984.

Camarlinghi, Carlo, *1915-1985: Settant'Anni di Pistole Beretta*, Florence, n.d. Bilingual text, English and Italian.
Caranta, Raymond, *Le Pistolet de Poche*, Paris, 1981.
Caranta, Raymond, *Pistolets à Grande Puissance de Feu*, Paris, 1985.
Caranta, Raymond and Yves Cadiou, *Le Guide des Collectionneurs d'Armes de Poing*, Paris, 1971.
Caranta, Raymond and Pierre Cantegrit, *L'Aristocratie du Pistolet*, Paris, 1971.
Caranta, Raymond and Jean Jordanoglou, *Postilets et Revolvers d'Autrefois (1829-1870)*, Paris, 1974.
Carmichel, Jim, *The Modern Rifle*, New York, 1975.
Carmichel, Jim, *Jim Carmichel's Book of the Rifle*, New York, 1985.
Cary, Lucian, *The New Lucian Cary on Guns*, New York, 1957.
Cassidy, William L., *Quick or Dead*, Boulder, Colorado, 1978.
Chandler, John, *The Target Gun Book of Pistol Coaching*, Droitwich, Worcestershire, 1983.
Clapp, Wiley M., *Modern Law Enforcement Weapons & Tactics*, Northbrook, Illinois, 1987.
Cole, Howard N., *The Story of Bisley*, Aldershot, Hampshire, 1960.
Cornfield, Susie, *The Queen's Prize: The Story of the National Rifle Association*, London, 1987.
Courtney, Andrew, *Muzzle Loading Today*, London, 1981.
Cradock, Chris, *A Manual of Clayshooting*, New York, 1983.
Crossman, Colonel Jim, *Olympic Shooting*, Washington, 1978.
Crudgington, Ian M. and D. J. Baker, *The British Shotgun, Volume 1: 1850-1870*, London, 1979.

Darling, Anthony D., *Red Coat and Brown Bess*, Bloomfield, Ontario, 1970.
Datig, Fred A., *The Luger Pistol (Pistole Parabellum)*, Los Angeles, 1962.
de Haas, Frank, *Bolt Action Rifles*, Northfield, Illinois, revised edition 1984; first published, 1971.
de Haas, Frank, *Single Shot Rifles and Actions*, Northfield, Illinois, 1969.
Derby, Harry, *The Hand Cannons of Imperial Japan*, Charlotte, North Carolina, 1981.
Devouges, Marcel, *L'Avenement des Armes Automatiques*, Paris, 1925.
Dougan, John C., *Know Your Ruger Single Action Revolvers, 1953-63*, Southport, Connecticut, 1981.
Douglas, James, *The Sporting Gun*, Newton Abbot, Devon, 1983.

Dove, Patrick Edward, *The Revolver, Its Description, Management and Use*, London, 1858. Reprint Houston, Texas, 1968.
Dowell, William Chipchase, *The Webley Story*, Leeds, 1962.
Dugelby, Thomas B., *EM-2: Concept & Design*, Toronto, 1980.

Erlmeier, Hans A. and Jakob H. Brandt, *Manual of Pistol and Revolver Cartridges: Volume 1, Centerfire, Metric Calibres*, Wiesbaden, 1967.
Erlmeier, Hans A. and Jakob H. Brandt, *Manual of Pistol and Revolver Cartridges: Volume 2, Centerfire, American and British Calibres*, Schwäbisch Hall, Germany, 1980.
Ezell, Edward C. (ed), *George Nonte's Combat Handguns*, London, 1980.
Ezell, Edward C., *Handguns of the World: Military Revolvers and Self-Loaders from 1870-1945*, London, 1981.
Ezell, Edward C., *Small Arms Today: Latest Reports on the World's Weapons and Ammunition*, Harrisburg, Pennsylvania, 1984.
Ezell, Edward C., *The Great Rifle Controversy: Search for the Ultimate Infantry Weapon from World War II Through Viet Nam and Beyond*, Harrisburg, Pennsylvania, 1984.
Ezell, Edward C., *The AK47 Story: Evolution of the Kalashnikov Weapons*, Harrisburg, Pennsylvania, 1986.

Fadala, Sam, *The Black Powder Handgun*, Northfield, Illinois, 1981.
Farrar, C. L. and D. W. Leeming, *Military Ballistics: A Basic Manual*, Oxford, 1983.
Flayderman, Norm, *Flayderman's Guide to Antique American Firearms and Their Values, 4th Edition*, Northbrook, Illinois, 1987.
Fletcher, John and Philip Upton, *Shooting Magazine Introduction to Clay Shooting*, London, 1987.
Forsyth, Lt. James O., *The Sporting Rifle and its Projectiles*, n.p., 1863. Reprint Big Timber, Montana, 1978.
Freeman, Peter C., *Target Pistol Shooting: Eliminating the Variables*, London, 1981.
Fuller, W. H., *Small-Bore Target Shooting*, London, 1963. Revised by A. J. Palmer, 3rd edition, 1977.

Gamma, Martin, et al, *Album Commemoratif du Centenaire de la Société Suisse des Carabiniers, 1824-1924*, n.p., 1924. Various parts in German, French and Italian.
Gates, Elgin, *Gun Digest Book of Metallic Silhouette Shooting*, Northfield, Illinois, 1979.
George, John Nigel, *English Pistols and Revolvers*, New York, 1962.
Gildersleeve, Judge H. A. et al, *Rifles & Marksmanship*, New York, 1878. Reprint Bedford, 1986.
Glen, John, *Bisley Stories & Others*, Brig O'Turk, Scotland, 1985.
Gould, A. C., *Modern American Pistols & Revolvers*, Boston, 1894. Reprint Plantersville, South Carolina, 1946.
Gould, Robert W. and Michael J. Waldren, *London's Armed Police: 1829 to the Present*, London, 1986.
Grant, James C., *More Single Shot Rifles*, Highland Park, New Jersey, 1976.
Greener, W. W., *The Gun & Its Development, 9th ed*, n.p., 1910. Reprint Poole, Dorset, 1988.
Grennell, Dean A. et al, *Handgun Digest*, Northfield, Illinois, 1987.
Grennell, Dean A. et al, *Pistol & Revolver Digest, 3rd Edition*, Northfield, Illinois, 1982.
Grennell, Dean A. et al, *Gun Digest Book of Autoloading Pistols*, Northfield, Illinois, 1983.

Harvey, Clay, *Popular Sporting Rifle Cartridges*, Northfield, Illinois, 1984.
Hastings, Macdonald (ed), *Churchills' Game Shooting*, London, 1979.
Hatcher, Julian S., *Hatcher's Notebook*, Harrisburg, Pennsylvania, 1962.
Hatcher, Julian S. with Frank J. Jury and Jac Weller, *Firearms Investigation, Identification and Evidence*, Harrisburg, Pennsylvania, 1957.
Hatcher, Julian S., *Textbook of Pistols & Revolvers: Their Ammunition, Ballistics and Use*, Plantersville, South Carolina, 1935.
Hatsumi, Dr. Yoshaki, *Knife and Pistol Fighting*, Boulder, Colorado, 1987.
Häusler, Fritz and Max Häusler, *Schweizer Faustfeuerwaffen seit 1818*, Frauenfeld, Switzerland, 1970.
Haven, Charles T. and Frank A. Belden, *A History of the Colt Revolver and the Other Arms Made by Colt's Patent Fire Arms Manufacturing Company from 1836 to 1940*, New York, 1940.
Hebard, Gil (ed), *The Pistol Shooter's Treasury*, Knoxville Illinois, 1969.
Hellstrom, Carl R., *"S&W" 100 Years of Gunmaking (1852-1952)*, New York, 1952; 3rd printing, 1960.
Hercisse, Colonel Jean, *Initiation au Tir de Compétition*, Paris, 1971.
Hillegas, Howard C., *With the Boer Forces, 2nd ed*, London, 1901.
Hinchliffe, K. B., *Target Pistol Shooting*, Newton Abbot, Devon, 1981.
Hinman, Bob, *The Golden Age of Shotgunning*, Prescott, Arizona, 1982.
Hoffschmidt, E. J., *Know Your Walther P.38 Pistols*, Southport, Connecticut, 1974.
Hoffschmidt, E. J., *Know Your Walther PP & PPK Pistols*, Southport, Connecticut, 1975.
Hogg, Ian V. and John Weeks, *Military Small Arms of the 20th Century, 5th Edition*, London, 1985. First edition 1973.
Hogg, Ian V. and John Weeks, *Pistols of the World*, Northfield, Illinois, 1982.
Hogg, Ian V., *Revolvers, 1870-1940: An Illustrated Reference Guide for Collectors*, London, 1984.
Hogg, Ian V., *Jane's Directory of Military Small Arms Ammunition*, London, 1985.
Hogg, Ian V., *Military Pistols & Revolvers*, London, 1987.
Howe, James V., *The Modern Gunsmith*, New York, 1982. The three-volume original reissued as a single volume.
Howe, Walter J. (ed), *NRA Firearms & Ammunition Fact Book*, Washington, n.d.
Hoyem, George A., *The History & Development of Small Arms Ammunition, Volume 3: British Sporting Rifle*, Tacoma, Washington, 1985.
Hübner, Siegfried F., *Der Erste Treffer Zählt*, Schwäbisch Hall, Germany, 1968.
Hughes, Major-General B. P., *Firepower: Weapons Effectiveness on the Battlefield, 1630-1850*, London, 1974.
Humphreys, John, *The Do-it-Yourself Game Shoot*, Newton Abbot, Devon, 1983

Jackson, Tony, *Shotguns & Shooting*, London, 1982.
James, Frank W. *Sub-Guns & Full-Auto Games*, Cornville, Arizona, 1987.
Johnson, Derek E., *Victorian Shooting Days: East Anglia, 1810-1910*, Woodbridge, Suffolk, 1981.
Johnson, George B. and Hans Bert Lockhoven, *International Armament, Volume 1*, Cologne, Germany, 1965.
Josserand, Michel H. and Jan A. Stevenson, *Pistols, Revolvers and Ammunition*, New York, 1972.
Journée, Général, *Le Tir des Fusils de Chasse, 4th Edition*, n.p. 1949. Second edition, 1902; 3rd edition, 1920.

Kaisertreu, *Die Prinzipiellen Eigenschaften der Automatischen Feuerwaffen*, n.p., n.d.
Keith, Elmer, *Sixguns by Keith*, Harrisburg, Pennsylvania, 1961.
Kelver, Gerald O., *100 Years of Shooters and Gunmakers of Single Shot Rifles*, Brighton, Colorado, 1975.
Kelver, Gerald O., *Schuetzen Rifles, History and Loading*, Brighton, Colorado, 1972.
Kelver, Gerald O. (ed), *Ned H. Roberts and the Schuetzen Rifle*, Brighton, Colorado, 1982. Anthology of magazine articles by Major Roberts.
Kerr, Charles Lee, Jr. and Carol Robbins Carr, *Remington Handguns*, Harrisburg, Pennsylvania, 1960.
King, Peter, *The Shooting Field: One Hundred and Fifty Years of Holland & Holland*, Southport, Connecticut, 1985.
Klein, Chuck, *Instinct Combat Shooting: Defensive Handgunning for Police*, Patriot, Indiana, 1986.
Klingner, Bernd, *Rifle Shooting as a Sport*, San Diego, California, 1980. Translated from German.
Krcma, Vaclav, *The Identification and Registration of Firearms*, Springfield, Illinois, 1971.

Labbett, P., *Military Small Arms Ammunition of the World, 1945-1980*, London, 1980.
Labiche, Capitaine, *Cours d'Artillerie—Armes Portatives*, Paris, 1879.
Labiche, Capitaine, *Les Armes Actuelles et Leurs Munitions*, Paris, 1893.
Leleu, Lt. Col. Victor, *Armes à Feu Portatives de Guerre à l'Exposition Universelle de 1900*, Paris, 1902.
Leleu, Lt. Col. Victor, *Les Révolvers et Pistolets Automatiques*, Paris, 1903.
Lenz, Ellis Christian, *Rifleman's Progress*, Huntington, West Virginia, 1946.
Lewis, Jack, *Gun Digest Book of Single Action Revolvers*, Northfield, Illinois, 1982.
Lewis, Jack, *Gun Digest Book of Modern Gun Values, 6th ed*, Northfield, Illinois, 1987.
Lewis, Jack (ed), *Gun Digest Book of Assault Weapons*, Northfield, Illinois, 1987.
Logan, Herschel C., *Cartridges*, New York, 1959.
Long, Duncan, *The AR-15/M16: A Practical Guide*. Boulder, Colorado, 1985.
Long, Duncan, *Automatics: Fast Firepower, Tactical Superiority*, Boulder, Colorado, 1986
Long, Duncan, *Streetsweepers: The Complete Book of Combat Shotguns*, Boulder, Colorado, 1987.
Long, Duncan, *Firearms for Survival*, Boulder, Colorado, 1987.
Long, Duncan, *The Mini-14: The Plinker, Hunter, Assault and Everything Else Rifle*, Boulder, Colorado, 1987.
Long, Duncan, *The Sturm, Ruger 10/22 Rifle and .44 Magnum Carbine*, Boulder, Colorado, 1988
Lugs, Jaroslav, *A History of Shooting*, Feltham, Middlesex, 1968.
Lugs, Jaroslav, *Firearms Past and Present*, (2 vol), London, 1973.

Madis, George, *The Winchester Handbook*, Brownsboro, Texas, 1981.
Mann, Franklin, *The Bullet's Flight*, Prescott, Arizona, 1980. A reprint of Harry Pope's annotated copy of a classic ballistics text.
Marchington, John, *Shooting: A Complete Guide for Beginners*, London, 1972. Reprint, 1982.
Marcot, Roy M, *Spencer Repeating Firearms*, Irvine, California, 1984.
Marshall-Ball, Robin, *The Sporting Rifle: A User's Handbook*, London, 1986.
Mathews, J. Howard, *Firearms Identification, Volume 1*, Madison, Wisconsin, 1962.
Maurel de Silvera, P., *Les Carabines .22 Long Rifle à la Chasse et au Tir*, Paris, 1976.
McBride, H. W., *A Rifleman Went to War*, Plantersville, South Carolina, 1935; Reprint Mt. Ida, Arkansas, 1987.
McGivern, Ed, *Fast and Fancy Revolver Shooting*, Chicago, 1975, 8th printing.
McHenry, Roy C. and Walter F. Roper, *Smith & Wesson Handguns*, Harrisburg, Pennsylvania, 1958.
Meyrick, Samuel Rush, *Observations upon the History of Hand Fire-arms and their Appurtenances*, London, 1829. Reprint Richmond, Surrey, 1971.
Mullin, Captain Timothy John, *Training the Gunfighter*, London, 1981.
Myatt, Major Frederick, *The Soldier's Trade: British Military Developments, 1660-1914*, London, 1974.
Myatt, Major Frederick, *Modern Small Arms*, London, 1978.
Myatt, Major Frederick, *The Illustrated Encyclopedia of Pistols & Revolvers*, London, 1980.
Myatt, Major Frederick, *The Illustrated Encyclopedia of 19th Century Firearms*, London, 1979.

Naramore, Earl, *Principles and Practice of Loading Ammunition*, Harrisburg, Pennsylvania, 1954.
Neal, Robert J. and Roy G. Jinks, *Smith and Wesson, 1857-1945*, New York, 1966.
Neal, W. Keith, *Collecting Duelling Pistols*, London, 1968. First published 1966.
Nichols, Bob, *The Secrets of Double Action Shooting*, New York, 1950.
Niotan, Capitaine, *Etude sur les Pistolets Automatiques*, Brussels, 1910.
Nonte, Major George C., *The Walther P.38 Pistol*, Cornville, Arizona, 1968.

O'Connor, Jack, et al, *Complete Book of Shooting*, New York, 1965.
O'Connor, Jack, *The Rifle Book*, New York, 1978.
O'Connor, Jack, *The Shotgun Book*, New York, 1981. 2nd edition.
Otteson, Stuart, *The Bolt Action: A Design Analysis*, Piscataway, New Jersey, 1976.
Otteson, Stuart, *Benchrest Actions & Triggers*, Prescott, Arizona, 1983.
Otteson, Stuart, *The Bolt Action: A Design Analysis, Volume 2*, Prescott, Arizona, 1985.

Page, Warren, *The Accurate Rifle*, South Hackensack, New Jersey, 1975; 6th printing, 1984.
Parra, Capitaine N., *Pistolets Automatiques*, n.p., 1899. Reprint Paris, 1976.
Parsons, John E., *The Peacemaker and Its Rivals*, New York, 1950.
Parsons, John E., *Smith & Wesson Revolvers: The Pioneer Single Action Models*, New York, 1957.
Peterson, Harold L., *The Treasury of the Gun*, New York, 1962.
Pollard, Captain Hugh B. C., *The Book of the Pistol & Revolver*, London, 1917.
Powell, George H., *Duelling Stories of the Sixteenth Century, from the French of Brantome*, London, 1904.
Pridham, Major C. H. B., *Superiority of Fire: A Short History of Rifles and Machine-Guns*, London, 1945.

Rae, William E. (ed), *A Treasury of Outdoor Life*, Harrisburg, Pennsylvania, 1983. An anthology of articles from the magazine of the same name.
Rankin, James L., *Walther, Volume III, 1908-1980*, Coral Gables, Florida, 1981.
Reid, William, *Weapons Through the Ages*, London, 1984. First published 1976.
Rikhoff, Jim, *Mixed Bag*, Washington, 1981.
Roads, Dr. Christopher, *The Gun*, London, 1978.
Robinson, Roger H., *The Police Shotgun Manual*, Sprinfield, Illinois, 1973.
Ronin, Paul, *L'Arme en France*, Saint-Etienne, 1957.
Rosa, Joseph G., *The Gunfighter, Man or Myth?*, Norman, Oklahoma, 1969.
Rosa, Joseph G., *Guns of the American West*, Poole, Dorset, 1988. 1st Edition London, 1985.
Ruffer, J. E. M., *Good Shooting*, Newton Abbot, Devon, 1983.
Rutterford, Ken, *Collecting Shotgun Cartridges*, London, 1987.

Sasia, Raymond, *Le Tir Rapide*, Paris, 1977.
Schenker, Urs, *150 Ans, Société Suisse des Carabiniers, 1824-1974*, n.p., 1974.
Schmidt, R., *Die Handfeuerwaffen*, Basel, 1875.
Schroeder, Joseph J. (ed), *Gun Collector's Digest, 3 vol*, Vols 1 & 2, Chicago, 1974 & 1977; Vol. 3. Northfield, Illinois, 1981.
Senich, Peter R., *The German Assault Rifle, 1935-1945*, Boulder, Colorado, 1987.
Senich, Peter R., *The German Sniper, 1914-1945*, London, 1982.
Serven, James E. (ed), *The Collecting of Guns*, Harrisburg, Pennsylvania, 1964.
Serven, James E., *Colt Firearms, 1836-1958*, Santa Ana, California, 1958.
Sharpe, Philip B., *Complete Guide to Handloading*, New York, 1937; 3rd edition, 2nd revision, 1953.
Shaw, John and Michael Bane, *You Can't Miss*, Memphis, Tennessee, 1983.
Smith, Gene P. and Chris C. Curtis, *The Pinfire System*, San Francisco, 1983.
Smith, Walter H. B., *The Book of Pistols and Revolvers*, Harrisburg, Pennsylvania, 1962.
Smith, Walter H. B., *Mauser Rifles and Pistols*, Harrisburg, Pennsylvania, 1946.
Smith, Walter H. B., *Walther Pistols and Rifles*, Harrisburg, Pennsylvania, 1962.
Smith, W. H. B. and Joseph E. Smith, *Small Arms of the World, 7th Edition*, Harrisburg, Pennsylvania, 1962.
Speirs, Martyn, *A Guide to Practical Pistol Shooting*, n.p., 1983.
Stadt, Ronald W., *Winchester Shotguns and Shotshells*, Tacoma, Washington, 1984.
Standl, Hans, *Pistol Shooting as a Sport*, London, 1975. First published Munich, 1973. Translated from German by Anita Pennington.
Stevens, R. Blake, *North American FAL's*, Toronto, 1979.
Stevens, R. Blake, *U.K. and Commonwealth FAL's*, Toronto, 1980.
Stevens, R. Blake and Jean E. Van Rutten, *The Metric FAL*, Toronto, 1981.
Stevens, R. Blake, *The Inglis-Browning Hi-Power Pistol*, Ottawa, 1974.
Stevens, R. Blake, *U.S. Rifle M14: From John Garand to the M21*, Toronto, 1983.
Stevens, R. Blake, *The Browning High Power Automatic Pistol*, Toronto, 1984.
Stevens, R. Blake and Edward C. Ezell, *The SPIW: The Deadliest Weapon that Never Was*, Toronto, 1985.
Swearengen, Thomas F., *The World's Fighting Shotguns*, Alexandria, Virginia, 1978.
Sweeting, Sergeant R. C., *Modern Infantry Weapons & Training in their Use*, Aldershot, Hampshire, 1962.

Taylerson, A. W. F., *Revolving Arms*, New York, 1967.
Taylerson, A. W. F., *The Revolver, 1865-1888*, New York, 1966.
Taylerson, A. W. F., *The Revolver, 1889-1914*, New York, 1971.
Taylerson, A. W. F. with R. A. N. Andrews and J. Frith, *The Revolver, 1818-1865*, New York, 1968.
Taylor, Chuck, *The Complete Book of Combat Handgunning*, Cornville, Arizona, 1982.
Teasdale-Buckell, G. T., *Experts on Guns & Shooting*, n.p., 1900. Reprint Sedfield, Hampshire, 1986.
Temple, B. A. and Ian D. Skennerton, *A Treatise on the British Military Martini: The Martini-Henry, 1869-1900*, Burbank, Australia, 1983.
Thierbach, M., *Die Geschichtliche Entwicklung der Handfeuerwaffen*, Dresden, 1899.
Thurlow Craig, C. W. and Eric G. Bewley, *Webley & Scott, 1790-1968*, Birmingham, 1968; 1st edition, 1953.
Trefethen, James B., *Americans and Their Guns*, Harrisburg, Pennsylvania, 1967.
Trench, Charles Chenevix, *A History of Marksmanship*, London, 1972.
Tubby, Pamela (ed), *The Book of Shooting for Sport and Skill*, London, 1980.

Wallack, L. R., *American Shotgun Design and Performance*, Piscataway, New Jersey, 1977.
Walter, John, *German Military Handguns, 1879-1918*, London, 1980.
Walter, John, *The Pistol Book*, London, 1983.
Walter, John, *Handgun: from Matchlock to Laser Sighted Weapon*, London, 1988.
Warner, Ken, *The Practical Book of Guns*, Piscataway, New Jersey, 1978.
Warner, Ken (ed), *Gun Digest Review of Custom Guns*, Northfield, Illinois, 1980.
Weeks, Colonel John (ed), *Jane's Infantry Weapons, 7th Edition*, London, 1981.
Westlake, Ray, *The Rifle Volunteers*, Chippenham, Wiltshire, 1982.
Whelen, Townsend, *Small Arms Design and Ballistics, 2 Volumes*, Georgetown, South Carolina, 1945.
Whelen, Colonel Townsend and Bradford Angier, *Mister Rifleman*, Los Angeles, 1965.
White, Henry P. and Burton D. Munhall, *Pistol and Revolver Cartridges*, New York, 1967.
Whitehead, G. Kenneth, *Practical Deer Stalking*, London, 1986.
Wilber, Dr. Charles G., *Ballistic Science for the Law Enforcement Officer*, Springfield, Illinois, 1977.
Wilkinson, Frederick, *Sporting Guns: An Illustrated Reference Guide for Collectors*, London, 1984.
Wilkinson, Henry, *Observations (Theoretical and Practical) on Muskets, Rifles and Projectiles* (2nd ed), London, 1852. Reprint Bedford, 1983.
Wille, Ulrich, *Waffenlehre*, n.p., 1896.
Wille, Ulrich, *Selbstlader Fragen*, n.p., n.d.
Williams, Mason, *The Sporting Use of the Handgun*, Springfield, Illinois, 1979.
Williamson, Harold F., *Winchester: The Gun that Won the West*, New York, 1952; 3rd printing, 1963.
Wilson, R. K. and Ian V. Hogg, *Textbook of Automatic Pistols*, London, 1975. First published 1943.
Winans, Walter, *The Art of Revolver Shooting*, New York, 1901.
Winokur, Jon, *Master Tips*, Pacific Palisades, California, 1985.
Woodend, Herbert, *Catalogue of the Enfield Pattern Room: British Rifles*, London, 1981.

Zutz, Don, *The Double Shotgun*, Piscataway, New Jersey, 1978.

Page numbers in *italic* type indicate
the subjects of illustrations
mentioned in captions.

INDEX

Picture Credits

Getting all the variety of firearms illustrated in this book to the same studio for photography presented, as one may well imagine, a logistical challenge that was only overcome thanks to the generosity and assistance of many people, some of whom put themselves to a quite remarkable degree of inconvenience in order to be of help. We are indeed grateful to each of them.

George Swenson, Bill Curtis, Nigel Hinton, Peter Eliot, Norman Cooper and Peter Sarony lent us guns from their personal collections, as did a number of other kind people who prefer not to be mentioned. The rest of the guns came to us through trade channels and we are very thankful to the many gunsmiths, manufacturers and distributors who let us borrow items from their stock for study and photography.

Among them are Accuracy International and Accuracy UK of Portsmouth; Swing Target Rifles of Tonbridge; Gunmark of Fareham; Hull Cartridge Co and Remington Arms of Humberside; A.S.I. of Saxmundham; Viking Arms (Ruger, Colt, Manurhin) of Harrogate; Shield Gunmakers of Poole; The Gun Room of Bishops Stortford; *Handgunner* Magazine of Brightlingsea; Holland and Holland Ltd of Bruton Street, London; Parker-Hale Ltd of Birmingham; Smith & Wesson at Liège; Coach Harness, the black powder specialist, at Stowmarket; Practisport of Harrowby Street, London; O J Gowers (Thompson/Center) of Leighton Buzzard; Delta Training of Great Saling; Browning Sports UK of Abingdon; Beechwood Equipment (S.I.G.) of Weybridge; Conjay Arms of London; Gunner 1 & Co of St Albans; Hill's Small Arms of Shenfield; Intergun of Truro; John Slough of Hereford; Sterling Armament of Dagenham and Winchester UK of Droitwich.

The author and publisher would like to thank the following people and companies who kindly supplied photographs for inclusion in this book. The photographs are here credited by page number.

All-Sport Photographic Ltd: 32/3.
Ardea London Ltd: 116/7.
BBC Hulton Picture Library: 82 right.
Pietro Beretta SpA: 118; 146 right; 150; 153; 161.
Blaser GmbH: 17; 29.
Browning: 118/9; 119 upper; 119 lower; 157.
Bruce Coleman Ltd: 117.
Norman Cooper: 127 right; 145 lower; 146 left.
John Darling: Back of jacket upper and lower; half title; title; 78/9; 79; 124 right; 125; 127 left; 138/9; 139; 144; 162/3; 163; 164 upper; 171 lower; 173.
Mary Evans Picture Library: 121; 141 left; 143.
W. W. Greener's *The Gun and its Development*: 129; 132.
Hämmerli GmbH: 85 upper left.
Handgunner: 38 upper; 39; 41 upper left; 41 lower right; 68 lower; 85 lower left; 87 upper left; 87 lower; 148; 149 left; 149 right.
Clay Harvey: 9; 12 upper left; 13 right; 14 lower left; 16 upper.
Hatfield Rifle Works: 165.
Heckler & Koch GmbH: 37 diagram; 126 left.

Hege GmbH: 169 upper; 180.
Hicks Photographic Services: 33; 35; 40; 41 lower left; 80; 83 lower; 85 right; 170/1; 171 upper.
Holland & Holland: 124 lower left.
The Image Bank (Guido Rossi): Front jacket inset.
Eduard Kettner: 166.
Israel Military Industries: 14 upper left.
The Mansell Collection: 37 lower left; 120 upper left; 120 lower left; 120/1; 142/3; 179.
Marlin Firearms Co: 8/9; 13 left; 15.
Miroku: 145 upper.
Anthony Morgan: Back of jacket centre; 84; 86; 87 upper right; 168; 169 lower.
Peter Newark's Western Americana and Historical Pictures: 82 left; 122 upper; 122 lower; 122/3; 142; 162.
NRA of Great Britain: 34 right; 36; 37 lower right; 164 lower.
Redfield Accu-Trac: 12 upper right.
Sako-Valmet: 10; 10/11.
J. P. Sauer & Sohn: 16 lower.
Schmidt & Bender: 12 lower.
Sporting Pictures: 140; 147; 155.
Steyr Defence Division: 41 upper right.
Hal Swiggett: 64/5; 65; 67 lower left; 67 lower right; 68 upper.
US Department of Defence: 67 upper right.
US Repeating Arms Co: 14 upper right.
Valmet: 126 right.
Carl Walther Waffenfabrik (via Accuracy International): 38 lower.
Weatherby Inc.: 11.

PRINTED IN BELGIUM BY

proost
INTERNATIONAL BOOK PRODUCTION